Emirati Arabic

Emirati Arabic: A Comprehensive Grammar offers readers a reference tool for discovering and studying in detail the specific dialect of Arabic spoken in the United Arab Emirates.

It covers all major areas of Emirati Arabic grammar, describing in detail its phonological, morphological, syntactic, and semantic systems. Each grammatical point is illustrated with numerous examples drawn from native Emirati Arabic speakers and is thoroughly discussed providing both accessible and linguistically informed grammatical description.

This book is a useful reference for students of Gulf Arabic and/or Modern Standard Arabic or other Arabic dialects with an interest in the dialect spoken in the UAE, researchers interested in Arabic language and linguistics as well as graduate students and scholars interested in Arabic studies.

Tommi Tsz-Cheung Leung is Associate Professor in the Department of Cognitive Sciences at the United Arab Emirates University. His research specializes in syntax, phonology, typology, and psycholinguistics.

Dimitrios Ntelitheos is Associate Professor in the Department of Cognitive Sciences at the United Arab Emirates University. His research interests include the investigation of morphological and syntactic structures from a theoretical perspective, as well as their cross-linguistic realization and their development in child language.

Meera Al Kaabi is Assistant Professor and Chair in the Department of Cognitive Sciences at the United Arab Emirates University and a visiting academic at New York University Abu Dhabi. Her research interests include neurolinguistics, psycholinguistics, language disorders, morphology, and Semitic languages.

Routledge Comprehensive Grammars

Titles in this series:

French Creoles
A Comprehensive Grammar
Anand Syea

Dutch
A Comprehensive Grammar, 3rd Edition
Bruce Donaldson

Finnish
A Comprehensive Grammar
Fred Karlsson

Persian
A Comprehensive Grammar
Saeed Yousef

Norwegian
A Comprehensive Grammar
Philip Holmes, Hans-Olav Enger

Korean
A Comprehensive Grammar, 2nd edition
Jaehoon Yeon, Lucien Brown

Modern Irish
A Comprehensive Grammar
Nancy Stenson

Lithuanian
A Comprehensive Grammar
Meilutė Ramonienė, Joana Pribušauskaitė, Jogilė Teresa Ramonaitė and Loreta Vilkienė

Máku
A Comprehensive Grammar
Chris Rogers

Emirati Arabic
A Comprehensive Grammar
Tommi Tsz-Cheung Leung, Dimitrios Ntelitheos and Meera Al Kaabi

For more information on this series, please visit: www.routledge.com/Routledge-Comprehensive-Grammars/book-series/SE0550

Emirati Arabic

A Comprehensive Grammar

Tommi Tsz-Cheung Leung,
Dimitrios Ntelitheos and
Meera Al Kaabi

Routledge
Taylor & Francis Group
LONDON AND NEW YORK

First published 2021
by Routledge
2 Park Square, Milton Park, Abingdon, Oxon OX14 4RN

and by Routledge
52 Vanderbilt Avenue, New York, NY 10017

Routledge is an imprint of the Taylor & Francis Group, an informa business

British Library Cataloguing-in-Publication Data
A catalogue record for this book is available from the British Library

Library of Congress Cataloging-in-Publication Data
A catalog record for this book has been requested

ISBN: 978-0-367-22082-2 (hbk)
ISBN: 978-0-367-22080-8 (pbk)
ISBN: 978-0-429-27316-2 (ebk)

Typeset in Sabon & Gill Sans
by Apex CoVantage, LLC

'To my mother Nerissa for her unconditional support, and to Seri, my source of joy and energy.'

—Tommi

'To Rachel, Alexi, and Lukas and to my friends, colleagues, and students who have inspired me over the years.'

—Dimitrios

'To my beloved parents, who will never read this book, and to those who inspire it.'

—Meera

Contents

Figures

Tables

Acknowledgements

The idea to compile a comprehensive grammar of Emirati Arabic dates back to 2007 when Tommi Leung and Dimitrios Ntelitheos first set foot in Al Ain, the 'garden city' of the United Arab Emirates, as Assistant Professors of Linguistics. During course material preparation for the undergraduate linguistics courses offered to the (mostly Emirati) Arabic students, they noticed that almost all 'Arabic' examples used in teaching materials were dismissed by the students as 'unnatural' or 'utterly formal.' To their surprise, although the situation had slightly improved after incorporating several examples from 'Gulf Arabic' grammars, students still dismissed particular usage as 'non-Emirati,' with a strong 'Iraqi' or 'Kuwaiti' flavor. This feedback from their students confirmed the existence of an Emirati-specific variety of Arabic, which had more or less been established and mostly agreed upon by Emirati speakers. Given the paucity of reliable language sources for the purpose of teaching and research, the need was felt for a comprehensive description of Emirati Arabic as a largely uniform spoken variety. Many hours of consultation with native speakers of Emirati Arabic followed, along with the collection of a one-million-word Emirati Arabic corpus, a labor which began in 2010 (Halefom et al., 2013). The team was later joined by Meera Al Kaabi, an alumna of the UAEU who finished her PhD studies in Linguistics at New York University. She brought a native speaker's perspective to the process and helped lay the foundations for the present volume.

We would like to express our gratitude to the continuous assistance from the following colleagues, research assistants, and students at the United Arab Emirates University and elsewhere, without whom this grammar would never have been completed: Eiman Al Ahbabi, Salama Al Dhahri, Noor Al Hashmi, Souad Al Helou, Fatima Al Kaabi, Sara Alkamali, Mariam Alneyadi, Hind

Alnuaimi, Haya Alsayegh, Maryam Alsereidi, Fatima Al Shamsi, Fatma Al Suwaidi, Abeer Bader, Uhood Bahr, Fatima Boush, Ali Idrissi, Meriem Madi, Wafa Mubarak, Mariam Omar, Mariam Poolad, Sara Qahtani, and Bakhita Raeisi. In particular, Fatima Boush, Souad Al Helou, Meriam Madi, Mariam Omar, and Bakhita Raeisi deserve additional acknowledgment for undertaking the painstaking task to proofread all examples and descriptions.

In addition, we express our gratitude for the continuous support from the College of Humanities and Social Sciences at UAEU and our colleagues in the Department of Cognitive Sciences (Linguistics). We also thank the reviewers and Editorial Board of the *Routledge Comprehensive Grammars Series*, especially Andrea Hartill and Claire Margerison for their support in the publication process, and Ellie Auton for her editorial assistance.

We hope that Emirati speakers cherish this comprehensive description of their 'dialect' as a highly convergent language variety which deserves the attention of both a general and academic readership. However, we conclude with a word of caution: all living languages/dialects are subject to change. This is especially true for Emirati Arabic, as the UAE is a cultural and financial hub, which facilitates contact between people from all over the Gulf region and beyond, fueling a linguistic *koineization* process. Therefore, this comprehensive grammar offers just a snapshot of the language spoken within the UAE at the beginning of the 21st century. We can only hope that continuous research engagement with this language variety will maintain an accurate reflection of the dynamicity of its transformation in the future.

Tommi Leung
Dimitrios Ntelitheos
Meera Al Kaabi
Al Ain, July 2020

Abbreviations

adj	adjectival
caus	causative
du	dual
EA	Emirati Arabic
e.o	each other
f	feminine
imp	imperative
imperf	imperfective
lnk	linking particle
m	masculine
MSA	Modern Standard Arabic
part	participle
pass	passive
perf	perfective
pers	person
pl	plural
poss	possessive particle
refl	reflexives
sg	singular
s.o	someone
s.th	something
var	phonological variant
/ /	phoneme/morpheme
[]	actual pronunciation

Chapter 1

Introduction

1.1 Emirati Arabic

This book is a comprehensive grammar of Emirati Arabic, the variety of Arabic spoken in the United Arab Emirates (UAE). The Arabic dialect spoken in the wider area around the Arabic Gulf is known as Gulf Arabic (خليجي khaliji in Arabic). Gulf Arabic is classified as an Afro-Asiatic, Semitic, Central South Arabic language. It belongs to the Semitic language subgroup which also includes languages such as Hebrew, Aramaic, and Amharic. Semitic languages form part of the larger Afro-Asiatic family of languages, which includes the Chad, Cushitic, and Berber languages, all spoken in territories within North Africa.

Gulf Arabic is a kind of accepted *koine*, an educated 'standard' dialect which has emerged through contact between several smaller, mutually intelligible colloquial varieties spoken in areas within and around both shores of the Gulf, including Kuwait, Saudi Arabia, Bahrain, Qatar, UAE, and parts of Oman, Iran, and Iraq. Gulf Arabic is a widely accepted term in Arabic dialectology, designating it as a separate dialect within the Arabic dialect spectrum. The current edition of *Ethnologue* (Eberhard et al., 2020), an authoritative database with statistics on all languages in the world, lists Gulf Arabic as the main Arabic dialect spoken by the majority of nationals in the UAE, Qatar, Bahrain, Kuwait, and in small areas in Saudi Arabia, Oman, southern Iran, and Iraq. The *Ethnologue* further classifies Gulf Arabic into smaller, named varieties. These include the varieties of Gulf Arabic spoken in Kuwait (Gulf Arabic, Kuwaiti), Qatar (Gulf Arabic, Qatari), Bahrain (Bahraini Gulf Arabic), and pockets within Saudi Arabia (Eastern Province and Najran region: inland from the southeast Kuwaiti border, east to the Gulf north of Al Damman; south, near the Yemeni and Omani borders), Oman (Omani Bedawi Arabic), Iraq (Al Basrah governorate: south of Basra city, near the Gulf), Iran (Hormozgan province and nearby Gulf islands; also Bushehr, Fars, Kerman, and Yazd provinces).

This area is vast, with many differences between local varieties, although several dialects have not been studied or described as well as would be desirable. It is perhaps more accurate to think of 'Gulf Arabic' as a dialectal continuum with core similarities rather than as a single dialect. Gulf Arabic remains a koine, but the dialect allows significant variation. Early studies of the varieties of Arabic spoken in the Arabian Peninsula describe in detail the different regional sub-dialects within Gulf Arabic. Johnston (1967) refers to the varieties spoken in the region as the 'Eastern Arabian dialects,' a subgroup within the Northern Arabian dialects, which also include the Syro-Mesopotamian, Shammari, and Anazi dialects. These dialects originate from the northeastern Arabian Peninsula, the region known as Najd, and especially the tribes of Aniza and Shammar (see Ingham, 1982; Palva, 1991; Versteegh, 1997). Gulf Arabic varieties originate from the Anazi subgroup of dialects and includes the varieties spoken in the geographical areas described previously. Johnstone (1967, p. 18) notes that 'the coastal dialects from Kuwait to Khor Fakkān[1] have many more features in common than differences, and can be clearly distinguished as a group from the dialects of Oman, SW Arabia, Central Neij, S. Iraq, and the Syrian Desert.' The map in Figure 1.1 shows the broader region in which Gulf Arabic is used as a koine.

Oil, and later, tourism, brought financial advancement to the Gulf region, and with them ease of communication and travel. These in turn allowed for a greater degree of contact between different peoples in the region, and a 'smoothing out' of cross-dialectal variation. As a result a Gulf Arabic koine began to emerge among well-educated Arabs. Holes (1990) describes a general educated spoken variety, common in the area extending roughly from the southern Iraqi port of Basra to Kuwait, Bahrain, Qatar, and the UAE, and including the eastern region (al-Hasa) of Saudi Arabia. However, Holes (1990, p. xi) indicates that

> even in a region as ethnically and topographically homogenous as the Gulf littoral, in which ancient tribal and familial ties cut across the boundaries of the more recently established political entities, there has always been and still remains, a good deal of both geographically and socially based dialectal diversity.

To the extent that this diversity has been considerably leveled by modern travel and communication, access to education has given Modern Standard Arabic (MSA) a greater influence on the educated spoken koine. Nonetheless, speakers of the different varieties (especially regional or administratively defined varieties)

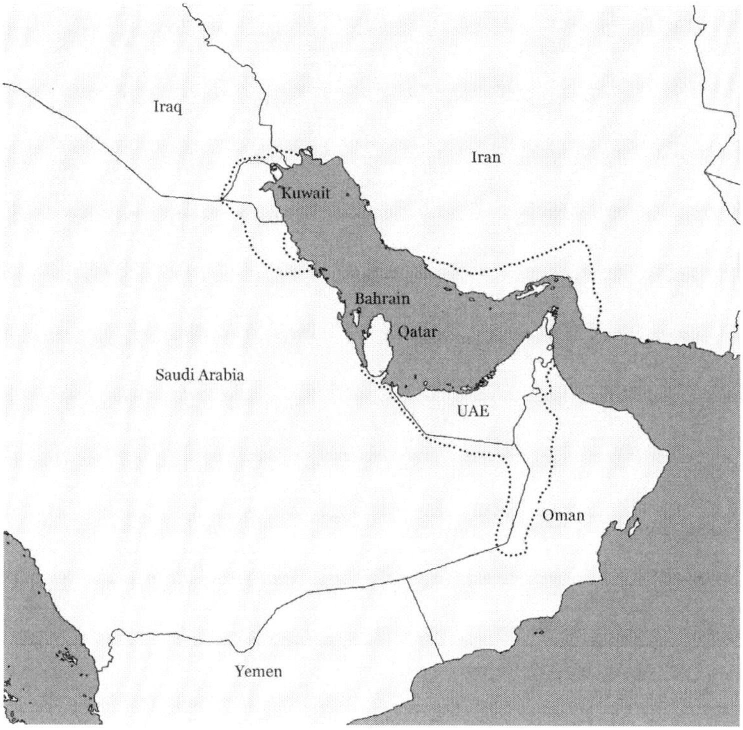

Figure 1.1 Gulf Arabic and the Arabian Peninsula

continue to recognize whether individual speech belongs to their own variety or originates from elsewhere in the region.

The term 'Emirati Arabic' is neither listed in the *Ethnologue* database nor the all-encompassing *Encyclopedia of Arabic Language and Linguistics* (Versteegh et al., 2006), and it is not widely used among Arabic dialectologists. The term is occasionally used in the linguistic literature to refer to that set of varieties specific to the people living within the confines of the UAE, as shown in Figure 1.2.

Under this rubric, Emirati Arabic is infrequently used in linguistic discourse that originates in academic institutions in the UAE and the broader region. In this, Emirati Arabic refers to a group of varieties that share core characteristics with specific phonological, lexical, and morphosyntactic idiosyncrasies and a certain degree of intra-dialectal variation, which is mostly geographically defined. It incorporates grammatical properties of smaller varieties within the UAE, mainly of tribal nature, which may be grouped roughly into three broader sub-varieties: the first spoken in the Northern Emirates of Dubai, Sharjah, Ajman, Umm al-Quwain, and part

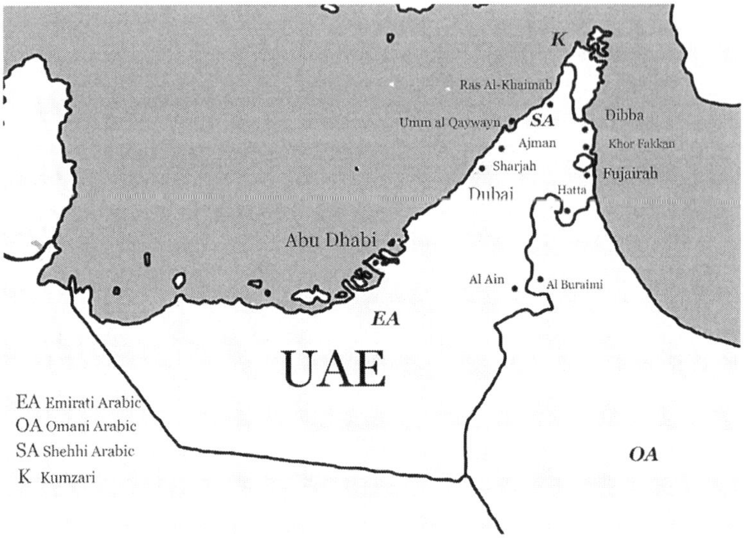

Figure 1.2 Dialects spoken in the United Arab Emirates

of Ras al-Khaimah; the second in the eastern part of the country, mainly in the Emirate of Fujairah, the Khawr Fakkan region, and the eastern part of Ras al-Khaimah; and the third in the Abu Dhabi region, including the oasis city of Al Ain. The dialect spoken in the Emirates is also attested in the Omani area close to the Al Ain region. The variety spoken in the Omani territory of Al Buraimi, across the border from Al Ain, is closely related to the variety spoken in Al Ain in the Emirates.

Speakers of Emirati Arabic identify themselves as speakers of a distinct variety (as compared with neighboring dialects such as Qatari Arabic or Kuwaiti Arabic), based on several phonological, morphological, and syntactic properties that distinguish Emirati Arabic from other Gulf Arabic varieties.

1.2 Triglossia in the UAE

The rich linguistic diversity of the region poses difficulties in clearly defining a distinct Emirati Arabic variety. An additional problem stems from the widespread use of more than one language in the UAE. While Emirati Arabic is the colloquial variety used in everyday communication between Emirati people, more formal contexts require the use of MSA, for instance, in education, public speeches, Arabic literature, and Islamic studies classes, and in news reports on UAE television channels such as تلفزيون دبي 'Dubai TV' and سما دبي 'Sama Dubai.' The extent to which MSA is used in these contexts depends on both the occasion and the speaker's awareness of language register. It is not surprising to hear Emirati Arabic spoken in public speeches, mixed with some high-register vocabulary or fixed expressions drawn from MSA. In addition, the English language has become the lingua franca in the UAE, especially when non-Arabic speaking people are involved in the communication. The influence of English in the Gulf first rose with the growth of British naval power in the 19th century. Later, in the 1960s, the British Council began to offer English classes to students in the Gulf region. In 1991, the UAE's national curriculum was approved, and, since 1994–1995, the English language has been formally taught in all grades beyond kindergarten. To date, the numbers of weekly teaching hours for English and Arabic are similar, and, since Grade 10, students spend more classroom hours learning English than Arabic. The UAE's National Admissions and Placement Office (NAPO), established in 1996 to oversee the transition from secondary to higher education, requires all students applying to study abroad or attend the three national universities (United Arab Emirates University, Higher Colleges of Technology, and Zayed University) to take the Common Educational Proficiency Assessment (CEPA), which consists of an English and a mathematics examination.

The intermingling use of three languages—MSA as the 'high' (primarily written) variety, Emirati Arabic as the 'low' (spoken) register, and English as the lingua franca for non-Arabic speaking communities—constitutes a 'triglossic' situation. An Emirati speaker, especially a young person, will normally converse in Emirati Arabic with a friend, switch to MSA in reading an Arabic newspaper or Arabic literature, and to English in the classroom. This gives rise to code-switching in everyday communication (e.g. the use of Arabic interjections in English sentences, or the use of 'trendy' English expressions in Emirati Arabic). Older generations, including Emiratis and non-Emirati Arabs, are likely to view this as a 'bad' form of language use.

Finally, the large expatriate population of South Asians in the UAE since the recruitment of South Asian skilled laborers, which commenced in 1990, has contributed to the creation of a pidginized Arabic which uses Arabic vocabulary inserted into grammatical structures influenced by South Asian languages. This pidgin is heard among the expatriates mentioned in their communicative exchanges with native Arab speakers, including Emiratis.

1.3 The descriptive approach to Emirati Arabic

The present Emirati Arabic grammar follows a descriptive approach, that is, the book aims to describe the set of rules which native speakers unconsciously manipulate when speaking in natural environments. A descriptive grammar embodies the full language intuition of native speakers as a result of years of language exposure since their birth. This approach stands in contrast with a prescriptive approach to grammar in which learners are advised to speak and (mostly) write their language in a 'proper' way. The disparity between 'prescriptive grammar' and 'descriptive grammar' is evident in many languages. In English, 'split infinitives' are considered a bad practice in writing, but they are unconsciously recognized as acceptable usage in spoken English. In Arabic, the contrast between prescriptive and descriptive grammar is sharpened because MSA (as a written language) is widely considered as prestigious, whereas other spoken vernacular varieties are seen as substandard and unsystematic. This is a misconceived view which primarily stems from the unscientific belief that a spoken language must be paired with a standardized writing system to be considered as standard. While the writing system and the prescriptive grammar of MSA remain highly valuable, the present work seeks to emphasize the view that a comprehensive descriptive grammar such as this provides the best snapshot of the spoken Arabic produced by Emirati speakers. The examples used in the book depict the actual usage and intuition of the spoken language by Emirati speakers, and what is considered as grammatical by native speakers. The data which form the basis for this grammatical description have been drawn from fieldwork sessions with native speakers of the language.

Thus, the grammar will be particularly useful for learners who seek to study Emirati Arabic as a 'live' language, and for language researchers from various perspectives who wish to investigate how the language is actually used. The intended audience for this work includes non-native speakers of Arabic who want to study the Gulf dialect of Emirati Arabic as spoken in the touristic and business hubs of Dubai and Abu Dhabi, as well as in the emerging centers of the rest of the Emirates. The audience additionally includes native speakers of other Arabic dialects with an interest in the linguistic idiosyncrasies of the Arabic dialect spoken in the UAE. Its comprehensive coverage of Emirati Arabic grammatical properties makes it valuable for language teachers who need a reference tool for teaching, non-native students who study Emirati Arabic as a second or foreign language, and anyone with an interest in language studies. The work also targets scholars and researchers of MSA who seek a better understanding of a contemporary spoken dialect of the language. Finally, given the thorough use of current linguistic research in compiling the grammar, albeit without a particular theoretical framework, the grammar is a resource for teachers, students, and researchers working in linguistics, linguistic theory, or typological studies of Semitic and Afro-Asiatic languages.

1.4 Transcription

All examples in this grammar are transcribed in Arabic script and the International Phonetic Alphabet (IPA). However, the use of Arabic script in examples diverges at times from the standard method for transcribing, for instance, MSA. The adopted spelling system corresponds closely with the actual pronunciation of the variety as commonly used by Emirati Arabic speakers, as shown in Table 1.1.

Table 1.1 Correspondences between Arabic letters and IPA symbols in transcription

Letter	*IPA*	*Example*	*Meaning*	*Letter*	*IPA*	*Example*	*Meaning*
ا	[ʔ]	ʔana	'I'	ق	[q]	lqaahəra	'Cairo'
	[aa]	ktaab	'book'		[g]	galam	'pen'
ب	[b]	baabaah	'father'		[dʒ]	tˤəriidʒ	'road'
ت	[t]	təlʕab	'she is playing'	ك	[k]	kəriim	'generous'
ث	[θ]	θalaaθa	'three'		[tʃ]	baʕtˤiitʃ	'I will give you'
ج	[dʒ]	maʕdʒuun	'toothpaste'	ل	[l]	leeʃ	'why'
	[j]	jəbal	'mountain'		[lˤ]	ʔalˤlˤa	'God'
ح	[ħ]	ħaraami	'robber'	م	[m]	mħammad	'Mohammed'
خ	[x]	ʔaxðˤar	'green'	ن	[n]	nʕaal	'slipper'
د	[d]	daraj	'stairs'	ه	[h]	saagha	'he drove it'
ذ	[ð]	haaða	'this'	و	[w]	ħəlwa	'beautiful'
ر	[r]	raaħ	'he left'		[oo]	dəktoor	'doctor'
ز	[z]	ʕəziiz	'Aziz'/'dear'		[uu]	maksuur	'broken'
س	[s]	sajjaara	'car'		[aw]	ʔawlaad	'boys'
ش	[ʃ]	ʃuu	'what'	ي	[j]	waajəd	'a lot'
	[tʃ]	tʃaaf	'saw'		[ii]	ʕətiidʒ	'old'
ص	[sˤ]	tsˤiiħiin	'you are crying'		[ee]	ween	'where'
ط	[tˤ]	tˤəmaatˤ	'tomato'		[aɪ]	dbaɪ	'Dubai'
ظ	[ðˤ]	ðˤruus	'teeth'	ى	[aa]	daraa	'knew'
غ	[ɣ]	maɣrəfa	'spoon'	ع	[ʕ]	ʕətiidʒ	'old'
ف	[f]	faatˤmah	'Fatima'				

1.5 Glossing

This grammar adopts a version of the Leipzig Glossing Rules as its glossing system (Comrie et al., 2008). These rules comprise an interlinear morpheme-by-morpheme glossing system which indicates the lexical and grammatical properties of individual words and morphemes. The system is theory-neutral, with merely the necessary information about the relevant morphemes. All sentence examples are given in four lines. The first line is the sentence written in Arabic script. The second presents a broad IPA transcription, representing as closely as possible the actual Emirati Arabic pronunciation. The third provides a morpheme-by-morpheme gloss in English. The fourth is a free English translation. While the morphological analysis of Arabic words may be intricate (e.g. the so-called 'root-and-pattern' morphological structure), to ease the reader's task, only linear morphemes are glossed. The transcriptional scheme is shown in the following example:

الكوفي أقوى من الشاي

əl-koofi	ʔa-gwa	mən	ətʃ-tʃaaj.
the-coffee	more-strong	than	the-tea

'Coffee is stronger than tea.'

1.6 Abbreviations

In glossing the different examples, standard abbreviations for grammatical functional properties are followed but the glossing system is simplified to improve readability (see Abbreviations). For instance, pronouns such as 'he' are used instead of more descriptive linguistic terms such as '3sm' (third-person singular masculine), and 'the' is used instead of 'det' for the determiner. The gloss 'they' (and similarly for other pronouns), as in 'meet.perf-they,' represents an agreement feature 'third-person plural.' The grammatical gender of nouns and adjectives is not explicitly indicated unless relevant to the discussion. The glosses 'you' and 'they' are by default masculine, while 'you.f' and 'they.f' express the feminine counterparts. Morphologically segmentable morphemes are separated by a hyphen, e.g. 'the-boy,' and dots are used to combine morphemes that do not possess clear boundaries, e.g. 'book.pl.' We also adopt the linguistic convention in using / / and [] to represent a phoneme/morpheme and its actual pronunciation, respectively.

Further reading

For a discussion of the historical development of Gulf Arabic dialects and how they correlate with the movement of nomadic groups from the north into the coastal regions, see Ingham (1982), Palva (1991), Versteegh (1997), and Holes (2007). For a detailed discussion of the demography of Gulf Arabic, see Johnstone (1967), Holes (1989, 1990, 2007), and Gazsi (2017). For the original discussion of Emirati Arabic as an independent spoken variety, see Hoffiz (1995), Mazid (2006), Blodgett et al. (2007), and work in the EMALAC project (Ntelitheos & Idrissi, 2017). The original discussion of 'diglossia' was from Ferguson (1959). Saiegh-Haddad and Henkin (2014) has a good summary of the diglossic situation of Arabic. For a discussion of current language policies in the UAE, see Boyle (2012) and Al Hussein and Gitsaki (2018) and the references therein. For information on the development of the Gulf Arabic pidgin, see Smart (1990).

As all Emirati Arabic is written in Arabic script, readers may refer to any Arabic grammar (e.g. MSA) for an overall description of the pronunciation and various ligatures of Arabic letters, e.g. Badawi et al. (2004), Ryding (2005), and Abu-Chacra (2007).

Note

1 A town in the Emirate of Sharjah, located along the Gulf of Oman on the east coast of the United Arab Emirates.

Chapter 2

The sounds of Emirati Arabic

In this chapter, we provide a description of the inventory of sounds in Emirati Arabic. Variation in languages and dialects is often encoded at the level of sounds. This generalization easily applies to all Arabic dialects spoken in the Gulf Arabic region. Traditionally, some linguists define Gulf Arabic as a distinct dialect that distinguishes it from other Arabic dialects primarily at the level of sound. For example, Johnstone (1967, pp. 2–18) lists several defining characteristics of the Eastern Arabian phonology, e.g. the affrication of [g] to [ʤ] and [k] to [ʧ], the effect of pharyngeal sounds on syllable structure, and the syllable structure of certain nominal and verbal forms. In the following two sections we list the consonant and vowel sounds in the dialect, with examples.

2.1 Consonants

2.1.1 *Simple consonants*

Table 2.1 shows the consonant inventory of Emirati Arabic.

Emirati Arabic consonants occupy various positions (e.g. onsets and coda) within the syllabic structure. For instance:

Table 2.1 International Phonetic Alphabets (IPA) chart for consonants of Emirati Arabic

	Bilabial	*Labio-dental*	*Interdental*	*Alveolar*	*Alveopalatal*	*Palatal*	*Velar*	*Uvular*	*Pharyngeal*	*Glottal*
Stops	b			t d			k g	q		ʔ
				tˤ						
Fricatives		f	θ ð	s z	ʃ		x ɣ		ħ ʕ	h
			ðˤ	sˤ						
Affricates					ʧ ʤ					
Nasals	m			n						
Laterals				l						
				lˤ						
Trills				r						
Glides	w					j				

Table 2.2 Consonants of Emirati Arabic

ا	[ʔ]	أنا	[ʔana]	'I'
		المسألة	[lmasʔala]	'the issue'
ب	[b]	باب	[baab]	'door'
		حبر	[ħibər]	'ink'
ت	[t]	تعال	[taʕaal]	'come!'
		بيت	[beet]	'house
ث	[θ]	ثلث	[θəlθ]	'one-third'
		مثلث	[muθallaθ]	'triangle'
ج	[ʤ]	طريجنا	[tˤəriiʤna]	'our way'
		جامعة	[ʤaamʕa]	'university'
	[j]	جدار	[jədaar]	'wall'
	[j]	فنجان	[fənjaan]	'coffee cup'
ح	[ħ]	حرامي	[ħaraami]	'robber'
		مفتاح	[məftaaħ]	'key'
خ	[x]	أخضر	[ʔaxðˤar]	'green'
		طباخ	[tˤabbaax]	'cook'

(*Continued*)

Table 2.2 (Continued)

		خل	[xall]	'vinegar'
د	[d]	درَج	[daraj]	'stairs'
		إتحاد	[ʔəttiħaad]	'union'
ذ	[ð]	هذا	[haaða]	'this'
		لذيذ	[laðiið]	'delicious'
ر	[r]	راح	[raaħ]	'he left'
		شكر	[ʃəkar]	'sugar'
ز	[z]	عزيز	[ʕəziiz]	'Aziz' or 'dear'
		زين	[zeen]	'well; fine'
س	[s]	سيارة	[sajjaara]	'car'
		مستانس	[məstaanəs]	'happy'
ش	[ʃ]	شو	[ʃuu]	'what'
		نش	[naʃʃ]	'he woke up'
	[ʧ]	شاف	[ʧaaf]	'saw'
ص	[sˤ]	تصيحين	[tsˤiiħiin]	'you are crying'
		صح	[sˤaħ]	'right'
		مقص	[məgasˤsˤ]	'scissors'
ط	[tˤ]	طاح	[tˤaaħ]	'he fell down'
		ضغط	[ðˤaɣtˤ]	'pressure'
		يطير	[jtˤiir]	'flies'
ظ	[ðˤ]	بيض	[beeðˤ]	'eggs'
		مريضة	[məriiðˤa]	'sick'
		ضروري	[ðˤaruuri]	'necessary'
ع	[ʕ]	عتيج	[ʕətiiʤ]	'old'
		ربع	[rəbəʕ]	'quarter'
غ	[ɣ]	مغرفة	[maɣrəfa]	'spoon'
		غترة	[ɣətra]	'head dress'
		صبغ	[sˤəbaɣ]	'he painted'
ف	[f]	فاطمة	[faatˤmah]	'Fatima'
		فتر	[ftarr]	'turned around'
		نفاف	[nəfaaf]	'light rain'
ق	[q]	القاهرة	[lqaahəra]	'Cairo'
		قرآن	[qurʔaan]	'Quran'
		صديق	[sˤadiiq]	'friend'

		مقاول	[mqaawel]	'contractor'
	[g]	قلم	[galam]	'pen'
		أزرق	[ʔazrag]	'blue'
		سقم	[səgam]	'sickness'
		مقطوع	[magtˤuuʕ]	'cut'
		ذوق	[ðoog]	'taste'
ك	[k]	كريم	[kəriim]	'generous'
		محرك	[mħarrik]	'engine'
	[ʧ]	بعطيج	[baʕtˤiiʧ]	'I will give you'
ل	[l]	ليش	[leeʃ]	'why'
		بدال	[bdaal]	'instead of'
	[lˤ]	طالبات	[tˤaalˤbaat]	'students'
م	[m]	محمد	[mħammad]	'Mohammed'
		تمام	[tamaam]	'exactly'
ن	[n]	نعال	[nʕaal]	'slipper'
		كان	[kaan]	'was'
ه	[h]	هذا	[haaða]	'this'
		أباه	[ʔabaah]	'I want it'
و	[w]	حلوة	[ħəlwa]	'beautiful'
		ورد	[ward]	'flowers'
ي	[j]	وايد	[waajəd]	'a lot'
		ماي	[maaj]	'water'
ا	[ʔ]	أنا	[ʔana]	'I'

Most Emirati Arabic consonants overlap with other Gulf Arabic dialects and MSA. The realization of MSA words with the letter ق as [g] is one of the major identifying properties of the Gulf Arabic varieties (including in the UAE). In Emirati Arabic, there are local varieties where [q] emerges more frequently but, in most cases, words in which [q] is pronounced are loanwords from MSA.

قرآن	[qurʔaan]	'Quran'
قاهرة	[qaahəra]	'Cairo'
قاموس	[qaamuus]	'dictionary'
قناة	[qanaah]	'channel'
قطار	[qətˤaar]	'train'
قانون	[qaanuun]	'law'

قرين	[qariin]	'consort'
دقيق	[daqiiq]	'precise'
قرية	[qaryah]	'village'

Phonetic variation is evident in the actual pronunciation of [g], and many Emirati speakers vary between the voiced uvular stop [ɢ] and the voiced velar stop [g], e.g. قريب gəriib/ɢəriib 'near, relative' and قادر gaadər/ɢaadər 'capable.'

The Gulf-specific consonant [ʧ] diachronically evolved from a historical *k in the context of (mid-)high (and front) vowels (كيف/ keef/ [ʧeef] 'how'). There is still free variation between [k], [ʧ] across UAE regions, and even between individuals. A similar variation occurs between the voiced counterparts [ʤ] and [g] in certain contexts, with the former in free variation with the glide [j]. Chapter 3 provides more information about the properties of these allophonic alternations.

Emphatic consonants in Emirati Arabic comprise a set of complex sounds produced by a primary coronal articulation, with the tip of the tongue touching the alveolar ridge behind the upper teeth, and a secondary articulation involving the retraction of the tongue body into the pharyngeal space. The secondary articulation distinguishes the emphatic sounds from their non-emphatic counterparts. However, these are separate sounds in the dialect. This is confirmed by the abundant existence of minimal pairs, words with distinct meanings which differ only in the emphatic/non-emphatic sound, e.g. سفر [safar] 'journey' vs. صفر [sˤafar] 'second month in the Muslim calendar,' تين [tiin] 'figs' vs. طين [tˤiin] 'clay,' and so on. The status of the emphatic lateral [lˤ] as a separate sound (phoneme) in Emirati Arabic is not definitive. [lˤ] occurs as an allophone of the phoneme /l/ in the environment of emphatic consonants, pharyngeals and velars, when the two are not separated by the front high vowel [i]. For example, اطلب 'ask for' is pronounced as [ʔətˤlˤib] and أطول 'longer' is pronounced as [ʔatˤwalˤ]. In some cases one finds minimal pairs formed by [l] and [lˤ]. For example, a commonly cited minimal pair is ولاه [wɛllæhu] 'he appointed him' vs. والله [wɛlˤlˤæhu] 'by God,' the sacred expressions which are used across dialects (Chapter 18).

2.1.2 *Double consonants (geminates)*

Emirati Arabic distinguishes between simple and double consonants or *geminates*. Geminates are pronounced by lengthening a single consonant. In Arabic script, gemination may be indicated by a diacritic symbol called 'shadda.' Geminates in Emirati Arabic can be word-final, and sometimes word-medial, according to the actual pronunciation and theoretical analysis. It is plausible to analyze the word-medial geminate consonants as belonging to separate syllables, e.g. [ʔalˁ.lˁah] 'Allah'/'God' ألله; thus they are considered by some phonologists as ambisyllabic.

Word-medial geminates

بعّد	[baʕ.ʕad]	'moved s.th away'	كبّر	[kab.bar]	'enlarged'
أذّن	[ʔað.ðan]	'called to prayer'	لحّف	[laħ.ħaf]	'covered'
طلّق	[tˁal.lag]	'divorced'	تعشّى	[tʕaʃ.ʃa]	'had dinner'
سوّس	[saw.was]	'had tooth decay'	شوّت	[ʃaw.wat]	'kicked'
ذكّر	[ðak.kar]	'reminded'	عوّر	[ʕaw.war]	'caused pain'
روّع	[raw.waʕ]	'frightened'	حصّل	[ħasˁ.sˁal]	'found'

Word-final geminates

فك	[fatʃtʃ]	'opened'	كد	[kadd]	'worked hard'
ضم	[ðˁamm]	'gathered'	عد	[ʕadd]	'counted'
رد	[radd]	'answered'	لم	[lamm]	'collected'
مد	[madd]	'extended'	شد	[ʃadd]	'pulled'
سد	[sadd]	'closed'	يد	[jadd]	'cut'
نط	[natˁtˁ]	'jumped'	بس	[bass]	'enough'

While morpheme-level word-initial geminates are generally unattested in Emirati Arabic, in natural conversations the definite determiner الـ [əl-] 'the' may be pronounced without [ə], which in turns creates apparent cases of word-initial geminates.

الطمّاع	[ətˁ-tˁammaʕ]	>	[tˁ-tˁammaʕ]	'the greedy'
الثمان	[əθ-θəmaan]	>	[θ-θəmaan]	'the eight'
الدمعة	[əd-damʕa]	>	[d-damʕa]	'the tear'
الشمس	[əʃ-ʃams]	>	[ʃ-ʃams]	'the sun'
الذنوب	[əð-ðənuub]	>	[ð-ðənuub]	'the sins'
الدوام	[əd-dəwaam]	>	[d-dəwaam]	'the work shift'

2.2 Vowels

The vowel system is probably the most elusive aspect of Emirati (and also Gulf) Arabic phonology. Moreover, it is the core of the differences between various Gulf Arabic dialects.

A problem faced by Arabic linguists and grammarians when depicting the vowel inventory of Arabic dialects stems partly from the fact that short vowels are not normally transcribed in Arabic writing. Satisfactory description or analysis of the vowel inventory is also hindered by the use of MSA words or expressions by speakers in formal contexts. Depending on the language register and formal education of MSA, native speakers may manipulate the two overlapping phonological systems.

Given the lack of research in the vowel inventory of Emirati Arabic, the vowel chart in Figure 2.1 depicts the actual pronunciation of Emirati Arabic words by Emirati speakers in naturalistic settings. We have made use of accurate measurements from the field of acoustics, especially for the inventory of short vowels.

Phonetic variations occur for short vowels in certain unstressed environments (and occasionally even in stressed syllables). It is possible all three short vowels (i.e. [a], [i], and [u]) are shifted to the neutral mid-central [ə]. In some cases, the high vowels may be pronounced as a high-central vowel [ɨ]. Some examples of vowel phonetic variation accepted by all native speakers are:

مسمار	[mismaar]/[məsmaar]	'nail'
جمعة	[jimʕa]/[jəmʕa]	'Friday'
سكت	[sikat]/[səkat]	'he silenced'
شكر	[ʃikar]/[ʃəkar]	'sugar'
متروس	[matruus]/[mətruus]	'full'

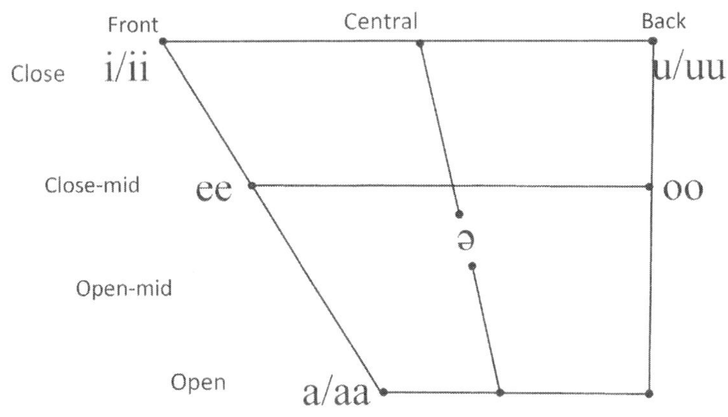

Figure 2.1 Vowels of Emirati Arabic

In many cases, even stressed vowels, especially in short bisyllabic words, require the vowel to be centralized to [ə], e.g. لقى [ləga] 'he found' and كتب [kətəb] 'books.'

Otherwise, short vowels are always pronounced as such at word-final positions.

بقا/بقى	[bəga]	'It remained'
ثلاثة	[θalaaθa]	'three'
ادري	[ʔadri]	'I know'
كتابي	[ktaabi]	'my book'
ابو	[ʔəbu]	'father'
شافوا	[ʧaafu]	'They saw'

To avoid confusion, we use [ə] throughout this grammar to summarize this vowel neutralization. In contrast, if the short vowel, e.g. [a], [i], or [u] is used, it indicates that the vowel may or may not be neutralized. For instance, the short vowel [a] is more stable in the vicinity of guttural and velar consonants, e.g. قلب [galˤb] 'heart' and ضمير [ðˤameer] 'conscience.' The feminine suffix -a/-ah and the third-person masculine singular pronoun suffix -ah seem to maintain the full vowel [a], e.g. الطالبة [ətˤtˤaaləba] 'the student' and اعتبره [ʔaʕtibrah] 'I consider him.'

Long vowels are pronounced with a duration approximately double that of their singleton counterparts. In addition to the peripheral long vowels [aa], [ii], and [uu], Emirati Arabic has two additional middle long vowels, [oo] and [ee].

[ii] [ي, jaa] or [ي kasrah jaa]			*[uu] [و, waaw] or [و dˤammah waaw]*		
سكين	[səʧʧiin]	'knife'	مجموعات	[məʤmuuʕaat]	'groups'
ذيب	[ðiib]	'wolf'	اسبوع	[ʔəsbuuʕ]	'week'
حيب	[ħiib]	'palm tree core'	نروح	[ənruuħ]	'to go'
بير	[biir]	'well'	تقوم	[tguum]	'to get up'

[aa] [ا, ʔalif] or [ا fatħah ʔalif]			*[oo]*		
مرتاح	[mərtaaħ]	'at ease'	تلفون	[təlfoon]	'phone'
مار	[maar]	'passing'	دور	[door]	'role'
راد	[raad]	'coming back'	لون	[loon]	'color'
فار	[faar]	'mouse'	حول	[ħool]	'around'

[ee]		
كيك	[keek]	'cake'
زيت	[zeet]	'oil'

In many cases, the vowels [ee] and [oo] seem to have emerged through a process of de-diphthongization, whereas the MSA diphthongs [aɪ] and [aʊ] have lost the gliding second part and raised or lengthened the first vowel part: [aɪ] > [ee] and [aʊ] > [oo]. The following shows the phonological correspondence between MSA and Emirati Arabic words regarding the pronunciation of diphthongs vs. [ee] and [oo]:

	MSA	*Emirati Arabic*	*Meaning*
بيت	[baɪt]	[beet]	'house'
ولدين	[waladaɪn]	[waladeen]	'two children'
خيل	[xaɪl]	[xeel]	'horses'
يوم	[jaʊm]	[joom]	'day'
خوف	[xaʊf]	[xoof]	'fear'

Long middle vowels also appear in borrowings. An underlying diphthong may not be theoretically motivated in such cases: تلفون [təlfoon] 'phone,' كيك [keek] 'cake,' تلفزون [talfizoon] 'television,' and others. The following minimal pairs further show that /ee/ and /oo/ are independent phonemes in Emirati Arabic:

شين	[ʃiin]	'the letter for [ʃ]'	شين	[ʃeen]	'bad'
دِين	[diin]	'religion'	دَين	[deen]	'loan'
لومي	[luumi]	'lemon'	لومي	[loomi]	'my blame'
كون	[kuun]	'become'	كون	[koon]	'universe'

Finally, in certain Emirati Arabic varieties and idiolects, the diphthongs are still clearly pronounced. Thus, the adjective/adverb 'good, well' is pronounced as either [zeen] or [zeɪn] in different varieties. Other examples include دبي [dbaɪ] 'Dubai,' شوي [ʃwaɪ] 'a little,' and لو [law] 'if.'

Further reading

Detailed descriptions of the phonemic inventories of Gulf Arabic varieties are given in Al-Ani (1970), Qafisheh (1977), Hassan (1981), and Holes (1990). Mustafawi (2006) provides a very detailed discussion of the alternations between [k]/[ʧ], [g]/[ʤ], and [q]/[g], based on data on the closely related variety of Qatari Arabic. For certain accounts for the phonological realization of [g], see Al-Ani (1978, p. 108), Johnstone (1978, p. 285), and Alamadidhi (1985, p. 85); while for others, [q] and [g] are separate phonemes in the target dialect (Bukshaisha, 1985, p. 17; Hussain, 1985, p. 8; Al-Sulaiti, 1993, pp. 6–7, Mustafawi, 2006, p. 19).

Chapter 3

Phonological processes

This chapter discusses several sound changes observed in Emirati Arabic, including processes also observed in other Arabic dialects. It provides descriptions of the syllable structure, stress assignment, and phonotactic rules. Many of these properties play an important role in identifying Emirati Arabic as a distinct variety within the Gulf Arabic dialect continuum.

3.1 Feature-level processes

Emirati Arabic is characterized by a number of assimilatory processes also common in other Arabic varieties. Assimilation causes a change in the features of a sound, in most cases to make it more similar to an immediately preceding or following sound, resulting in easier articulation of the sound sequence. In the case of consonants, this change may affect either the place of articulation, the manner of articulation, or the voicing specification of the segment.

3.1.1 *Nasal place assimilation*

A typical example of this process is *place assimilation.* As Table 3.1 shows, the nasal consonant /n/, which is pronounced by touching the tip of the tongue to the alveolar ridge behind the upper teeth, acquires the place of articulation of the following consonant.

3.1.2 *Palatalization*

Another widely attested assimilatory process is palatalization. In addition to the well-known variation between [k]~[ʧ] and [g]~[ʤ], which applies across almost all Gulf Arabic varieties, velar plosives undergo palatalization (i.e. the articulation and constriction within the oral cavity is shifted towards the middle-front region), especially if followed by front vowels.

Table 3.1 Place assimilation

alveolar (-palatal) place assimilation			
سنطرة	/sˤantˤara/	[sˤantˤara]	'mandarin' (fruit)
كندورة	/kandoora/	[kandoora]	'dress' (cultural dress)
سمج	/səmatʃ/	[səmatʃ]	'fish'
شمعة	/ʃamʕa/	[ʃamʕa]	'candle'
velar place assimilation			
نقرى	/ngaraa/	[ŋgaraa]	'was read'
نكوى	/nkəwaa/	[ŋkəwaa]	'was ironed'
نكتم	/nkətam/	[ŋkətam]	'was filled' or 'was silenced'
bilabial place assimilation			
نمصع	/ənməsˤaʕ/	[əmmesˤaʕ]	'was pulled out'
نمسك	/ənməsak/	[əmməsak]	'got caught'
نمط	/ənmatˤtˤ/	[əmmatˤtˤ]	'got stretched'
labio-dental place assimilation			
منفاخ	[mənfaax]	[məɱfaax]	'air pump'
منفر	[mənfarr]	[məɱfarr]	'thrown'
انفصل	[ənfəsˤalˤ]	[əɱfəsˤalˤ]	'separated'
منفعص	[mənfəʕəsˤ]	[məɱfəʕəsˤ]	'squished'

قبلة	/giblˤa/	[gʲiblˤa]	'direction of prayer'
قر	/girr/	[gʲirr]	'sit'
قيتار	/giitaar/	[gʲiitaar]	'guitar'
قيس	/giis/	[gʲiis]	'measure'
قيمه	/giimah/	[gʲiimah]	'value

Similar processes apply to the voiceless velar consonant [k], i.e. it is palatalized to [kʲ].

مسكين	/miskiin/	[miskʲiin]	'poor'
ذكي	/ðaki/	[ðakʲi]	'smart'
كيمرا	/keemara/	[kʲeemara]	'camera'
كيلو	/kiilu/	[kʲiilu]	'kilogram'

3.1.3 Phonological variation

A salient phonological property of Emirati Arabic is the observation of free variation [g]~[ʤ] and [k]~[ʧ], especially when preceded or followed by a front (i.e. non-back) vowel.

[g]~[ʤ]

حريق	[ħəriig]	حريج	[ħəriiʤ]	'fire'
قدر	[gədər]	جدر	[ʤədər]	'cooking pot'
ثقيل	[θəgiil]	ثجيل	[θəʤiil]	'heavy'
رفقة	[rəfga]	رفجة	[rəfʤa]	'friends' (used for swearing by God)
طريق	[tˤəriig]	طريج	[tˤəriiʤ]	'road'
عتيق	[ʕətiig]	عتيج	[ʕətiiʤ]	'old'
عميق	[ʕəmiig]	عميج	[ʕəmiiʤ]	'deep'

[k]~[ʧ]

كم	[kamm]	جم	[ʧamm]	'How much?'
كيس	[kiis]	جيس	[ʧiis]	'bag'
شوكة	[ʃooka]	شوجة	[ʃooʧa]	'thorn'
كحال	[kħaal]	جحال	[ʧħaal]	'eyeliner'
كلب	[kalb]	جلب	[ʧalb]	'dog'
كتف	[katf]	جتف	[ʧatf]	'shoulder'
كبد	[kabd]	جبد	[ʧabd]	'liver'
كنعد	[kanʕad]	جنعد	[ʧanʕad]	'mackerel fish'
باكر	[baakər]	باجر	[baaʧər]	'tomorrow'

Sometimes, the [g]~[ʤ] variation applies even when the front/non-back vowel is separated by an intervening consonant.

قبال	[gbaal]	جبال	[ʤbaal]	'across'
قريب	[griib]	جريب	[ʤriib]	'close to'
عرق	[ʕərg]	عرج	[ʕərʤ]	'vein'
صدق	[sˤədg]	صدج	[sˤəʤ]	'truth'
حلق	[ħalg]	حلج	[ħalʤ]	'pharynx, mouth'

In Emirati (and other Gulf) Arabic, the phonological realization of [k] and [ʧ] is also morphologically conditioned. For the expression of the second-person singular suffix (Section 5.8), its phonological exponence hinges upon its gender, i.e. ك- [-ək] for masculine and ج- [-əʧ] for feminine.

وياك/وياج	بيتك/بيتج
wəjja-k/ʧ	beet-ək/əʧ
with-you/you.f	house-your/your.f
'with you'	'your house'

كلّمك/كلّمج	عندك/عندج
kallam-k/ʧ.	ʕənd-ək/əʧ?
spoke.perf-you/you.f	with-you/you.f
'He spoke to you.'	'Do you have?'

3.1.4 *Affricate lenition*

Lenition is a phonological process through which a consonant becomes more sonorous. In Emirati Arabic, the [ʤ]~[j] variation is one such example. Sociolinguistic factors play a role in this alternation; for example, [ʤ] is more frequently used in educated or formal contexts. People living in rural areas, such as the Emirates of Fujairah or Ras Al Khaimah, are more likely to use the [j] variant.

رجل	[raʤəl]	ريل	[rajəl]	'husband'
جعل	[ʤəʕal]	يعل	[jəʕal]	'may it'
جديد	[ʤədiid]	يديد	[jədiid]	'new'
جواز	[ʤəwaaz]	يواز	[jəwaaz]	'passport'
شجر	[ʃəʤar]	شير	[ʃəjar]	'trees'

In addition, distribution seems to be somewhat phonologically and lexically conditioned. Overall, [ʤ]~[j] variation is quite common at the onset position.

مجلس	[maʤləs]	ميلس	[majləs]	'guest room/hall'
جزر	[ʤəzar]	يزر	[jəzar]	'carrot'
فنجان	[fənʤaan]	فنيان	[fənjaan]	'coffee cup'
مسجد	[masʤəd]	مسيد	[masjəd/məsiid]	'mosque'
جيران	[ʤiiraan]	يران	[jiiraan]	'neighbors'
جبل	[ʤəbal]	يبل	[jəbal]	'mountain'

جار	[ʤaar]	يار	[jaar]	'neighbor'
جاب	[ʤaab]	ياب	[jaab]	'brought'
جر	[ʤarr]	ير	[jarr]	'pulled'
جانب	[ʤaanəb]	يانب	[jaanəb]	'side'
مجنون	[maʤnuun]	مينون	[majnuun]	'crazy'

For unknown reasons, the [ʤ]~[j] variation at the onset position for the following list is not available, i.e. [ʤ] in this list is the only pronunciation. Some of these words stem from lexical borrowing.

جبن	[ʤə.bən]	'cheese'
جهاز	[ʤə.haaz]	'machine'
جندي	[ʤən.di]	'soldier'
معجزة	[muʕ.ʤə.zah]	'miracle'
جريدة	[ʤa.rii.da]	'newspapers'
نجار	[naʤ.ʤaar]	'carpenter'
تاجر	[taa.ʤər]	'merchant'
جرس	[ʤa.ras]	'bell'
جدول	[ʤad.wal]	'schedule'
مهرجان	[mah.ra.ʤaan]	'festival' (<Persian)
جاكيت	[ʤaa.keet]	'jacket' (<English)
رجيم	[rəʤiim]	'diet' (<Latin)

3.1.5 *Pharyngealization*

Emirati Arabic pharyngeal and emphatic consonants affect the pronunciation of neighboring vowels. The effect is mainly realized as a lowering and retraction of the tongue in the articulation of vowels, resulting in more open and back vowels. Pharyngealization may also be spread across consonants, resulting in a secondary articulation with tongue retraction towards the pharyngeal wall, essentially producing emphatic allophones of the target consonants. The process is unidirectional and iterative, resulting in pharyngealization of adjacent consonants. In Emirati Arabic, such an 'emphatic spread' can be left-to-right and right-to-left.

طالب	/tˤaalˤəb/	[tˤaalˤəbˤ]	'student'
صام	/sˤaam/	[sˤaamˤ]	'he fasted'

طب	/tˤibb/	[tˤəbˤbˤ]	'medicine'
صفر	/sˤifr/	[sˤəfˤərˤ]	'zero'
ضرب	/ðˤarb/	[ðˤarˤbˤ]	'beating'
صف	/sˤaff/	[sˤafˤfˤ]	'row'
ظلام	/ðˤalaam/	[ðˤalˤaamˤ]	'darkness'
مظلة	/mðˤalla/	[mˤðˤalˤlˤa]	'umbrella'
حطب	/ħatˤab/	[ħətˤabˤ]	'wood'
طالعة	/tˤaalʕah/	[tˤaalˤʕah]	'getting out'
صالة	/sˤaalah/	[sˤaalˤah]	'living room'
ظلم	/ðˤelm/	[ðˤelˤm]	'injustice'

During emphatic spread, in some cases (depending on the speaker), the high long vowels can be lowered.

ضمير	/ðˤəmiir/	[ðˤəmeer]	'conscience'
صريح	/sˤariiħ/	[sˤəreeħ]	'frank'
طابور	/tˤaabuur/	[tˤaaboor]	'queue'
حصير	/ħasˤiir/	[ħəsˤeer]	'carpet'

The bilabial nasal [m] and the two liquids [l] and [r] appear pharyngealized in additional contexts (again, depending on the speaker).

مابا	/maaba/	[mˤaaba]	'I don't want'
عاملة	/ʕaamla/	[ʕaamˤlˤa]	'worker'
حمار	/ħmaar/	[ħmˤaarˤ]	'donkey'
امايه	/ʔəmmaaja/	[ʔəmˤmˤaaja]	'my mother'
امّرّة	/əmmarra/	[əmˤmˤarˤrˤa]	'at all'
مر	/marr/	[mˤarˤrˤ]	'passed'

[lˤ] contrasts with [l] in words like والا [wəlla] 'or' and والله [wɒlˤlˤa] 'by God' and it appears mainly (almost exclusively) in derivatives of the word الله [ʔalˤlˤaah] 'God.' Therefore, it occupies a place as a distinct sound in the inventory of Emirati Arabic, as discussed in Chapter 2.

3.1.6 *Complete assimilation*

A few cases of complete assimilation occur in Emirati Arabic; in these the affected sound becomes identical to the sound causing the change. As with other Arabic dialects, the lateral consonant [l] of the definite determiner prefix ال əl- 'the' assimilates to the initial segment of the following noun (or nominal modifier) when the latter is one of the coronal consonants [t, d, θ, ð, tˤ, ðˤ, s, z, sˤ, ʃ, n, r, l], which are produced with the front part of the tongue, including the tip and tongue blade. These letters are usually termed 'sun' letters (حروف شمسية ħuruuf ʃamsijjah) in Arabic grammars, to distinguish them from all other consonants, termed 'moon' letters (حروف قمرية ħuruuf gamarijjah), which do not trigger assimilation.

Sun letters

الشمس	[əʃʃams]	'the sun'
الذنوب	[əððənuub]	'the sins'
الدوام	[əddəwaam]	'the work shift'
السؤال	[əssuʔaal]	'the question'
الظلام	[əðˤðˤalˤaam]	'the darkness'

Moon letters

البيض	[əlbeeðˤ]	'the egg'
الاوراق	[əlʔawraag]	'the papers'
الاقلام	[əlʔaglaam]	'the pens'
الفاضية	[əlfaaðˤja]	'the empty (f)'
الورد	[əlward]	'the flowers'

There seem to be a few exceptions to the rule of determiner assimilation and certain cases where inter-speaker variation is evident. Thus, while the voiceless affricate [ʧ] seems to always assimilate, its voiced counterpart [ʤ] sometimes does not, depending on the speaker.

الجلب	[əlʧalb]/[əʧʧalb]	'the dog'
الجواب	[əlʤawaab]/[əʤʤawaab]	'the answer'
الجيب	[əlʤeeb]/[əʤʤeeb]	'the army'

A second case of complete assimilation takes place with affixation of pronominal suffixes to consonant-final words. The voiceless glottal fricative [h] in an affix-initial position frequently assimilates fully to the stem-final voiceless pharyngeal fricative [ħ] and stem-final voiceless stop [t].

جرح	/jarħ/ + /hum/	[jarħħum]	'their wound'
فرّح	/farraħ/ + /hum/	[farraħħum]	'made them happy'
مسح	/məsaħ/ + /ha/	[məsaħħa]	'deleted it (f)'
فتح	/fətaħ/ + /ha/	[fətaħħa]	'he opened it'
ليت	/leet/ + /hum/	[leettum]	'their light'
كليت	/kaleet/ + /hum/	[kaleettum]	'I ate them'
فرّت	/farrat/ + /ha/	[farratta]	'she threw it (f)'
زخّيتّم	/zaxxeet/ +/-hum/	[zaxxeettum]	'I caught them'
قريتّا	/gareet/ + /-ha/	[gareetta]	'I read it (f)'
خالتّا	/xalat/ + /-ha/	[xalatta]	'her aunt (mother side)'
ليت	/leet/ + /ha/	[leetta]	'her light'

Finally, the reflexive prefix /t-/ (Sections 5.2.7 and 5.2.8) assimilates fully to verbal stem-initial coronal consonants.

ادّعم	/t-/ + /daʕʕam/	[əddaʕʕəm]	'she hits'
ادّمع	/t-/ + /damməʕ/	[əddamməʕ]	'she tears up'
اطرّش	/t-/ + /tˤarrəʃ/	[ətˤtˤarrəʃ]	'she sends'
ادّور	/t-/ + /duur/	[əduur]	'she spins'
اثّبت	/t-/ + /θabbat/	[əθθabbat]	'it was fixed'
اطّقم	/t-/ + /tˤaqqam/	[ətˤtˤaqqəm]	'she coordinates'

Word-final consonants are devoiced in utterance-final position, especially when they form the final segment of a consonant cluster.

صب	[sˤab] > [sˤab̥]	'pour'
حب	[ħab] > [ħab̥]	'sunflower seeds'

Several vowels seem to be underlyingly long yet appear short in word-final positions. The long counterparts emerge when the word is suffixed and thus the vowels appear word-medially.

لقى	[ləga]	'he found'	لقاه	[ləgaah]	'he found it/him'
تعنّى	[tʕanna]	'he made an effort'	تعنّاله	[tʕannaala]	'he made effort for him'
تريّا	[trajja]	'he waited'	تريّاكم	[trajjaakum]	'he waited for you (pl)'

عشا	[ʕəʃa]	'dinner'	عشانا	[ʕəʃaana]	'our dinner'
أدري	[ʔadri]	'I know'	ادريبه	[ʔadriibah]	'I know him'
غنّى	[ɣanna]	'he sang'	غنّاها	[ɣannaaha]	'he sang it (f)'
قرينا	[gareena]	'we read'	قريناها	[gareenaaha]	'we read it (f)'
خلّينا	[xalleena]	'we let'	خلّيناكم	[xalleenaakum]	'we let you (pl)'
سمعو	[səmʕaw]	'they (m) saw'	سمعوك	[səmʕook]	'they heard you'
قريتي	[gəreeti]	'you (f) read'	قريتيها	[gəreetiiha]	'you read it (f)'
شفتي	[ʧəfti]	'you (f) saw'	شفتيهم	[ʧəftiihum]	'you saw them'
مشى	[maʃʃa]	'he made s.o walk'	مشاكم	[maʃʃaakum]	'he walked you (pl)'
سقى	[səga]	'watered'	سقاها	[səgaaha]	'he watered it (f)'
حنّى	[ħənna]	'dye'	حناكم	[ħənnaakum]	'your (pl) dye'

3.2 Segment-level processes

3.2.1 *Consonant deletion*

Consonant deletion is a consonant cluster simplification process implemented in Emirati Arabic to reduce sequences of consonants, usually derived by affixation. Thus, when a double consonant is followed by a single consonant in the same word or between word boundaries, the double consonant is reduced to a single consonant.

بسهم	/bass/ + /-hum/	[bashum]	'enough for them'
لفهم	/ləff/ + /-hum/	[ləfhum]	'wrap them'
خلها	/xall/ + /-ha/	[xalha]	'let her'
بس ملح	/bass/ + /məlħ/	[bas məlħ]	'enough salt'
عقهن	/ʕəgg/ + /-hən/	[ʕəghən]	'throw them (f) away'

A second case of consonant deletion affects glottal stops in word-initial position. In many instances, the glottal stops are dropped, especially if the word preceding the target word ends in a consonant, e.g. with the addition of the definite determiner prefix الـ- əl- 'the.'

إلخضر	/əl-/ + /ʔaxðˤar/	[əlxaðˤar]	'the green'

Word-final geminates are also usually pronounced as their singlet counterparts, the geminates emerging again when in a non-final position, e.g. with the addition of a suffix.

عض	/ʕaðˤðˤ/	[ʕaðˤ]	'bite'	(but: عضة [ʕaðˤðˤa] 'a bite')
شل	/ʃall/	[ʃal]	'carry'	(but: شله [ʃallah] 'he carried it')
خض	/xaðˤðˤ/	[xaðˤ]	'shake'	(but: خضه [xaðˤðˤah] 'shake it')

3.2.2 *Vowel insertion/epenthesis*

Another process which functions to simplify consonant clusters is vowel insertion (*epenthesis*), where an epenthetic vowel [ə] (or occasionally [ɨ]) is inserted between consonants in the cluster. There seems to be variation in the place where the epenthetic vowel is inserted. For words ending in a double consonant, epenthesis can take place within a morpheme or at word boundaries. However, in cases where the word ends in a two-consonant cluster of different consonants, for some speakers the epenthetic vowel is inserted between these two consonants.

بنتنا	/bint/ + /-na/	[binitna]	'our daughter'
لبسنا	/ləbs/ + /-na/	[ləbisna]	'our outfit'
كسرت	/kəsart/ + /-hum/	[kəsarəthum]	'he broke them'

Vowel epenthesis is productive across morpheme boundaries, especially if combining two morphemes/words would result in 'heavy' consonant clusters (e.g. CCC and CCCC).

لأنه مسكر	/lannah/ + /msakkar/	[lannah əmsakkar]	'because it's close'
الولد مخلّص	/əlwalad/ + /mxalləsˤ/	[əlwalad əmxalləsˤ]	'the boy is finished'
لأنه تراب	/lannah/ + /traab/	[lannah ətraab]	'because it's sand'
الريال مكابر	/ərrajjaal/ + /mkaabər/	[ərrajjaal əmkaabər]	'the man is arrogant'
بنت مركزة	/bənt/ + /mrakza/	[bənt əmrakza]	'an attentive girl'

In the same vein, if the definite determiner prefix -ال /əl-/ is added to a noun starting with a two-consonant cluster, an epenthetic vowel is inserted after the prefixed lateral (note: the underlying onset /ʔ/ will become the vowel [a] after -ال /əl-/ prefixation).

الولاد	/əl-/ + /ʔawlaad/	[lawlaad]	'the boys'
المخبّل	/əl-/ + /mxabbalˤ/	[ləmxabbalˤ]	'the crazy one'
البيوت	/əl-/ + /bjuut/	[ləbjuut]	'the houses'
الفلوس	/əl-/ + /fluus/	[ləfluus]	'the money'

In contrast, epenthesis is not observed if the two morphemes do not form a single prosodic unit. The second words in the following examples are proper names, prepositional phrases, and noun phrases, respectively. They are independent prosodic units and therefore do not permit epenthesis.

حق أحمد	/ħagg/ + /ʔaħmad/	[ħagg ʔaħmad]	'for Ahmad'
حلوة منّك	/ħəlwa/ + /mənnək/	[ħəlwa mənnək]	'nice coming from you'
فك حلجك	/fətʧʧ/ + /ħalʤək/	[fətʧʧ ħalʤək]	'open your mouth!'

3.2.3 *Vowel deletion*

Unstressed short vowels, in a non-final position, are usually deleted, subject to dialectal variation.

كتاب	/kətaab/	[ktaab]	'book'
سرور	/səruur/	[sruur]	'Emirati name'
قصور	/gəsʕuur/	[gsʕuur]	'palaces'
قلمي	/galˤam/ + /-i/	[glˤəmi]	'my pen'
بحور	/bəħuur/	[bħuur]	'seas'

If a word ends with an unstressed vowel-consonant sequence and a vowel-initial suffix is added to it, then the unstressed vowel is dropped.

اسمي	/ʔəsəm/ + /-i/	[ʔəsmi]	'my name'
رسمي	/rasəm/ + /-i/	[rasmi]	'my paintings'

3.2.4 *Metathesis*

Some speakers avoid initial closed syllables (e.g. CVC) where the vowel is [a] and the coda consonant is a guttural fricative (x, ɣ, ħ, ʕ, h). The coda consonant is shifted to form a cluster onset, i.e. CCV.

قهوة	/gahwa/	[ghawa]	'coffee'
نخلة	/naxla/	[nxala]	'palm tree'
ورقة	/wərga/	[wrəga]	'paper'

3.3 Suprasegmental processes and phonotactics

3.3.1 *Syllable structure*

Emirati Arabic words may be monosyllabic or polysyllabic. Each syllable may have a short or long vowel; and if a coda is available it may have one or two consonants. Emirati Arabic has the following types of syllabic structures:

CV

ب	[ba]	'will'	يا	[ja]	'Hey!'
ف	[fa]	'so'	كِسر	[ki.sar]	'broke'
ها	[ha]	'this'	و	[wa]	'and'

CVC

حس	[ħəs]	'voice'	هم	[hum]	'them'
قص	[gəsˤ]	'cut'	رش	[raʃ]	'splash'
شم	[ʃəm]	'smell'	عن	[ʕan]	'instead'

CVCC

درب	[darb]	'path'	قلب	[galb]	'heart'
كلب	[tʃalb]	'dog'	ظرف	[ðˤarf]	'envelope'
بنت	[bənt]	'girl'	تحت	[taħt]	'under'

CCV

بقرة	[bga.ra]	'cow'	بركة	[brə.kah]	'blessing'
عنبة	[ʕnə.ba]	'grape'	اشتريت	[ʃtə.reet]	'I bought'
انحرق	[nħə.rag]	'was burned'	سمكة	[smə.tʃa]	'a fish'
انتبهت	[ntə.baht]	'I paid attention'	افعصته	[fʕə.sˤata]	'she squeezed (it)'
استحيت	[stə.ħeet]	'I felt shy'	سلقته	[slə.gata]	'she boiled (it)'

CCVC

مكسر	[mkas.sar]	'broken'	ستعيل	[staʕ.jal]	'rushed'
ملون	[mlaw.wan]	'colored'	صغيّر	[sˤɣaj.jər]	'small'
تفتح	[tfat.taħ]	'opened up'	ستعبط	[staʕ.batˤ]	'acted foolish'
تبطل	[tbatˤ.tˤal]	'was opened/s.th turned on'	مبلّغ	[mbal.ləɣ]	'notifier'

$CCVC_1C_1$ (C_1C_1 are geminates)

فتر	[ftarr]	'turned around'	حتل	[ħtall]	'invaded'
انشل	[nʃall]	'was lifted'	انفر	[nfarr]	'was thrown'
امتن	[mtann]	'gained weight'	اسمر	[smarr]	'tanned'
نجب	[ntʃabb]	'was spilled'	مقص	[mgasˤsˤ]	'scissors'
نعد	[nʕadd]	'was counted'	نعق	[nʕagg]	'was thrown'
ندق	[ndagg]	'was hit'	انشل	[nʃall]	'was paralyzed'

CVV

لا	[laa]	'no'	ما	[maa]	'not'
في	[fii]	'there is'	شو	[ʃuu]	'what'
جي	[tʃii]	'like this'	واحد	[waa.ħəd]	'one'

CCVV

دبي	[dbaɪ]	'Dubai'	شوي	[ʃwaɪ]	'a little'
يديده	[jdii.da]	'new'	صغيره	[sˤɣii.ra]	'small'
تسيخف	[tsee.xaf]	'acted silly'	معاند	[mʕaa.nəd]	'bullheaded'

CVVC

قار	[gaar]	'asphalt'	غاز	[ɣaaz]	'gas'
فاز	[faaz]	'won'	مات	[maat]	'died'
صوب	[sˤoob]	'near'	كان	[kaan]	'was'

CCVVC

فلوس	[fluus]	'money'	حمار	[ħmaar]	'donkey'
كتاب	[ktaab]	'book'	بعير	[bʕiir]	'camel'
نعال	[nʕaal]	'shoes'	فطور	[ftˤuur]	'breakfast'

تقول	[tguul]	'she said'	اختار	[xtaar]	'chose'
ربيع	[rbiiʕ]	'friend'	خبال	[xbaal]	'craziness'

3.3.2 *Stress*

In the domain of phonology, stress is defined as the perceived prominence attached to a particular syllable. Stress is identified phonetically by the syllable's duration, pitch, or intensity, although the stressed status may also be agreed among native speakers without any phonetic correlate. In this grammar, we define a stressed syllable as the syllable bearing the longest duration, highest pitch, and highest intensity (compared with others). The following acoustic measurement of the word ماله [maaləh] 'belongs to him' is illustrative. Figure 3.1 shows that the pitch of the first (i.e. penultimate) syllable is higher than in the remaining part of the word. The first syllable is also longer in duration than the second syllable. This suggests that the first syllable is the stressed syllable (i.e. [<u>maa</u>ləh]).

Stress assignment depends on the number of syllables of the word and the syllabic structure of each syllable.

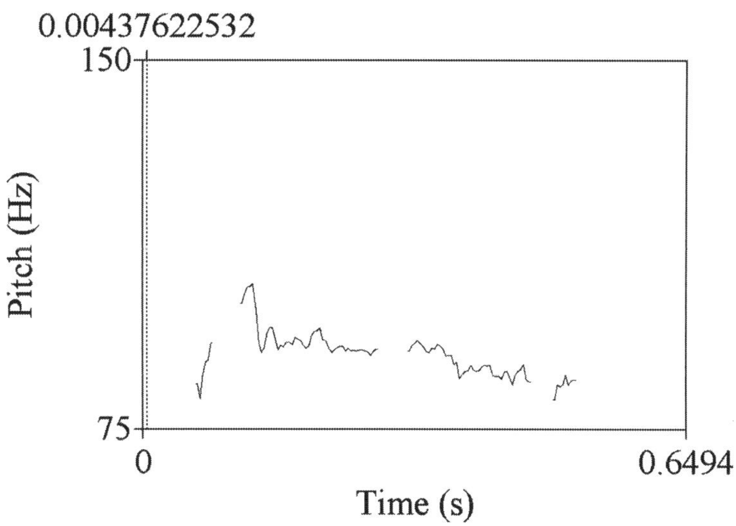

Figure 3.1 The pitch pattern for penultimate stress

3.3.2.1 *Monosyllabic words*

Monosyllabic words will be stressed if they are 'closed' (with a coda) or 'long' (e.g. CVV, CVC, CVCC, or CVVC).

بس	[bas]	'enough'	عيد	[ʕiid]	'feast'
درب	[darb]	'path'	بيت	[beet]	'house'
يوم	[joom]	'day'	حولْ	[ħool]	'around'

3.3.2.2 *Bisyllabic words*

For bisyllabic words, stress will fall on the final syllable if it is super-heavy (e.g. CVCC or CVVC); otherwise it will fall on the penultimate syllable.

Penultimate stress

ضرب	[ðˤa.rab]	'hit'	ولد	[wa.lad]	'boy'
ضحّك	[ðˤaħ.ħak]	'made s.o laugh'	عطني	[ʕatˤ.ni]	'give me!'
درى	[da.ra]	'knew'	قتل	[gə.tal]	'killed'
سرق	[sə.rag]	'stole'	خرب	[xə.rab]	'went bad'
شرشح	[ʃar.ʃaħ]	'scolded'	قاسي	[gaa.si]	'cruel'

Final stress

مشغول	[maʃ.ɣuul]	'busy'	تعبير	[taʕ.biir]	'expression'
مسمار	[məs.maar]	'nail'	زَعلان	[zaʕ.laan]	'sad'
مسكين	[məs.kiin]	'poor man'	أساس	[ʔa.saas]	'base'
يبون	[jə.boon]	'They want'	يكون	[jə.kuun]	'He is'

3.3.2.3 *Polysyllabic words*

For polysyllabic words, stress will fall on the final syllable if it is super-heavy; otherwise it will fall on the penultimate syllable if it is heavy. If neither condition is met, stress will fall on the antepenultimate syllable.

Final stress

مُطربين	[mutˤ.rə.biin]	'singers'	مبتدئات	[mub.ta.di.ʔaat]	'beginners'
الدولتين	[əd.daw.lə.teen]	'the two countries'	الطلاب	[ətˤ.tˤəl.laab]	'the students'
بيضيعون	[baj.ðˤii.ʕuun]	'They will lose'	هالمفتاح	[hal.məf.taaħ]	'this key'
هدّافين	[had.da.feen]	'two goalkeepers'	مناحيز	[ma.naa.ħiiz]	'mincing tool(s)'

Penultimate stress

بشكارة	[bəʃ.kaa.ra]	'housekeeper'	نسينا	[nə.see.na]	'we forgot'
الحاسر	[əl.ħaa.sər]	'newborn girl'	حضنها	[ħə.ðˤan.ha]	'he hugged her'
حدعشر	[ħi.daʕ.ʃar]	'eleven'	الحرارة	[l.ħa.raa.ra]	'the heat'
بالوعة	[bal.luu.ʕa]	'sewer'	دراجة	[dar.raa.dʒa]	'motorcycle'

Antepenultimate stress

مثلًا	[ma.θa.lan]	'for example'	مزرعة	[maz.ra.ʕa]	'farm'
درجة	[da.ra.dʒa]	'degree'	مكّاوي	[mak.kaa.wi]	'person from Mecca'

Further reading

For general discussions of Arabic phonology, see Watson (2002) and Youssef (2013). A discussion of Gulf Arabic phonology is found in Qafisheh (1977) and Holes (1990), and of Emirati Arabic phonology, in Al Ameri (2009). Emphasis spread/pharyngealization is considered under different theoretical frameworks in Davis (1995) and Watson (1999). The full assimilation of the definite article onto the first consonant of the following noun for 'sun' letters is discussed for several dialects by Watson (2002, p. 217), who also provides an extended list of references.

Chapter 4

Morphology and word formation

Morphology is the subfield in grammar which encompasses the representation of word structure and the structure-building mechanisms thereof. Emirati Arabic, along with other Arabic dialects, and Semitic languages in a broader sense, distinguishes itself from other languages in possessing non-linear morphological processes. Cross-linguistically, a new lexical item may be derived by applying morphological operations on a basic form ('stem'). Some operations are linear or concatenative in the sense that a morpheme is directly affixed to the right/left periphery of the stem, e.g. English 'cat' vs. 'cat-s.' Semitic languages employ an additional dimension of morphological processes, in which word formation takes place within the stem. This type of non-linear/non-concatenative operation applies productively in the formation of most complex words in Emirati Arabic.

4.1 Non-linear morphological processes

According to consensus, lexical items in Semitic languages stem from the notion of *root*, which consists of a small number (e.g. 2–5) of meaning-defining consonants or 'radicals.' These lexical items are derived by mapping the consonantal root with a fixed morphological pattern or template. The pattern consists of a fixed linear arrangement of segments formed by consonants (C) and vowels (V). Based on a single consonantal root, various patterns can produce a list of lexical items, all of which bearing related meanings. Linguists usually call this the *root-and-pattern morphology*. Since the pattern formed by a sequence of vowels and consonants encodes the syllabic/prosodic information of the lexical item, the theoretical study of the root-and-pattern morphology falls within the realm of phonology-morphology interface and is sometimes known as *prosodic morphology*. The detailed discussion of how the consonant root is mapped onto the pattern is examined in various sections of this work on grammatical categories

Table 4.1 Examples of morphological derivations in Emirati Arabic

Locative nouns			
Root consonants	Root meaning		Meaning
ك-ت-ب	k-t-b 'write'	مكتبة	maktəba 'library'
د-ر-س	d-r-s 'study'	مدرسة	madrəsa 'school'
Result nouns			
ل-ع-ب	l-ʕ-b 'play'	لعبة	ləʕba 'a game/toy'
س-ب-ح	s-b-ħ 'shower'	سبحة	sabħa 'a shower'
Diminutives			
ه-ش-ل	h-ʃ-l 'night visitor'	هويشل	hweeʃəl 'Hashil (name)'
ر-ش-د	r-ʃ-d 'to lead'	رويشد	rweeʃəd 'Rashed (name)'

(Sections 5.1, 5.2, and 5.3). Readers without prior knowledge of Arabic (or Semitic) word formation processes should bear in mind that consonant roots are merely abstract mental representations of lexical items. It is the non-linear morphological operations that apply to the consonantal roots to form all 'pronounceable' words. That is to say, even basic nouns such as كتاب ktaab 'book' and جلب tʃalb 'dog,' and verbs such as كِسر kisar 'broke' and أخذ ʔaxað 'took,' are morphological derivatives. In the domain of morphology, the operation to produce a new lexical item is called *morphological derivation*. On the other hand, non-linear morphological operations also yield lexical items which encode further grammatical information, e.g. aspect such as 'perfective' vs. 'imperfective' (Chapter 8), number distinction such as 'singular' vs. 'plural' vs. 'dual' (Section 5.1), and degree comparison such as comparatives and superlatives (Section 5.3). Linguists call these *morphological inflections* (Tables 4.1, 4.2, 4.3).

4.2 Affixation

Morphological affixations in Emirati Arabic are inflections that indicate grammatical information such as person, number, gender, and modality. In addition to prefixes and suffixes, circumfixes which encode a single grammatical feature may be used. The imperfective aspect of verbs presents a typical example of prefixation and

Table 4.2 Forms of verbal inflections in Emirati Arabic

Root consonants		*Form I*		*Form II*		*Root meaning*
ق-ر-ء	g-r-ʔ	قرا	gəra	قرّا	garra	'made s.o read'
د-ر-ي	d-r-j	درى	dəra	درّى	darra	'made s.o know (m)'
ر-ف-ع	r-f-ʕ	رفع	rəfaʕ	رفّع	raffaʕ	'raise'
ك-س-ر	k-s-r	كسر	kəsar	كسّر	kassar	'broke'
م-س-ك	m-s-k	مسك	məsak	مسّك	massak	'made s.o hold'
ف-ت-ح	f-t-ħ	فتح	fətaħ	فتّح	fattaħ	'opened'
ف-ظ-ح	f-ðˤ-ħ	فضح	fəðˤaħ	فضّح	faðˤðˤaħ	'exposed'

Table 4.3 Other morphological inflections in Emirati Arabic

Root consonants		*Root meaning*	*Broken plural*		*Meaning*
ن-خ-ل	n-x-l	'palm'	نخل	naxal	'palm tree(s)'
ع-ن-ب	ʕ-n-b	'berry'	عنب	ʕənab	'grape(s)'
			Active participle		
ر-ق-د	r-g-d	'sleep'	راقد	raagəd	'sleeping'
و-ق-ف	w-g-f	'stand'	واقف	waagəf	'standing'
			Comparatives		
ك-ب-ر	k-b-r	'big'	أكبر	ʔakbar	'bigger'
ص-غ-ر	sˤ-ɣ-r	'small'	أصغر	ʔasˤɣar	'smaller'

circumfixation in Emirati Arabic (Table 4.4). On the other hand, the perfective verb is derived by suffixation (Table 4.5).

4.3 Reduplication

Reduplication is a morpho-phonological process where the complete stem or some part of it is repeated. Cross-linguistically, reduplication may be total or partial—that is, the entire word base or only part of the base is reduplicated. Total reduplications in

Table 4.4 Prefixes and circumfixes of imperfective verbs

أكسر ʔa-ksər. I-break.imperf 'I break.'	تكسر tə-ksər. you-break.imperf 'You break.'	تكسرين tə-ksər-iin. you.f-break.imperf-you.f 'You (f) break.'
يكسر jə-ksər. he-break.imperf 'He breaks.'	تكسر tə-ksər. she-break.imperf 'She breaks.'	نكسر nə-ksər. we-break.imperf 'We break.'
تكسرون tə-ksər-uun. you.pl-break.imperf-you.pl 'You (pl) break.'	يكسرون jə-ksər-uun. they-break.imperf-they 'They break.'	يكسرن jə-ksər-ən. they.f-break.imperf-they.f 'They (f) break.'

Table 4.5 Suffixes of perfective verbs

كسرت kəsar-t. break.perf-I 'I broke.'	كسرت kəsar-t. break.perf-you 'You broke.'	كسرتي kəsar-ti. break.perf-you.f 'You (f) broke.'
كسر kəsar. break.perf-he 'He broke.'	كسرت kəsr-at. break.perf-she 'She broke.'	كسرنا kəsar-na. break.perf-we 'We broke.'
كسرتوا kəsar-tu. break.perf-you.pl 'You (pl) broke.'	كسروا ksər-aw. break.perf-they 'They broke.'	كسرن kəsr-an. break.perf-they.f 'They (f) broke.'

Emirati Arabic, if considered productive at all, are limited to the expression of universal quantification (Section 5.6) of nouns. This type of universal quantification may only exist as an object of the sentence. On the other hand, reduplication of nouns is generally not permitted at the subject position.

بفتش بيت بيت لين أحصلها

b-a-fattəʃ	beet	beet	leen	ʔa-ħasˤsˤəl-ha.
will-I-search.imperf	house	house	until	I-find.imperf-her

'I will search in each house until I find her.'

بقرا هالكتاب كلمة كلمة

b-a-gra	ha-l-ktaab	kəlma	kəlma.
will-I-read.imperf	this-the-book	word	word

'I will read this book word by word.'

بسألهن وحدة وحدة

b-a-sʔal-hən	wəħd-a	wəħd-a.
will-I-ask.imperf-them.f	one-f	one-f

'I will ask each single one of them.'

Total noun reduplication may also express a distributive quantificational meaning.

اقري كلمة كلمة

ʔə-gra-j	kəlma	kəlma.
you.f-read.imp-you.f	word	word

'Read word by word.'

دخلوا وحدة وحدة

dəxl-u	wəħd-a	wəħd-a.
enter.imp-you.pl	one-f	one-f

'Enter one by one.'

There exist a few cases of total reduplication which express an idiomatic meaning. For example:

علميها حبة حبة

ʕalmii-ha	ħabba	ħabba.
teach.imp-her	unit	unit

'Teach her deliberately/little by little.'

امشي شوي شوي

ʔəmʃ-i	ʃwaj	ʃwaj.
walk.imp-you	little	little

'Walk slowly.'

نص نص		بدخل غرفة غرفة	
nəsˤ	nəsˤ	b-a-dxəl	ɣərfa ɣərfa
half	half	will-I-enter.imperf	room room
'sort of'		'I will enter room by room.'	

Other apparent cases of total reduplication stem from onomatopoeic (i.e. sound-symbolic) expressions. The following table shows that the monosyllable (usually with a CVC syllable structure, see Chapter 2) may be reduplicated to form a verb. In linguistic approaches to reduplication, this type may not be considered as real reduplication, as the monosyllable bears no meaning.

قرقر	gargar	'gossiped'	تمتم	tam tam	'stuttered'
يريز	jarjar	'dragged s.th aggressively'	دندن	dandan	'hummed'
طر طر	tˤartˤar	'tore (paper)'	غرغر	ɣarɣar	'gurgled'
كركر	karkar	'laughed'	بح بح	baħbaħ	'lived in prosperity'
حب حب	ħabħab	'became rough in surface'	بربر	barbar	'prattled'
رب رب	rabrab	'became fat'	بسبس	basbas	'murmured'
سب سب	sabsab	'swore'	زرزر	zarzar	'salivated'

These 'reduplicated' verbs function like other typical verbs which carry further aspectual or modality marker and pronoun suffixes.

طبطبي عليها يوم تصيح

tˤabtˤəb-i	ʕalee-ha	joom	t-sˤiiħ.
pat.imperf-you.f	on-her	when	she-cry.imperf

'Pat on her when she cries.'

طقطقنا عالجيران أمس

tˤagtˤag-na	ʕ-al-jiiraan	ʔams.
gossip.perf-we	on-the-neighbour.pl	yesterday

'We gossiped (to make fun) about the neighbors yesterday.'

الشيطان وسوسلها تسوي تشي

əʃ-ʃajtˤaan	waswasə-l-ha	t-sawwi	ʧii.
the-Satan	advocate.perf-he-to-her	she-do.imperf	this

'The devil advocated for her to do this.'

غرغري بماي وملح يوم تمرضين

ɣarɣər-i	b-maaj	w	məlħ	joom	tə-mrəðˤ-iin.
gargle.imp-you.f	with-water	and	salt	when	you.f-get.sick.imperf-you.f

'Gargle with water and salt when you get sick.'

In a very few cases, the monosyllable itself bears a semantic meaning which is almost identical to its reduplicated counterpart. The reduplicated verb is considered as more colloquial.

قصقصنا الخضره رباعة

gasˤgasˤ-na	l-xəðˤra	rbaaʕa.
cut.perf-we	the-vegetable.pl	together

'We cut the vegetables together.'

أحمد طرطر أوراق أخته

ʔaħmad	tˤartˤar	ʔawraag	ʔəxt-ah.
Ahmad	cut.perf-he	paper.pl	sister-his

'Ahmad cut his sisters' papers.'

On the other hand, partial reduplication is not generally attested in Emirati Arabic. Perhaps the only marginal case of partial reduplication is observed in gemination (Section 2.1.2). For instance, causative verbs may be derived by geminating the word-medial root consonant.

طلع	tˤəlaʕ	'went out'	طلّع	tˤallaʕ	'expelled'
نزل	nəzal	'went down'	نزّل	nazzal	'lowered'
خرب	xarab	'went bad'	خرّب	xarrab	'ruined'
كل/كلا	kal/kala	'ate'	أكّل	ʔakkal	'fed'

4.4 Compounding

It remains controversial as to whether compounds exist in Emirati Arabic on a par with other languages such as English. In

Emirati Arabic, all noun compounds are formed by phrasal constructions or *construct states* (Section 6.2). A number of non-decompositional construct states combine the possessor and the possessed to give rise to an independent (and therefore lexical) meaning. The following table of noun compounds may also be attested in other Arabic dialects, though their pronunciation has been localized according to Emirati Arabic phonology (Chapter 2):

ماي الويه

maaj	l-wajh
water	the-face

'the dignity'

عروس البحر

ʕaruus	əl-bahar
bride	the-sea

'mermaid'

عصا موسى

ʕəsˤaa	muusa
staff	Moses

'a divine object (the staff of Moses)'

قوي القلب

gəwi	l-galb
strong	heart

'strict (brave-hearted)'

حجر الأساس

ħədʒar	əl-ʔasaas
stone	the-base

'the foundation'

البحر الأبيض المتوسط

əl-baħr əl-ʔabjaðˤ əl-mətwassətˤ

the-sea the-white the-Mediterranean

'the Mediterranean Sea'

المحيط الهادي

əl-məħiitˤ	əl-haadi
the-ocean	the-pacific

'the Pacific Ocean'

البحر الأحمر

əl-baħr əl-aħmar

the-sea the-red

'the Red Sea'

رايد الفضاء

raajəd	l-faðˤaaʔ
pioneer	the-space

'the astronaut'

الاقتصاد الجزئي

lə-qtəsˤaad	əl-ʤəzʔi
the-economy	the-partial

'microeconomics'

بيت الدوا

beet	əd-dəwaa
house	the-medicine

'the pharmacy'

عيوز النار

ʕəyuuz	ən-naar
old.woman	the-fire

'an evil woman'

On the other hand, there are compounds which correspond to English bound roots, i.e. morphemes that possess lexical meanings yet do not exist independently, e.g. 'mono-,' 'anti-,' and 'semi-.' However, in Emirati Arabic the corresponding morphemes are free morphemes, e.g. the negative particle mub مب 'not' (Section 10.2). In these cases, it is not clear whether we are dealing with compound formation or a derivational morphological process.

مضاد حيوي
məðˤaad ħajawi
anti biotic
'antibiotic'

مب اجتماعي
mub ʔədʒtəmaaʕi
not social
'antisocial'

نص دايرة
nəsˤ daajra
half circle
'semi-circle'

لافقاري
laa faqaari
no vertebrate
'invertebrate'

لاسلكي
laa səlki
non wired
'wireless'

أبيض واسود
ʔabjaðˤ w aswad
white and black
'monochrome'

محد فيه صبر ع أسلوبه المب اجتماعي
ma-ħħad fii-h sˤabər ʕa-ʔəsluub-ah əl-mub ʔədʒtəmaaʕii.
no-one in-him patience on-attitude-him the-not social
'No one is patient with his antisocial attitude.'

هالمحل بعده يبيع تلفزيون أبيض واسود
ha-l-maħal baʕda-h j-biiʕ talfəzjoon ʔabjaðˤ w aswad.
this-the-store still-it it-sell.imperf television white and black
'This store still sells monochrome TV.'

الغرفة مافيها نت لاسلكي
əl-ɣərfa maa-fii-ha nət laa-səlki.
the-room not-in-it internet non-wired
'The room does not have wireless internet.'

4.5 Loanwords

Given the UAE's geographical closeness to its neighboring countries and its current development as an economic and cultural hub in the

Middle East, Emirati Arabic people have borrowed many lexical items and expressions from other foreign languages. Loanwords, while bearing an origin in a foreign language, are fully incorporated in the borrowing language regarding the linguistic properties (e.g. phonological and morphological structure, grammatical categories) and are commonly used by monolinguals without any knowledge of the donor language (i.e. the language from which the loanword was borrowed). In addition to loanwords, there are also loan translations in which a word taken from the donor language is literally translated into the borrowing language. Table 4.6 presents a short list of loanwords from popular donor languages.

Table 4.6 Loanwords in Emirati Arabic

Loanwords from English					
جرج	ʧarʧ	'charge'	بوت	buut	'boots'
سيكل	seekal	'bicycle'	ميكب	meekab	'makeup'
سندويتش	sandəwiiʧ	'sandwich'	كيك	keek	'cake'
كاب	kaab	'cap'	بنك	bank	'bank'
قلاص	glˤaasˤ	'glass'	أسكريم	ʔaskəriim	'ice-cream'
باسوورد	baaswoord	'password'	جبس	ʧəbs	'chips'
دكتور	dəktoor	'doctor'	لابتوب	labtoob	'laptop'
Loanwords from Persian					
كمان	kamaan	'violin'	برواز	bərwaaz	'frame'
دكان	dəkkaan	'store'	أستاذ	ʔəstaað	'teacher'
صروال	sˤərwaal	'trousers'	بخت	baxt	'luck'
شطرنج	ʃatˤrandʒ	'chess'	كيسة	kiisa	'bag'
دفتر	daftar	'notebook'	بازار	baazaar	'bazaar'
Loanwords from French					
بنطلون	bantˤəloon	'trousers'	ديكور	diikoor	'decor'
بانيو	baanjo	'bathtub'	رجيم	rədʒiim	'regime'
كافتيريا	kaftiirja	'cafeteria'	كوافيرة	kwaafeera	'hairdresser'
موضة	moodˤa	'fashion'	بوفيه	boofeeh	'buffet'

(*Continued*)

Table 4.6 (Continued)

Loanwords from Hindi/Urdu					
جوتي	dʒuuti	'shoes'			
ربيّة	rəbbijja	'Dirham'			
Loanwords from Turkish					
شنطة	ʃantˤa	'bag'	جمارك	dʒamaarik	'customs'
ابلة	ʔabla	'teacher'	طز	tˤəzz	'whatever'
شاكوش	ʃaakuuʃ	'hammer'	طابور	tˤaabuur	'line'
بقشيش	baqʃiiʃ	'tips'			

Table 4.7 Loanwords in Emirati Arabic

غسيل دماغ		الحرب الباردة	
ɣasiil	dəmaaɣ	l-ħarb	l-baard-a
washing	brain	the-war	the-cold-f
'brainwashing'		'the Cold War'	
كرة السلة		تفاحة آدم	
kura-t	əs-salla	təffaaħa-t	ʔaadam
ball-f	the-basket	apple-f	Adam
'basketball'		'Adam's apple'	
عالخط		ناطحة سحاب	
ʕa-l-xatˤ		naatˤħa-t	saħaab
on-the-line		scraper-f	cloud.pl
'online'		'skyscraper'	
خط أحمر			
xatˤ	ʔaħmar		
'line	red'		
'red line'			

Finally, Table 4.7 presents a list of structures derived from translations of equivalent structures in other languages.

4.6 Acronyms, abbreviations, and blending

Most cases of acronyms and abbreviations are drawn from names of organizations and institutes. In Emirati Arabic, most of the acronyms and abbreviations attested stem from English.

ديوا	DEWA (Dubai Electricity and Water Authority)
ناسا	NASA (National Aeronautics and Space Administration)
أدنوك	ADNOC (Abu Dhabi National Oil Company)
أديك	ADEC (Abu Dhabi Education Council)
أديب	ADIB (Abu Dhabi Islamic Bank)
فاب	FAB (First Abu Dhabi Bank)

Blending is another word formation process in which two (or more) words are merged together by 'clipping' individual words, e.g. 'smog' (< 'smoke' + 'fog') and 'brunch' (< 'breakfast' + 'lunch'). In Emirati Arabic, the cases of blending usually stem from borrowing.

ترانسكو TRANSCO (Abu Dhabi Transmission and Despatch Company)

It is also common to borrow acronyms and abbreviations directly from English.

اليونيسكو UNESCO
اليونيسيف UNICEF

Very rarely, an acronym or abbreviation is constructed purely from Emirati Arabic expressions. The following is one such example:

وام wam < وكالة أنباء الإمارات underline م 'Emirates News Agency'

4.7 Back formation

As most word derivation stems from the consonant root, it is unusual to find examples of back formation in which new words are created by erasing a supposed morpheme. The derivation of a country's people is one such example:

ألمانيا	ʔalmaanja	Germany	ألمان	ʔalmaan	German (people)
ألبانيا	ʔalbaanja	Albania	ألبان	ʔalbaan	Albanian (people)
أسبانيا	ʔəsbaanja	Spain	أسبان	ʔəsbaan	Spanish (people)

4.8 Conversion

In contrast to English, the grammatical category of a single lexical item (in terms of bearing a single spelling and pronunciation) is largely fixed and unalterable in Emirati Arabic. Overall, it is not possible to derive a lexical item from another without applying a morphological operation (such as those defined earlier). Probably the only possible case in which a word's category may change without any morphological change is the use of adjectives without a head noun, cf. English 'the rich' and 'the impossible.' However, a caveat is in order. While the following examples may be considered as potential cases of category change, it is equally plausible to analyze each as an adjectival phrase (Chapter 6) which modifies an elliptical noun phrase (Section 16.3).

لفقير	لغني	لحمر	لحلو
l-faqiir	l-ɣani	l-aħmar	l-ħəlu
The-poor	the-rich	the-red	the-beautiful
'the poor (people)'	'the rich (people)'	'the red (thing)'	'the beautiful (thing)'

Further reading

The classical discussion of prosodic and non-linear morphology originated in McCarthy (1979, 1981) and McCarthy and Prince (1990). For a general introduction to word formation processes, see Katamba (2005) and Katamba and Stonham (2006). For the morphological analysis of compound formation, see Borer (2009) for Hebrew and Altakhaineh (2018) for Arabic.

Chapter 5

Syntactic categories and parts of speech

5.1 Nouns

The category of nouns semantically refers to those words which denote entities in the world, usually referring to people, places, things, abstract ideas, and so on. In terms of morphosyntactic distribution, nouns are usually inflected for grammatical categories such as gender, number, and definiteness; in terms of word order, they appear adjacent to modifiers such as adjectives (Section 5.3), numerals, quantifiers (Section 5.6), and (in-)definiteness markers.

5.1.1 Noun inflection

5.1.1.1 Gender

Emirati Arabic nouns may be masculine or feminine. The masculine feature carries no morphology; hence, masculine nouns are morphologically unmarked. Feminine nouns are usually marked with the suffix ة- -a(h), with the final voiceless fricative [h] left unpronounced in most cases. Table 5.1 gives examples of nouns where both feminine and masculine exemplars are available.

Table 5.1 Masculine and feminine nouns

Masculine		*Feminine*		
مدرّب	mudarrəb	مدرّبة	mudarrəba	'coach'
متسابق	mətsaabəg	متسابقة	mətsaabga	'contestant'
مشارك	mʃaarək	مشاركة	mʃaarka	'participant'
ربيع	rbiiʕ	ربيعة	rbiiʕa	'friend'
شاعر	ʃaaʕər	شاعرة	ʃaaʕra	'poet'
مجابل	mdʒaabəl	مجابلة	mdʒaabla	'opponent'

(*Continued*)

Table 5.1 (Continued)

Masculine		*Feminine*		
إستاذ	ʔəstaað	إستاذة	ʔəstaaða	'professor'
مهندس	mhandəs	مهندسة	mhandəsa	'engineer'
لاعب	laaʕəb	لاعبة	laaʕba	'player'
متحدّث	məthaddəθ	متحدّثة	məthadθa	'speaker'

However, in several cases, the noun has no overt morphology for the feminine gender, and the only way to identify it as feminine is if it triggers feminine agreement on noun modifiers such as adjectives and numerals (Sections 5.3 and 5.6). This is true for most body parts.

عيون	ʕjuun	'eyes'
إيد	ʔiid	'hand'
ريل	riil	'foot'
حوايب	ħəwaajəb	'eyebrows'
إذن	ʔəðən	'ear'

5.1.1.2 Number

The plural may be expressed in two ways. Some nouns use linear morphology in the form of suffixes to express the plural for both masculine and feminine nouns ('sound plural'). Other nouns form the plural in a morphologically non-linear fashion, by using specific vocalic patterns with the consonants of the noun root. The usual term for this second kind of plural noun formation is 'broken plural.' In the formation of sound plurals, the masculine and feminine nouns end with suffixes which express gender and number features simultaneously. For masculine nouns, their plurals are marked by the suffix ين- -iin (Table 5.2), while feminine plurals are suffixed by ات- -aat (Table 5.3).

A noun may also be dual and refer to two entities. The dual is formed by the suffix ين- -een (Table 5.4), and, for the feminine nouns, the suffix ت- -t will be added between the stem noun and the dual suffix (Table 5.5). This suffix ت- -t also appears productively in the expression of possessive structures (Section 6.2).

On a par with all other Arabic dialects, Emirati Arabic possesses the second type of plural, the broken plural, which is formed by mapping the consonantal roots with a number of vocalic templates. Note that all vocalic templates stated in this grammar are phonological representations (Table 5.6). On the other hand, it is

Table 5.2 Masculine plural paradigm

Singular		*Plural*		
مهندس	muhandəs	مهندسين	muhandəsiin	'engineer(s)'
مساعد	musaaʕəd	مساعدين	musaaʕdiin	'assistant(s)'
مُطرب	mutˤrəb	مُطربين	mutˤrəbiin	'singer(s)'
صيّاد	sˤajjaad	صيّادين	sˤajjaadiin	'hunter(s)'
مُراقب	muraqəb	مُراقبين	muraqbiin	'monitor(s)'

Table 5.3 Feminine plural paradigm

Singular		*Plural*		
مبتدئة	mubtadəʔa	مبتدئات	mubtadiʔaat	'beginner(s)'
مُستجدّة	mustadʒədda	مُستجدّات	mustadʒəddaat	'college freshman (-men)'
معلمة	mʕalma	معلمات	mʕalmaat	'teacher(s)'
ممرضة	mumarrədˤa	ممرضات	mumarrədˤaat	'nurse(s)'

Table 5.4 Masculine dual paradigm

Singular		*Dual*		
مدرّب	mudarrəb	مدرّبين	mudarrəbeen	'(two) trainer(s)'
مُعلّم	mʕalləm	معلّمين	mʕallmeen	'(two) teacher(s)'
هدّاف	haddaf	هدّافين	haddafeen	'(two) striker(s)'
طالب	tˤalˤəb	طالبين	tˤaalˤbeen	'(two) student(s)'
عامل	ʕaaməl	عاملين	ʕamleen	'(two) worker(s)'

Table 5.5 Feminine dual paradigm

Singular		*Dual*		
بشكارة	bəʃkaara	بشكارتين	bəʃkaarteen	'(two) housekeeper(s) (f)'
حرمة	ħərma	حرمتين	ħərməteen	'(two) women (f)'
علبة	ʕəlba	علبتين	ʕəlbəteen	'(two) box(es)'
عاملة	ʕaamla	عاملتين	ʕaaməlteen	'(two) worker(s) (f)'
دراجة	darraadʒa	دراجتين	darraadʒteen	'(two) motorcycle(s)'

Table 5.6 Non-linear plural templates and examples

Pattern	*Singular*		*Plural*		
CaCaa-CiiC	طراد	tˤarraad	طراريد	tˤaraariid	'boat(s)'
	سروود	saruud	سراريد	saraariid	'traditional tablecloth(s)'
	خياط	xajjatˤ	خياييط	xajaajiitˤ	'tailor(s)'
CəCaa-CiiC	منحاز	mənħaaz	مناحيز	mənaaħiiz	'mincing tool(s)'
	بالوعة	balluuʕa	بواليع	bəwaaliiʕ	'sewer(s)'
	دبدوب	dabduub	دباديب	dəbaadiib	'teddy bear(s)'
	سكين	sətʃtʃiin	سكاكين	sətʃaatʃiin	'knife/knives'
	مسكين	məskiin	مساكين	məsaakiin	'poor'
	مسمار	məsmaar	مسامير	məsaamiir	'nail(s)'
	نفاخة	nəffaaxa	نفافيخ	nəfaafiix	'balloon(s)'
CəCaaCiC	منحل	manħal	مناحل	mənaaħəl	'bee farm(s)'
	مطرقة	matˤrəga	مطارق	mətˤaarəg	'hammer(s)'
CuCCaaC/ CəCCaaC	سايح	saajəħ	سواح	suwwaaħ	'tourist(s)'
	طالب	tˤaaləb	طلاب	tˤəllaab	'student(s)'
	قارئ	gaari	قراء	gərraaʔ	'reader(s)'
	كاتب	kaatəb	كتاب	kəttaab/ kuttab	'writer(s)'
ʔaCCaaC	سور	suur	أسوار	ʔaswaar	'fence(s)'
	بوك	buuk	أبواك	ʔabwaak	'wallet(s)'
	لون	loon	ألوان	ʔalwaan	'color(s)'
	باب	baab	ابواب	ʔabwaab	'door(s)'
	جرس	dʒaras	أجراس	ʔadʒraas	'bell(s)'
	عود	ʕuud	أعواد	ʔaʕwaad	'stick(s)'
	سوق	suug	أسواق	ʔaswaag	'markets'
CaCaC/ CəCaC	نخلة	naxla	نخل	naxal	'palm tree(s)'
	عنبة	ʕnəba	عنب	ʕənab	'grape(s)'
	ياعدة	jaaʕda	يعد	jaʕad	'sheep'
	بقرة	bgara	بقر	bəgar	'cow(s)'

Pattern	*Singular*		*Plural*		
CuCuC	سحابة	saħaba	سحب	suħub	'cloud(s)'
CuCuuC	جزيرة	dʒaziira	جزر	dʒuzur	'island(s)'
	طريقة	tˁariiqa	طرق	tˁuruq	'method(s)'
	كتاب	ktaab	كتب	kutub	'book(s)'
	أساس	ʔasaas	أسس	ʔusus	'base(s)'
	غيمة	ɣeema	غيوم	ɣujuum	'cloud(s)'
	اسد	ʔasad	اسود	ʔusuud	'lion(s)'
CiCaC/	شنطة	ʃantˁa	شنط	ʃinatˁ	'bag(s)'
CəCaC	حفرة	ħəfra	حفر	ħəfar	'hole(s)'
	فلة	vəlla	فلل	vəlal	'villa(s)'
	خيمة	xeema	خيم	xejam	'tent(s)'
	ريشة	reeʃa	ريش	rejaʃ	'feather(s)'
C(ə)CuuC	شمعة	ʃamʕa	شموع	ʃmuuʕ	'candle(s)'
	حصن	ħəsˁən	حصون	ħəsˁuun	'castle(s)'
	غصن	ɣəsˁən	غصون	ɣəsˁuun	'log(s)'
	عين	ʕeen	عيون	ʕjuun	'eye(s)'
CiiCaaC	جار	jaar	جيران	jiiraan	'neighbor(s)'
	فار	faar	فيران	fiiraan	'mouse/mice'
	حوت	ħoot	حيتان	ħiitaan	'whale(s)'
	شايب	ʃaajəb	شيبان	ʃiibaan	'old man/men'
	باب	baab	بيبان	biibaan	'door(s)'
	عود	ʕuud	عيدان	ʕiidaan	'stick(s)'
CəCiiC	حمار	ħmaar	حمير	ħəmiir	'donkey(s)'
	عبد	ʕabd	عبيد	ʕəbiid	'slave(s)'
CCuuC	حرف	ħarf	أحرف/ حروف	ʔaħruf/ ħruuf	'letter(s)'
	سطح	satˁħ	اسطح	stˁuuħ	'roof(s)'
	رف	raf	ارفف	rfuuf	'shelf/shelves'
	فلس	fəls	فلوس	fluus	'fils/money'
	دمعة	damʕa	دموع	dmuuʕ	'tear(s)'

(*Continued*)

Table 5.6 (Continued)

Pattern	*Singular*		*Plural*		
	سطر	satˤər	سطور	stˤuur	'line(s)'
ʔaCaaCi	أرض	ʔarð	أراضي	ʔaraaðˤi	'land(s)'
	امنيه	ʔəmnija	اماني	ʔamaani	'wish(es)'
	اغنية	ʔəɣniya	اغاني	ʔaɣaani	'song(s)'
CiCCaan/	بعير	bʕiir	بعران	bəʕraan	'camel(s)'
CəCCaan	عمود	ʕamuud	عمدان	ʕəmdaan	'column(s)/ pole(s)'
	سبال	səbaal	سبلان	səblaan	'monkey(s)'
maCaa-CəC	مزرعة	mazraʕa	مزارع	məzaarəʕ	farm(s)
məCaa-CəC	ملعب	malʕab	ملاعب	malaaʕəb	'playground(s)'
	مصنع	masˤnaʕ	مصانع	məsˤaanəʕ	'factory/ factories'
	مصعد	masˤʕad	مصاعد	masˤaaʕəd	'elevator(s)'
	مطبخ	matˤbax	مطابخ	mətˤaabəx	'kitchen(s)'
	مكتب	maktab	مكاتب	məkaatəb	'office(s)'
CaCCaa-Ciin	سراق	sarraag	سراقين	sarraagiin	'thief/thieves'
	سواق	sawwaag	سواقين	sawwaagiin	'driver(s)'
	طباخ	tˤabbaax	طباخين	tˤabbaxiin	'cook(s)'
	شحّات	ʃaħħaat	شحّاتين	ʃaħħaatiin	'beggar(s)'

likely that the actual pronunciation of some broken plurals may deviate from their underlying representations (especially when the pronunciation of vowels is concerned).

5.1.2 Noun derivation

5.1.2.1 *Derivations from nouns*

Nouns may be derived from other grammatical categories through linear derivational morphology, usually with the addition of suffixes. Thus, the ethnicity or place of origin of a person is derived from their geographical location, with the addition of the suffix [-i] (Table 5.7). (See also its adjectival use in Section 5.3.3).

Table 5.7 Ethnicity nouns

شارجة	ʃaardʒah	'Sharjah'	شرجاوي	ʃaardʒaawi	'a person from Sharjah'
عمان	ʕmaan	'Oman'	عماني	ʕmaani	'an Omani'
مصر	masˤr	'Egypt'	مصري	masˤri	'an Egyptian'
يابان	jaabaan	'Japan'	ياباني	jaabaani	'a Japanese'
جدّة	dʒaddah	'Jeddah'	جدّاوي	dʒəddaawi	'a person from Jeddah'
مكّة	makkah	'Mecca'	مكّاوي	makkaawi	'a person from Mecca'

A second case of derived nouns is in the expression of a counting unit. This is done by the suffix ة- -a, with occasional phonological processes altering the source stem (Table 5.8).

Table 5.8 Unit nouns

Noun		*Unit noun*		*Meaning*
بطاط	bətˤaatˤ	بطاطة	batˤaatˤa	'(a) potato'
بصل	bəsˤalˤ	بصلة	bsˤala	'(an) onion'
عنز	ʕanz	عنزة	ʕanza	'(a) goat'
تفّاح	təffaaħ	تفّاحة	təffaaħa	'(an) apple'
لبس	ləbs	لبسة	labsa	'(an) outfit'

شريت بصلة وتفاحة

ʃaree-t bsˤala w təffaaħa.
buy.perf-I an.onion and an.apple
'I bought an onion and an apple.'

5.1.2.2 *Derivations from adjectives*

Abstract nouns may be derived from the corresponding adjectives which denote the property the nouns refer to. This is accomplished by adding the suffix ية- -ijja to the corresponding adjective (Table 5.9).

5.1.2.3 *Agentive nouns*

Agentive or subjective nouns are nouns which refer to the actor or agent participant in the event described by the verb. Many agentive nouns further denote professionals related to the base verb. A few vocalic patterns turn the verb into an agentive noun (Table 5.10).

Table 5.9 Adjective-to-noun derivation

صادق	sˤaadəg	'honest'	مصداقية	məsˤdaaqijja	'honesty'
عاقل	ʕaagəl	'rational'	عقلانية	ʕaglaanijja	'mentality'
علمي	ʕaalami	'global'	علمية	ʕaalamijja	'globality'
حيادي	ħəjaadi	'neutral'	إنحيادية	ʔənħəjaadijja	'neutrality'
إنحيازي	ʔənħəjaazi	'biased'	إنحيازية	ʔənħəjaazijja	'bias'
عاطفي	ʕaatˤifi	'emotional'	عاطفية	ʕaatˤəfijja	'emotionality'
إستثنائي	ʔəstəθnaaʔi	'exceptional'	إستثنائية	ʔəstəθnaaʔijja	'exception'

Table 5.10 Agentive noun derivation

	CəCa/CaCa			*CaaCi*	
قرا	gara	'read'	قاري	gaari	'reader'
درى	dara	'knew'	داري	daari	'knower'
بنى	bəna	'built'	باني	baani	'builder'
نسى	nəsa	'forgot'	ناسي	naasi	'forgetter'
سقى	səga	'watered'	ساقي	saagi	'waterer'
رعى	rəʕa	'herded'	راعي	raaʕi	'shepherd'
روى	rəwa	'told'	راوي	raawi	'narrator'
	CeCaC			*CaCCaaC*	
رسم	rəsam	'drew'	رسّام	rassaam	'artist'
رقد	rəgad	'slept'	رقّاد	raggaad	'(big) sleeper'
طبخ	tˤəbax	'cooked'	طبّاخ	tˤabbaax	'chef'
باع	baaʕ	'sold'	بيّاع	bajjaaʕ	'seller'
سبح	səbaħ	'swam'	سبّاح	sabbaaħ	'swimmer'
خيّط	xajjatˤ	'sewed'	خياط	xajjaatˤ	'tailor'
	CaCCaC			*mCaCCaC*	
حلّق	ħallag	'shaved'	محلّق	mħalləg	'one who's shaved'
علّق	ʕallag	'commented'	معلّق	mʕalləg	'commentator'
بلّغ	ballaɣ	'announced'	مبلّغ	mballəɣ	'notifier'
دقق	daqqaq	'proofread'	مدقق	mdaqqəq	'proofreader'

The agentive noun of the first template in Table 5.10 is derived from Form I verbs, while the nouns in the third template derive their agentive nominal from Form II (causative) verbs. The second template shows that nouns may have verbal or nominal sources (Section 5.2).

An additional template is usually listed together with مصدر masdars (Section 5.1.2.7) but this pattern sometimes produces agentive nouns.

			CaaCəC		
ضرب	dˁərab	'stroke'	ضارب	dˁaarəb	'striker'
ربح	rəbaħ	'won'	رابح	raabəħ	'winner'
نهب	nəhab	'stole'	ناهب	naahəb	'thief'

5.1.2.4 *Instrumental nouns*

An instrumental noun usually expresses a tool or means with or by which the action denoted by the verb is accomplished. An instrumental noun is most frequently a physical entity but it could also refer to an abstract entity (e.g. a place), depending on the semantic properties of the source verb. Some instrumental nouns, especially those borrowed from other languages (Section 4.5), do not have a base verb (Table 5.11).

5.1.2.5 *Locative nouns*

Locative deverbal nouns denote the location where the action described by the verb happens habitually (Table 5.12).

5.1.2.6 *Result nouns*

Some deverbal nouns refer to a single occurrence of the action denoted by the source verb or the result of applying such action. The derived noun is usually called a *result noun* in the relevant literature (Table 5.13). The phonological structure of result nouns is CVCCa.

عندي طلعة ويا ربيعاتي بعدين

ʕənd-i	tˁalʕa	wijja	rbiiʕ-aat-i	baʕdeen.
with-me	outing	with	friend-f.pl-my	later

'I have an outing with my friends later.'

Table 5.11 Instrumental noun derivation

məCCaaC	سبّح	sabbaħ	'prayed'	مسباح	məsbaaħ	'prayer beads'
	فتح	fətaħ	'opened'	مفتاح	məftaaħ	'key'
	داخ	daax	'smoked'	مدواخ	mədwaax	'smoking pipe'
	نفخ	nəfax	'inflated'	منفاخ	mənfaax	'air pump'
	سحل	səħal	'filed a knife'	مسحال	məshaal	'knife filer'
məCCaC	دخان	dəxxaan	'burned incense'	مدخن	mədxan	'incense burner'
	برد	barad	'filed'	مبرد	məbrad	'nail filer'
maCCəCa	سطر	satˤər	'line'	مسطرة	mastˤara	'ruler'
	قلم	galam	'pencil'	مقلمة	magləma	'pencil case'
	نجر	nədʒar	'carpented'	منجرة	mandʒara	'carpentry'
CajjaaCa	سار	saar	'left (go)'	سيارة	sajjaara	'car'
	طار	tˤaar	'flew'	طيارة	tˤajjaara	'airplane'
CaCCa				لمبة	lamba	'light' (fr. English)
				بنكة	banka	'fan' (fr. Hindi)
				قفشة	gafʃa	'spoon' (fr. Turkish)

يبالي سبحة بعد هالمباراة

jə-baa-l-i	sabħa	baʕd	ha-l-əmbaaraa.
it-want.imperf-for-me	shower	after	this-the-match

'I need a shower after this match.'

5.1.2.7 مصدر *masdar*

مصدر masdar is a verbal noun, i.e. a form derived through a morphological process which transforms the base verb into

Table 5.12 Locative noun derivation

məCCəCa	كتب	kətab	'wrote'	مكتبة	maktəba	'library'
	درس	dəras	'studied'	مدرسة	madrəsa	'school'
	قصب	gəsˁab	'butchered'	مقصبة	magsˁəba	'butchery'
maCCaC	عبد	ʕəbad	'worshipped'	معبد	maʕbad	'temple'
	لعب	ləʕab	'played'	ملعب	malʕab	'court/ playground'
	كتب	kətab	'wrote'	مكتب	maktab	'office'
	خزن	xazzan	'stored'	مخزن	maxzan	'storage room'
	شغل	ʃaɣɣal	'turned on'	مشغل	maʃɣal	'workshop'
məCCiC	سجد	sədʒad	'prostrated'	مسجد	məsiid/ masjəd	'mosque'
	يلس	jəlas	'sat down'	ميلس	miilas/ majləs	'living room'
	ضيف	ðˁeef	'guest'	مضيف	məðˁiif	'guest house'

Table 5.13 Result noun derivation

لِعَب	ləʕab	'played'	لعبة	ləʕba	'a game'
سِبَح	səbaħ	'showered'	سبحة	sabħa	'a shower'
احَتفل	ʔəhtəfal	'to party oneself'	حفلة	ħafla	'a party'
رقد	rəgad	'slept'	رقدة	ragda	'a period of sleep'
طِلَع	tˁəlaʕ	'left/went out'	طلعة	tˁalʕa	'an outing'

a noun, while keeping the semantic meaning of the verb intact (Section 5.2). It is sometimes called a *(de)verbal noun* or *verbal nominalization*. In most cases, masdars denote the action or the event expressed by the base verb, e.g. ركض rəkadˁ 'ran' vs. rakədˁ 'running.' There are several cases of semantic extension in which masdars denote the participants of the event, e.g. كل kal 'ate' vs. أكل ʔakəl 'food' (Table 5.14).

Table 5.14 Masdar templates and examples

Form I						
C(ə)CuuC	لجأ	lədʒaʔ	'sought refuge'	لجوء	lədʒuuʔ	'refuge'
	سكت	səkat	'went silent'	سكوت	səkuut	'silence'
	تريّق	trajjag	'had an early breakfast'	ريوق	rjuug	'early breakfast'
	فطر	fətˤar	'had breakfast'	فطور	ftˤuur	'breakfast'
CaCaC	ركض	rəkadˤ	'ran'	ركض	rakədˤ	'running'
	كل	kal	'ate'	أكل	ʔakəl	'food'
	فكر	fakkar	'thought'	فكر	fəkər	'thinking'
	لعب	ləʕab	'played'	لعب	ləʕəb	'playing'
	سكن	səkan	'lived at'	سكن	sakan	'hostel'
C(ə)CaaCa	عادا	ʕaada	'be infected'	عدوى	ʕadwa	'infection'
	وقى	wuga	'prevented'	وقاية	wəgaaja	'prevention'
CiCC/	حلم	ħəlam	'dreamed'	حلم	ħəlm	'dream'
CəCC	فلم	fallam	'dramatized'	فلم	fəlm	'film'
CuCC	صَلَب	sˤalab	'fixed attitude'	صُلب	sˤulb	'toughness'
	قرب	gərab	'came closer'	قُرب	gurb	'closeness'
	ملك	məlak	'owned'	ملك	mulk	'property'
	ظلم	dˤəlam	'did injustice'	ظلم	dˤulm	'injustice'
ʔiCCaaʔ	خلى	xəla	'emptied'	إخلاء	ʔəxlaaʔ	'evacuation'
	عفى	ʕəfa	'exempted'	إعفاء	ʔəʕfaaʔ	'exemption'
Form II						
taCCja	ربّى	rabba	'raised'	تربية	tarbija	'upbringing'
	حلّى	ħalla	'had dessert'	تحلية	taħlija	'dessert'
	سمّى	samma	'named'	تسمية	tasmija	'naming'
taCCiiC	رطّب	ratˤtˤab	'moisturized'	ترطيب	tartˤiib	'moisturizing'
	رتّب	rattab	'organized'	ترتيب	tartiib	'organizing'
	درّب	darrab	'trained'	تدريب	tadriib	'training'
ʔiCaaCa	دور	dawwar	'administered'	إدارة	ʔədaara	'administration'
	ثور	θawwar	'erupted'	إثارة	ʔəθaara	'excitement'

Form III

m(u)CaCCa	حكم	ħəkam	'judged'	محاكمة	muħaakama	'trial'
	طلب	tˤəlab	'claimed'	مطالبة	mutˤaalaba	'claim'
	نقر	nəgar	'hit'	مناقرة	munaagara	'dispute'
m(u)CaaCa	دارى	daara	'took care'	مداراة	mdaaraa	'taking care'
	بارى	baara	'played against'	مباراة	mbaaraa	'game'

Form V

taCa-CCuC	خصص	xasˤsˤasˤ	'devoted'	تخصص	taxasˤsˤusˤ	'specialty'
	كبر	kabbar	'grew'	تكبر	takabbur	'arrogance'

Form VIII

iCtiCaac(a)	ابتكر	btəkar	'invented'	ابتكار	btəkaar	'innovation'
	اختار	xtaar	'chose'	اختيار	xtijaar	'selection'

Form X

(ʔə)sti-CCaaC	خدم	xədam	'served'	استخدام	(ʔə)stəxdaam	'usage'
	نسخ	nəsax	'copy'	استنساخ	(ʔə)stənsaax	'copying'
	عرض	ʕaraðˤ	'showed'	استعراض	(ʔə)stəʕraaðˤ	'showing off'

مصدر masdar nominals function as typical nouns which may carry further affixation and assume grammatical functions such as subjects and objects (Chapter 6).

وايد أحب تخصصي

waajəd	ʔa-ħəb	taxasˤsˤəsˤ-i.
very	I-love.imperf	major-my

'I really love my major.'

ترتيب المدرسة للفعالية وايد حلو

tartiib	l-madrəsa	l-əl-faʕaalijja	waajəd	ħəlw.
organizing	the-school	for-the-event	very	beautiful

'The school's organization of the event is excellent.'

التعليم وايد مهم للأجيال الصغيرة

ət-taʕliim	waajəd	mhəm	l-əl-ʔadʒjaal	əsˤ-sˤəɣiir-a.
the-education	very	important	for-the-generations	the-young-f

'Education is important for the young generation.'

5.1.2.8 *Diminutives*

Diminutives convey a slighter degree, size, or age of the meaning the source noun usually conveys. This may be interpreted as referring to objects or ideas which are smaller or 'less' than the usual size or quality of the source noun; or, in many cases, to convey a sense of intimacy or endearment to the referent. The formation of diminutives in Emirati Arabic adopts a list of vocalic patterns, depending on the phonological structure of the base stem (Table 5.15).

Additionally, the diminutive of other proper names, or 'hypocorism' (cf. English 'Thomas' vs. 'Tom,' 'Andrew' vs. 'Andy,' etc.) is formed by adding و -oo at the end of the base noun if it is an open syllable; otherwise, before the coda consonant of the base noun.

Table 5.15 Diminutives

CaaCəC	*Base*	*CweeCiC*	*Diminutive*	
هاشل	haaʃəl	هويشل	hweeʃəl	'Hashil'
راشد	raaʃəd	رويشد	rweeʃəd	'Rashed'
هاشم	haaʃəm	هويشم	hweeʃəm	'Hashim'
كاتب	kaatəb	كويتب	kweetəb	'writer'
CəCaC/CəCiiC	*Base*	*CCajjiC*	*Diminutive*	
صغير	sˤəɣiir	صغيّر	sˤɣajjər	'small'
غدير	ɣədiir	غديّر	ɣdajjər	'deep pond'
نتفه	nətfah	نتيف	ntajjəf	'little bit'
قصير	gəsˤiir	قصيّر	gsˤajjər	'short'
CeeC/CuuC	*Base*	*CwaCCiC*	*Diminutive*	
زين	zeen	زويّن	zwajjən	'good'
نورة	nuura	نويّر	nwajjər	'Noora'

	Base		Diminutive	
روضة	rooðˤa	روضو	rooðˤoo	'Rauda'
علي	ʕəlii	علَو	ʕalloo	'Ali'
حمد	ħamad	حمّود	ħammuud	'Hammed'
سعيد	sʕiid	سعّود	saʕʕuud	'Said'
ميثة	meeθa	ميثو	meeθoo	'Maitha'

5.2 Verbs

Verbs are a lexical category associated semantically *inter alia* with actions, events, activities, accomplishments, and states. As mentioned in Chapter 4, Emirati verbs are derived by mapping the consonantal root with a specific phonological template/pattern associated with a particular meaning or function. The templatic system for the derivations of verbs is so rich that a single consonant root can yield up to nine different forms, each bearing a related meaning. The various derived forms express a plethora of grammatical lexical and grammatical information such as intensification, causation, and reflexivization. While this grammar is self-contained in the sense that it may be studied independently with little reference to MSA, it is important to note that the templatic systems of verbs for MSA and Emirati Arabic (EA) are highly compatible with each other. Consequently, the form class system is adopted from MSA. Table 5.16 shows that variations

Table 5.16 The verbal forms of MSA and Emirati Arabic

Form	*Modern Standard Arabic*	*Emirati Arabic*
I	$C_1aC_2aC_3$	$C_1əC_2aC_3$
II	$C_1aC_2C_2aC_3$	$C_1aC_2C_2aC_3$
III	$C_1aaC_2aC_3$	$C_1aaC_2aC_3$
IV	$C_1aC_2C_2aC_3$	—
V	$taC_1aC_2C_2aC_3$	$tC_1aC_2C_2aC_3$
VI	$taC_1aaC_2aC_3$	$tC_1aaC_2aC_3$
VII	$(ʔi)nC_1aC_2aC_3$	$nC_1əC_2aC_3$
VIII	$(ʔi)C_1taC_2aC_3$	$C_1təC_2aC_3$
IX	$(ʔi)C_1C_2aC_3C_3$	$C_1C_2aC_3C_3$
X	$(ʔi)staC_1C_2aC_3$	$staC_1C_2aC_3$

exist between the two dialects for most of the form classes. In addition, Form IV is not attested in Emirati Arabic.

As this grammar discusses in the following sections, all forms carry the perfective aspect as the default aspectual value (Section 8.1). Distinct from many languages such as English, which considers the infinitival form as the basic verbal form (e.g. 'go,' 'eat,' 'walk'), Emirati Arabic (as with other Arabic dialects) does not make a distinction between finite and infinitival verbs. Verbs are either perfective or imperfective. Both specify the physical time in which the verbal event happens; in that sense, all verbs are finite. The third-person singular masculine agreement of the perfective verb is normally considered as the default verbal form, as it is homographic with its underlying consonant root, e.g. ك-ت-ب k-t-b vs كتب kitab 'he wrote.' On the other hand, while some Arabic grammarians claim that nonfinite verbs exist in Arabic, e.g. active/passive participles and verbal nouns, there is strong evidence they should not be categorized as prototypical verbs.

5.2.1 Weak verbs

Weak verbs are verbs formed by a weak consonant as part of the root. The weak consonants are the glottal stop ا [ʔ], which is articulatorily 'weak,' و [w] and ي [j], which are semi-vowels, and the word-final long vowel ى [aa], which stems from the phoneme /j/. A weak verb, in which the initial and/or last radical is weak, is traditionally called a 'defective' verb, e.g. نسى nəsa 'forgot' and بقى bəga 'stayed' (Table 5.17). On the other hand, a 'hollow' verb

Table 5.17 Defective verbs

Root consonants		*Derived words*		
ن-س-ي	n-s-j	نسى	nəsa	'forgot'
ب-ق-ي	b-g-j	بقى	bəga	'stayed'
م-ش-ي	m-ʃ-j	مشى	məʃa	'walked'
ر-ض-ي	r-ðˤ-j	رضى	rəðˤa	'settled'
و-ف-ي	w-f-j	وفى	wəfa	'kept (a promise)'
أ-ك-ل	ʔ-k-l	كلا	kal(a)	'ate'
ل-ع-ي	l-ʕ-j	لعى	ləʕa	'cried loudly'
ر-ق-ي	r-g-j	رقى	rəga	'climbed'
ع-ط-ي	ʕ-tˤ-j	عطى	ʕatˤa	'gave'

Table 5.18 Hollow verbs

Root consonants		*Derived words*		
ق-و-ل	g-w-l	قال	gaal	'said'
ر-و-ح	r-w-ħ	راح	raaħ	'went'
س-ي-ر	s-j-r	سار	saar	'left'
م-و-ت	m-w-t	مات	maat	'died'
ط-ي-ر	tˤ-j-r	طار	tˤaar	'flew'
ف-و-ت	f-w-t	فات	faat	'passed'
ص-ي-ح	sˤ-j-ħ	صاح	sˤaaħ	'cried'
س-ي-ح	s-j-ħ	ساح	saaħ	'melted/swallowed'
ب-ي-ع	b-j-ʕ	باع	baaʕ	'sold'
م-ي-ل	m-j-l	مال	maal	'tipped/leaned'

is defined by having a medial long vowel ا [aa] and no medial consonant in pronunciation (hence its name), e.g. قال gaal 'said' and راح raaħ 'went.' These hollow verbs (Table 5.18) always contain an underlying weak medial radical consonant (i.e. [ʔ], [w], or [j]) as part of their abstract mental representation (Section 2.1.1). Certain phonological processes derive the long vowel from a representation which deletes the underlying weak medial radical consonant. Because of the presence of weak consonants, weak verbs are susceptible to phonological changes which are not observed in normal 'sound' verbs, as discussed in Sections 8.1 and 8.2.

5.2.2 *Doubled verbs*

Doubled verbs are triconsonantal root verbs in which the second and third radical consonants are identical (Table 5.19). It is not possible for Emirati Arabic (and other Arabic dialects) to have an initial and medial radical which are identical.

5.2.3 *Quadriliteral verbs*

Quadriliteral verbs are verbs which have four radical consonants. Some quadriliteral verbs share a historical origin with other Arabic dialects (including MSA) and the quadriliteral roots bear a conceptual meaning (albeit an abstract one). There are also quadriliteral verbs which result from reduplication, onomatopoeia, and

Table 5.19 Doubled verbs

Root consonants		*Derived words*		
د-ش	d-ʃ	دش	daʃʃ	'entered'
ن-ش	n-ʃ	نش	naʃʃ	'woke up'
ل-ف	l-f	لف	laff	'turned'
ص-ك	sˤ-k	صك	sˤakk	'closed'
ح-ب	ħ-b	حب	ħabb	'loved'
م-ر	m-r	مر	marr	'passed'
ب-ر	b-r	بر	barr	'obeyed'
ز-ر	z-r	زر	zarr	'tightened'
ح-ر	ħ-r	حر	ħarr	'heated'
ي-ر	j-r	ير	jarr	'pulled'
ف-ر	f-r	فر	farr	'threw'

borrowing (Chapter 4). The quadriliteral root may be formed by completely distinct, partially identical, or reduplicated consonants. In addition, there is a class of derived quadriliteral roots formed by a prefix تـ t- (Table 5.20).

Table 5.20 Quadriliteral roots

$C_1C_2C_3C_4$		
زخرف	zaxraf	'decorated'
شخبط	ʃaxbatˤ	'messed up'
دربح	darbaħ	'rolled'
خربط	xarbatˤ	'mistaken'
طنقر	tˤangar	'irritated'
برطم	bartˤam	'hummed'
لخبط	laxbatˤ	'messed up or 'mixed up'
وهدن	wahdan	'made motionless/immobile'
$C_1C_2C_1C_2$		
مضمض	maðˤmaðˤ	'rinsed out'
فضفض	faðˤfaðˤ	'let out/let loose'

فصفص	fasˁfasˁ	'separated into small units'
فتفت	fatfat	'shattered into small bits'
قرقر	gargar	'talked much'
صحصح	sˁaħsˁaħ	'woke from sleep'
كركر	karkar	'laughed loudly'
$C_1C_2C_1C_3$		
سرسح	sarsaħ	'drank refreshingly'
شرشح	ʃarʃaħ	'scolded'
كركب	karkab	'made a mess'
نعنش	naʕnaʃ	'freshened'
فرفش	farfaʃ	'became energetic and happy'
مرمط	marmatˁ	'chided'
قرقع	gargaʕ	'created a smashing sound'
$C_1C_2C_3C_3$		
بهسس	bahsas	'donated generously'
بخشش	baxʃaʃ	'gave tips'
Borrowing		
بستر	bastar	'pasteurized'
كنسل	kansal	'canceled'
بنجر	bantʃar	'punctured'
فرمت	farmat	'formatted'
فوّل	fawwal	'became full'/'became upset'
سشور	saʃwar	'blow-dried'
بركن	barkan	'parked'

Base			tCaCCaC		
قهوة	gahwa	'coffee'	تقهوا	tgahwa	'drank coffee'
بهدل	bahdal	'messed'	تبهدل	tbahdal	'was embarrassed'
بلم	blamm	'wordless'	تبلّم	tballam	'became wordless'
قطع	gətˁaʕ	'cut'	تقطّع	tgatˁtˁaʕ	'was cut'
رقّع	raggaʕ	'patched'	ترقّع	traggaʕ	'was patched'

(*Continued*)

Table 5.20 (Continued)

Base			tCeeCaC		
سخيف	saxiif	'silly'	تسيخف	tseexaf	'acted silly'
نحس	naħs	'jinxed'	تنيحس	tneeħas	'acted stubbornly'

5.2.4 Form I

Form I is the simplest inflectional class (Table 5.21). It is marked by the mid-central vowel [ə] or the high-front vowel [i] after the first radical. The vowel may be lowered to [a] if the initial radical is a pharyngeal or velar consonant.

The semantic interpretation of Form I verbs is not restricted and allows for a wide range of possible meanings. Verbs of different syntactic valency (i.e. intransitive, transitive, ditransitive)

Table 5.21 Form I

فضح	fəðˁaħ	'exposed'	شل	ʃall	'removed'
كسر	kəsar	'broke'	خذ	xað(a)	'took'
شل	ʃall	'carried'	ضم	ðˁamm	'hid'
ضرب	ðˁarab	'hit'	مسك	məsak	'held'
دش	daʃʃ	'entered'	كتب	kətab	'wrote'
شات	ʃaat	'shot'	باع	baaʕ	'sold'
حل	ħall	'solved'	خاف	xaaf	'feared'
سمع	səmaʕ	'heard'	دق	dagg	'knocked'
صار	sˁaar	'became'	وقف	wəgaf	'stopped'
كان	kaan	'was'	قعد	gaʕad	'sat, stayed'
شاف	ʧaaf	'saw'	رسم	rəsam	'drew'
قام	gaam	'rose'	برز	bəraz	'stood out'
يا	jaa	'came'	شرد	ʃarad	'ran away'
كبر	kəbar	'grew old'	حس	ħass	'felt'
مات	maat	'died'	رقص	rəgasˁ	'danced'
نام	naam	'slept'	راح	raaħ	'went'

and argument structures (e.g. unergative and unaccusative) may appear in Form I (Chapter 7).

الممثل نطق

əl-mumaθθəl nətˤag.

the-actor speak.perf-he

'The actor spoke.'

أحمد شبع

ʔaħmad ʃəbaʕ.

Ahmad get.full.perf-he

'Ahmad got full.'

الماي برد

əl-maaj bərad.

the-water get.cold.perf-it

'The water got cold.'

الجيش رفعوا العلم الوطني

əl-ʤeeʃ rəfʕ-aw əl-ʕalam əl-watˤanı.

the-army raise.perf-they the-flag the-national

'The army raised the national flag.'

هالوثايق فضحت الحكومة

ha-l-wəθaajəg fəðˤħ-at əl-ħəkuuma.

these-the-documents expose.perf-f the-government

'These documents exposed the government.'

علي كسر الكوب بالغلط

ʕəli kəsar l-koob b-əl-ɣalatˤ

Ali break.perf-he the-cup by-the-mistake

'Ali broke the cup by accident.'

5.2.5 *Form II*

Form II has an almost identical pattern as Form I, with the exception that the medial consonant of the triconsonantal root is doubled. Form II usually expresses the meaning of causatives, and

Table 5.22 Form II

Form I			*Form II*		
ضحك	ðˤaħak	'laughed'	ضحّك	ðˤaħħak	'made s.o laugh'
خلص	xəlasˤ	'finished'	خلّص	xalˤlˤasˤ	'finished s.th'
نام	naam	'slept'	نوّم	nawwam	'put s.o to sleep'
طلع	tˤalaʕ	'went out'	طلّع	tˤalˤlˤaʕ	'brought s.th out'
نزل	nəzal	'went down'	نزّل	nazzal	'lowered'
طاح	tˤaaħ	'fell'	طيّح	tˤajjaħ	'knocked down'
خرب	xarab	'went bad'	خرّب	xarrab	'ruined'
نظف	nəðˤaf	'became clean'	نظّف	naðˤðˤaf	'cleaned'
قصر	gəsˤar	'became short'	قصّر	gasˤsˤar	'shortened'
Noun/Adjectives					
وصخ	wəsˤax	'dirt'	وصّخ	wasˤsˤax	'made s.th dirty'
فنش	fanaʃ	'end of service'	فنّش	fannaʃ	'terminated s.o'
عوار	ʕawaar	'pain'	عوّر	ʕawwar	'inflicted pain'
قيض	geeðˤ	'summer'	قيّض	gajjaðˤ	'spent the summer'
خيمة	xeema	'tent'	خيّم	xajjam	'camped'
فصل	fəsˤal	'disconnected'	فصّل	fasˤsˤal	'tailored s.o'
يديد	jediid	'new'	يدّد	jaddaad	'renewed'
غنيَّة	ɣnijja	'song'	غنّى	ɣanna	'sang'

occasionally the intensification of an action. Form II verbs also possess a different argument structure to Form I, which may be intransitive. Table 5.22 shows the relation between Form I and Form II verbs. Note that Form II verbs may also be denominal or deadjectival, as a number of triconsonantal roots on which Form II verbs are formed express nominal (e.g. قيض geeðˤ 'summer') or adjectival (e.g. وصخ wasˤx 'dirty') meanings.

The grammatical distinctions between Form I and II verbs are illustrated by the following examples. In the formation of causative structures, the causee functions as the object of the causative (i.e. Form II) verbs (Chapter 7).

السيارة وقفت

əs-səjjaara wəgf-at.
the-car stop.perf-it.f
'The car stopped.'

علي ركب على الناقة

ʕəli	rəkab	ʕala	ən-naaga.
Ali	ride.perf-he	on	the-camel

'Ali rode on the camel.'

حامد فرح

ħaamed	fəraħ.
Hamid	happy.perf-he

'Hamid was happy.'

عمر وقف السيارة

ʕumar	waggaf	əs-sajjaara.
Omar	caus.stop.perf-he	the-car

'Omar stopped the car.'

خالد ركّب فاطمة على الناقة

xaled	rakkab	fatˁma	ʕala	ən-naaga.
khalid	caus.ride.perf-he	fatima	on	the-camel

'Khalid helped Fatma (to ride) on the camel.'

علي فرّح فاطمة

ʕəli	farraħ	fatˁma.
Ali	caus.happy.perf-he	fatma

'Ali made Fatma happy.'

5.2.6 *Form III*

Form III (Table 5.23) is characterized by the first vowel lengthening, i.e. CaaCaC. It expresses an associative meaning and introduces the associated participant (e.g. the indirect object) of the verbal action as an argument. In some cases, Form III also expresses the meaning of reciprocity. In Emirati Arabic, the two arguments of Form III are almost always animate participants.

علي لاعب الولد

ʕəli	laaʕab	əl-walad.
Ali	play.with.perf	the-boy

'Ali played with the boy.'

Table 5.23 Form III

Root		*Form III*		
ج-و-ب	ʤ-w-b	جاوب	ʤaawab	'answered (to s.o)'
ز-ع-ق	z-ʕ-g	زاعق	zaaʕag	'yelled at s.o'
خ-ص-م	x-sˤ-m	خاصم	xaasˤam	'antagonized s.o (traditionally)'
ب-ر-ك	b-r-k	بارك	baarak	'gave blessings to s.o'
و-ف-ق	w-f-g	وافق	waafag	'agreed with s.o'
ر-س-ل	r-s-l	راسل	raasal	'corresponded with s.o'
ش-ر-ك	ʃ-r-k	شارك	ʃaarak	'shared with s.o'
ع-ل-ج	ʕ-l-ʤ	عالج	ʕaalaʤ	'dealt with s.th/s.o'
س-ب-ق	s-b-g	سابق	saabag	'competed with s.o'

In many other cases, Form III is used on non-action verbs which involve an event associate. For instance, verbs such as عاقب ʕaaqab 'punished' and عاون ʕaawan 'helped' are Form III.

علي عاقب أحمد

ʕəli ʕaaqab ʔaħmad.

Ali punish.perf-he Ahmad

'Ali punished Ahmad.'

علي عاون فاطمة

ʕəli ʕaawan faatˤma.

Ali help.perf-he Fatma

'Ali helped Fatma.'

فاطمة رابعت شيخة

fatˤma raabaʕ-at ʃeexa.

Fatma befriend.perf-she Shaikha

'Fatma befriended Shaikha.'

It is also possible for Form III verbs to select indirect objects. For instance, بارك baarak 'blessed' and وايق waajag 'gazed' select the indirect objects which are marked by a preposition.

علي بارك لأحمد

ʕəli baarak l-ʔaħmad.
Ali bless.perf-he for-Ahmad
'Ali congratulated Ahmad.'

علي وايق من الباب على الولد

ʕəli waajag mən əl-baab ʕala l-walad.
Ali gaze.perf-he from the-door on the-boy
'Ali peeped (through the door) at the boy.'

5.2.7 *Form V*

Form V is derived by adding the prefix تـ t- to Form II. In contrast with Form II, Form V is valency-decreasing, which can be interpreted in different ways. The most common usage is to reflexivize and passivize the base verb. Compare the interpretations of Form II and Form V verbs in Table 5.24.

Table 5.24 Form V

Form II			*Form V*		
علّم	ʕallam	'taught'	تعلّم	tʕallam	'learned'
زوّج	zawwadʒ	'married s.o to s.o'	تزوّج	tzawwadʒ	'got married'
غيّر	ɣajjar	'changed s.th'	تغيّر	tɣajjar	'changed'
ونّس	wannas	'showed s.o a good time'	تونّس	twannas	'had a good time'
غدّا	ɣadda	'gave lunch to s.o'	تغدّا	tɣadda	'had lunch'
فصّخ	fasˁsˁax	'took off s.th'	تفصّخ	tfasˁsˁax	'took off clothes'
ذكّر	ðakkar	'reminded'	تذكّر	tðakkar	'remembered'
بنّد	bannad	'shut s.th'	تبنّد	tbannad	'was shut'
ثمّن	θamman	'priced s.th'	تثمّن	tθamman	'was priced'
وهّق	wahhag	'involved s.o'	توهّق	twahhag	'was involved'
عوّر	ʕawwar	'inflicted pain to s.o'	تعوّر	tʕawwar	'was injured'
طرّش	tˁarraʃ	'sent s.th'	اتطرّش	əttˁarraʃ	'was sent'

Some examples are:

فاطمة تعلّمت السواقة

fatma	t-ʕalləm-at	əs-swaaga.
Fatma	refl-caus.teach.perf-she	the-driving

'Fatma learned how to drive.'

علي تذكر الرقم

ʕəli	t-ðakkar	ər-ragəm.
Ali	refl-caus.remind.perf-he	the-number

'Ali remembered the number.'

أحمد تسلى

ʔaħmad	tə-salla.
Ahmad	refl-caus.enjoy.perf-he

'Ahmad enjoyed himself.'

الحبل تقطّع

əl-ħabəl	t-gatˁtˁaʕ.
the-rope	pass-caus.cut.perf-it

'The rope was cut.'

اللحم تنشّف

əl-laħam	t-naʃʃaf.
the-meat	pass-caus.dry.perf

'The meat dried.'

أحمد تيبّس

ʔaħmad	t-jabbas.
Ahmad	refl-caus.freeze-he

'Ahmad froze in his place.'

حسن تسدّح

ħasan	t-saddaħ.
Hasan	refl-caus.lie.down-he

'Hasan lay (himself) down.'

أحمد تقطّع

ʔaħmad	t-gatˤtˤaʕ.
Ahmad	pass-caus.criticize.perf-he

'Ahmad was criticized.'

أحمد تعيّن مدير

ʔaħmad	t-ʕayyan	mudiir.
Ahmad	pass-caus.appoint.perf-he	director

'Ahmad was appointed as director.'

5.2.8 Form VI

Form VI (Table 5.25) is formed by attaching the same mediopassive prefix تـ t- to Form III. Similarly to Form V, Form VI also bears a valency-decreasing function. Semantically, Form VI expresses two interpretations: reciprocality and mediopassives. It is mostly used with plural or conjoined subjects (Chapter 15), or with two participants which bear the same thematic role.

تبارت العين مع الوحدة

t-baar-at	əl-ʕeen	maʕa	l-wəħda.
refl-play.perf-it.f	Al Ain	with	Al-Weħda

'Al Ain team played a match against Al-Wehda team.' (lit. Al Ain and Al Wehda played with each other.)

Table 5.25 Form VI

Form III			*Form VI*		
شاور	ʃaawar	'consulted s.o'	تشاور	tʃaawar	'deliberated with e.o'
قابل	gaabal	'met s.o'	تقابل	tgaabal	'met e.o'
خابر	xaabar	'telephoned s.o'	تخابر	txaabar	'telephoned e.o'
جاوب	ʤaawab	'responded to s.o'	تجاوب	tʤaawab	'responded to e.o'
وافق	waafag	'agreed with s.o'	توافق	twaafag	'agreed with e.o'
ساعد	saaʕad	'helped s.o'	تساعد	tsaaʕad	'helped e.o'
فاهم	faaham	'understood'	تفاهم	tfaaham	'understood e.o'

تسابق أحمد مع علي

t-saabag	ʔahmad	maʕ	ʕəli.
refl-race.perf-he	Ahmad	with	Ali

'Ahmad raced with Ali.'

تضارب أحمد مع علي

t-ð^{ʕ}aarab	ʔahmad	maʕ	ʕəli.
refl-fight.perf-he	Ahmad	with	Ali

'Ahmad fought with Ali.'

الريابيل تضاربوا

ər-rəjaajiil	t-ð^{ʕ}aarəb-aw
the-men	refl-fight.perf-they

'The men fought with each other.'

تضايق أحمد من علي

t-ð^{ʕ}aajag	ʔahmad	mən	ʕəli.
refl-get.annoyed.perf-he	Ahmad	from	Ali

'Ahmad got annoyed by Ali.'

5.2.9 *Form VII*

Form VII is formed by adding the prefix نـ n- to Form I. Form VII expresses a range of mediopassive meanings, including middle, reflexive, resultative, and passive (Table 5.26).

خالد انضرب

xaaləd	n-ð^{ʕ}ərab.
Khalid	pass-hit.perf-he

'Khalid was hit.'

انكسر الكوب

n-kəsar	l-koob.
pass-break.perf-it	the-glass

'The glass was broken.'

انقطع الخيط

n-get^{ʕ}aʕ	l-xeet^{ʕ}.
pass-cut.perf-it	the-thread

'The thread was cut.'

انغسل اللحاف

n-ɣəsal	əl-laħaaf.
pass-wash.perf-it	the-blanket

'The blanket was washed.'

Table 5.26 Form VII

Form I			*Form VII*		
ترس	təras	'filled'	انترس	ntəras	'was filled'
عرف	ʕaraf	'knew'	انعرف	nʕaraf	'was known'
ترك	tərak	'left'	انترك	ntərak	'was left'
سمع	səmaʕ	'heard'	انسمع	nsəmaʕ	'was heard'
درى	dara	'knew'	اندرى	ndara	'was known'
رمس	rəmas	'talked'	انرمس	nrəmas	'was talked about'
سرق	sərag	'stole'	انسرق	nsərag	'was stolen'
شال	ʃaal	'lifted'	انشل	nʃall	'was lifted'
قتل	gətal	'killed'	انقتل	ngətal	'was killed'
عق	ʕagg	'threw away'	انعق	nʕagg	'was discarded'

انشغل علي
n-ʃeɣal ʕəli.
pass-busy.perf-he Ali
'Ali was (made) busy.'

انسرق الكتاب
n-sərag lə-ktaab.
pass-steal.perf-it the-book
'The book was stolen.'

الاكل اناٍكل كله
əl-ʔakəl n-ʔəkal kəll-a.
the-food pass-eat.perf-it all-it
'The food was eaten entirely.'

الملابس انغسلن عدل
l-malaabəs n-ɣasl-an ʕadəl.
the-clothes pass-wash.perf-they well
'The clothes were washed well.'

Some Form VII verbs are intransitive themselves and do not seem to derive from any interpretable Form I verbs.

سالم انخمد
saaləm n-xəmad.
Salim pass-sleep.perf-he
'Salim slept.'

طارق انطب
tˤaarəg n-tˤabb.
Tarig pass-shut.up.perf-he
'Tariq shut his mouth.'

5.2.10 *Form VIII*

Form VIII (Table 5.27) is marked by infixing the morpheme تـ -t- after the first Form I radical. Verbs belonging to this form can

Table 5.27 Form VIII

Form I			*Form VIII*		
حرق	ħərag	'burned'	احترق	(ə)ħtərag	'was burned'
سند	sənad	'supported'	استند	(ə)stənad	'leaned on'
بعد	bəʕad	'pushed away'	ابتعد	(ə)btəʕad	'went far'
كشف	kəʃaf	'exposed'	اكتشف	(ə)ktəʃaf	'discovered'
قصد	gəsˤad	'meant'	اقتصد	(ə)gtəsˤad	'used efficiently'
ربط	rəbatˤ	'linked'	ارتبط	(ə)rtəbatˤ	'got engaged'
Form II			*Form VIII*		
فرق	farrag	'separated s.th'	افترق	(ə)ftərag	'got separated'
عدل	ʕaddal	'fixed'	اعتدل	(ə)ʕtədal	'was fixed'
سلم	sallam	'delivered'	استلم	(ə)stəlam	'received'

have a number of different interpretations, including reflexive, mediopassive, resultative, and reciprocal meanings. Some Form VIII verbs may stem from a legitimate Form II word (e.g. افترق ftərag 'separated' < فرق farrag 'separated' (Form II)).

خالد انتحر

xaləd n-taħar.

Khalid refl-kill.perf-he

'Khalid committed suicide.'

أحمد ارتاح

ʔaħmad ərtaaħ.

Ahmad refl.rest.perf-he

'Ahmad reposed himself.'

افتضح الولد

ftəðˤaħ l-welad.

refl.embarrass.perf-he the-boy

'The boy got embarrassed.'

اشتغل التلفزيون

ʃtaɣal ət-tәlfəzjoon.

refl.work.perf-it the-TV

'The TV worked.'

انتفخ خشمي

ntəfax xaʃm-i.

refl.swell.perf-it nose-my

'My nose got swollen.'

احترق البيت

ħtərag əl-beet.

refl.burn.perf-it the-house

'The house was burned.'

5.2.11 Form IX

Form IX is marked by geminating/doubling the third radical consonant, although some Form IX verbs do not observe gemination (e.g. متن mtann 'became fat' can also be pronounced as [mətan]). Form IX is mainly interpreted as stative, denoting colors and physical defects, but it may also denote a change in physical appearance. Mostly, Form IX verbs are related to corresponding adjectives (Table 5.28).

متن الولد

mtann l-walad.
become.fat.perf-he the-boy
'The boy became fat.'

وسعت الكندورة

wsaʕʕ-at l-kandoor-a.
become.loose-it.f the-dress-f
'The dress became loose.'

احلوّ الولد

ħlaww l-walad.
become.handsome.perf-he the-boy
'The boy became handsome.'

اضعف الولد

ðˤʕaff l-walad.
become.thin.perf-he the-boy
'The boy became thin.'

اخضرّت الشجرة

xðˤarr-at lə-ʃjara.
become.green.perf-it.f the-tree
'The tree turned green.'

اسود البيت

swadd l-beet.
become.black.perf-it the-house
'The house turned black.'

Table 5.28 Form IX

Form IX					
متن	mtiin	'fat'	متن	mtann	'became fat'
وسيع	wsiiʕ	'loose'	وسع	wsaʕʕ	'became loose'
حلو	ħilw	'handsome'	احلوّ	ħlaww	'became handsome'
ضعيف	ðˤʕiif	'thin, weak'	اضعف	ðˤʕaff	'became thin/weak'
احول	ʔaħwal	'cross-eyed'	احول	ħwall	'became cross-eyed'
اخضر	ʔaxðˤar	'green'	اخضر	xðˤarr	'turned green'
اسود	ʔaswad	'black'	اسود	swadd	'turned black'
طويل	tˤwiil	'long'	اطول	tˤwall	'became long'
صغير	sˤɣiirr	'small'	اصغر	sˤɣarr	'became small'
ازرق	azrag	'arrogant'	ازرق	zragg	'turned blue'

5.2.12 *Form X*

Form X is not widely attested in Emirati Arabic; if used at all, it is mostly borrowed from MSA or other Arabic (in particular Egyptian) varieties. Form X seems to be built on Form IV (the causatives in MSA), and in Emirati Arabic is associated with the general meaning of reflexivity. Some examples are in Table 5.29.

محمد استقال
mħammad əsta-qaal.
mohammed refl-resign.perf-he
'Mohammed resigned'

أحمد استعبط
ʔaħmad əsta-ʕbatˤ.
Ahmad refl-caus.stupid.perf-he
'Ahmad acted stupidly.'

خالد استقوا علينا
xaaləd əsta-gwaa ʕal-eena.
Khalid refl-caus.strong.perf on-us
'Khalid acted tough on us.'

علي استخدم القلم
ʕəli sta-xdam əl-galam.
Ali refl-caus.perf-he the-pen
'Ali used the pen.'

5.2.13 *The perfective aspectual marker*

All typical verbs are inflected for a particular verbal aspect (Chapter 8), and the perfective aspect is considered the 'basic' verbal form (cf. English infinitives). The perfective verbal stem is further inflected for subject agreement morphology, which encodes information about the person, number, and gender of the sentence subject. Sometimes it is possible for the verbal stem to be suffixed

Table 5.29 Form X

Form I			*Form X*		
عبط	ʕabatˤ	'naïvety'	استعبط	(ə)staʕabatˤ	'acted naïvely/ stupidly'
عيل	ʕjal	'hurried'	استعيل	(ə)staʕjal	'rushed'
كبر	kəbar	'became bigger'	استكبر	(ə)stakbar	'acted arrogantly'
حمل	ħəmal	'carried'	استحمل	(ə)staħmal	'tolerated s.th'
عمل	ʕəmal	'worked'	استعمل	(ə)staʕmal	'used s.th'
رجع	rədʒaʕ	'returned'	استرجع	(ə)stardʒaʕ	'returned s.th'

Table 5.30 The perfective aspect of sound verbs

Person	*Gender*	*Number*					
first	m/f	singular	ـت	-t	كسرت	kəsart	'(I) broke'
second	m	singular	ـت	-t	كسرت	kəsart	'(You) broke'
second	f	singular	ـتي	-ti	كسرتي	kəsarti	'(You.f) broke'
third	m	singular	—	—	كسر	kəsar	'(He) broke'
third	f	singular	ـت	-at	كسرت	kəsrat	'(She) broke'
first	m/f	plural	ـنا	-na	كسرنا	kəsarna	'(We) broke'
second	m	plural	ـتوا	-tu	كسرتوا	kəsartu	'(You.pl) broke'
second	f	plural	ـتن	-tin	كسرتن	kəsartən	'(You.f.pl) broke'
third	m	plural	ـوا	-aw	كسروا	kəsraw/ ksəraw	'(They) broke'
third	f	plural	ـن	-an	كسرن	kəsran/ ksəran	'(They.f.pl) broke'

by the object pronoun (Section 5.8.1). In total, up to ten morphological inflections are observed. Variation exists among speakers as to whether the subject agreement for the second-person plural feminine is actually attested in natural conversation (Table 5.30).

The morphology of weak verbs (Section 5.2.1) in the perfective aspect differs from that of sound verbs and double verbs (Section 5.2.2, Table 5.35) mainly in terms of phonological realization. For defective verbs formed by root-final weak radicals (i.e. [ʔ], [w], [j], and [aa]), the actual pronunciation of the root-final weak radicals changes, depending on the subject agreement. For the third-person (masculine/feminine, singular/plural) subject agreement, the vowel quality of the root-final ى [aa] stays intact, e.g. نست [nəsat] '(she) forgot.' For non-third-persons, ى [aa] changes to [ee], e.g. نسيت nəseet '(I) forgot' (Table 5.31). On the other hand, the root-initial weak radical [ʔ] is not be pronounced in all forms of the perfective verb, e.g. كلت kelt '(I) ate' and كل kal '(he) ate' (Table 5.32). For hollow verbs that contain the root-medial weak consonants و /w/ or ي /j/, as shown in Table 5.34 and Table 5.33 respectively, some phonological change will apply to their non-third-person inflection. The underlying hollow phoneme surfaces as [ə] in the first and second person inflections (e.g. قلت gəlt '(I) said') and as the long vowel [aa] for the third-person (e.g. قال gaal '(He) said').

Table 5.31 The perfective aspect of defective verbs with a final /j/ or /aa/

Person	*Gender*	*Number*			
first	m/f	singular	نسيت	nəseet	'(I) forgot'
second	m	singular	نسيت	nəseet	'(You) forgot'
second	f	singular	نسيتي	nəseeti	'(You.f) forgot'
third	m	singular	نسى	nəsa	'(He) forgot'
third	f	singular	نست	nəsat	'(She) forgot'
first	m/f	plural	نسينا	nəseena	'(We) forgot'
second	m	plural	نسيتوا	nəseetu	'(You.pl) forgot'
second	f	plural	نسيتن	nəseetən	'(You.f.pl) forgot'
third	m	plural	نسوا	nəsaw	'(They) forgot'
third	f	plural	نسن	nəsan	'(They.f.pl) forgot'

Table 5.32 The perfective aspect of defective verbs with an initial /ʔ/

Person	*Gender*	*Number*			
first	m/f	singular	كلت/كليت	kalt/kaleet	'(I) ate'
second	m	singular	كلت/كليت	kalt/kaleet	'(You) ate'
second	f	singular	كلتي/كليتي	kalti/kaleeti	'(You.f) ate'
third	m	singular	كل/كلا	kal/kala	'(He) ate'
third	f	singular	كلت	kalat	'(She) ate'
first	m/f	plural	كلنا/كلينا	kalna/kaleena	'(We) ate'
second	m	plural	كلتوا/كليتوا	kaltu/kaleetu	'(You.pl) ate'
second	f	plural	كلتن/كليتن	kaltən/kaleetən	'(You.f.pl) ate'
third	m	plural	كلوا	kalaw	'(They) ate'
third	f	plural	كلن	kalan	'(They.f.pl) ate'

Table 5.33 The perfective aspect of hollow verbs with a medial /aa/

Person	*Gender*	*Number*			
first	m/f	singular	بعت	bəʕt	'(I) sold'
second	m	singular	بعت	bəʕt	'(You) sold'

Person	Gender	Number			
second	f	singular	بعتي	bəʕti	'(You.f) sold'
third	m	singular	باع	baaʕ	'(He) sold'
third	f	singular	باعت	baaʕat	'(She) sold'
first	m/f	plural	بعنا	bəʕna	'(We) sold'
second	m	plural	بعتوا	bəʕtu	'(You.pl) sold'
second	f	plural	بعتن	bəʕtən	'(You.f.pl) sold'
third	m	plural	باعوا	baaʕaw	'(They) sold'
third	f	plural	باعن	baaʕan	'(They.f.pl) sold'

Table 5.34 The perfective aspect of hollow verbs with an underlying /w/

Person	Gender	Number			
first	m/f	singular	مت	mətt	'(I) died'
second	m	singular	مت	mətt	'(You) died'
second	f	singular	متي	mətti	'(You.f) died'
third	m	singular	مات	maat	'(He) died'
third	f	singular	ماتت	maatat	'(She) died'
first	m/f	plural	متنا	mətna	'(We) died'
second	m	plural	متّوا	məttuu	'(You.pl) died'
second	f	plural	متّن	məttən	'(You.f.pl) died'
third	m	plural	ماتوا	maataw	'(They) died'
third	f	plural	ماتن	maatan	'(They.f.pl) died'

Table 5.35 The perfective aspect of doubled verbs

Person	Gender	Number			
first	m/f	singular	دشيت	daʃʃeet	'(I) entered'
second	m	singular	دشيت	daʃʃeet	'(You) entered'
second	f	singular	دشيتي	daʃʃeeti	'(You.f) entered'

(*Continued*)

Table 5.35 (Continued)

Person	*Gender*	*Number*			
third	m	singular	دش	daʃʃ	'(He) entered'
third	f	singular	دشت	daʃʃat	'(She) entered'
first	m/f	plural	دشينا	daʃʃeena	'(We) entered'
second	m	plural	دشيتوا	daʃʃeetu	'(You.pl) entered'
second	f	plural	دشيتن	daʃʃeetən	'(You.f.pl) entered'
third	m	plural	دشوا	daʃʃaw	'(They) entered'
third	f	plural	دشن	daʃʃan	'(They.f.pl) entered'

5.2.14 *The imperfective aspectual marker*

In Emirati Arabic, the imperfective verbal stem (Table 5.36) usually contains the vowel [ə], i.e. CCəC. Subject agreement on the imperfective verb form is realized with a separate series of affixes—in this case, prefixes and some circumfixes (Chapter 4).

As observed in the perfective aspect, weak verbs in the imperfective aspect also deviate from sound verbs and double verbs (Table 5.42) in the actual phonological realization. For defective verbs with root-initial consonant أ /ʔ/ (Table 5.38), /ʔ/ is replaced by the vowel [a] (e.g. ياكل jaakəl 'He eats'). The root-initial و /w/ (Table 5.39) and يـ /j/ (Table 5.40) remain intact, with the same inflectional morphology as sound verbs (e.g. أوفّي ʔawaffi 'I fulfill' and ايدّد ʔajaddid 'I renew'). If root-final, ي /j/ (Table 5.37) becomes the vowel [a] if the imperfective verb is not suffixed (e.g. أبقى ʔabga 'I stay'). For hollow verbs (Table 5.41), the root-medial يـ /j/ becomes the long vowel [ii] (e.g. أصيح ʔasˤiiħ 'I cry').

5.2.15 *Imperatives*

Imperatives are used to express commands, instructions, requests, and so on. In contrast with other typical verbs, which bear aspectual morphology and grammatical information about the subject, the imperative verb consists of an imperfective verb stem. Since commands and requests are always addressed from the speaker to the hearer (i.e. the second person), the imperfective verb stem conflates

Table 5.36 The imperfective aspect of sound verbs

Person	*Gender*	*Number*					
first	m/f	singular	اـ	ʔ(a)-	أكسر	ʔaksər	'(I) break'
second	m	singular	تـ	t(ə)-	تكسر	təksər	'(You) break'
second	f	singular	تـ . . . ـين	t(ə)- . . . -iin	تكسرين	təksərriin	'(You.f) break'
third	m	singular	يـ	j(ə)-	يكسر	jəksər	'(He) breaks'
third	f	singular	تـ	t(ə)-	تكسر	təksər	'(She) breaks'
first	m/f	plural	نـ	n(ə)-	نكسر	nəksər	'(We) break'
second	m	plural	تـ . . . ـون	t(ə)- . . . -uun	تكسرون	təksəruun	'(You.pl) break'
second	f	plural	تـ . . . ـين	t(ə)- . . . -n	تكسرن	təksərən	'(You.f.pl) break'
third	m	plural	يـ . . . ـون	j(ə)- . . . -uun	يكسرون	jəksəruun	'(They) break'
third	f	plural	يـ . . . ـن	j(ə)- . . . -ən	يكسرن	jəksərən	'(They.f.pl) stay'

Table 5.37 The imperfective aspect of defective verbs with a final /j/

Person	*Gender*	*Number*			
first	m/f	singular	أبقى	ʔabga	'(I) stay'
second	m	singular	تبقى	təbga	'(You) stay'
second	f	singular	تبقين	təbgeen	'(You.f) stay'
third	m	singular	يبقى	jəbga	'(He) stays'
third	f	singular	تبقى	təbga	'(She) stays'
first	m/f	plural	نبقى	nəbga	'(We) stay'
second	m	plural	تبقون	təbgoon	'(You.pl) stay'
second	f	plural	تبقن	təbgan	'(You.f.pl) stay'
third	m	plural	يبقون	jəbgoon	'(They) stay'
third	f	plural	يبقن	jəbgan	'(They.f.pl) stay'

Table 5.38 The imperfective aspect of defective verbs with an initial /ʔ/

Person	*Gender*	*Number*			
first	m/f	singular	آكل	ʔaakəl	'(I) eat'
second	m	singular	تاكل	taakəl	'(You) eat'
second	f	singular	تاكلين	taakliin	'(You.f) eat'
third	m	singular	ياكل	jaakəl	'(He) eats'
third	f	singular	تاكل	taakəl	'(She) eats'
first	m/f	plural	ناكل	naakəl	'(We) eat'
second	m	plural	تاكلون	taakluun	'(You.pl) eat'
second	f	plural	تاكلن	taaklən	'(You.f.pl) eat'
third	m	plural	ياكلون	jaakluun	'(They) eat'
third	f	plural	ياكلن	jaaklən	'(They.f.pl) eat'

Table 5.39 The imperfective aspect of defective verbs with an initial /w/

Person	*Gender*	*Number*			
first	m/f	singular	أوفّي	ʔawaffi	'(I) fulfill'
second	m	singular	توفّي	təwaffi	'(You) fulfill'

Person	*Gender*	*Number*			
second	f	singular	توفّين	twaffiin	'(You.f) fulfill'
third	m	singular	يوفّي	jəwaffi	'(He) fulfills'
third	f	singular	توفّي	twaffi	'(She) fulfills'
first	m/f	plural	نوفّي	nwaffi	'(We) fulfill'
second	m	plural	توفّون	twaffuun	'(You.pl) fulfill'
second	f	plural	توفّن	twaffən	'(You.f.pl) fulfill'
third	m	plural	يوفّون	jəwaffuun	'(They) fulfill'
third	f	plural	يوفّن	jtwaffən	'(They.f.pl) fulfill'

Table 5.40 The imperfective aspect of defective verbs with an initial /j/

Person	*Gender*	*Number*			
first	m/f	singular	أيدد	ʔajaddəd	'(I) renew'
second	m	singular	تيدد	tjaddəd	'(You) renew'
second	f	singular	تيددين	tjaddədiin	'(You.f) renew'
third	m	singular	ايدد	ijjaddəd	'(He) renews'
third	f	singular	تيدد	tjaddəd	'(She) renews'
first	m/f	plural	نيدد	njaddəd	'(We) renew'
second	m	plural	تيددون	tjaddəduun	'(You.pl) renew'
second	f	plural	تيددن	tjaddədən	'(You.f.pl) renew'
third	m	plural	ايددون	ijaddəduun	'(They) renew'
third	f	plural	ايددن	ijaddədən	'(They.f.pl) renew'

Table 5.41 The imperfective aspect of hollow verbs

Person	*Gender*	*Number*			
first	m/f	singular	أصيح	ʔasˤiiħ	'(I) cry'
second	m	singular	تصيح	tsˤiiħ	'(You) cry'
second	f	singular	تصيحين	tsˤiiħiin	'(You.f) cry'
third	m	singular	يصيح	jsˤiiħ	'(He) cries'
third	f	singular	تصيح	tsˤiiħ	'(She) cries'

(*Continued*)

Table 5.41 (Continued)

Person	*Gender*	*Number*			
first	m/f	plural	نصيح	nsˤiiħ	'(We) cry'
second	m	plural	تصيحون	tsˤiiħuun	'(You.pl) cry'
second	f	plural	تصيحن	tsˤiiħən	'(You.f.pl) cry'
third	m	plural	يصيحون	jsˤiiħuun	'(They) cry'
third	f	plural	يصيحن	jsˤiiħən	'(They.f.pl) cry'

Table 5.42 The imperfective aspect of doubled verbs

Person	*Gender*	*Number*			
first	m/f	singular	أصبّ	ʔasˤəbb	'(I) pull'
second	m	singular	تصبّ	tsˤəbb	'(You) pull'
second	f	singular	تصبّين	tsˤəbbiin	'(You.f) pull'
third	m	singular	يصبّ	jsˤəbb	'(He) pulls'
third	f	singular	تصبّ	tsˤəbb	'(She) pulls'
first	m/f	plural	نصب	nsˤəbb	'(We) pull'
second	m	plural	تصبّون	tsˤəbbuun	'(You.pl) pull'
second	f	plural	تصبّن	tsˤəbbən	'(You.f.pl) pull'
third	m	plural	يصبّون	jsˤəbbuun	'(They) pull'
third	f	plural	يصبّن	jsˤəbbən	'(They.f.pl) pull'

Table 5.43 The imperfective aspect of quadriliteral verbs

Person	*Gender*	*Number*			
first	m/f	singular	أطنقر	ʔatˤangər	'(I) irritate'
second	m	singular	تطنقر	ətˤtˤangər	'(You) irritate'
second	f	singular	تطنقرين	ətˤtˤangəriin	'(You.f) irritate'
third	m	singular	يطنقر	jətˤangər	'(He) irritates'
third	f	singular	تطنقر	ətˤtˤangər	'(She) irritates'
first	m/f	plural	نطنقر	ntˤangər	'(We) irritate'

Person	Gender	Number			
second	m	plural	تطنقرون	ətˁtˁangəruun	'(You.pl) irritate'
second	f	plural	تطنقرن	ətˁtˁangərən	'(You.f.pl) irritate'
third	m	plural	يطنقرون	jtˁangəruun	'(They) irritate'
third	f	plural	يطنقرن	jtˁangərən	'(They.f.pl) irritate'

the second person as a grammatical agreement feature. The morphological realization of the second-person subject agreement depends on the gender and number features of the implied subject.

اطلع	ʔətˁlaʕ	'(You) get out!'
طلعي	tˁləʕi/tˁəlʕi	'(You.f) get out!'
طلعو	tˁəlʕu	'(You.pl) get out!'
طلعن	tˁəlʕən	'(You.f.pl) get out!'

The imperfective stem of the imperative is augmented with a prefix -إ [ʔə-].

إقراه	ʔə-graa-h	'(You) read it!'
إقريه	ʔə-grii-h	'(You.f) read it!'
إقروه	ʔə-groo-h	'(You.pl) read it!'
إقرنه	ʔə-grənn-ah	'(You.f.pl) read it!'

5.2.16 *The irrealis modality prefix* -ب *b-*

Future events may be expressed by prefixing the irrealis modal marker b- to the imperfective verb stem (Table 5.44). For the case of 'future perfect,' the prefix -ب b- is attached to the modal auxiliary كان kaan 'be' (Chapter 7).

5.2.17 *The negative prefix* -ما *maa- 'not'*

The negative marker ما maa 'not' (Table 5.45) may be attached to the verbs and become a prefix -ما maa- (Chapter 10). The negative prefix linearly precedes all aspectual and modal markers.

Table 5.44 The irrealis modality prefix -ب b-

بيي	bajji	'(I) will come'
بتي	batti	'(You) will come'
بتين	bəttin	'(You.f) will come'
بيي	bijji	'(He) will come'
بتي	bəti/bətji	'(She) will come'
بني	bəni/bənji	'(We) will come'
بتون	bətjuun	'(You.pl) will come'
بتن	bəttən	'(You.f.pl) will come'
بيون	bijjuun	'(They) will come'
بين	bijjən	'(They.f.pl) will come'
بكون روّحت	bakuun rawwaħt	'(I) will have left'
بتكون روّحت	batkuun rawwaħt	'(You) will have left'
بتكونين روّحتي	batkuuniin rawwaħti	'(You.f) will have left'
بيكون روّح	bajkuun rawwaaħ	'(He) will have left'
بتكونن روّحتن	batkuun rawwəħat	'(She) will have left'
بنكون روّحنا	bankuun rawwaħna	'(We) will have left'
بتكونون روّحتوا	batkuunuun rawwaħtu	'(You.pl) will have left'
بتكونن روّحتن	batkuunən rawwaħtən	'(You.f.pl) will have left'
بيكونون روّحوا	bajkuunuun rawwəħaw	'(They) will have left'
بيكونن روّحن	bajkuunən rawwəħan	'(They.f.pl) will have left'

Table 5.45 The negative prefix -ما maa- 'not'

ما بي	maa baji	'(I) will not come'
ما بتي	maa bətii	'(You) will not come'
ما بتين	maa bətiin	'(You.f) will not come'
ما بيي	maa bijji	'(He) will not come'
ما بتي/بتيي	maa bətii/bətjji	'(She) will not come'
ما بني	maa bənji	'(We) will not come'
ما بتون	maa bətjuun	'(You.pl) will not come'
ما بتن/بتين	maa bəttən/bətjjən	'(You.f.pl) will not come'
ما بيون	maa bijjuun	'(They) will not come'
ما بين	maa bijjən	'(They.f.pl) will not come'

5.3 Adjectives

Based on the consonantal roots, on which lexical words are formed in Arabic, adjectives in Emirati Arabic surface in various phonological forms. The relation between the form and meaning of Emirati Arabic adjectives is largely ambiguous, although there are cases in which a particular adjectival form corresponds to a particular (class of) meaning. Adjectives may be derived from verbs (Sections 5.3.2.1 and 5.3.2.2) or nouns (Section 5.1). Adjectives further provide the morphological bases for the derivation of comparatives and superlatives, although the latter is also formed by periphrastic expressions.

5.3.1 *Forms of adjectives*

Emirati Arabic adjectives surface in different consonant-vowel templatic forms (Section 5.2). For instance (C: consonant, V: vowel):

CCiiC

Masculine		Feminine		Meaning
يديد	jdiid	يديده	jdiida	'new'
كبير	kbiir	كبيره	kbiira	'big'
صغير	sˤɣiir	صغيره	sˤɣiira	'small'
بعيد	bʕiid	بعيده	bʕiida	'far'

CVCC

Masculine		Feminine		Meaning
وصخ	wasˤx	وصخه	wasˤxa	'dirty'
خشن	xaʃn	خشنه	xaʃna	'coarse'
سهل	sahl	سهله	sahla	'easy'

Some phonological structures express a particular class of meaning, e.g. emotion.

CaCCaan

Masculine		Feminine		Meaning
زَعلان	zaʕlaan	زعلانه	zaʕlaana	'sad'
فرحان	farħaan	فرحانه	farħaana	'happy'
ندمان	nadmaan	ندمانه	nadmaana	'regretful'

CaaCaC

Masculine		Feminine		Meaning
ساكت	saakət	ساكته	saakta	'quiet'
ناعم	naaʕəm	ناعمه	naaʕma	'soft'
ناجح	naadʒəħ	ناجحه	naadʒħa	'successful'

Color adjectives and some (but not all) bodily defects are expressed by ʔaCCaC (for masculine) and CVCCa (for feminine).

ʔaCCaC		CaCCa		
Masculine		Feminine		Meaning
أسود	ʔaswad	سودا	sooda	'black'
أبيض	ʔabjað^ʕ	بيضا	beeð^{ʕ}a	'white'
أصفر	ʔas^{ʕ}far	صفرا	s^{ʕ}afra	'yellow'
أحمر	ʔaħmar	حمرا	ħamra	'red'
أزرق	ʔazrag	زرقا	zarga	'blue'
أخضر	ʔaxð^{ʕ}ar	خضرا	xað^{ʕ}ra	'green'
أعمى	ʔaʕma	عميا	ʕamja	'blind'
أصلع	ʔas^{ʕ}laʕ	صلعا	s^{ʕ}alʕa	'bald'
أبهق	ʔabhag	بهقا	bahga	'has vitiligo'
أبلم	ʔablam	بلما	balma	'mute'
أحول	ʔaħwal	حولة	ħoola	'cross-eyed'

Some adjectives are based on roots with geminate medial radicals.

CVCCVVC

Masculine		Feminine		Meaning
دلوع	dalluuʕ	دلوعه	dalluuʕah	'spoiled'
كذاب	ʧaððaab	كذابه	ʧaððaabah	'liar'
خراط	xarraat^ʕ	خراطه	xarraat^{ʕ}ah	'liar'

Some adjectives consist of quadrilateral roots.

CVCCVVC

Masculine		Feminine		Meaning
لعلوع	laʕluuʕ	لعلوعة	laʕluuʕa	'talkative'
ثرثار	θarθaar	ثرثاره	θarθaara	'talkative'

Some derived forms of adjectives, for instance participles (Sections 5.3.2.1 and 5.3.2.2), contain additional affixal consonants, e.g. مـ /m-/ and مستـ /məst-/.

maCCuuC

Masculine		Feminine		Meaning
مقهور	maqhuur	مقهوره	maqhuura	'annoyed'
مستور	mastuur	مستوره	mastuura	'hidden'
مطرور	matˤruur	مطروره	matˤruura	'torn'
مينون	majnuun	مينونه	majnuuna	'crazy'
مفرور	mafruur	مفروره	mafruura	'thrown'
محبوس	maħbuus	محبوسه	maħbuusa	'trapped'
مستانس	məstaanəs	مستانسه	məstaansa	'happy'
مستعيل	məstaʕjəl	مستعيله	məstaʕjəla	'rushing'
مستمتع	məstamtəʕ	مستمتعه	məstamtəʕa	'enjoying'

Adjectives may function attributively (e.g. 'the *smart* student') and predicatively (e.g. 'Ahmad is *smart*'). Both attributive and predicative adjectives agree with the head noun in gender. Moreover, the attributive adjective agrees with the head noun in definiteness (Section 6.1).

البنت الحلوه اللي هناك اختي

əl-bənt	əl-ħəlw-a	ʔəlli	hnaak	ʔəxt-i.
the-girl	the-beautiful-f	that	there	sister-my

'The beautiful girl there is my sister.'

5.3.2 *Active and passive participles*

Participles are deverbal forms which serve various grammatical functions. Participles may be active or passive with distinct argument structures. Active participles denote or modify the doer of a verbal action, whereas passive participles denote or modify the entity which undergoes the action. In English, active participles are derived by suffixing -ing to the verbal stems, as in 'the dancing queen' and 'the smiling face,' and may function as adjectives. On the other hand, the form, ending in -ed/-en, is used to derive passive participles such as 'the broken vase' and 'the rejected application.' Emirati Arabic allows the use of active and passive participles to function as adjectives.

5.3.2.1 *Active participles*

رقد	rəgad	'sleep'	راقد	raagəd	'sleeping'
وقف	wəgaf	'stand'	واقف	waagəf	'standing'
سكن	səkan	'lived at'	ساكن	saakən	'living'
قعد	gəʕad	'sit'	قاعد	gaaʕəd	'sitting'
يلس	jəlas	'sit'	يالس	jaaləs	'sitting'
قال	gaal	'say'	قايل	gaajəl	'saying'
زار	zaar	'visit'	زاير	zaajər	'visiting/visitor'
لعب	ləʕab	'play'	لاعب	laaʕəb	'playing'
شغل	ʃəɣlˤ	'work'	شغّال	ʃaɣɣalˤ	'working'
ازعاج	əzʕaadʒ	'bother'	مزعج	muzʕədʒ	'annoying'

5.3.2.2 *Passive Participles*

كسر	kəsar	'break'	مكسور	maksuur	'broken'
طر	tˤarr	'tear'	مطرور	matˤruur	'torn'
فر	farr	'throw'	مفرور	mafruur	'thrown'
دعس	dəʕas	'step'	مدعوس	madʕuus	'stepped'
فعص	fəʕasˤ	'squash'	مفعوص	mafʕuusˤ	'squashed'
حرق	ħərag	'burn'	محروق	maħruug	'burned'
سرق	sˤərag	'steal'	مسروق	masruug	'stolen'
خرب	xərab	'destroy'	مخترب	məxtərəb	'destroyed'
طبخ	tˤəbax	'cook'	مطبوخ	matˤbuux	'cooked'
استخدم	ʔəstəxdam	'use'	مستخدم	məstaxdam	'used'
خلّص	xalˤlˤasˤ	'finish'	مخلّص	mxalˤlˤəsˤ	'finished'
استبعد	ʔəstəbʕad	'exclude'	مستبعد	məstabʕad	'excluded'

The active or passive adjectival participle agrees with the head noun in gender and definiteness. Note that while adjectival participles are acceptable in Emirati Arabic (in both attributive and predicative positions), they are not the preferred way to express adjectival modification (Chapter 6).

الحرمه اليالسه حامل

əl-ħərmah	əl-jaals-a	ħaaməl.
the-woman	the-part.sit-f	pregnant

'The sitting woman is pregnant.'

الكرسي المكسور عور أحمد

əl-kərsii	əl-ma-ksuur	ʕawwar	ʔaħmad.
the-chair	the-part-pass.break	caus.hurt.perf-it	Ahmad

'The broken chair hurt Ahmad.'

الأوراق المفروره في الزبالة مالت حسين

l-awraag	əl-ma-fruur-ah	fə-z-zəbaalah	maal-at	ħseen.
the-paper.pl	the-part-pass.throw-f	in-the-garbage	poss-f	Husain

'The papers thrown in the garbage belong to Husain.'

In their predicative function, passive participles agree with the subject in gender but they cannot be definite.

الشبرية مكسوره

əʃ-ʃəbrəjjah	ma-ksuur-ah.
the-bed	part-pass.break.perf-f

'The bed (is) broken.'

القوطي مفرور

əl-guutˤi	ma-froor.
the-bottle	part-pass.throw.perf

'The bottle (is) thrown.'

العصير مشروب نصه

əl-ʕasˤiir	ma-ʃruub	nəsˤsˤ-ah.
the-juice	part-pass.drink.perf	half-it

'The juice (is) half drunk.'

In Emirati Arabic, a small number of variants of passive participles are formed by the prefix مـ m- and the passive verb stem with an initial نـ n- consonant. This morphological derivation is unproductive and there is a preference for 'normal' passive participles (see also Chapter 6).

منكسر/متكسر	mənkəsər/mətkassər	'broken'
منطر	məntˤarr	'torn'
منفر	mənfarr	'thrown'
منفعص	mənfəʕəsˤ	'squashed'
منحرق/محترق	mənħərəg/məħtərəg	'burned'
منسرق	mənsˤərəg	'stolen'
منجب/منصب	məntʃabb/mənsˤabb	'spilled'
منخش/مخشوش	mənxaʃʃ/maxʃuuʃ	'hidden'
مندس/مدسوس	məndass/madsuus	'hidden'

حصلت المرايه منكسره

ħasˤsˤalˤ-t əl-məraaj-ah mə-nkəsr-ah.
find.perf-I the-mirror-f part-pass.break.perf-f
'I found the mirror broken.'

حصلت العصير منجب في الصاله

ħasˤsˤalˤ-t əl-ʕəsˤiir mə-ntʃabb f-əsˤ-sˤaalˤah.
find.perf-I the-juice part-pass.spill.perf in-the-living.room
'I found the juice spilled in the living room.'

أختي منخشه في الكبت

ʔəxt-i mə-nxaʃʃ-ah f-əl-kabat.
sister-my part-pass.hide.perf-f in-the-wardrobe
'My sister is hidden in the wardrobe.'

Overall, the use of adjective participles is less preferred than relative clauses (Chapter 12).

البيت اللي انحرق كان بيتنا

əl-beet ʔəlli n-ħərag kaan beet-na.
the-house that pass-burn.perf be.perf-it house-our
'The house that was burned was our house.'

الولد اللي يصيح هو ولدي

əl-walad ʔəlli j-sˤiiħ huu wəld-i.
the-boy that he-cry.imperf he son-my
'The boy who is crying is my son.'

ابوي تعب وهو يوعي اخوي اللي راقد

ʔubuu-j təʕab w hu j-waʕʕi ʔuxuu-j ʔəlli raagəd.
father-my get.tired.perf and he he-wake.up.imperf brother-my that asleep
'My father is tired of waking up my sleeping brother.'

البنت اللي تدرس هناك عندها الكتاب

əl-bənt ʔəlli tə-drəs hnaak ʕənd-ha əl-ktaab.
the-girl that she-study.imperf there with-her the-book
'The girl over there who studies has the book.'

5.3.3 *Derivation of adjectives from nouns*

Adjectives may be productively derived from nouns (cf. English '-al' and '-ese'). In Emirati Arabic, the derivational suffix ـي -i expresses such a function. Some derivations are not entirely transparent, e.g. كوريا kuurja 'Korea' ~ كوري kuuri 'Korean' (Table 5.46).

احمد اشترى كتاب إماراتي

ʔaħmad	əʃtara	ktaab	ʔəmaara-at-i.
Ahmad	refl.buy.perf-he	book	Emirate-f.pl-adj

'Ahmad just bought an Emirati book.'

هذا حدث تاريخي

haaða	ħadaθ	tariix-i.
this	event	history-adj

'This event is historical.'

هذي الفعاليات أهدافها تعليمية

haaði	əl-faʕaaljj-aat	ʔahdaaf-ha	taʕliim-ijj-a.
these	the-event-f.pl	purposes-f	education-adj-f

'These activities are for educational purposes.'

5.3.4 *Comparatives*

Comparative adjectives are formed by prefixing أ- /ʔ-/ to the adjectival stem. Depending on the phonological structure of the stem, further phonological change (especially for the vowel) will result.

CCiiC			ʔaCCaC		
كبير	kbiir	'big'	أكبر	ʔakbar	'bigger'
صغير	sˤɣiir	'small'	أصغر	ʔasˤɣar	'smaller'
طويل	tˤwiil	'tall'	أطول	ʔatˤwalˤ	'taller'
خطير	xətˤiir	'dangerous'	أخطر	ʔaxtˤar	'more dangerous'
سريع	səriiʕ	'fast'	أسرع	ʔasraʕ	'faster'
فظيع	fəðˤiiʕ	'horrible'	أفظع	ʔafðˤaʕ	'more horrible'
جميل	ʤamiil	'handsome'	أجمل	ʔaʤmal	'more handsome'

Table 5.46 Derivation of adjectives from nouns

Noun			*Adj*	*Adj (f)*			
صين	sˤiin	'China'	صيني	صينية	sˤiini	sˤiinijja	'Chinese'
إمارات	ʔəmaaraat	'Emirates'	إماراتي	إماراتية	ʔəmaaraati	ʔimaaraatijjah	'Emirati'
تاريخ	taariix	'history'	تاريخي	تاريخية	tariixi	tariixijah	'historical'
كوريا	kuurja	'Korea'	كوري	كورية	kuuri	kuurijjah	'Korean'
تعليم	taʕliim	'education'	تعليمي	تعليمية	taʕliimi	taʕliimijjah	'educational'
دين	diin	'religion'	ديني	دينية	diini	diinijjah	'religious'

CCuu			ʔaCCa		
حلو	ħəluu	'pretty'	احلى	ʔaħla	'prettier'
CeeC			ʔaCjaC		
زين	zeen	'good'	أحسن	ʔaħsan[1]	'better'
شين	ʃeen	'bad'	أشين	ʔaʃjan	'worse'
خير	xeer	'good/wealth'	أخير	ʔaxjar	'better'
CaaC(ə)C			ʔaCCaC		
واضح	waaðˤəħ	'clear'	أوضح	ʔawðˤaħ	'clearer'
واسع	waasəʕ	'wide'	أوسع	ʔawsaʕ	'wider'
فاتح	faatəħ	'light'	أفتح	ʔaftaħ	'lighter'
C(ə)CiiC			ʔaCCaC		
يديد	jdiid	'new'	أيدد	ʔajdad	'newer'
بعيد	bəʕiid	'far'	أبعد	ʔabʕad	'farther'
وسيع	wəsiiʕ	'wide'	أوسع	ʔawsaʕ	'wider'
CaaCii/ CaCi/ CəCi/ CuCi			ʔaCCa		
راقي	raaqii	'sophisticated'	أرقى	ʔarqa	'more sophisticated'
غالي	ɣaalii	'expensive'	أغلى	ʔaɣla	'more expensive'
عالي	ʕaalii	'high'	أعلى	ʔaʕla	'higher'
قوي	guwii	'strong'	أقوى	ʔagwa	'stronger'
ذكي	ðakii	'smart'	أذكى	ʔaðka	'smarter'
غبي	ɣabii	'stupid'	أغبى	ʔaɣba	'more stupid'

Some adjectives add the prefix /ʔa-/ without any further sound change.

مرّ	mərr	'bitter'	أمر	ʔamarr	'more bitter'
حرّ/حار	ħarr/ħaar	'hot'	أحر	ʔaħarr	'hotter'

If the comparative adjective is used to compare two entities, it is followed by the preposition عن ʕan 'than' (Section 5.5). Emirati Arabic speakers prefer عن ʕan to the preposition من min 'from' in the expression of comparison.

أحمد أذكى عن أخوه

ʔaħmad ʔa-ðka ʕan ʔəxuu-h
Ahmad more-smart than brother-his
'Ahmad is smarter than his brother.'

In the expression of comparisons between two events, the comparative adjective أكثر ʔakθar 'more' is used. Morphologically, أكثر ʔakθar itself is the comparative form of كثير kθiir 'much.'

أحمد كل أكثر عن مريم

ʔaħmad kal ʔakθar ʕan marjam.
Ahmad eat.perf-he more than Mariam
'Ahmad ate more than Mariam.'

بعد ما دخلت الجامعة شيخه استوت تتكلم أكثر عن قبل

baʕad maa dəxla-t əl-ʤaamʕah ʃeexa ʔəstəwa-t tə-tkallam ʔakθar ʕan gabəl.
after that enter.perf-she the-university Shaikha become.perf-she she-speak.imperf more than before
'After entering university, Shaikha became more talkative than before.'

سالم يرسم أكثر عن ما يطالع أفلام

saaləm je-rsəm ʔakθar ʕan maa j-tˤaaləʕ ʔaflaam.
Salem he-draw.imperf more than that he-watch.imperf movie.pl
'Salem draws more than he watches movies.'

When functioning as an attributive adjective, the comparative adjective precedes the head noun. Note that the following noun phrase is specific even though no determiner is needed:

أطول طالب هو ولد عمي

ʔa-tˤwal tˤaaləb huu wəld ʕamm-i.
more-tall student he son uncle-my
'(The) taller student is my cousin.'

The expression أقل عن ʔagal ʕan 'less than' (أقل ʔagal 'less' stems from the comparative form of قليل gəliil 'little') is considered uncommon in Emirati Arabic.

الأهالي يرقدون أقل بعد مايكون عندهم يهال

əl-ʔahaali jə-rgəd-uun ʔagal baʕd maa-j-jkuun ʕəndə-hum jəhhaal.

the-parents they-sleep.imperf-they less after part-it-become with-them children

'Parents sleep less after they have children.'

فاطمة تاكل أقل عن السنة اللي طافت عشان تضعف

faatˤma t-aakəl ʔagal ʕan əs-səna ʔəlli tˤaaf-at ʕaʃaan tə-ðˤʕaf.

Fatima she-eat.imperf less than the-year.f that pass.perf-she in.order.to she-lose.weight.imperf

'Fatima eats less than last year to lose weight.'

5.3.5 *Superlatives*

Emirati Arabic does not seem to possess an independent expression of superlatives. Instead the superlative meaning may be inferred by the use of comparatives with a set of entities (rather than a single entity). The following examples are comparative adjectives which are interpreted as superlative in the relevant context:

أغنى واحد في العالم هو جيف بيزوس

ʔa-ɣna waaħəd f-əl-ʕaalam huu dʒeff beezos.

more-rich one in-the-world he Jeff Bezos

'The richest person in the world is Jeff Bezos.'

أحلى بنت في مسابقة هالسنه هي اختي

ʔa-ħla bənt fi məsaabaq-at ha-s-səna hii ʔəxt-ii.

more-pretty girl in tournament-f this-the-year she sister-my

'The prettiest girl in the tournament this year is my sister.'

كوكب المشتري هو أكبر كوكب في المجموعة الشمسية
kawkab əl-muʃtari huu ʔa-kbar kawkab f-əl-madʒmuuʕa əʃ-ʃamsijj-ah.
planet the-Jupiter it more-large planet in-the-system the-solar-f
'Jupiter is the largest planet in the solar system.'

نعوم تشومسكي هو أكثر لغوي مأثر على وايد ناس
naʕuum tʃooməski huu ʔakθar laɣawi mʔaθθər ʕala waajəd naas.
Noam Chomsky he most linguist part-influence-he on many people
'Noam Chomsky is the most influential linguist to many people.'

شيخة أطول طالبة هنيه
ʃeexa ʔa-tˤwalˤ tˤaalˤb-ah hnii.
Shaikha more-tall student-f here
'Shaikha is the tallest student here.'

مريم يابت أعلى درجة فالصف
marjam jaab-at ʔa-ʕla daradʒ-ah fe-sˤ-sˤaf.
Mariam bring.imperf-she more-high grade-f in-the-class
'Mariam got the highest scores in the whole class.'

مريم اجمل بنت شفتها
marjam ʔa-dʒmal bənt ʃəf-t-ha.
Mariam more-pretty girl see.perf-I-her
'Mariam is the prettiest girl I have ever seen.'

أعقل ولد هو احمد
ʔa-ʕgal walad huu ʔaħmad
more-rational boy he Ahmad
'The most rational boy is Ahmad.'

The superlatives can interact with the definite plural noun phrases to express a partitive meaning (Sections 5.6.5 and 6.1.1).

مريم من أحلى البنات اللي شفتهم
marjam mən ʔa-ħla l-banaat ʔəlli ʧəf-t-hum.
Mariam from most-pretty the-girl.pl that see.perf-I-them
'Mariam is the prettiest among the girls I have seen.'

أحمد اعقل الاولاد فالمدرسة

ʔaħmad ʔa-ʕgal əl-awlaad f-əl-mədrəsa.
Ahmad most-rational the-boy.pl in-the-school
'Ahmad is the most rational among the boys in school.'

5.3.6 *Equatives*

The equative expression 'as X as' (where X is an adjective) may be expressed by the preposition شرات ʃaraat 'like/as.'

إيمان ذكية شرات موزه

ʔimaan ðakijj-ah ʃaraat moozah.
Eiman smart-f like Moza
'Eiman is as smart as Moza.'

علي يركض سريع شرات محمد

ʕəli jə-rkəðˤ sariiʕ ʃaraat mħammad.
Ali he-run.imperf fast like Mohammed
'Ali runs as fast as Mohammed.'

For equatives between two verbal events (cf. English 'as much as'), the conjunctions كثر kəθər and قد gadd 'as much as' are used.

هذي السنة قسم اللغويات عندهم طلاب قد قسم علم النفس

haaðii əs-səna qəsm əl-luɣawijjaat ʕənd-hum tˤəlˤlˤaab gadd qəsəm ʕəlm ən-nafs.
this the-year department the-linguistics with-them students as.much.as department science the-mind
'This year the Department of Linguistics has as many students as the Department of Psychology.'

عندي شغل كثر شعر راسي

ʕənd-i ʃəɣəl kəθər ʃaʕar raas-i.
with-me work as.much.as hair head-my
'I have many things to do.' (شعر راسي ʃaʕar raasi 'hairs on my head' is an idiomatic expression which means 'a lot.')

أحبك كثر ماحب نفسي

ʔa-ħəbb-ək	kəθər	maa-ħəbb	nafs-i.
I-love.imperf-you	as.much.as	part-love	self-my

'I love you as much as I love myself.'

5.3.7 *Order of adjectives*

Adjectives are ordered according to their semantic category, when they are stacked together within a noun phrase. Adjectives that categorically define the intrinsic properties of the head noun are closer to the noun, whereas adjectives that modify the head noun in other non-defining aspects are further from it. The following examples exemplify the preferred linear ordering of adjectival modifiers:

numeral > noun > size > color > property (>: linearly precede)

ثلاث صواني صغار بيض حلوات

θalaaθ	sˤəwaanii	sˤɣaar	beeðˤ	ħəlw-aat
three	chinese.plates	little.pl	white.pl	beautiful-f.pl

'three beautiful little white Chinese plates'

noun > material > color

طاولة خشبية صفرا

tˤaawl-ah	xaʃabijj-ah	saˤfr-a
table-f	wooden-f	yellow-f

'a yellow wooden table'

Sometimes adjectives are not linearly ordered but conjoined by the coordinator و wa- 'and' (Chapter 15), e.g. adjectives of age and size.

noun > nationality > size, age

طالبة عربية كبيره و قصيره

tˤaalˤb-ah	ʕarabijj-ah	kbiir-ah	w	gəsˤiir-ah
student-f	Arab-f	old-f	and	short-f

'A short old Arabic student'

It is also possible to have more than one linear ordering between adjectives. The following examples are grammatical and semantically equivalent:

color > size

البيت الأخضر الكبير

l-beet ǝl-ʔaxðˁar ǝl-kbiir
the-house the-green the-big
'The big green house'

size > color

بيت كبير أخضر

beet kbiir ʔaxðˁar
house big green
'A green big house'

5.4 Adverbs and adverbial expressions

Adverbs and adverbial expressions generally modify verbs (e.g. 'run slowly/quickly'), adjectives (e.g. 'very/so/rather quick'), and sentences (e.g. 'Unfortunately, John failed the examination'). Semantically, they can provide additional information such as time (Section 5.4.1), place (Section 5.4.2), manner (Section 5.4.3), degree (Section 5.4.4), frequency (Section 5.4.5), and further speech acts (Section 5.4.6). Grammatically, they function as adjuncts, i.e. optional expressions which are not obligatorily required by the predicate's argument structure (Chapter 7). Some adverbs occupy various positions within the sentence (shown here with the use of parentheses), and these positions may correspond to different semantic or pragmatic interpretations (Chapter 11).

5.4.1 *Adverbs of time*

Adverbs of time express the time at which an event takes place (Table 5.47).

(أمس) ريم (أمس) رايحة (أمس) عند الدكتور (أمس)

(ʔams) riim (ʔams) raaj-ħa (ʔams) ʕǝnd ǝd-dǝktor (ʔams)
yesterday reem yesterday go.perf-he yesterday to the-doctor yesterday
'Reem went to the doctor yesterday.'

Table 5.47 Adverbs of time

أحّين/الحين	aħħiin/ əl-ħiin	'now'	جريب	ʤəriib	'soon'
أمس	ʔams	'yesterday'	من جريب	mən ʤəriib	'recently'
البارحة	əl-baarħa	'yesterday'	الليلة	əl-leela	'tonight'
باجر	baatʃər	'tomorrow'	بعدين	baʕdeen	'later'
اليوم	əl-joom	'today'	توّا	tawwa	'just'

(الحين) أمي (الحين) سايرة السوق (الحين)
(əl-ħiin) ʔumm-i (əl-ħiin) saajr-a əs-suug (əl-ħiin).
the-now mother-my the-now part.go-f the-market the-now
'My mother is going to the market now.'

(جريب) بسير (جريب) صوب يدوتي (جريب)
(ʤəriib) b-a-siir (ʤəriib) s^{ʕ}oob jəduut-ti (ʤəriib).
soon will-I-go.imperf soon to grandparents-my soon
'I will visit my grandparents soon.'

Adverbials of time can be expressed by prepositional phrases. For example:

الموظفين خذوا رواتبهم من جريب
əl-mwaðˁðˁaf-iin xað-aw ruwaatəb-hum mən ʤəriib.
the-employee-pl get.perf-they payment-their from recent.time
'The employees got their salary recently.'

5.4.2 *Adverbs of location and direction*

Adverbs may indicate the location where the verbal event occurs (locative adverb), or the direction in which the verbal event proceeds (directional adverb) (Table 5.48). They are mostly postverbal, although occasionally they occupy other positions. Given their semantic functions, most locative and directional adverbs double as prepositions (Section 5.5).

Table 5.48 Adverbs of place and direction

منّي/هني	mənnii/hnii	'here'	فوق/على	foog/ʕala	'over'
هناك	hnaak	'there'	حول	ħool	'around'
منّاك	mənnaak	'there'	متواطي	mətwaatˤi	'down'
تحت	taħat	'down'	شمالي	ʃəmaali	'northward'
فوق	foog	'up'	جنوبي	dʒənuubi	'southward'
جدام	dʒəddaam	'in front of'	غربي	ɣarbi	'westward'
ورا	wara	'behind'	شرقي	ʃargi	'eastward'
برا/برّع	barra/ barraʕ	'outside'	داخل/في	daaxəl/fi	'inside'

دخيلك تعال هني ولاتّم هناك!

dəxiil-ək taʕaal hnii w-laa t-tam hnaak!

please-your come.imperf here and-not you-stay.imperf there

'Please come here, and do not stay there!'

الطلاب قاعدين يتريون برا

ətˤ-tˤəllab gaaʕd-iin jə-trajj-oon barra.

the-students part.sit-pl they-wait.imperf-they outside

'The students are waiting outside.'

أحمد كان عايش برا البلاد سنين طويلة

ʔaħmad kaan ʕaajəʃ barra l-blaad sniin tˤəwiil-a.

Aħmad be.perf-he part.live outside the-country years long-f

'Ahmad has been living abroad for many years.'

بنمشي شمالي مب جنوبي

ba-nə-mʃi ʃəmal-i mub jənuub-i.

will-we-walk.imperf north-ward not south-ward

'We will walk northward, not southward.'

خلنا نسوق متواطيين فالشارع ونصف قدام المحل
xal-na n-suug mə-twatˤi-in f-əʃ-ʃaarəʕ w n-sˤəff dʒəddaam əl-maħal.
let-us we-drive.imperf part-down-m.pl in-the-street and we-park.imperf in.front.of the-store
'Let us drive down the street and park in front of the store.'

تجربة وايد حلوة انه نشوف العين تحت من فوق جبل حفيت
tadʒrəba waajəd ħəlw-a ʔən-na n-tʃuuf əl-ʕeen taħat mən foog jəbal ħəfiit.
experience very good-f that-it we-see.imperf Al.Ain down from above mountain Hafeet
'It is a great experience to see the city of Al Ain from the top of Jabel Hafeet.'

5.4.3 Adverbs of manner

Adverbs of manner (Table 5.49) describe the way in which the verbal event takes place. In Emirati Arabic, adverbs of manner are usually expressed by prepositional phrases, e.g. 'with speed' to express 'quickly' and 'with care' to express 'carefully.'

أحمد يسبح وايد بسرعة وبشكل دقيق
ʔaħmad jə-sbaħ waajəd b-sərʕa w b-ʃakəl daqeeq.
Ahmad he-swim.imperf very with-speed and with-form accurate
'Ahmad swims very quickly (i.e. with speed) and accurately (i.e. in accurate form).'

Table 5.49 Adverbs of manner

بسرعة	bsərʕa	'quickly'	بوناسة	bwanaasa	'happily'
بهدوء	bhəduuʔ	'quietly'	بشويش	bəʃweeʃ	'carefully'
شوي شوي	ʃwaj ʃwaj	'slowly'	بإهمال	bəhmaal	'carelessly'
بصوت عالي	bsˤoot ʕaali	'loudly'	بحزن	bħəzən	'sadly'
زين	zeen	'well'	حلو	ħəlu	'beautifully'
سيدة	siida	'directly'	بقوّة	bguwwa	'strongly'/ 'forcefully'

الياهل ربع بوناسة عند أمه

l-jaahəl	rəbaʕ	b-wanaasa	ʕənd	ʔumm-ah.
the-child	run.perf-he	with-happiness	to	mother-his

'The child ran happily to his mother.'

البلاد كبرت بسرعة من القرن العشرين

əl-blaad	kəbra-t	b-sərʕa	mən	əl-qarn	əl-ʕəʃriin.
the-town	grow.perf-it.f	with-speed	from	the-century	the-twentieth

'The town grew quickly since the twentieth century.'

الطلاب تريوا الدكتور بصبر

ətˤ-tˤəlˤlˤaab	trajj-aw	əd-dəktoor	b-sˤabər.
the-student.pl	wait.perf-they	the-professor	with-patience

'The students waited for the professor patiently.'

5.4.4 *Adverbs of degree*

Adverbs of degree (Table 5.50) describe the extent to which the verbal event is complete or the degree to which a property denoted by an adjective is expressed by the modified noun.

وايد waajəd 'very, quite, absolutely'

The degree adverb وايد waajəd includes a range of meanings, including 'very,' 'quite,' and 'absolutely.' وايد waajəd can either precede or follow an adjective, although the former order is preferred by native speakers. If it is post-adjectival, a pause is usually added before, which renders the use of وايد waajəd as an afterthought (Chapter 11).

الجو فالعين (وايد) جاف، (وايد)

əl-dʒaw	f-əl-ʕeen	(waajəd)	dʒaaf	(waajəd).
the-weather	in-Al Ain	very	dry	very

'The weather in Al Ain is very dry.'

Table 5.50 Adverbs of degree

وايد	waajəd	'very/quite'	شوية	ʃwajja	'little'
أكيد	ʔakiid	'absolutely'	ياالاً ياالاً	jaalla jaalla	'barely'
بالتمام	bittamaam	'completely'	شوية و	ʃwajja/ʃwajj w	'almost'

المحاضرة كانت وايد مملة
əl-muħaaðˁara kaan-at (waajəd) mumәll-a, (waajəd).
the-lecture be.perf-it.f quite boring-f quite
'The lecture was quite boring.'

الفلم (وايد) كان (وايد) حلو، (وايد)
əl-fələm (waajəd) kaan (waajəd) ħəlu, (waajəd).
the-movie very be.perf-it very nice very
'The movie was very nice.'

It is possible to reduplicate وايد waajəd for degree intensification (cf. English 'very very').

سويسرا كانت وايد وايد غاليه
sweesra kan-at waajəd waajəd ɣaalj-ah.
Switzerland be.perf-it.f very very expensive-f
'Switzerland was very very expensive.'

Moreover, وايد waajəd can modify the verbal event (cf. English 'very much').

أحمد (وايد) يحب الرياضيات، (وايد)
ʔaħmad (waajəd) j-ħəb ər-rəjaaðˁijjaat (waajəd).
Ahmad very he-like.imperf the-mathematics very
'Ahmad likes mathematics very much.'

مريم (وايد) درست مادة اللغويات عشان الامتحان، (وايد)
Marjam (waajəd) dərs-at maaddat əl-ləɣawijj-aat ʕaʃaan əl-əmtəħaan (waajəd).
Mariam very study.perf-she subject the-linguistics-f for the-exam very
'Mariam studied linguistics for the examination a lot.'

شيخة (وايد) تحب الأفلام الرومانسية، (وايد)
ʃeexa (waajəd) ət-ħəb əl-aflaam ər-roomansj-ja (waajəd).
Sheikha quite she-love.imperf the-movie.pl the-romantic-f quite
'Sheikha quite loves romantic movies.'

أحمد (وايد) يكره الدراسة، (وايد)

ʔaħmad (waajəd) jə-krah əd-dəraas-a (waajəd).
Ahmad absolutely he-hate.imperf the-studying-f absolutely
'Ahmad absolutely hates studying.'

In some contexts, e.g. negation, the position of وايد waajəd is preferred to be clause-final (Chapter 10).

هذاك المكان مب زين وايد

haðaak əl-məkaan mub zeen waajəd.
that the-place not good very
'That place is not very good.'

بيتي مب بعيد وايد

beet-ii mub bʕiid waajəd.
house-my not far very
'My house is not very far.'

شوية و ʃwajja w 'almost'

شوية و ʃwajja w 'almost,' which lexically stems from the quantifier شوية ʃwajja 'little' and the coordinator و w 'and,' is interpreted as a degree adverb. It immediately precedes the main verb, and can be positioned between the main verb and the auxiliary verb.

كنت شوية وبصيح

kənt ʃwajja w b-a-sˤiiħ.
be.perf-I little and will-I-cry.imperf
'I almost cried.'

أحمد شوي ويكون جاهز للرحلة

ʔaħmad ʃwajj w j-kuun ʤaahəz l-ər-rəħla.
Ahmad little and he-be.imperf ready for-the-trip
'Ahmad is almost ready for the trip.'

فيدرر كان شوية وبيخسر المباراة أمس المسا

federer kaan ʃwajja w ba-jə-xsar l-mubaaraa ʔams l-məsa.
Federer be.perf-he little and will-he-lose.imperf the-match yesterday the-night
'Federer almost lost the match last night.'

يالاً يالاً jalla jalla 'barely'

يالَّا يالَّا jalla jalla is formed by reduplication of يالَّا jalla (which may further stem from from ja Allah 'oh God') and denotes the slightest degree similar to English 'barely.'

أحمد يالَّا يالَّا يفهم شوي صيني عقب سنة من الدراسة

ʔaħmad	jalla jalla	jə-fham	ʃwajj	sˤiini	ʕəgəb	səna
mən	əd-dəraas-a.					
Ahmad	barely	he-understand.imperf	little	Chinese	after	year
from	the-studying-f					

'Ahmad can barely understand some Chinese after one year of study.'

صوته يالاً يالاً ينسمع

sˤoot-a	jaalla jaalla	jə-n-səməʕ.
voice-his	barely	it-pass-hear.perf

'His voice is barely audible.'

شوية ʃwajja 'somewhat'

شوية ʃwajja 'somewhat' as a degree adverb is homophonous with as شوية ʃwajja 'little' as a quantifier (Section 5.6).

الجودة شوية مب نفس ما كنت متوقعة

əl-ʤawda	ʃwajja	mub	nafs	maa	kən-t	mə-t-waqqʕ-a.
the-quality	little	not	like	what	be.perf-I	part-refl-caus. expect.imperf-f

'The quality is somewhat unlike what I was expecting.'

5.4.5 *Adverbs of frequency*

Adverbs of frequency (Table 5.51) indicate how often the verbal event occurs. In Emirati Arabic, adverbs of frequency may be expressed by a single lexical item (e.g. دايماً daajman 'always') or temporal nouns (e.g. كل يوم kil joom 'everyday').

دايما daajman 'always'

Table 5.51 Adverbs of frequency

دايماً	daajman	'always'	أبداً	ʔabadan	'ever'
مرات	marraat	'sometimes'	عمر	ʕəmər	'ever'
نادر	naadər	'rarely'	كل سنة	kəl səna	'annually' (every year)
كل فترة	kəl fatra	'regularly' (every period)	كل يوم	kəl joom	'daily' (every day)
مرة	marra	'once'	كل ساعة	kəl saaʕa	'hourly' (every hour)
مرتين	marteen	'twice'	كل شهر	kəl ʃaħar	'monthly' (every month)

(دايماً) بتذكر هذاك اليوم ، (دايماً)
(daajman) b-a-ððakkar haaðaak əl-joom (daajman).
always will-I-remember.imperf that the-day always
'I will always remember that day.'

مرات marraat 'sometimes'

(مرات) لازم (مرات) أشتغل (مرات) لين وقت متأخر فالمكتب (مرات)
(marraat) laazəm (marraat) ʔa-ʃtəɣəl (marraat) leen wagt mə-t-ʔaxxər f-əl-maktab (marraat).
sometimes must sometimes I-work.imperf sometimes until time part-refl-caus.late-imperf in-the-office sometimes
'I sometimes have to work late in the office.'

عمر ʕəmər 'ever/never'

The notion of negative degree adverbs such as 'never' is expressed by عمر ʕəmər 'ever' followed by the negative marker ما ma (Chapter 10). In the expression of an irrealis event which 'never' occurs (i.e. the frequency is zero), the negative marker obligatorily follows the degree adverb عمر ʕəmər. Different from other degree adverbs of frequency, عمر ʕəmər needs to be suffixed by a pronoun which denotes the sentential subject. While عمر ʕəmər bears the semantic function of expressing the degree adverb of frequency, its grammatical function is more compatible to a preposition (Section 5.5).

(عمره)علي (عمره) ما سافر أمريكا

(ʕəmr-a)	ʕəli	(ʕəmr-a)	maa	saafar	ʔamriika.
ever-him	Ali	ever-him	not	part.travel	America

'Ali never traveled to America.'

عمر ʕəmər is also used in forming yes-no questions. In such case, the negative marker is not needed (Chapter 13).

عمرك سافرت بروحك؟

ʕəmr-ək	saafar-t	əb-ruuħ-ək?
ever-you	travel.perf-you	by-self-your

'Have you ever traveled alone?'

Note that عمر ʕəmər may not be used alone, for instance, in elliptical expressions. The following answer is preferred by native speakers to express the answer 'never':

ولا مره

wala	marra.
and.not	once

'Not once.'

Another word ابدا ʔabadan 'never' is mostly used as a marker of negative imperatives. Note that negative imperatives always begin with the negative marker لا la.

لا تسمع راي أي حد أبدا

la	tə-smaʕ	raaj	ʔaj	ħad	ʔabadan.
don't	you-listen.imperf	opinion	any	one	never

'Do not ever listen to anyone's opinion.'

Other frequentative adverbial expressions such as 'annually,' 'daily,' or 'every two years' are usually expressed in clause-final position.

كل السواقين لازم يجددون سجلهم كل سنة

kəl əs-sawwag-iin laazəm j-ʤaddəd-uun sədʒəl-hom kəl səna.

all the-driver-m.pl must they-renew.imperf-they record-their every year

'All drivers have to renew their record annually.'

5.4.6 *Adverbs of speech act*

Speech-act adverbs, or occasionally called speaker-oriented adverbs, expose the speaker's attitude toward the proposition. Speaker-oriented adverbs may be evaluative (e.g. 'unfortunately' and 'sadly'), modal (e.g. 'probably' and 'evidently'), or performative (e.g. 'confidentially' and 'personally'). Morphologically, all speech-act adverbs are decompositional and consist of prepositions such as بـ b- 'with,' مع maʕ 'with,' and عن ʕan 'about' (Section 5.5).

Speech-act adverbs are always sentence-initial (Table 5.52).

بصراحة، ماعرف أي شي عن اللغويات

b-sˤaraaħa maa-ʕarf ʔaj ʃaj ʕan əl-luɣawijjaat.

with-honesty not-I.know.imperf any thing about the-linguistics

'Honestly, I don't know anything about linguistics.'

Table 5.52 Adverbs of speech act

بصراحة	bsˤaraaħa	'honestly'	الحمدلله	əlħamdəllaah	'fortunately'
مع احترامي	maʕ əħtəraami	'with due respect'	عن نفسي	ʕan nafsi	'personally'
للأسف	ləlʔasaf	'unfortunately'	بلغلط	bəlɣalatˤ	'accidentally'
بلختصار	bəxtəsˤaar	'in short'			

الحمدلله الجو بيكون وايد أحسن باجر
l-ħamdəllaah əl-ʤaw ba-j-kunn waajəd ʔaħsan baatʃər.
fortunately the-weather will-it-be.imperf much better tomorrow
'Fortunately, the weather will be much better tomorrow.'

عن نفسي، أحس هالطريقة ما بتنجح
ʕan nafs-i ʔa-ħəss ha-tˤ-tˤariiqa maa b-tə-nʤaħ.
about self-my I-feel.imperf this-the-method not will-it-succeed.imperf
'Personally, I think this method will not succeed.'

بالغلط ضرب ربيعه بالسلاح
bə-l-ɣalatˤ ðˤərab rbiiʕ-ah b-əs-səlaaħ.
by-the-mistake hit.perf-he friend-his by-the-weapon
'He accidentally shot his best friend with the gun.'

للأسف مشروعه خسر
l-əl-ʔasaf maʃruuʕ-ah xəsar.
for-the-regret project-his fail.perf-it
'Unfortunately, his project failed.'

بصراحه، ماريدك تروح
b-sˤaraaħa maa-riid-ək t-ruuħ.
with-honesty not-I.want.imperf-you you-leave.imperf
'Honestly, I don't want you to leave.'

باختصار كلامي انا صح
b-əxtəsˤar kalam-ii ʔana sˤaħ.
by-brief word-my I right
'In short, what I said is right.'

للأسف عندي خطط ثانيه في الويكند
lə-l-asaf ʕənd-ii xətˤatˤ θaanj-ah f-əl-wiikand.
for-the-regret with-me plan.pl other-f in-the-weekend
'Unfortunately, I have made other plans for the weekend.'

مع احترامي بس ماتوقع اللي انت سويته صح

maʕ əħtəram-i bas maa ʔa-t-waqqaʕ ʔəlli sawwee-t-ah sˤaħ.

with respect-my but not I-refl-guess.imperf that do.perf-you-it right

'With due respect, I don't think that what you did was right.'

5.5 Prepositions

Prepositions are semi-lexical items which express a relation between the grammatical constituents which they precede and other constituents within the sentence. In most cases, prepositions sub-categorize for a nominal argument and form a prepositional phrase, although other types of arguments may also be selected. The prepositional phrase as formed further expresses various meanings such as time, space, manner, instrument, and reason. Prepositions may also express part-whole relations such as possession, or combine with verbs or adjectives to express particular predicate relations (Chapter 7).

5.5.1 *Simple prepositions*

Simple prepositions are the most frequently used prepositions—they may assume various meanings depending on the context. Phonologically, they consist of one or two consonants which can always be truncated and *cliticized* to their following hosts. Grammatically, the prepositional phrases formed by some simple prepositions function as arguments. Simple prepositions may assume concrete (e.g. spatiotemporal) and abstract (e.g. metaphorical) meanings depending on the context. Some simple prepositions are sub-categorized by verbs to express an idiomatic meaning. Unlike complex prepositions (Section 5.5.2), simple prepositions are not preceded by other prepositions within the same sentence. Instead, simple prepositions may combine with other words to form a complex preposition.

شي كوكاكولا فالثلاجة

ʃaj kookakoola f-əθ-θallaadʒa.

there.is Coca-Cola in-the-fridge

'There is some Coca-Cola in the fridge.'

رسمت اللوحة بالألوان الشمعية

rəsma-t əl-looħah b-l-ʔalwaan əʃ-ʃamʕijja
draw.perf-she the-painting with-the-colors the-waxy
'She drew the painting with wax colors.'

الباب تبطل بهالمفتاح

əl-baab t-batˤtˤal b-ha-l-məftaaħ.
the-door pass-caus.open.perf by-this-the-key
'The door was opened by this key.'

الفلم بيبدا الساعة ٩ فليل

əl-fəlm ba-jə-bda əs-saaʕa təsəʕ f-əl-leel.
the-movie will-it-start.imperf the-hour nine in-the-night
'The movie will start at 9pm.'

أحمد بيشتغل في البيت من اليوم لين باجر

ʔaħmad ba-jə-ʃtəɣəlˤ f-əl-beet mən əl-joom leen baatʃər.
ahmad will-he-work.imperf in-the-house from the-today until tomorrow
'Ahmad will work at home from now until tomorrow.'

السيارة مرت من النفق

əs-sajjaara maarr-at mən ən-nafaq.
the-car pass.perf-it.f from the-tunnel
'The car passed through the tunnel.'

هالفلم عن تاريخ فرنسا

ha-l-fəlm ʕan taariix faransa.
this-the-movie about history France
'This movie is about French history.'

عالاسبوع الياي، لازم تسلم الواجب

ʕa-l-əsbuuʕ əl-jaaj laazəm t-salləm əl-waadʒəb.
by-the-week the-next must you-refl.submit.imperf the-assignment
'By next week, you need to submit the assignment.'

مادريت عنه إلّا من قريب

maa	daree-t	ʕann-ah	ʔəlla	mən-ʤəriib.
not	know.perf-I	about-it	except	from-near

'I didn't know about it until recently.'

يلس عالكرسي

jəlas	ʕa-l-kərsi.
sit.perf-he	on-the-chair

'He sat on the chair.'

رحت البيت ويا ربيعتي

rəħ-t	əl-beet	wəjja	rbiiʕ-ti.
go.perf-I	the-home	with	friend-my

'I went home with my friend.'

بطلع ويا أهلي

b-a-tˤlaʕ	wəjja	ʔahl-i.
will-I-go.out.imperf	with	family-my

'I will go out with my family.'

Simple prepositions (Table 5.53), regardless of their phonological truncation, must precede another constituent and form a prepositional phrase. They cannot exist in isolation.

5.5.2 *Complex prepositions*

Complex prepositions (Table 5.54) have a phonological structure analogous to typical Emirati Arabic words (e.g. triconsonantal) (Section 3.3.1). They are independent lexical items and are not

Table 5.53 Simple prepositions

في/فـ	fii/f-	'in/at'	بـ	b-	'in/by/with'
ويا/مع-	wəjja/maʕ	'with'	على/عـ	ʕala/ʕ-	'on'
من/مـ	mən/m-	'from/since/than'	لـ	lee/l-	'to/until'
عن	ʕan	'about/than'			

truncated or cliticized to the following hosts. Grammatically, the prepositional phrases formed by complex prepositions are adverbials which are not the core arguments of the sentence. Semantically, their meaning is fixed and remains unaltered regardless of the preceding contexts.

عقب باجر بنسافر ايطاليا

ʕəgəb	baaʧər	ba-n-saafər	ʔiitˤaalja.
after	tomorrow	will-we-travel.imperf	Italy

'After tomorrow, we will travel to Italy.'

لو سمحت قابلني قبل الساعة عشر الصبح

law	səmaħ-t	gaabəl-ni	gabəl	əs-saaʕa	ʕaʃər	əsˤ-sˤəbħ.
if	allow-you	meet.imp-me	before	the-hour	ten	the-morning

'Please (lit. if you allow) come to see me before 10am.'

دزوها تحت الشبرية

dazz-oo-ha	taħt	əʃ-ʃəbrəjja.
push.perf-they-it.f	under	the-bed

'They pushed it under the bed.'

الياهل رقى فوق الطاولة

əl-jaahəl	rəga	foog	ətˤ-tˤaawla.
the-baby	go.up.perf-he	above	the-table

'The baby climbed onto the table.'

المشي لساعة كاملة يحرق وايد سعرات حرارية

əl-maʃi	lə-saaʕa	kaaml-ah	jə-ħrəg	waajəd	səʕra-at
the-walking	for-hour	whole-f	it-burn.imperf	a.lot	unit-f.pl

ħaraarij-jah.
heat.adj-f

'Walking for an hour burns a lot of calories.'

كانوا قاعدين عدال الشجرة

kaan-aw	gaaʕd-iin	ʕəddaal	əʃ-ʃjara.
be.perf-they	part.sit-they	next	the-tree

'They were sitting next (to) the tree.'

الكرسي ورا التلفزيون

əl-kərsii waraa əl-təlfəzjoon.

the-chair behind the-television

'The chair is behind the television.'

قعد جبال مريم

gəʕad dʒbaal marjam.

sit.perf-he across Mariam

'He sat across from Mariam.'

الأرض اتدور حول الشمس

əl-ʔarðˁ əd-duur ħool əʃ-ʃams.

the-Earth it-revolve.imperf around the-sun

'The Earth revolves around the sun.'

لقى هالفندق بدون تعب

ləga ha-l-fəndəq bduun taʕab.

find.perf-he this-the-hotel without exhaustion

'He found this hotel without difficulty.'

كلهم نجحوا فالامتحان إلا أحمد

kəl-hum nədʒħ-aw f-əl-əmtəħaan ʔəlla ʔaħmad.

every-them pass.perf-they in-the-test except Ahmad

'Everyone passed the test, except Ahmad.'

الكتاب مال سارة

lə-ktaab maal saara.

the-book poss Sarah

'The book belongs to Sarah.'

عحسب كلام الشرطة، أحمد انمسك فمسرح جريمة السرقة

ʕa-ħasab kalaam əʃ-ʃərtˁa ʕaħmad ən-məsak f-masraħ dʒariima-t əs-sərga.

on-accordance speech the-police Ahmad pass-arrest.perf-he in-scene crime-f the-stealing

'According to police, Ahmad was arrested at the scene of the robbery.'

عكلام الموظفين باجر ماشي دوام

ʕa-kalam	əl-mwaðˤaf-iin	baatʃər	maa	ʃaj	dəwaam.
on-talk	the-employee-pl	tomorrow	not	have	work

'Based (on) the employees' talk there is no work tomorrow.'

Some complex prepositions may be (and sometimes must be) preceded by a simple preposition to create grammatical expressions.

كنا فنص العاصفة

kən-na	f-nəsˤsˤ	əl-ʕaasˤfa.
be.perf-we	in-middle	the-storm

'We were in the middle of the storm.'

شل الفلس من تحت الكرسي

ʃall	əl-fəls	mən	taħt	əl-kərsi.
pick.perf-he	the-fils	from	under	the-couch

'He picked up the fils from under the couch.'

ركبي الواير من ورا الشاشة

rakb-i	l-waajər	mən	wara	əʃ-ʃaaʃa.
plug-imp	the-wire	from	behind	the-screen

'Plug in the wire from behind the screen.'

تقدر تاخذ السيكل من داخل الحوش

tə-gdar	t-aaxəð	əs-seekal	mən	daaxəl	əl-ħooʃ.
you-can.imperf	you-take.imperf	the-bike	from	inside	the-area

'You can take the bike from inside the front yard.'

لقيت الرسالة امبين اوراقه

ləgee-t	ər-rəsaala	əm-been	ʔawraag-ah.
find.perf-I	the-letter	from-among	paper.pl-his

'I found the letter (from) among his papers.'

من غير ما آخذ راي مريم فالموضوع

mən	ɣeer	maa	ʔaa-xəð	raaj	marjam	f-əl-mawðˤuuʕ
from	without	that	I-take.imperf	opinion	mariam	in-the-topic

'Without asking for Mariam's opinion on the topic'

Table 5.54 Complex prepositions

عقب	ʕəg(ə)b	'after'	صوب	sˤoob	'near'
قبل	gabəl	'before'	جبال	ʤbaal/gbaal	'across'
تحت	taħt	'under'	جدام	ʤəddaam/gəddam	'front'
فوق	foog	'above'	ورا	wara	'behind'
داخل	daaxəl	'inside'	برع	barraʕ	'outside'
حق	ħagg	'for'	مال	maal	'belong to'
فنص	f(ə)nəsˤsˤ	'in the middle'	بدون	bduun	'without'
إلا	ʔella	'except'	من (بين)	(mən) been	'between'
حذال	ħðaal	'beside'	مثل	məθəl	'as/like'
عند	ʕənd	'with/of'	حول/حوالي/حولي	ħooli/ħawali/ħool	'about'
حول	ħool	'around'	عدال	ʕəddaal	'beside'
ضد	ðˤədd	'against'	عحسب	ʕaħasab	'according to'
بدال	bdaal	'instead of'	مادام	maa daam	'as long as'
اول ما	ʔawwal maa	'as soon as'	يانب	jaanəb	'beside'
مقابل	mgaabəl/mʤaabəl	'opposite'	قريب	griib/ʤriib	'close to'
جدا	ʤəda	'near'	من غير	mən ɣeer	'without'

بدون لا اراوي اختي الشنطة اشتريتها

bduun laa ʔa-raawii əxt-ii əʃ-ʃantˤah əʃtəree-t-ha.

without that I-show.imperf sister-my the-bag refl.buy.perf-I-it.f

'Without showing my sister the bag, I bought it.'

بدون ما تشوفني مريم شليت الكتاب

bduun maa t-ʧuuf-ni marjam ʃall-eet lə-ktaab.

without that she-see.imperf-me Mariam take.perf-I the-book

'Without Mariam's noticing, I took the book.'

بدال ما تكلميني كلميها عنه

bdaal maa t-kalm-ii-ni kalmii-ha ʕanna-h.

instead that you-talk.imperf-you.f-me talk.imp-her about-it

'Instead of talking to me, talk to her about it.'

دام ها رايج يامريم خليه لنفسج

daam haa raajə-ʧ jaa-marjam xaal-iih l-nafs-əʧ.

as.long.as this opinion-your you-mariam keep.imp-her for-self-you.f

'As long as this is your opinion, Mariam, keep it to yourself.'

اول ماتخرجت من الجامعة توظفت

ʔawwal maa t-xaradʒ-t mən əl-dʒaamʕa twaðˤðˤaf-t.

as.soon as that refl-graduated.perf-I from the-university employ.perf-I

'As soon as I graduated from university, I got a job.'

بتلقين التلفون عجانب الشبرية

ba-tə-lgeen əl-təlfoon ʕa-jaanəb əʃ-ʃəbriija.

will-you-find.imperf the-phone on-side the-bed

'You will find the phone beside the bed.'

المحل بتلقينه مقابل الشارع العام

əl-maħal ba-tə-lgeen-a mgaabəl əʃ-ʃaarəʕ əl-ʕaam.

the-shop will-you-find.imperf-it opposite the-street the-main

'You will find the shop opposite the main street.'

هو واقف قريب بيتنا

huu waagəf griib beet-naa.

he part.stand close house-our

'He is standing near our house.'

Complex prepositions, given their semantic content, may be used without a following complement and function as adverbial predicates.

كتابك فوق

ktaabə-k foog.

book-your above

'Your book is on top.'

الطلاب برع

ətˤ-tˤəllaab barraʕ.

the-students outside

'The students are outside.'

حطيته تحت

ħatˤtˤee-t-a taħat.

put.perf-I-it down

'I put it down.'

Moreover, they may be suffixed by object pronoun suffixes (Section 5.8.1.8).

خولة كسرت الدريشة بها

xawla kəsr-at əd-dəriiʃa b-haa.

Khawla break.perf-she the-window by-it

'Khawla broke the window with it.'

حطيت كل الكتب عليه

ħatˤtee-t kəl əl-kətəb ʕalee-h.

put.perf-I all the-books on-it

'I put all the books on it.'

احمد بيغني جدامهم

ʔaħmad ba-j-ɣanni ʤəddaam-hum.

Ahmad will-he-sing.imperf in.front.of-them

'Ahmad will sing in front of them.'

ريم توها مشت (من) بينهم

Riim	taw-ha	məʃa-t	(mən)	been-hum.
Reem	just-her	walk.perf-she	from	between-them

'Reem just walked between them.'

الكتاب كان مالها

lə-ktaab	kaan	maal-ha.
the-book	be.perf-it	poss-her

'The book belonged to her.'

بلبس فستان مثلهم

b-a-lbas	fəstan	məθəl-hum
will-I-wear.imperf	dress	like-them

'I will wear a dress like them.'

عادي ايلس حذالج؟

ʕaad-ii	ʔa-jləs	ħðaal-ətʃ?
can-me	I-sit.imperf	by-you.f

'Can I sit by you?'

يصير اكل عداله والا لا؟

jsˤiir	ʔaa-kəl	ʕəddaal-a	wəlla	laa?
can	I-eat.imperf	next.to-him	or	not

'Can I eat next to him or not?'

الله يخليج تعالي ويّاي

ʔalˤlˤah	j-xallii-tʃ	taʕaal-ii	wijjaa-j
Allah	he-protect.imperf-you.f	come.imp-you.f	with-me

'May Allah protect you, come with me.'

الله معاكن

ʔalˤlˤah	maʕa-kən.
Allah	with-you.f

'Allah is with you.'

5.5.3 *Selection of prepositions*

Some nouns, verbs, and adjectives impose a specific requirement for the following prepositions (cf. English 'live in Dubai,' 'happy with the result,' and 'proud of you'). The following is a non-exhaustive list:

بـ b- 'by/with'

فكرت باللي قلته

fakkar-t	b-əlli	gəl-t-ah.
think.perf-I	about-that	say.perf-you-it

'I thought about what you said.'

بدلناه بنموذج يديد

baddal-naa-h	b-namuuðadʒ	jdiid.
caus.change.perf-we-it	with-model	new

'We exchanged it for a new model.'

من mən 'from'

متفشل من عمري

mə-t-faʃʃəl	mən	ʕəmr-i.
part-refl-caus.shame.perf	of	self-my

'I feel ashamed of myself.'

زين منك ساعدت

zeen	mənn-ək	saaʕad-t.
good	from-you	help.perf-you

'It is good of you to help.'

مريم تفشلت من اللي سوته اول

marjam	t-faʃʃəl-at	mən	ʔəlli	sawwə-t-ah	ʔawwal.
Mariam	refl- caus.shame.perf-she	from	that	do.perf-she-it	past

'Mariam felt ashamed of what she did in the past.'

على/عـ ʕalaa/ʕ- 'on'

يعتمد عالتكلفة

jə-ʕtəməd	ʕa-t-takləfa.
it-depend.imperf	on-the-cost

'It depends on the cost.'

لامني عالتاخير

laam-ni	ʕa-t-taʔxiir.
blame.perf-he-me	on-the-delay

'He blamed me for the delay.'

لاتعتمد عليه

laa	tə-ʕtəməd	ʕalee-h.
don't	you-rely.imperf	on-him

'Don't rely on him.'

دفعت خمس دراهم عليه

dəfaʕ-t	xams	daraahəm	ʕalee-h.
pay.perf-I	five	Dirham.pl	on-it

'I paid five Dirhams for it.'

جايزة عالشجاعة

ʤaajzah	ʕa-ʃ-ʃaʤaaʕ
reward	on-the-bravery

'a reward for bravery'

ريم حصلت جايزة على أدائها فالحفلة

riim	ħasˤsˤəl-at	ʤaajza	ʕala-ʔadaaʔ-ha	f-əl-ħafla.
Reem	get.perf-she	award	on-performance-her	in-the-concert

'Reem received an award for her performance during the concert.'

أحمد اتخالف على ليت سيارته المكسور

ʔaħmad	t-xaalaf	ʕala-leet	sajjaart-ah	əl-maksuur.
Ahmad	refl-fine.perf-he	on-light	car-his	the-broken

'Ahmad got fined for his car's broken headlight.'

قص عليه

gasˤsˤ	ʕalee-h.
lie.perf-he	to-him

'He lied to him.'

بموت عليه

b-a-muut	ʕalee-h.
will-I-die.imperf	on-him

'I admire him.'

مريت ع بالي

marr-eet	ʕa	baal-i.
pass.perf-you	on	mind-my

'You crossed my mind.'

حق ħagg 'for'

المشي السريع ممكن يكون مب زين حقك

əl-maʃi	əs-sareeʕ	mumkən	j-kuun	mub	zeen	ħagg-ək.
the-walking	the-fast	can	it-be.imperf	not	good	for-you

'Jogging can be bad for you.'

الأكل الزايد مب زين حقي

əl-ʔakəl	əz-zaajəd	mub	zeen	ħagg-i.
the-food	the-excessive	not	good	for-me

'Excessive food is not good for me.'

فـ fii/f- 'in'

ما روم أتطور فها

maa	ruum	ʔa-t-tˁawwər	f-haa.
not	can.perf-I	I-refl-caus.develop.imperf	in-that

'I could not improve on that.'

شو مستوي فالسودان؟

ʃuu	mə-stəwii	f-əs-suudaan?
what	part-refl.happen	in-the-sudan

'What is happening in Sudan?'

أحمد شارك فالمسابقة

ʔaħmad ʃaarak f-əl-musaabaqa.

Ahmad join.perf-he in-the-competition

'Ahmad joined the competition.'

مدرس اللغة العربية أثر فولدي

mdarrəs əl-luɣa əl-ʕarabijja ʔaθθar f-wəld-ii.

teacher the-language the-Arabic caus.influence.perf-he in-son-my

'The Arabic language teacher had an impact on my son.'

طاح في الغلط

tˤaaħ f-əl-ɣalatˤ.

fell.perf-he in-the-mistake

'He made a mistake.'

لـ l- 'to'

وصلت لحل

wəsˤal-t l-ħall

reach-perf-I to-solution

'I reached a solution.'

فوق foog 'above'

يشتغل فوق طاقته

jə-ʃtəɣəl foog tˤaaqt-ah.

he-work.imperf above capacity-his

'He works beyond his capacity.'

ورا wara 'behind'

يركض ورا حلمه

jə-rkəðˤ wara ħəlm-ah.

he-run.imperf behind dream-his

'He chases his dream.'

يركض ورا البيت

jə-rkəð^{ʕ}	wara	əl-beet.
he-run.imperf	behind	the-house

'He runs behind the house.'

ضد ð^{ʕ}ədd 'against'

يوقف ضد الغلط

j-uugaf	ð^{ʕ}ədd	əl-ɣalat^{ʕ}.
he-stand.imperf	against	the-wrong

'He stands in the way of wrongdoing.'

5.6 Quantification: numerals and quantifiers

The system of numerals in Emirati Arabic shares almost all its features with other Arabic dialects, including MSA. The basic cardinal numerals (Section 5.6.1) run from zero to ten, with higher numerals formed by morphological derivation (e.g. suffixation (Section 4.2)) and grammatical rules such as coordination (Chapter 15). On the other hand, ordinal numerals (Section 5.6.2), decimals (Section 5.6.3), and fractions (Section 5.6.4) are derived from the cardinal numeral system (Table 5.55), each possessing a distinct phonological and morphological structure.

5.6.1 *Cardinal numbers*

The cardinal numeral system consists of a number of classes, each bearing distinct phonological, morphological, and grammatical properties.

5.6.1.1 *The numeral* صفر *s^{ʕ}əfər 'zero'*

The numeral صفر s^{ʕ}əfər 'zero' is only used in scientific and mathematical contexts, and never as a numeral quantifier (cf. English 'zero solution'). As a numeral, it grammatically functions as a noun which may be made definite by adding the determiner (Section 6.1.1).

Table 5.55 Cardinal numerals[2]

صفر	sˤəfər	0	ثلاثين	θalaaθiin	30
واحد	waaħəd	1	تسعة وثلاثين	təsʕa wa θalaaθiin	39
اثنان	ʔθneen	2	أربعين	ʔarbəʕiin	40
ثلاثة	θalaaθa	3	خمسين	xamsiin	50
أربعة	ʔarbaʕa	4	ستين	səttiin	60
خمسة	xamsa	5	سبعين	sabʕiin	70
ستة	sətta	6	ثمانين	θəmaaniin	80
سبعة	sabʕa	7	تسعين	təsʕiin	90
ثمانية	θəmaanja	8	تسعة وتسعين	təsʕa wa tisʕiin	99
تسعة	təsʕa	9	مئة	ʔəmja	100
عشرة	ʕaʃar(a)	10	مئة وواحد	ʔəmja w waaħəd	101
أحد عشر	ħidaʕʃ(ar)	11	مئة وعشرة	ʔəmja w ʕaʃra	110
إثنا عشر	θnaʕʃ(ar)	12	مئتين	miiteen	200
ثلاثة عشر	θalatˤtˤaʕʃ(ar)	13	ثلاثمائه	θalaaθ-əmja	300
أربعة عشر	ʔarbaʕtˤaʕʃ(ar)	14	أربع مائة	ʔarbaʕ-əmja	400
خمسة عشر	xaməstˤaʕʃ(ar)	15	ألف	ʔalf	1000
ستة عشر	sətˤtˤaʕʃ(ar)	16	ألف وواحد	ʔalf w waħəd	1001
سبعة عشر	sabəʕtˤaʕʃ(ar)	17	عشرة آلاف	ʕaʃər-talaaf	10000
ثمانية عشر	θəməntˤaʕʃ(ar)	18	مئة ألف	ʔəmjat-ʔalf	100000
تسعة عشر	təsəʕtˤaʕʃ(ar)	19	عشرة ملايين	ʕaʃrat-malajiin	10000000
عشرين	ʕəʃriin	20	بليون	bəljoon	100000000

درجة الحرارة فالعين عمرها ما وصلت تحت الصفر

daradʒ-at əl-ħaraara f-əl-ʕeen ʕəmər-ha maa wəsˤl-at taħt əsˤ-sˤəfər.

degree-f the-heat in-Al Ain ever-it not reach.perf-it.f under the-zero

'The temperature in Al Ain has never reached below zero.'

احتمالية الفوز بالمباراة قريبة من الصفر

ʔəħtəmaalijj-at əl-fooz bə-l-əmbaaraa gəriib-ah mən əsˤ-sˤəfər.

chance.adj-f the-winning with-the-match close-f from the-zero

'The chance of winning the match is close to zero.'

As a numeral, صفر sˤəfər 'zero' can be used in forming a decimal (Section 5.6.3).

واحد فاصلة صفر واحد

waaħəd (faasˤla) sˤəfər waaħəd

one comma zero one

'one point zero one (1.01)'

5.6.1.2 *The numerals* واحد *waaħəd 'one' and* اثنين *ʔθneen 'two'*

In addition to the numeral interpretation, the numerals واحد waaħəd 'one' and اثنين ʔəθneen 'two' are used to express the meaning of indefiniteness (for the numeral 'one') (Section 6.1) and pairs (for the numeral 'two').

هالكورس فيه بس طالب واحد وطالبتين

ha-l-koors fii-h bas tˤaaləb waaħəd w tˤaaləb-t-een.

this-the-course in-it only student one and student-f-du

'This course has only one male student and two female students.'

The numerals 'one' and 'two' are not generally required to quantify objects, unless a contrast needs to be emphasized.

حسن اشترى كتابين صح؟ لا، اشترى بس كتاب واحد

ħasan əʃtar-a ktaab-een, sˤaħ? laa, əʃtar-a bas ktaab waaħəd.

Hasan refl.buy.perf-he book-du right no refl.buy.perf-he only book one

'Hasan bought two books, right? No, he bought only ONE book.'

حسن بس اشترى كتاب، لكن ريم اشترت اثنين

ħasan bas əʃtar-a ktaab, laakən reem əʃtar-at ʔəθneen.

Hasan only refl.buy.perf-he book but Reem refl.buy.perf-she two

'Hasan only bought one book, but Reem bought TWO (books).'

If 'one' and 'two' are overtly expressed, they need to follow the head noun and agree with it in gender (Section 5.1). Interestingly, the dual form of the noun may still be used even if the numeral 'two' is overtly expressed (Section 6.5).

ولد واحد/بنت واحدة

walad waaħəd/ bənt wəħd-ah

boy one girl one-f

'one boy/one girl'

ولدين/بنتين

walad-een / bənt-een

boy-du girl-du

'two boys/two girls'

طالبين اثنين

tˤaalb-een ʔəθneen

student-du two

'two (male) students'

Masculine		Feminine		Meaning
واحد	waaħəd	واحدة	wəħda	'one'
اثنين	ʔəθneen	اثنتين	θənteen	'two'

5.6.1.3 *The numerals* ثلاث *θalaaθ 'three' to* عشرة *ʕaʃər 'ten'*

Masculine		Feminine		Meaning
ثلاث	θalaaθ	ثلاثة	θalaaθa	'three'
أربع	ʔarbaʕ	أربعة	ʔarbaʕa	'four'
خمس	xams	خمسة	xamsa	'five'
ست	sətt	ستة	sətta	'six'
سبع	sabəʕ	سبعة	sabʕa	'seven'
ثمان	θəmaan	ثمانية	θəmaanja	'eight'
تسع	təsəʕ	تسعة	təsʕa	'nine'
عشر	ʕaʃər	عشرة	ʕaʃra	'ten'

The numerals ثلاث θalaaθ 'three' to عشر ʕaʃər 'ten' precede the plural noun they quantify (Section 5.1.1.2). The agreement between the numeral ثلاث θalaaθ 'three' to عشر ʕaʃər 'ten' and the quantified noun is intricate and, at times, unsystematic. Variations exist between groups of Emirati speakers and sometimes within individuals about whether there is gender agreement or gender polarity (i.e. opposite gender specifications) between the numerals 'three' to 'ten' and the head noun. For instance, the numeral can agree in gender with the plural masculine noun.

Plural masculine noun

ثلاث طلاب
θalaaθ tˤəlˤlˤaab
three students
'three students'

أربع دفاتر
ʔarbaʕ dəfaatər
four notebooks
'four notebooks'

خمس دكاترة
xams dəkaatra
five doctors
'five doctors'

سبع بناطلين
sabəʕ bənaatˤl-iin
seven trouser-pl
'seven pairs of trousers'

Sound/broken plural feminine noun

ثلاث طالبات
θalaaθ tˤaalb-aat
three student-f.pl
'three (female) students'

أربع سيايير/سيارات
ʔarbaʕ səjaajiir/sajjaar-aat
four cars car-f.pl
'four cars'

خمس طبيبات		ست وردات	
xams	tˤabiib-aat	sətt	ward-aat
five	doctor-f.pl	six	rose-f.pl
'five (female) doctors'		'six roses'	
سبع مرات		ثمان غراش	
sabəʕ	marr-aat	θəmaan	ɣraaʃ
seven	time-f.pl	eight	bottles
'seven times'		'eight bottles'	
تسع أوراق		عشر علب	
təsəʕ	ʔawraag	ʕaʃər	ʕəlab
nine	papers	ten	cans
'nine (pieces of) paper'		'ten cans'	

Overall, there is a general intuition by Emirati speakers that gender agreement is more acceptable if the agreement is masculine (numeral)-masculine (noun), as the masculine form is morphologically unmarked.

نبى نشتري ثلاث كتب، أربع كراسي، خمس شباري وست كمبيوترات

nə-ba nə-ʃtəri θalaaθ kətəb, ʔarbaʕ karaasi xams ʃəbaari w sətt kambjuutar-aat.

we-want.imperf we-buy.imperf three books four chairs five beds and six computer-f.pl

'We want to buy three books, four chairs, five beds, and six computers.'

5.6.1.4 *The numerals أحد عشر ħidaʕʃ 'eleven' to تسعة عشر tisaʕtˤaʕʃ 'nineteen'*

The numerals أحد عشر ħidaʕʃ 'eleven' to تسعة عشر tisaʕtˤaʕʃ 'nineteen' contain the suffix عشر- -aʕʃ(r), which corresponds to the English '-teen.' Except for the numerals أحد عشر ħidaʕʃ 'eleven' and اثنا عشر θnaʕʃ 'twelve,' the numerals ثلاثة عشر θalatˤtˤaʕʃ 'thirteen' to تسعة عشر tisaʕtˤaʕʃ 'nineteen' contain the stem which refers to the single-digit numeral. An intervening consonant ة [tˤ] is used to separate the stem and the suffix:[3]

ثلاثة عشر θalattˤaʕʃ < θalat-tˤ-aʕʃ (three-teen) 'thirteen'

خمسة عشر xaməstˤaʕʃ < xamas-tˤ-aʕʃ (five-teen) 'fifteen'

The numerals احد عشر ħidaʕʃ(ar) 'eleven' to تسعة عشر tisaʕtˤaʕʃ(ar) 'nineteen' always precede the head noun, which is always singular, and are unmarked for gender (i.e. masculine), regardless of the gender of the head noun.

أحد عشر طالبة وخمسة عشر طالب

ħidaʕʃar tˤaaləb-ah w xamstˤaʕʃar tˤaaləb

eleven student-f and fifteen student

'eleven female students and fifteen male students'

في اثنا عشر طالب وخمسة عشر طالبة مسجلين فهالمادة

fii θnaʕʃar tˤaaləb w xamstˤaʕʃar tˤaaləb-a msadʒliin f-ha-l-maadda.

there.is twelve student and fifteen student-f registered.pl in-this-the-course

'There are twelve male students and fifteen female students registered in this course.'

5.6.1.5 *The tens from عشرين ʕəʃriin 'twenty' onwards*

From the numeral عشرين ʕəʃriin 'twenty' and subsequent tens, the numerals consist of the suffix ين- -iin, which corresponds to English '-ty.'

ثلاثين θalaaθ-iin 'thirty' (three-ty)

أربعين ʔarbəʕ-iin 'forty' (four-ty)

خمسين xams-iin 'fifty' (five-ty)

5.6.1.6 *Hundreds, thousands, and so on*

The expression of hundreds, thousands, and so on, follow the same strategies as many other languages, such as English. Multiples of hundreds (e.g. 'three hundred' and 'four hundred') are directly expressed by placing the single-digit numeral right before the hundreds (except 'two hundred' which is in the dual form).

ثلاثمائة θalaaθ-əmja (three-hundred) '300'

ثلاثمائة ʔarbaʕ-əmja (four-hundred) '400'

ثلاثة الاف θalaaθ-t-aalaaf(three-thousand) '3000'

أربعة آلاف ʔarbaʕ-t-aalaaf (four-thousand) '4000'

ثلاث ملايين/ثلاثة مليون	θalaaθ malajiin/θalaaθa məljoon (three-million) '3000000'
أربع ملايين/أربعة مليون	ʔarbaʕ malajiin/ʔarbaaʕa məljoon (four-million) '4000000'
عشر ملايين/عشرة مليون	ʕaʃər malajiin/ʕaʃra məljoon (ten-million) '10000000'

ثلاث بلايين/ثلاثة بليون	θalaaθ balajiin/θalaaθa bəljoon (three-billion) '3000000000'
أربع بلايين/أربعة بليون	ʔarbaʕ balajiin/ʔarbaʕa bəljoon (four-billion) '4000000000'

5.6.1.7 *Coordination in the formation of higher numerals*

For numerals which consist of different units such as ones, tens, hundreds, and so on, the coordinator و wa 'and' (Chapter 15) must be used.

مئة و عشرين ألف و ثلاثمائه و خمس و أربعين

ʔəmja w-ʕəʃriin ʔalf w-θalaaθ-əmja w-xamsa w-ʔarbəʕiin
hundred and-twenty thousand and-three hundred and-five and-forty
'One hundred and twenty thousand three hundred and forty-five'

أربع و عشرين ألف و أربع مائة و ثمان

ʔarbaʕ w-ʔəʃriin ʔalf wa-ʔarbaʕ-əmja w-θəmaan
four and-twenty thousand and-four hundred and-eight
'Twenty-four thousand four hundred and eight'

5.6.1.8 *Numerals with comparatives*

It is possible to form comparative numerals such as 'more than ten' or 'less than one hundred' by the comparative structure (Section 5.3.4).

أكثر من ألف طالب تخرج من الجامعة هالسنة

ʔakθar mən ʔalf tˤaaləb t-xarradʒ mən əl-dʒaamʕa ha-s-sənah.
more than thousand student refl-caus.graduate.imperf from the-university this-the-year
'More than 1000 students graduated from the university this year.'

It is clear that the comparative marker 'more than' combines with the numerals (e.g. 1000) instead of the quantified nouns (e.g. 100 students). This is shown by the following coordination structure (Chapter 15), in which the head noun is separated from the coordinated quantifiers:

معاش أحمد الشهري أكثر من عشرين ألف بس أقل عن ثلاثين ألف درهم

maʕaaʃ ʔaħmad əʃ-ʃahri ʔakθar mən ʕəʃriin ʔalf bas ʔaqal ʕan θalaaθiin ʔalf dərham.
salary Ahmad the-monthly more than twenty thousand but less than thirty thousand Dirham
'Ahmad's monthly salary is more than 20000 but less than 30000 Dirhams.'

5.6.1.9 *Partitives*

Numerical bases such as ten, hundred, and thousand may be used in partitive constructions (Section 6.1.1). In such cases, these bases function as a typical noun which is inflected for number (i.e. plural). Moreover, the determiner may be affixed (both for the partitive noun and the head noun).

آلاف من المتظاهرين ساروا البرلمان

ʔaalaaf mən əl-mə-tðˁaahr-iin saar-aw əl-barlamaan.
thousands of the-part-refl.protester-pl go.perf-they the-parliament
'Thousands of protesters marched to the parliament.'

الشركة استثمرت ملايين الدراهم في هذا المشروع الكبير

əʃ-ʃarika staθmər-at malaaj-iin əd-daraahəm f haaða l-maʃruuʕ əl-kəbiir.
the-company invest.perf-it.f million-pl the-Dirhams in this the-project the-grand
'The company has invested millions of Dirhams in this grand project.'

5.6.1.10 *Numerals in ellipsis*

Numerals, in their quantifying function, may be used in elliptical contexts (Chapter 16).

أحمد اشترى ثلاث كتب و أنا اشتريت اثنين
ʔaħmad əʃtara θalaaθ kətəb w ʔana ʃtaree-t ʔəθneen.
Ahmad refl.buy.perf-he three books and I buy.perf-I two
'Ahmad bought three books, and I bought two.'

كم إمارة موجودة في الإمارات ؟ سبع
kam ʔəmaara ma-wdʒuud-a f-əl-əmaaraat? sabʕa.
how.many Emirate part-exist.perf-f in-the-UAE? seven
'How many emirates are there in UAE? Seven.'

5.6.1.11 *Numerals in complex expressions*

A numeral may be used to form a complex expression (Chapter 4) which further modifies the head noun.

علاقة من طرف واحد
ʕalaaqa mən tˤaraf waaħəd
relationship from side one
'one-sided relationship'

شخص بويهيين
ʃaxsˤ b-wajh-een
person with-face-du
'two-faced person'

فندق خمس نجوم
funduq xams ndʒuum
hotel five stars
'five-star hotel'

ثمان ساعات استراحة
θəmaan saaʕ-aat əstəraaħa
eight hour-f.pl break
'eight-hour break'

5.6.2 ***Ordinal numbers***

The classification of ordinal numbers is similar to that of cardinal numbers. أول ʔawwal 'first' and ثاني θaani 'second' possess their own syllabic structure, whereas ثالث θaaləθ 'third' to عاشر ʕaaʃər 'tenth' have the unified syllabic template CaaCiC (for masculine) and CaaCCah (for feminine). The ordinal numbers from إحدى عشر ħidaʕʃ 'eleventh' onwards are lexically identical to their cardinal number counterparts, the major difference being that ordinal numbers can be prenominal or postnominal. If the ordinal number is postnominal, it behaves adjectivally and agrees with the head noun in gender. Only the ordinal number أول ʔawwal 'first' to عاشر ʕaaʃər 'tenth' has a feminine form, whereas إحدى عشر ħidaʕʃ 'eleventh' onwards only have one unmarked (hence masculine) form (Table 5.56).

Table 5.56 Ordinal numerals

	Masculine	*Feminine*	*Meaning*			*Meaning*
أول /أولى	ʔawwal	ʔuula	'first'	عشرين	ʕəʃriin	'20th'
ثاني/ثانية	θaani	θaanjah	'second'	واحد وعشرين	waaħəd w ʕəʃriin	'21st'
ثالث/ثالثة	θaaləθ	θaalθah	'third'	اثنين وعشرين	ʔəθneen w ʕəʃriin	'22nd'
رابع/رابعة	raabəʕ	raabʕah	'fourth'	ثلاثين	θalaθiin	'30th'
خامس/خامسة	xaaməs	xaamsah	'fifth'	أربعين	ʔarbəʕiin	'40th'
سادس/سادسة	saadəs	saadsah	'sixth'	خمسين	xamsiin	'50th'
سابع/سابعة	saabəʕ	saabʕah	'seventh'	ستين	səttiin	'60th'
ثامن/ثامنة	θaamən	θaamnah	'eighth'	سبعين	sabʕiin	'70th'
تاسع/تاسعة	taasəʕ	taasʕah	'ninth'	ثمانين	θəmaaniin	'80th'
عاشر/عاشرة	ʕaaʃər	ʕaaʃrah	'tenth'	تسعين	təsʕiin	'90th'
إحدى عشر	ħidaʕʃ		'11th'	مئة	ʔəmja	'100th'
إثنى عشر	əθnaʕʃ		'12th'	ألف	ʔalf	'1000th'
ثلاثة عشر	θalat[ʕ]t[ʕ]aʕʃ		'13th'	مليون	məljoon	'millionth'

(*Continued*)

Table 5.56 (Continued)

	Masculine	*Feminine*	*Meaning*	*Meaning*
أربعة عشر	ʔrbaʕtˁaʕʃ		'14th'	
خمسة عشر	xamastˁaʕʃ		'15th'	
ستة عشر	sətˁtˁaʕʃ		'16th'	
سبعة عشر	sabaʕtˁaʕʃ		'17th'	
ثمانية عشر	θəmantˁaʕʃ		'18th'	
تسعة عشر	təsəʕtˁaʕʃ		'19th'	

Postnominal ordinal number

الكتاب الأول/الثالث السيارة الأولى

əl-ktaab	əl-ʔawwal/əθ-θaaləθ	əs-sajjaara	əl-ʔuula
the-book	the-first/the-third	the-car.f	the-first.f
'the first/third book'		'the first car'	

Prenominal ordinal number

ثالث كتاب/ريال/بنت

θaaləθ	ktaab	/rajjaal/bənt
third	book	/man /girl

'the third book (masculine)/man (masculine)/girl (feminine)'

The ordinal number is used productively in date expressions.

ثاني يوم من شهر ستة

θaani	joom	mən	ʃahar	sətta
second	day	from	month	six

'The second of June'

Ordinal numbers may also be used in ellipsis (Chapter 16).

أول طالب كان يريد ياخذ لغويات، بس الثاني لا

ʔawwal	taaləb	kaan	j-riid	j-aaxəð
luɣawiijjaat		bas	əθ-θaani	laaʔ.
first	student	be.perf-he	he-want.imperf	he-take.imperf
linguistics		but	the-second	no

'The first student wanted to take linguistics, but the second (one) did not.'

5.6.3 Decimals

For the expression of decimals such as tenths and hundredths, they are indicated in the same way as cardinal numbers, and combine with the larger units (e.g. ones) by the word فاصلة faasˁla 'point.'

أربعة فاصلة سبعة أربعة فاصلة أربعة وسبعين

ʔarbaʕ-a	faasˁla	sabʕa	ʔarbaʕ-a	faasˁla	ʔarbaʕ-a	w	sabʕiin
four-f	point	seven	four-f	point	four	and	seventy
'4.7'			'4.74'				

أربعة فاصلة خمسة			
ʔarbaʕ-a	faasˤla	xams-a	
four-f	point	five-f	
'4.5'			

أربعة فاصلة خمسة و عشرين				
ʔarbaʕ-a	faasˤla	xams-a	w	ʕəʃriin
four-f	point	five-f	and	twenty
'4.25'				

For fractions such as 'half' and 'quarter,' the coordinator و w 'and' is used (Chapter 15).

أربعة ونص		
ʔarbaʕ-a	w	nəsˤ
four-f	and	half
'4.5' (lit. four and a half)		

أربعة وربع		
ʔarbaʕ-a	w	rəbəʕ
four-f	and	quarter
'4.25' (lit. four and a quarter)		

أربعة وثلاث أرباع		
ʔarbaʕ-a	w	θalaθaat-arbaaʕ
four-f	and	three-quater.pl
'4.75' (lit. four and three-quarters)		

5.6.4 Fractions

The fraction نص nəsˤ '1/2' lexically means 'half' and is independent of the cardinal numeral اثنين ʔθneen 'two.' The fractions ثلث θəlθ 'one-third' to عشر ʕəʃr 'one-tenth' are formed by the syllabic structure CəCC (Table 5.57).

ثلث	θəlθ	'1/3'
ربع	rəbəʕ	'1/4'
خمس	xəms	'1/5'

If the numerator of the fraction number is 'two,' the dual form is used.

ثلثين	θəlθ-een	'2/3 (the dual of 1/3)'
خمسين	xəms-een	'2/5 (the dual of 1/5)'

The numerator (except 'one' and 'two') is lexically identical to its cardinal number counterpart if the denominator is from 'four' to 'ten' (which is in the plural).

Table 5.57 Fractions

نص	nəsˤ	'1/2'	ثلثين	θəlθeen	'2/3'
ثلث	θəlθ	'1/3'	خُمسين	xəmseen	'2/5'
ربع	rəbəʕ	'1/4'	ثلاث أرباع	θalaaθ ʔarbaaʕ/θalattarbaaʕ	'3/4'
خمس	xəms	'1/5'	ثلاث أخماس	θalaaθ ʔaxmaas/θalattaxmaas	'3/5'
سدس	səds	'1/6'	أربع أخماس	ʔarbaʕ ʔaxmaas	'4/5'
سبع	səbʕ	'1/7'	أربع أسداس	ʔarbaʕ ʔasdaas	'4/6'
ثمن	θəmn	'1/8'	ثلاث من أحد عشر	θalaaθa mən ħidaʕʃ	'3/11'
تسع	təsʕ	'1/9'	اثنين من أحد عشر	ʔəθneen mən ħidaʕʃ	'2/11'
عشر	ʕəʃr	'1/10'			
واحد من أحد عشر	waaħəd mən ħidaʕʃ	'1/11'			
واحد من عشرين	waaħəd mən ʕəʃriin	'1/20'			
واحد من مئة	waaħəd mən ʔəmja	'1/100'			

ثلاث أرباع	ثلاث أخماس
θalaaθ ʔarbaaʕ/θalattarbaaʕ	θalaaθ ʔaxmaas/θalattaxmaas
three fours	three fives
'three-fourths'	'three-fifths'

أربع أخماس
ʔarbaʕ ʔaxmaas
four fives
'four-fifths'

For the denominator from 'eleven' onwards, the periphrastic expression formed by the preposition من mən 'from' is used (Section 5.5), except (again) if the numerator is 'two' and in the dual form.

واحد من أحد عشر	واحد من عشرين
waaħəd mən ħidaʕʃ	waaħəd mən ʕəʃriin
one from eleven	one from twenty
'1/11'	'1/20'

واحد من مئة
waaħəd mən əmja
one from hundred
'1/100'

5.6.5 *Quantifiers*

Quantifiers (Table 5.58) are a type of word class which denote quantity and specify to what extent the entire proposition, of which the quantificational expression is an argument, is true. Quantifiers can be further classified as universal ('universal quantifier') (e.g. 'all' and 'both'), distributive ('distributive quantifier') (e.g. 'each'), and existential ('existential quantifier') (e.g. 'some').

5.6.5.1 *Universal quantifier* كل *kəl 'all/every/each'*

The universal quantifier كل kəl 'all/every' modifies both count and mass nouns. The quantified noun is interpreted as definite-specific if it contains a determiner (e.g. 'all the books') (Section 6.1.1), a demonstrative (e.g. 'all those books') (Section 5.8.4), a possessive structure (e.g. 'all her friends') (Section 6.2), or a construct state

Table 5.58 Quantifiers

كل	kəl	'all/every/each'	نص	nəsˤ	'half'
وايد	waajəd	'many/much/a lot of'	بعض	baʕðˤ	'some/ several'
معظم	muʕðˤam	'most'	شوية	ʃwajjat	'some/little'
أي	ʔaj	'any'	نتفة	nətfa	'a bit of'

(e.g. 'all Ahmad's friends') (Section 6.2.1). The quantified count noun may be singular or plural, depending on the intended meaning. If singular, the quantification expresses the total part of it (e.g. 'the entire book' and 'the entire movie').

كل الكتب
kəl əl-kətəb
all the-books
'all the books' (plural count noun)

كل السكر
kəl əs-səkkar
all the-sugar
'all the sugar' (mass noun)

كل ربع أحمد
kəl rabəʕ ʔaħmad
all friends Ahmad
'All Ahmad's friends' (construct state)

كل هذي الكتب
kəl haaði əl-kətəb
all these the-books
'All these books' (demonstrative)

These definite quantified expressions may function as subject or object arguments.

في مكيف في كل الصفوف
fii mkajjəf f kəl əsˤ-sˤəfuuf.
there.is air.con in all the-classroom.pl
'There is an air-conditioner in all the classrooms.'

كل الطلاب بينظمون لحفل التخرج
kəl ətˤ-tˤəlˤlˤaab b- jə-ndˤamm-uun l-ħafl ət-taxarruudʒ.
all the-students will they-caus.arrange.imperf-they for-ceremony the-graduation
'All the students will join the graduation ceremony.'

أمين المكتبة ضيّع تقريبا كل النسخ
ʔamiin əl-maktəb-ah ðˤajjaʕ taqriiban kəl ən-nəsax.
secretary the-library-f lose.perf-he almost all the-copies
'The librarian lost almost all the copies.'

ما أتفق مع كل تعليقاتك
maa ʔa-t-təfəq maʕ kəl taʕliiq-aat-ək.
not I-refl.agree.imperf with all comment-f.pl-your
'I do not agree with all your comments.'

كل kəl can also be suffixed by the object pronoun (Section 5.8.1).

أنا توني سويت كم من أكلة الليلة. دخيلكم خلصوهن كلهن
ʔana taw-ni sawwee-t kam mən ʔakla əl-leelah
dəxiil-kum xalsˤu-hən kəl-hən.
I just-me make.perf-I few of dish the-tonight
please.imp-you.pl finish-them.f all-them.f
'I have just cooked a few dishes tonight. Please finish them all.'

On the other hand, when the universal quantifier combines with a bare singular noun, it is interpreted as 'every.' Note that the quantified expression is grammatically singular, as shown by the singular verbal agreement.

كل طالب في المدرسة يعرف مريم
kəl tˤaalˤəb f-əl-madrəsah jə-ʕarf marjam.
every student in-the-school he-know.imperf Mariam
'Every student in the school knows Mariam.'

الطلاب لازم ييون للصف كل صبح
ətˤ-tˤəlˤlˤaab laazəm əj-j-uun əsˤ-sˤaff kəl sˤəbħ.
the-students must they-come.imperf-they the-class every morning
'Students have to come to class every morning.'

كل واحد من الكلاس حصّل شهادة الدبلوم من المدرس
kəl waaħəd mən lə-klaas ħasˤsˤal ʃahaad-at
əd-dəbloom mən əl-mudarrəs.
every one from the-class receive.perf-he certificate-f
the-diploma from the-teacher
'Everyone in the class received the diploma from the teacher.'

The universal quantifier كل kəl 'all' functions as a definite noun when prefixed by the determiner الـ al- (Sections 5.1 and 6.1.1). In contrast, the bare كل kəl 'all' cannot function as a quantified noun itself.

منو ياي؟ الكل

mnuu jaaj? əl-kəl.

who he-come.imperf the-all

'Who's going to come? All (are).'

5.6.5.2 وايد *waajəd 'many/much/a lot of'*

The quantifier وايد waajəd 'many/much/a lot' may combine with bare plural count and mass nouns. As a quantifier, it precedes the noun that it quantifies. On the other hand, if وايد waajəd follows the noun, it behaves adjectivally and agrees with the head noun in gender (cf. English 'numerous').

في وايد أخطاء فهذي المقالة

fii waajəd ʔaxtˤaaʔ f-haaði əl-maqaala.

there.is many mistakes in-this the-essay

'There are many mistakes in this essay.'

الرئيس ما عنده وايد معلومات عن الحال

ər-raʔiis maa ʕənd-ah waajəd maʕluumaat ʕan əl-ħaal.

the-president not with-him much information-pl about the-current.situation

'The president does not have much information about the current situation.'

وايد waajəd can be used in elliptical structures (Chapter 16). For example:

أحمد قال لي إنه اشترى بعض الكتب بس مب وايد

ʔaħmad gaal l-i ənn-ah əʃtara baʕðˤ əl-kətəb bas mub waajəd.

Ahmad tell.perf-he to-me that-him refl.buy.perf.he few the-books but not many

'Ahmad told me that he bought a few books, but not many (books).'

علي يعرف وايد عن الوضع الحالي و أنا ما أعرف وايد

ʕəli jə-ʕarf waajəd ʕan əl-waðʕ əl-ħaali w ʔana maa ʕarf waajəd.

Ali he-know.imperf much about the-situation the-current and I not I.know.imperf much

'Ali knows much about the current situation, but I don't know much (about the current situation).'

وايد waajəd 'many/much' can be used in partitive constructions (Section 6.1.1).

وايد من الناس يقولون ان الاقتصاد سيء هالأيام

waajəd mən ən-naas j-guul-uun ʔənna l-əqtəsˤaad sajjəʔ ha-l-ʔajjaam.

many of the-people they-say.imperf-they that the-economy bad these-the-days

'Many people say that the economy is bad these days.'

هالأيام وايد من الحريم يشتغلون في المكاتب، ووايد منهم مستانسات للدولة

ha-l-ʔajjaam waajəd mən əl-ħariim jə-ʃtaɣl-oon f-əl-məkaatəb, w waajəd mən-hən məstaans-aat əb-ʃəɣəl-hən.

these-the-days many of the-women they-refl.work.imperf-they in-the-offices and many of-them.f happy-f.pl in-work-their.f

'Nowadays many women work in offices, and many of them enjoy their work.'

5.6.5.3 معظم *muʕðˤam 'most'*

The quantifier معظم muʕðˤam 'most' may combine directly with a definite expression. This quantifier is mainly used by well-educated people.

معظم الناس اتفقوا على أن الرئيس اشتغل زين للدولة

muʕðˤam ən-naas əttafg-aw ʕala ʔən ər-raʔiis əʃtəɣal zeen l-əd-doola.

most the-people agree.perf-they on that the-president refl.work.perf-he good for-the-country

'Most people agreed that the president has done a good job for the country.'

معظم الطلاب راح ياخذون كورسات صيفية هذا الفصل

muʕðˤam ətˤ-tˤəlˤlˤaab raħ j-aaxð-uun koors-aat sˤajfij-jah haaða əl-fasˤəl.

most the-student.pl will they-take.imperf-they course.f.pl summer.adj-f this the-semester

'Most students will take summer courses this semester.'

معظم muʕðˤam 'most' can also combine with a bare noun, but only if it forms a partitive structure.

معظم طلاب هذي الجامعة إماراتيين لأنها جامعة وطنية

muʕðˤam tˤəlˤlˤaab haðˤi əl-dʒaamʕ-a ʔəmaaraatijj-iin laʔan-ha dʒaamʕa watˤanijj-a.

most students this the-university-f Emirati -pl because-it university national-f

'Most students from this university are Emirati because it is a national university.'

معظم muʕðˤam can also take an object pronoun as a suffix to express a partitive meaning

في وايد تفاح في السوق. معظمه أحمر وشوي منه أخضر

fii waajəd təffaaħ f-əs-suug muʕðˤam-ah ʔaħmar w ʃwajj mənn-ah ʔaxðˤar.

there.is a.lot apple in-the-market most-it red and some of-it green

'There are lots of apples in the market. Most are red, but some are green.'

5.6.5.4 بعض *baʕðˤ 'some'*

بعض baʕðˤ 'some' combines with the definite noun. Similar to معظم muʕðˤam 'most,' بعض baʕðˤ is used primarily by educated people.

بعض الناس يآمنون بالحظ

baʕðˤ ən-naas jə-ʔaamn-uun b-əl-ħaðˤ

some the-people they-believe.imperf-they in-the-luck

'Some people believe in luck.'

بس بعض الأعضاء حضروا

bas baʕð̣ ʕ əl-ʔaʕðʕaaʔ ħəðʕr-aw.

only some the-members attend.perf-they

'Only some members attended.'

bas	baʕðʕ	əl-ʔaʕðʕaaʔ	ħəðʕr-aw.
only	some	the-members	attend.perf-they

'Only some members attended.'

بقترح عليك بعض الكتب

b-a-qtərəħ	ʕalee-k	baʕðʕ	əl-kətəb.
will-I-refl.recommend.imperf	on-you	some	the-books

'I will recommend some books to you.'

بعض baʕðʕ 'some' may take an object pronoun suffix. For example:

توني مجابل طلاب هارفارد السنة اللي طافت. بعضهم وايد أذكيا

taw-ni	m-ʤaabəl	tʕəlʕlʕaab	haarvərd	əs-səna	ʔəlli
just-me	part-meet	students	Harvard	the-year	that

tʕaaf-at	baʕðʕ-hum	waajəd	ʔaðakija.
pass.perf-she	some-them	much	intelligent.pl

'I just met some Harvard students last year. Some of them are very intelligent.'

5.6.5.5 شوية *ʃwajjat 'some/little'*

شوية ʃwajjat 'some/little' can directly combine with a bare noun. Similar to other numeral quantifiers, it cannot combine with a definite noun phrase. This quantified expression only appears as an object and is generally not allowed at the grammatical subject position; another quantifier بعض baʕðʕ 'some' should be used as a subject quantifier.

يدورون حد عنده شوية خبرة

j-dawr-uun	ħadd	ʕənd-a	ʃwajja-t	xəbra.
they-look.imperf-they	person	with-him	some-f	experience

'They're looking for someone with some experience.'

عطي الياهل شوية حلاوة

ʕatʕi	l-jaahəl	ʃwajja-t	ħalaawa.
give.imp	the-kid	some-f	candy

'Give the kid some candy.'

In contrast, the preposition في fi 'in' may be used in existential constructions (Section 7.7), and in these cases شوية ʃwajjat functions as a subject.

في شوية حلويات ع الطاولة
fii ʃwajja-t ħalawjj-aat ʕa-tˤ-tˤaawla.
there.is some-f sweet.adj-f.pl on-the-table
'There are some candies on the table.'

Another word شوية ʃwajja 'some' (or sometimes شوي ʃwaj) is used in partitive structures (Section 6.1.1). شوية ʃwajja also functions as a quantified noun itself without a following noun (cf. 'Some are good').

أعرف شوي من ربعه
ʔa-ʕarf ʃwaj-ja mən rabʕ-a.
I-know.imperf some-f of friends-his
'I know some of his friends.'

شوي منا يبون يغيرون الوضع
ʃwaj mən-na jə-b-oon jə-ɣajr-uun l-waðˤʕ.
some of-us they-want.imperf-they they-change.imperf-they the-situation
'Some of us want to change the situation.'

صرفت بس شويه من الفلوس
sˤaraf-t bas ʃwaj-ja mən əl-fluus.
spend.perf-I only some-f from the-money
'I have only spent some of the money.'

عطيتها شوي من البسكوت
ʕatˤee-t-ha ʃwaj mən əl-baskuut.
give.perf-I-her some from the-cookies
'I gave her some of the cookies.'

توني سويت دلة قهوة. تبا شوي؟
taw-ni sawwee-t dalla-t gahwa t-əba ʃwaj?
just-me make.perf-I pot-f coffee you-want.imperf some
'I have just made a pot of coffee. Do you want some?'

بسويلي خبز رقاق وبعطي الجيران شوي

b-a-sawwii-l-i xəbz rgaag w b-a-ʕtˤi l-ʤiiraan ʃwaj.

will-I-make.imperf-for-me bread Rugag and will-I-give.imperf the-neighbors some

'I will make myself Rugag bread and give the neighbors some.'

خذت أي خبرة عمل؟ هيه، بس شوية

xað-t ʔaj xəbra-t ʕamal? heeh bas ʃwaj-ja.

get.perf-you any experience-f work yes but little-f

'Did you get any working experience? Yes, but just a little.'

Note that شوية ʃwajja is interpreted partitively. In the following example, the quantified expression شوية طلاب ʃwajja tˤəlˤlˤaab 'some students' is interpreted as a subset of students in the relevant discourse:

بعض الطلاب مجتهدين بس في شوية طلاب كسلانين

baʕðˤ ətˤ-tˤəlˤlˤaab məʒtahd-iin bas fii ʃwajja-t tˤəllaab kaslaan-iin.

some the-students hard-working-pl but there.is some-f' student.pl lazy-pl

'Some students are hard workers, but there are some lazy students.'

شوي ʃwaj as a diminutive marker can be pragmatically interpreted as a politeness marker 'please.'

ممكن شوي؟

mumkən ʃwaj?

possible little

'Excuse me.'

ممكن تصب لي شاي شوي؟

mumkən t-sˤəbb l-i tʃaaj ʃwaj?

possible you-pour.imperf for-me tea little

'Could you pour me a little tea (please)?'

Similar to شوية ʃwajjat, another quantifier نتفة nətfah 'a little bit' may be used, typically in reference to food.

كلت نتفة من الكيكة اليوم الصبح

kal-t nətfah mən əl-keeka l-joom əsˤ-sˤəbħ.
eat.perf-I bit from the-cake the-day the-morning
'I just ate a bit of cake this morning.'

هو زين يوم تحطين نتيفة حلاوة فالكوفي

huu zeen joom t-ħətˤtˤ-iin nteef-at ħalaawa f-əl-koofi
It good when you.f-put.imperf-you.f bit-f chocolate in-the-coffee
'It is good to add a bit of chocolate to the coffee.'

5.6.5.6 كم من *kammin 'a number of'*

The quantifier كم من kammin 'a number of' possibly stems from the grammaticalization of كم kam 'quantity/number' and من mən 'from/of,' although native speakers consider this as a single lexical item. Its lexical meaning is 'a number of' and it combines only with a bare count noun. It cannot combine with a definite expression or form a partitive structure.

برد كم من كتاب للمكتبة

b-a-rəd kammən ktaab l-əl-maktəba.
will-I-return.imperf a.number.of book to-the-library
'I will return a number of books to the library.'

أنا توني سويت كم من أكلة الليلة. دخيلكم خلصوهن كلهن

ʔana taw-ni sawwee-t kammən ʔakl-a əl-leela dəxiil-kum xalsˤ-uu-hən kəl-hən.
I just-me make.cook.perf-I a.number.of dishes the-tonight please-you.pl finish-you.pl-them.f all-them.f
'I have just cooked a few dishes tonight. Please finish them all (of them).'

5.6.5.7 نص *nəsˤ 'half'*

نص nəsˤ 'half' (var. nəsˤsˤ if it is followed by a vowel) may function as a generalized quantifier (which quantifies over a set), in addition to being a numeral quantifier. It can combine with definite expressions, including construct states.

نص الشعب يستخدم التكاسي

nəsˤsˤ	əʃ-ʃaʕb	jə-staxdəm	ət-təkaasi.
half	the-people	they-use.imperf	the-taxis

'Half of the people use taxis.'

عرضوا يدفعون نص تكاليف التصليح

ʕərðˤ-aw	jə-dfəʕ-uun	nəsˤ	təkaaliif	ət-tasˤliiħ.
offer.perf-they	they-pay.imperf-they	half	cost.pl	the-repair

'They offered to pay half the cost of repairs.'

In addition, نص nəsˤ 'half' may form a partitive structure and take an object pronoun as a suffix.

أكثر من نص الأطفال في العالم الغربي يعيشون ويا واحد من الوالدين

ʔakθar	mən	nəsˤsˤ	əl-ʔatˤfaal	f-əl-ʕaalam	əl-ɣarbi
j-ʕiiʃ-uun			wəjja waaħəd	mən	əl-waald-een.
more	from	half	the-children	in-the-world	the-western
they-live.imperf-they			with one	from	the-parent-du

'Over half (of) the children in the Western world live in one-parent families.'

إذا شفت الجروب، تلاقي عالأقل نصهم حريم

ʔiða	ʧəf-t	əl-gruub	t-laagi	ʕa-l-laqal
nəsˤ-hum		ħəriim.		
if	see.perf-you	the-group	you-find.imperf	at-the-least
half-them		women		

'If you look at our members, you will find at least half of them are women.'

نصهم ما عندهم تعليم أبد

nəsˤ-hum	maa	ʕənd-hum	taʕliim	ʔabad.
half-them	not	with-them	education	not.at.all

'Half of them are not educated at all.'

5.6.5.8 أي *ʔaj 'any'*

The word ي ʔaj 'any' can denote zero quantity, especially if it functions as a negative polarity item in the context of negation (Chapter 10) and conditionals (Chapter 14). Interestingly, the use of ي ʔaj in polar questions (Chapter 13) is considered unnatural by Emirati speakers.

ما عزموا أي حد فينا

maa	ʕəzm-aw	ʔaj	ħad	fii-na.
not	invite.perf-they	any	one	in-us

'They didn't invite any of us.'

ي ʔaj 'any' as a free-choice item also has the flavor of a universal quantifier (cf. كل kəl 'all') (Section 5.6.5.1).

اي مرشح ياخذ ١٠٠٪ في الامتحان راح يحصل جايزة بقيمة مئة دولار

ʔaj	mraʃʃaaħ	jaa-xəð	ʔəmja	b-əl-əmja	f-əl-əmtəħaan
raaħ	j-ħasˤsˤəl		dʒaaʔəza	b-qiima-t	ʔəmja-t
doolaar.					
any	candidate	he-get.imperf	hundred	of-the-hundred	in-the-test
will	he-caus.receive.imperf		prize	with-value-f	hundred-f
dollar					

'Any candidate who got 100% on the test will receive a prize of 100 dollars.'

هذا السؤال كان وايد سهل! أي حد بيعرف الجواب بسرعة

haaða	əs-suʔaal	kaan	waajəd	sahəl!	ʔaj	ħad
ba-j-ʕarf		əl-dʒawaab		b-sərʕa.		
this	the-question	be.perf-it	very	easy	any	one
will-he-know.imperf		the-answer		with-speed		

'This question is too easy! Anyone (would) know the answer immediately!'

5.7 Complementizers

Complementizers comprise a functional category which marks a complement clause—that is, a clause which simultaneously functions as an argument or adjunct of another predicate. Across languages, complementizers may be an independent category, or they may fall into the class of subordinators (Chapter 14). In some cases, a complementizer functions as a relative clause marker (Chapter 12). The semantic function of complementizers varies depending on the type of the main predicate. In Emirati Arabic, the complement clause marked by the complementizer انه ʔən-n(ah) 'that' may assume various semantic functions (Table 5.60),

Table 5.59 The complementizer انه ʔənn(ah) 'that'

إن/إنه	ʔənn-ah/ʔənn	'that'	إنه	ʔən-nah	'that he/it'
إنك	ʔənn-ək	'that you'	إنها	ʔən-ha	'that she'
إنج	ʔənn-əʧ	'that you (f)'	إنا	ʔən-na	'that we'
إني	ʔənn-ii	'that I'	إنهم	ʔən-hum	'that they'

whereas another complementizer جنه ʧann(ah) 'as though' further encodes the speaker's modality (Table 5.61).

5.7.1 انه ʔənn(ah) 'that'

The complementizer انه ʔənn(ah) 'that' (Table 5.59) may appear independently or with the subject of the complement clause suffixed as a bound pronoun (Section 5.8.1.6).

The complement clause marked by the complementizer انه ʔənn(ah) 'that' may be selected by various types of main clause predicates. The most common semantic function is to be an argument of reporting verbs of saying (Section 5.2).

حميد قال انه بيسافر باجر

ħmeed	gaal	ʔənn-ah	ba-j-saafər	baaʧər.
Humaid	say.perf-he	that-him	will-he-travel.imperf	tomorrow

'Humaid said that he will travel tomorrow.'

شما خبرتني انها نجحت فالامتحان

ʃamma	xabbar-at-ni	ʔən-haa	nədʒħ-at	f-l-əmtħan.
shamma	tell.perf-she-me	that-her	pass.perf-f	in-the-exam

'Shamma told me that she passed the exam.'

Psychological verbs can also select complement clauses marked by انه ʔənn(ah). For example:

محمد يخاف انه يرسب فالامتحان

mħammad	j-xaaf	ʔənn-ah	jə-rsab	fə-l-əmtəħaan.
Mohammed	he-fear.imperf	that-him	he-fail.imperf	in-the-exam

'Mohammed fears that he will fail the exam.'

فاطمه تتمنى انها تحصل وظيفة بسرعة

faatˤmah tə-tmanna ʔən-ha t-ħasˤsˤel waðˤiifa b-sərʕa.

Fatima she-wish.imperf that-her she-find.imperf job with-speed

'Fatima wishes that she will find a job quickly.'

انه ʔənnah may also introduce a factive complement clause.

نحن آاسفين انكم خسرتوا فالمسابقة

nəħən ʔaasf-iin ʔən-kum xəsart-uu f-əl-musaabaqah.

we sorry-pl that-you lose.perf-you.pl in-the-competition

'We are sorry that you lost the competition.'

ينرفزني انك جذبت عليه

j-narfəz-ni ʔən-ək ʧaððab-t ʕala-jjah.

it-irritate.imperf-me that-you lie.perf-you on-me

'It irritates me that you lied to me.'

Control predicates such as 'try' and 'want' may be followed by the complement clause marked by انه ʔənn(ah) (Section 7.11).

حاول انك ما ترقد قبل ما تاكل

ħaawel ən-ək maa tə-rgəd gabəl maa t-aakəl.

try.imp that-you not you-sleep.imperf before that you-eat.imperf

'Try not to sleep before you eat.'

أنا ما أبا ان حميد يروح

ʔana maa ʔa-ba ʔənn ħmeed jə-rawwəħ.

I not I-want.imperf that Humaid he-leave.imperf

I don't want Humaid to leave.' (lit. I don't want that Humaid leaves.)

مهم جداً انك تشتغل زين

muhəm ʤəddan ʔənn-ək tə-ʃtəɣəl zeen.

important very that-you you-work.imperf well

'It is very important that you work hard.'

The complement clause may function as the subject of the main predicate. Note that the complementizer انه ʔənn(ah) is still required.

انج ذكية ها شيء واضح

ʔənn-ətʃ	ðakijj-a	haa	ʃajj	waað[ʕ]eħ.
that-you.f	smart-f	this	thing	clear

'It is obvious that you are smart.' (lit. that you are smart is a clear thing)

The complementizer انه ʔənn(ah) can also type a noun-complement clause. For example:

إشاعة أنه الإجازة اسبوعين مب مأكدة

ʔiʃaaʕat	ʔənna	l-ʔədʒaaza	sbuuʕ-een	mub	mʔakkad-a.
rumor	that	the-break	week-du	not	confirmed-f

'The rumor that the break is two weeks long is not confirmed.'

5.7.2 جنه *tʃann(ah) 'as though'*

جنه tʃann(ah) 'as though' is another complementizer which expresses irrealis modality (Chapter 9). Similar to انه ʔənn(ah), جنه tʃann(ah) has a list of morphological variants, depending on the subject pronoun suffix (Table 5.60).

جنه بيطيح سيل اليوم

tʃann-ah	ba-j-t[ʕ]iiħ	seel	əl-joom.
as.though-it	will-it-fall.imperf	rain	the-today

'(It seems) as though it will rain today.'

Table 5.60 The complementizer جنه tʃannah 'as though'

جني	tʃann-ii	'as though I'	جنك	tʃann-ək	'as though you'
جنه	tʃann-ah	'as though it/he'	جنج	tʃann-ətʃ	'as though you (f)'
جنها	tʃann-ha	'as though she'	جنه نحن	tʃanna -nəħən	'as though we'
جنهم	tʃan-hum	'as though they'	جنهن	tʃann-hən	'as though they (f)'

جنج ما خبرتيني انج بتروحين السينما

ʧann-əʧ maa xabbar-tii-ni ʔən-əʧ
bə-t-ruuħ-iin əs-seenəma.
as.though-you.f not tell.perf-you-me that-you.f
will-you.f-go.imperf-you.f the-cinema
'(It seems) as though you didn't tell me that you will go to the cinema.'

جنه ميثا ما اشتغلت اليوم

ʧann-ah meeθa maa ʃtaɣl-at əl-joom.
as.though-it Maitha not work.perf-she the-today
'(It seems) as though Maitha did not work today.'

مب جنه نحن اللي قلنا نبا الامتحان يكون الأحد؟

mub ʧann-ah neħen ʔəlli gəl-na n-əba
l-əmtəħaan j-kuun əl-ʔaħad?
not as.though.it we that say.perf-we we-want.imperf
the-exam it-be.imperf the-sunday
'Isn't it we who said that we want the exam to be on Sunday?'

جنه نحن راقدين من أمس

ʧann-ah nəħən raagd-iin mən ʔams.
as.though-it we part.sleep-pl since yesterday
'(It seems) as though we were asleep since yesterday.'

5.8 Pronouns

The term 'pronoun' traditionally refers to a class of lexical items that substitute for nouns. This is not entirely accurate, as pronouns usually substitute for larger syntactic elements than simple nouns, namely, noun phrases (Chapter 6). The usual function of a pronoun is to refer to an entity that has already been established in the discourse by a noun phrase—in other words, it has an 'anaphoric' function. The noun phrase that introduces the referent of the pronoun is called its antecedent. In certain cases, the pronoun may be used with no antecedent. This is done by pointing or referring to a person in the immediate environment of the speaker-addressee interaction.

There are different subclasses of pronouns, depending on their function in the sentence and their referential properties. Thus, most grammatical systems contain pronominal forms categorized as personal (Section 5.8.1), reflexive (Section 5.8.3), possessive (Section 5.8.2), and demonstrative (Section 5.8.4).

5.8.1 Personal pronouns

The system of personal pronouns in Emirati Arabic consists of a series of independent/free pronouns and a series of affixed pronouns whose form changes, based on the syntactic function they play in the sentence.

5.8.1.1 Free pronouns

Personal pronouns are marked for gender (masculine and feminine) and number (singular and plural). Contrary to nouns, pronouns are not marked for the dual number (Table 5.61).

There is some variation in the use of the second- and third-person plural feminine forms, which are predominantly used in the varieties spoken in the Northern Emirates and by older generations. Other varieties use the masculine forms for all second- and third-person plural pronouns.

Free pronouns may not be realized in natural conversations even if the lexical subject is absent in the sentence, as the verb morphology is rich enough to inform the identity of the sentence subject. This is the phenomenon called 'subject pro-drop,' in which the subject pronoun may be dropped, and its referent recovered by the verbal morphology (Section 5.2). However, subject pronouns may be mentioned in discourse, especially if they bring along the effect of emphasis. The following examples show that subject pronouns may be used to refer to various grammatical functions (e.g. object, possessives) in the sentence.

Table 5.61 Free pronouns in Emirati Arabic

	Singular			*Plural*		
First pers.	أنا	ʔana	'I'	نحن	nəħən	'we'
Second pers. m	إنت	ʔənt(a)	'you'	إنتوا	ʔintu/ ʔintum	'you (pl)'
Second pers. f	إنتي	ʔənti	'you (f)'	إنتن	ʔəntən	'you (f)'
Third pers. m	هو	huu/huwa	'he/it'	هم	hum	'they'
Third pers. f	هي	hii/hijja	'she'	هن	hin/hən	'they (f)'

هم مب نحن، اللي محتاجين يحلون المشكلة

hum mub nəħən ʔəlli məħtaadʒ-iin j-ħəll-uun əl-məʃkəla.

they not we that part.need-pl they-solve.imperf-they the-problem

'They, not we, are the ones who need to solve the problem.'

أحمد صدق يكرهها، هي

ʔaħmad sˤədəg jə-krah-ha, hii.

Ahmd really he-hate.imperf-her her

'Ahmad really hates *her*.'

هي هاي، أحمد صدق يكرهها

hii haaj ʔaħmad sˤədəg jə-krah-ha.

she this Ahmad really he-hate-imperf-her

'It's *her*, Ahmad really hates her.'

هذي فلوسي، أنا!

haaði fluus-i, ʔana!

this.f money-my I

'This is *my* money.'

5.8.1.2 *Bound pronouns*

Suffixed pronouns typically appear after various lexical (e.g. verbs) and functional (e.g. subordinator) categories and they usually serve to refer to an object in the sentence (Table 5.62). As compared with verbal agreement with subjects, which is obligatorily required for all verbal forms (Section 5.2), suffixed pronouns are only required if the object they refer to is not overtly present in a postverbal position. If the verb is transitive (Chapter 7), the suffixed pronoun always refers to the direct object of the sentence. If the verb is ditransitive (e.g. 'send' and 'give'), the suffixed pronoun refers to the indirect object of the sentence, and it is preceded by the preposition لـ l- 'to' (Section 5.5). Note that the set of suffixed pronouns is almost homographic with the possessive pronouns (Chapter 6). The most salient distinction of suffixed pronouns lies on the first-person singular ـني -ni 'me' (Table 5.62).

Table 5.62 Bound pronoun suffixes in Emirati Arabic

		Singular			
1st pers.	ـني	-ni	حبني	ħabni	'He liked me'
2nd pers. m	ـك	-(ə)k	حبك	ħabbək	'He liked you'
2nd pers. f	ـج	-(ə)ʧ	حبج	ħabbəʧ	'He liked you (f)'
3rd pers. m	ـه	-a/ah	حبه	ħabbah	'He liked him'
3rd pers. f	ـها	-ha	حبها	ħabha	'He liked her'
1st pers.	ـنا	-na	حبنا	ħabna	'He liked us'
2nd pers. m	ـكم	-kum	حبكم	ħabkum	'He liked you (pl)'
2nd pers. f	ـكن	-kən	حبكن	ħabkən	'He liked you (f.pl)'
3rd pers. m	ـهم	-hum	حبهم	ħabhum	'He liked them'
3rd pers. f	ـهن	-hin/hən	حبهن	ħabhən	'He liked them (f)'
		Singular			
1st pers.	ـي	-i	طرشلي	tˤarraʃli	'He sent me'
2nd pers. m	ـك	-(ə)k	طرشلك	tˤarraʃlək	'He sent you'
2nd pers. f	ـج	-(ə)ʧ	طرشلج	tˤarraʃləʧ	'He sent you (f)'
3rd pers. m	ـه	-a	طرشله	tˤarraʃla	'He sent him'
3rd pers. f	ـها	-ha	طرشلها	tˤarraʃəlha	'He sent her'
		Plural			
1st pers.	ـنا	-na	طرشلنا	tˤarraʃəlna	'He sent us'
2nd pers. m	ـكم	-kum	طرشلكم	tˤarraʃəlkum	'He sent you (pl.)'
2nd pers. f	ـكن	-kən	طرشلكن	tˤarraʃəlkən	'He sent you (f.pl)'
3rd pers. m	ـهم	-hum	طرشلهم	tˤarraʃəlhum	'He sent them'
3rd pers. f	ـهن	-hin/hən	طرشلهن	tˤarraʃəlhən	'He sent them (f)'

5.8.1.3 *Pronoun suffixes of verbs*

لا تكسره

la	t-kassər-ah.
don't	you-caus.break.imperf-it

'Don't break it.'

يعتبرونه طالب ذكي

jə-ʕtəbr-oon-ah	tˤaaləb	ðaki.
they-consider. imperf-they-him	student	smart

'They consider him a smart student.'

طنشهم

tˤannəʃ-hum.
ignore.imp-them
'Ignore them.'

حطيت كل الكتب عليه

ħatˤtˤ-eet kəl əl-kətəb ʕalee-h.
put.perf-I all the-book.pl on-it
'I put all the books on it.'

Verbal participles can also take an object pronoun suffix. For example:

نورة كانت مسوتنهم يوم تلاقينا

nuura kaan-at m-sawwə-tən-hum joom t-laagee-na.
noora be.perf-she part-do-f-them when refl-meet.perf-we
'Noora had done them when we met.'

كان اليار شالنهم يوم وصلت

kaan l-jaar aall-ən-hum joom wəsal-t.
be.perf-he the-neighbor part.take-them when arrive.perf-I
'The neighbor had taken them when I arrived.'

ابويا كان عاطنّه ايّاه

ʔəbuu-ja kaan ʕaatˤə-nn-a jja-ah.
dad-my be.perf-he part.give-him Ink-it
'Dad had given it to him.'

أخويا كان شالنها بدون ما يخبرني

ʔəxuu-ja kaan ʃaall-ən-ha bduun maa j-xabbər-ni.
brother-my be.perf-he part.take-her without not he-tell.imperf-me
'My brother had taken it without telling me.'

The object pronoun suffix is not realized if the object noun phrase is pronounced in the sentence.

لا تكسر القلاص

la tə-ksər lə-glaasˤ.
don't you-break.imperf the-glass
'Don't break the glass.'

طنش التعليقات الخايسة

tˤann-əʃ	ə-ttaʕliiq-aat	əl-xaajs-a.
ignore.imp-you.f	the-comment-f.pl	the-bad-f

'Ignore the bad comments.'

In the expression of double-object constructions by ditransitive verbs (Section 7.6), the ditransitive verb may be suffixed by the indirect object pronoun. However, the direct object pronoun suffix cannot be attached to the ditransitive verb; instead, it is attached to the linking particle ايّا (ə)jja.

عطني ياه

ʕatˤ-ni	jja-ah.
give.imp-me	lnk-it

'Give it to me.'

يابلها ياه

jaabə-l-ha	jja-ah.
bring.perf-he-to-her	lnk-it

'He brought it to her.'

خذت له ياها

xað-at	l-a	jjaa-ha.
take.perf-she	for-him	lnk-it

'She took it for him.'

5.8.1.4 *Pronoun suffixes of subordinators*

In many cases, the suffixed pronouns refer to a grammatical object, but there are structures in which they function as a grammatical subject. For instance, the pronoun suffix of subordinators such as لأن lann 'because' and دام daam 'as soon as' (Chapter 14) functions as the grammatical subject of the embedded clause (Table 5.63).

ما قدرت أداوم لاني كنت مريض

ma	gədar-t	ʔa-daawəm	lann-i	kənt	məriið.
not	can.perf-I	I-go.work.imperf	because-me	be.perf-I	sick

'I could not go to work because I was sick.'

ربيعتي ما تسير السينما لانها ما تحب الظلام

rbiiʕ-ti	ma	t-siir	əs-seenəma	lan-ha	ma	t-ħəb	əð-ðalaam.
friend-my	not	she-go.imperf	the-Cinema	because-her	not	she-like.imperf	the-darkness

'My friend does not go to the cinema because she does not like the darkness.'

Table 5.63 Pronoun suffixes of subordinators

لانّي	lanni	'because I'	لانها	lanha	'because she'
لانّك	lannək	'because you'	لانّا	lannna	'because we'
لانج	lannətʃ	'because you (f)'	لانهم	lanhum	'because they'
لانكم	lankum	'because you (pl)'	لانهن	lanhən	'because they (f)'
لانّه	lannah	'because he'			
دامني	daamni	'as long as I'	دامها	daamha	'as long as she'
دامك	daamək	'as long as you'	دامنا	daamna	'as long as we'
دامج	daamətʃ	'as long as you (f)'	دامهم	daamhum	'as long as they'
دامكم	daamkum	'as long as you (pl)'	دامهم/دامهن	daamhən/daamhum	'as long as they (f)'
دامه	daamah	'as long as he'			

دامج مب يايه لا تسإلين

daam-əʧ mub jaaj-a la tə-sʔəl-iin

as.long.as-you.f not come.perf-f not you.f-ask.imperf-you.f

'Since you are not coming, don't ask.'

بسويلكم اياها مرة ثانية دامها عيبتكم

ba-sawwii-l-kum jjaah-a mara θaanja daam-ha ʕijba-t-kum

will-I-do.imperf-for-you Ink-it.f once again as.long.as-it.f like.perf-f-you.pl

'I will make it again for you since you liked it.'

5.8.1.5 *Pronoun suffixes of wh-words*

The object pronoun suffixes may be attached to the wh-word وين ween 'where' (Chapter 13), except for the pronoun نحن nəħən 'we.' Other wh-words cannot take object pronoun suffixes.

ويني

weenn-i?

where-me

'Where am I?'

وينك/وينج

ween-ək/ween-əʧ?

where-you/where-you.f

'Where are you?'

وينه

ween-ah?

where-him

'Where is he?'

وينها

ween-ha?

where-her

'Where is she?'

نحن وين

nəħən ween?

we where

'Where are we?'

وينهم

ween-hum?

where-them

'Where are they?'

5.8.1.6 *Pronoun suffixes of complementizers*

The grammatical subject of the clause marked by the complementizer انه ʔənnah 'that' and جان ʧann 'as though' is morphologically realized as a pronominal suffix (Section 5.7) (Table 5.64).

Table 5.64 Pronoun suffixes of complementizers

انه	ʔənnah	'that/that it'	انه	ʔənn-ah	'that he'
انك	ʔənn-ək	'that you'	انها	ʔən-ha	'that she'
انج	ʔənn-əʧ	'that you (f)'	انا	ʔən-na	'that we'
اني	ʔənn-i	'that I'	انهم	ʔən-hum	'that they'
جني	ʧann-ii	'as though I'	جنك	ʧann-ək	'as though you (m)'
جنه	ʧann-ah	'as though it/he'	جنج	ʧann-əʧ	'as though you (f)'
جنها	ʧan-ha	'as though she'	جنه نحن	ʧann-ah nəħən	'as though we'
جنهم	ʧan-hum	'as though they'	جنهن	ʧan-hən	'as though they (f)'

زين انهم راقدين بدري والا ما بينشون الصبح

zeen ʔən-hum raagd-iin badri wəlla ma ba-j-nəʃʃ-uun əsˤ-sˤəbħ.

good that-them part.sleep-pl early otherwise not will-they-get.up.imperf-they the-morning

'It is good that they are asleep early, otherwise they won't get up in the morning.'

بيتنا جنه ثلاجة من البرد

beet-na ʧann-ah θallaaʤa mən əl-bard.

house-our as.though-it fridge from the-cold

'Our home feels like a fridge (from the cold).'

5.8.1.7 *Pronoun suffixes of adverbs*

Some adverbs, especially those used in negative contexts, may be suffixed with pronouns expressing the sentential subject (Sections 10.1 and 10.8).

بعده ما رجع البيت

baʕd-ah maa rəʤaʕ əl-beet

still-him not come.back.perf-he the-house

'He has not come home yet.'

بعدني ما تعودت عالمكان

baʕad-ni	maa	t-ʕawwad-t	ʕa-l-məkaan
still-me	not	refl-caus-accustom.perf-I	on-the-place

'I am still not used to the place.'

عمرها ما عطتني هدية

ʕəmər-ha	ma	ʕətˤa-t-ni	hədijja
never-her	not	give.perf-she-me	gift

'She never gave me a gift.'

عمري ما حبيت هاللعبة

ʕəmr-i	ma	ħabb-eet	h-al-ləʕba
ever-me	not	like.perf-I	this-the-game

'I never liked this game.'

5.8.1.8 *Pronoun suffixes of prepositions*

كله بسببها

kəll-ah	mən-ha.
all-it	from-her

'It is all because of her.'

بتطلعين وياي؟

bə-tə-tˤləʕ-iin	wijjaa-j ?
will-you.f-go.out.imperf-you.f	with-me

'Will you go out with me?'

بتشترين نفسي؟

bə-tə-ʃtər-iin	nafs-i?
will-you.f-buy.imperf-you.f	like-me

'Will you buy like what I bought?'

Note that object pronoun suffixes are never independent. Thus, in the following sentences, it is necessary to repeat the preposition to host the second-object pronoun:

ينعاد علينا و عليكم بالخير

jə-nʕaad	ʕalee-naa	w	ʕalee-kum	b-əl-xeer.
it-pass.return	on-us	and	on-you.pl	with-the-goodness

'May we and you celebrate it again with goodness.'/'(Wishing) Many good returns of the occasion.'

منا و منكم صالح الاعمال

mənn-a w mən-kum sˤaaləħ əl-ʔaʕmaal.

from-us and from-you righteous the-deeds

'From us and you the righteousness of deeds (idiomatic wish expression).'

5.8.1.9 *Resumptive pronouns*

Object pronoun suffixes also function as the resumptive pronouns, commonly used in the construction of relative clauses (Chapter 12).

الكتاب اللي اشتريته أمس غالي

lə-ktaab ʔəlli əʃtaree-t-ah ʔams ɣaali.

the-book that refl.buy.perf-I-it yesterday expensive

'The book that I bought yesterday is expensive.'

5.8.2 Possessive pronouns

The set of possessive pronouns is almost homographic with that of (objective) suffixed pronouns (Section 5.8.1.2) (Table 5.65).

5.8.3 Reflexive pronouns

There are three major reflexive pronouns in Emirati Arabic: روح ruuħ, عمر ʕəmr, and نفس nafs. These are suffixed with possessive pronouns (Section 5.8.2).

طرشت رسالة لعمري

tˤarraʃ-t rəsala l-ʕəmr-i.

send.perf-I letter to-self-my

'I sent a letter to myself.'

كتبت كتاب عن نفسي

kətab-t ktaab ʕan nafs-i

write.perf-I book about self-my

'I wrote a book about myself.'

Table 5.65 Possessive pronouns

ـي/يا	-i/j(a)	'my'	كتابي	ktaab-i	طاولتي	tˤaawl-ti
ـك	-(ə)k	'your'	كتابك	ktaab-ək	طاولتك	tˤaawl-tək
ـج	-(ə)ʧ	'your (f)'	كتابج	ktaab-əʧ	طاولتج	tˤaawl-ətʃ
ـه	-(a)h	'his'	كتابه	ktaab-ah	طاولته	tˤaawlə-tah
ـها	-(ə)ha	'her'	كتابها	ktaab-ha	طاولتها	tˤaawlə-tha
ـنا	-(ə)na	'our'	كتابنا	ktaab-na	طاولتنا	tˤaawlə-tna
ـكم	-(ə)kum	'your (pl)'	كتابكم	ktaab-kum	طاولتكم	tˤaawlə-tkum
ـكم ـكن	-(ə)kum -(ə)kən	'your (f.pl)'	كتابكن	ktaab-kən	طاولتكن	tˤaawlə-tkən
ـهم	-(ə)hum	'their'	كتابهم	ktaab-hum	طاولتهم	tˤaawl-thum
ـهم ـهن	-(ə)hum -(ə)hən	'their (f)'	كتابهن	ktaab-hən	طاولتهن	tˤaawl-thən

صب الشاي الحار على نفسه

sˤabb	ətʃ-tʃaaj	əl-ħaar	ʕala	nafs-ah
spill.perf-he	the-tea	the-hot	on	self-his

'He spilled the hot tea on himself.'

غسلت روحي أحسن عن أمي

ɣassal-t	ruuħ-i	ʔa-ħsan	ʕan	ʔumm-i.
caus.wash.perf-I	self-my	more-good	from	mom-my

'I washed myself better than my mom.'

In addition, reflexivity may be conveyed with the use of some of the verb forms (Sections 5.2 and 5.8.3).

5.8.4 Demonstrative pronouns

Demonstrative pronouns possess distinct forms for proximal (i.e. close to speaker) and distal (i.e. far from speaker) referents. They are inflected for number and gender (Table 5.66).

Table 5.66 Demonstrative pronouns

Proximal					
Singular				*Plural*	
هذا/ها	haaða/ ha-	'this'	ها/هذيل/ هاييل	ha/haaðeel/ haajeel	'these (m)'
هاي	haaj	'this (f)'	ها/هذيل/ هاييل	ha-, haðeel/ hajeel	'these (f)'
Distal					
Singular				Plural	
هذاك	haaðaak	'that'	هذيلاك/ هاييلاك	haaðeelaak/ haajeelaak	'those'
هاذيج/ هاييج	haaðiitʃ/ haajiitʃ	'that (f)'	هذيل/هاييل	haaðeel(a)/ haajeel(a)	'those (f)'

شو ها؟
ʃuu haa?
what this
'What is this?'

عطني ها
ʕatˤ-ni haa!
give.imp-me that
'Give me that!'

مابا هييل
maa-ba haajeel.
not-I-want.imperf those
'I don't want those.'

ها ما يبشر بالخير
haa ma jbaʃʃər b-əl-xeer.
this not caus.bode.perf with-the-good
'This is not good.'

Demonstratives also express the deictic function by combining with a definite noun phrase (Section 6.1.1).

أحب هالجواتي
ʔa-ħəb ha-dʒ-dʒəwaati.
I-like.imperf these-the-shoe.pl
'I like these shoes.'

أحمد خذ هالسيارة الحمرا
ʔaħmad xað ha-s-sajjaara əl-ħamra.
Ahmad take.perf-he this-the-car the-red.f
'Ahmad bought this red car.'

Finally, demonstrative pronouns are used to refer to an event. Consider the following exchange:

أ: أحمد قال انه لازم نطلع من وقت

ʔaħmad	gaal	ʔənnah	laazəm	nə-tˤlaʕ	mən	wagt.
Ahmad	say.perf-he	that	must	we-leave.imperf	from	time

A: 'Ahmad said that we should leave early.'

ب: أنا ما وافقت عها

ʔana	maa	waafag-t	ʕa-haa.
I	not	agree.perf-I	on-this

B: 'I didn't agree to that (i.e. we should leave early).'

Further reading

There has been very limited research into the properties of individual lexical and functional categories in Emirati Arabic and Gulf Arabic. General descriptions of categories in MSA and other Arabic dialects may be found in Holes (2004a) and Versteeghet al. (2006). For Gulf Arabic, the available grammars provide general descriptions (Qafisheh, 1977; Holes, 1990; Feghali, 2008). For a survey of quadriliteral roots in Gulf Arabic, refer to Holes (2004b) and Albader (2016). Qafisheh (1977) provides a detailed (albeit dated) description of the inflectional morphology of Gulf Arabic verbs, including sound and weak verbs. Al Kaabi and Ntelitheos (2019) discuss the various verb forms in Emirati Arabic. A discussion of morphology of Emirati and Gulf Arabic in general may also be found in Hoffiz (1995), Holes (2005), and Al Kaabi (2015), among others. Caubert (1991) and Persson (2006) discuss the properties of the active participles in Gulf Arabic. Brustad (2000) describes the demonstrative and quantification systems of the related Kuwaiti Arabic dialect.

Notes

1 The comparative adjective أحسن ʔaħsan 'better' may be the only exception to the rule.
2 The Arabic script for cardinal and ordinal numerals adopts MSA spelling to the extent that the script and actual pronunciation can be completely independent. This is especially true for the numerals احد عشر ħidaʕʃ 'eleven' to تسعة عشر təsəʕtˤaʕʃ 'nineteen,' and مائة ʔəmja

'hundred.' In contrast, it is considered unusual to adopt dialectal writing for numerals.

3 The emergence of [tˤ] potentially stems from its historical relation with ة Taa marbuta in MSA, which in general is pronounced as [-ah] word-finally and [-t] non-word-finally. The numerals 'three' to 'ten' contain a word-final Taa marbuta in MSA, e.g. ثلاثة 'three' and تسعة 'nine.' The fact that the numerals 'three' to 'nine' in Emirati Arabic do not contain a word-final [t] may be the result of some phonological rule (e.g. word-final deletion). On the other hand, it is plausible to hypothesize that the underlying phoneme /-t/ can emerge if it is not word-final/pausal, which is the case for the numerals 'thirteen' to 'nineteen.' A further emphatic spread from ع [ʕ] of the suffix may cause the pharyngealization of [t] to become [tˤ]. For a detailed discussion of the pronunciation of Taa marbuta in MSA, see Ryding (2005, pp. 21–24).

Chapter 6

The noun phrase

The noun phrase is the syntactic constituent of the sentence that contains the noun as a head and all its satellites (i.e. modifying items). We assume here the more traditional definition of a noun phrase as consisting of the head noun and its satellites, including definiteness and specificity markers such as determiners and demonstratives, modifiers such as adjectives, and other numerical expressions. Noun phrases occupy specific slots in the sentence, functioning as grammatical subjects, direct and indirect objects of verbs, or complements of prepositions. Some examples of noun phrases are provided in the following sentences:

الكوفي أقوى من الشاي

əl-koofi	ʔa-gwa	mən	ətʃ-tʃaaj.
the-coffee	more-strong	than	the-tea

'Coffee is stronger than tea.'

خلا لي قطعة كيك

xallaa-li	gətˤʕa-t	keek.
leave.perf-for.me	piece-f	cake

'He left me a piece of cake.'

في شوية سيايير في الشارع

fii	ʃwajj-at	səjaajiir	f-əʃ-ʃaarəʕ.
there.is	few-f	cars	on-the-road

'There are few cars on the road.'

وصلنا البيت وقت اللي كانو ياكلون

wəsˤal-na	l-beet	wagt	ʔəlli	kaan-aw	j-aakl-uun.
arrive.perf-we	to-the-house	time	that	be.perf-they	they-eat.imperf-they

'We arrived at the house when they were eating.'

Adjectives and numerals are sometimes used in the same positions without an accompanying nominal (cf. English 'the rich' and 'I just bought two'). In such use of substantives, we may assume either that the grammatical category of the target word is a noun (i.e. a deadjectivized or de-numeralized noun), or that the adjective/numeral modifies an unpronounced generic noun (e.g. 'person' or 'thing'). For the latter option, the referent of the generic noun can be recovered by the context (Section 16.3).

في ثلاثة في الحديقة

fii	θalaaθa	f-əl-ħadiiqa.
there.is	three	in-the-garden

'There are three (people) in the garden.'

أي سيارة عيبتك، الحمرة والا الزرقة؟

ʔaj	sajjaara	ʕiibat-k,	əl-ħamra	wəlla	əz-zarga?
which	car	like.perf-you	the-red.f	or	the-blue.f

'Which car did you like, the red (one) or the blue (one)?'

The term *noun satellite* refers to nominal modifiers such as adjectives, numerals, quantifiers, partitivity markers, determiners/articles, demonstratives, relative clauses, and modifying prepositional phrases. These follow in most cases a specific linear order, discussed in Section 6.7. The following sections describe each type of noun modifiers and discuss their distribution within the noun phrase.

6.1 Definiteness

Traditional Arabic grammars divide nouns into definite and indefinite, a standard dichotomy in most languages. However, morphological definiteness does not always coincide with semantic definiteness and the presence of a definiteness marker interacts with specificity, animacy, and pragmatic factors. In Emirati Arabic, noun phrases are morphologically marked as definite, while indefinite noun phrases are morphologically unmarked (or zero-marked). Indefinite nouns provide new information to the addressee, whereas the definite marker الـ əl- 'the,' indicates, in most cases, that the referent is salient to the discourse participants.

أبا أطرش حقنا أربع رسايل الأسبوع الياي

ʔa-ba ʔa-tˤarrəʃ ħag-na ʔarbaʕ rəsaajəl əl-əsbuuʕ əl-jaaj.

I-want.imperf I-caus.send.imperf for-us four letters the-week the-next

'I want to send us four letters next week.'

الأربع رسايل وصلن أمس

əl-ʔarbaʕ rəsaajəl wəsˤlˤ-an ʔams.

the-four letters arrive.perf-they.f yesterday

'The four letters arrived yesterday.'

6.1.1 *Definite noun phrases*

Definiteness is usually indicated by the definite determiner prefix الـ əl-/l-, which may be further subject to allophonic variation. The definiteness prefix is phonologically conditioned: الـ əl-/l- is prefixed to its following noun with a 'moon' initial consonant, while the prefix undergoes assimilation with the initial consonant of the following noun if this consonant is a 'sun' (i.e. coronal) consonant (Chapter 3).

كتاب	kətaab	'book'	الكتاب	əl-ktaab	'the book'
مدرسة	madrəsa	'school'	المدرسة	əl-madrəsa	'the school'
طفاية	tˤaffaaja	'ashtray'	الطّفاية	ətˤ-tˤaffaaja	'the ashtray'
شاي	ʧaaj	'tea'	الشاي	əʧ-ʧaaj	'the tea'
دلّة	dalla	'coffee pot'	الدّلة	əd-dalla	'the coffee pot'

Additionally, definiteness may be expressed by possession, expressed with the genitive structure إضافة idˤaafa 'construct state' (Section 6.2.1). A simple way of marking definiteness in this way is by attaching a possessive suffix (Section 5.8.2) to the possessor.

أخواني	أمّج	ربيعتها
ʔəxwaan-i	ʔumm-əʧ	rəbiiʕat-ha
brothers-my	mother-your.f	friend-her
'my brothers'	'your mother'	'her friend'

That the noun phrases in these examples are interpreted as definite is confirmed by the appearance of definiteness marking on the modifying adjective (Section 5.3), such as الجديدة əljədiida ‘new’ in the following sentence:

راويتها سيارتي الجديدة.

raawee-t-ha sajjaart-i l-jədiid-a.
show.perf-I-her car.f-my the-new-f
‘I showed her my new car.’

In certain environments the presence of the definite determiner is required by the syntactic context. Thus, in partitive constructions, the quantifier (e.g. كل kəl ‘all’) (Section 5.6.5) is always followed by a definite noun phrase, regardless of specificity.

كل الطلاب قدّمَو الامتحان و وايد منهم نجحَو

kəl ətˤ-tˤəlˤlˤaab gaddəm-aw l-əmtəħaan w waajəd mən-hum nəʤħ-aw.
all the-students take.perf-they the-exam and a.lot of-them pass.perf-they
‘All students took the exam and most of them passed.’

نص الطلاب سيدة روحو

nəsˤsˤ ətˤ-tˤəlˤlˤaab siida rawwəħ-aw.
half the-student.pl immediately leave.perf-they
‘Half of the students left immediately.’

أكثر الماي يستخدمونه حق هالغسالة

ʔakθar əl-maaj jə-staxdəm-uuna ħag h-al-ɣassaala.
much the-water they-refl.use.imperf-they for this-the-washing.machine
‘Much of the water is used for this washing machine.’

بشرب شوي من عصير الفواكه اللي اشتريته

ba-ʃrab ʃwajj mən ʕasˤiir əl-fawaakəh ʔəlli əʃtəree-t-a.
will-I-drink.imperf some of juice the-fruit.pl that refl.buy.perf-you-it
‘I will drink some of the fruit juice that you bought.’

وايد من ربيعاتي روحن بسرعة

waajəd mən rəbiiʕaat-i rawwəħ-an b-sərʕa.
many of friends-my leave.perf-they.fem with-speed
‘Many of my friends left early.’

This is also true of partitives formed by a numeral.

ثلاث من السيايير بنبيعهم بسرعة

θalaaθ mən əs-səjaajiir bə-n-biiʕ-hum b-sərʕa.
three of the-cars will-we-sell.imperf-them with-speed
'Three of the cars, we will sell them quickly.'

شفت ثلاثة من الأولاد

tʃəf-t θalaaθa mən əl-awlaad.
see.perf-I three from the-boys
'I saw three of the boys.'

شافت ثلاثة من ربايعي

tʃaaf-at θalaaθa mən rbaajʕ-i.
see.perf-she three of friends-my
'She saw three friends of mine.'

Finally, negative partitivity is usually expressed with the expression ولا واحد wala waaħəd 'not one,' as in the following examples (Chapter 10):

ولا واحد منهم سار الاجتماع

wala waaħəd mən-hum saar l-ədʒtəmaaʕ.
not one of-them come.perf-he the-meeting
'Not one of them came to the meeting.'

ولا واحد فيهم خلّص الواجب

wala waaħəd fii-hum xalˤlˤasˤ əl-waadʒəb.
not one of-them finish.perf-he the-assignment
'Not one of them finished the assignment.'

It should be noted that partitives may be expressed by count nouns (cf. English 'a piece of cake'). In the following example, the noun الكيك əlkeek 'the cake' is definite:

خلّالي قطعة من الكيك

xallaa-li gətˤʕa mən əl-keek.
leave.perf-for.me piece from the-cake
'He left a piece of the cake for me.'

In contrast, if an indefinite noun phrase follows the quantifier, the construction is not a partitive one, i.e. there is no pre-established set of the entities denoted by the noun phrase in the discourse. Consider the contrast in the following examples:

شفت مجموعة فيلة

tʃəf-t	madʒmuuʕa-t	fjəla.
see.perf-I	group-f	elephants

'I saw some elephants (that happened to be there).'

شفت مجموعة من الفيلة

tʃəf-t	madʒmuuʕa	mən	lə-fjela.
see.perf-I	group	of	the-elephants

'I saw some of the elephants.'

In the first example, there is no pre-established set of elephants familiar to the speaker and the addressee. In the second example with a definite noun phrase, the set of elephants has been established in the preceding discourse and the speaker refers to a part of that specific set. The expression of partitive constructions is considered as formal and close to MSA and is not frequently used in colloquial Emirati Arabic.

In addition to partitives, demonstrative determiners may only modify definite-marked noun phrases independently of position.

هذي/هاي الدريشة		الدريشة هذي/ هاي	
haaði/haaj	əd-dəriiʃa	əd-dəriiʃa	haaði/haaj
this	the-window	the-window	this
'this window'		'this window (in particular)'	

6.1.2 *Indefinite noun phrases*

Indefinite noun phrases are usually unmarked but may be modified by indefinite quantifiers, such as كم من kammin 'some,' وايد waajəd 'many,' and شويّة ʃwajjat 'few' (Section 5.6.5). A syntactic context in which indefinite noun phrases necessarily appear and definite noun phrases are excluded is in existential sentences formed by the existential preposition في fii 'there is' (Section 7.7).

في كتاب عالطاولة

fii	ktaab	ʕa-tˁ-tˁaawla.
there.is	book	on-the-table

'There is a book on the table.'

في ثلاث أشخاص في الحديقة

fii	θalaaθ	ʔaʃxaasˁ	f-əl-ħadiiqa.
there.is	three	persons	in-the-garden

'There are three people in the garden.'

في كم من طالب في الصف

fii	kammən	tˁaalˁəb	f-əsˁ-sˁaf.
there.is	some	students	in-the-classroom

'There are some students in the classroom.'

في وايد كتب عالطاولة

fii	waajəd	kətəb	ʕa-tˁ-tˁaawla.
there.is	a.lot	books	on-the-table

'There are many books on the table.'

في شويّة سيايير في الشارع

fii	ʃwajjat	səjaajiir	f-əʃ-ʃaareʕ.
there.is	few	cars	on-the-road.

'There are few cars on the road.'

Indefinite noun phrases may be used predicatively. In the following examples, the noun phrase denotes the property which functions as the predicate for the sentential subject:

أحمد دكتور

ʔaħmad	dəktoor.
Ahmad	doctor

'Ahmad is a doctor.'

أنا أعتبره عالم

ʔana	ʔa-ʕtəbr-ah	ʕaaləm.
I	I-consider.imperf-him	scientist

'I consider him a scientist.'

مارلن براندو كان ممثل حقيقي

maarlən	braandoo	kaan	mumaθθəl	ħaqiiqi.
Marlon	Brando	be.perf-he	actor	real

'Marlon Brando was a real actor.'

Indefinites sometimes implore the numeral واحد waaħəd 'one' (Section 5.6.5) to refer to an indefinite specific entity, sometimes interpreted as 'a certain.' The following is one such example, although native speakers prefer to omit واحد waaħəd if the indefinite noun phrase is nonspecific:

راحت حق واحد خبير

raaħ-at	ħagg	waaħəd	xabiir.
go.perf-she	to	one	expert

'She went to a (certain) expert.'

In any case, واحد waaħəd seems to modify only human nouns. By contrast, abstract, mass, collective, and generic nouns require the definite determiner marker.

الشاي غالي هالأيام

ətʃ-tʃaaj	ɣaali	ha-l-ʔajjaam.
the-tea	expensive	these-the-days

'Tea is expensive these days.'

مب كل الناس تعرف انه البوش يسون لبن

mub kəl ən-naas ət-ʕarf ʔənna əl-booʃ
j-saw-w-ən ləban
not every the-people they-know.imperf that the-camel.pl
they-refl.produce.imperf-they.f milk
'Not everyone knows camels can produce milk.'

الهوش ياكلون أي شي

əl-hooʃ	ja-akl-uun	ʔaj	ʃaj.
the-goats	they-eat.imperf-they	any	thing

'Goats eat anything.'

As can be seen in the previous examples, singular or plural generic nouns are marked as definite, which is contrary to their English counterparts, as the English translations indicate. This usage extends to some abstract nouns as well.

الصدق أحسن عن الكذب

əsˤ-sˤədg ʔa-ħsan ʕan əl-ʧaðb.
the-truth more-good than the-lie
'Truth is better than lies.'

The situation is not clear with proper names. While many Arabic proper names appear to be preceded by a definite determiner, others are not. The difference seems to be lexically determined.

أنا سرت العراق/السودان/القاهرة/الكويت

ʔana sər-t əl-ʕəraaq /əs-suudaan /əl-qaahəra /əl-kweet.
I go.perf-I the-Iraq /the-Sudan /the-Cairo /the-Kuwait
'I went to Iraq/Sudan/Cairo/Kuwait.'

إنت من عمان/أمريكا/قطر/لبنان/بو ظبي؟

ʔənt mən ʕmaan /ʔamriika /gətˤar /ləbnaan /buu ðˤabi?
you from Oman /America /Qatar /Lebanon /Abu Dhabi
'Are you from Oman/America/Qatar/Lebanon/Abu Dhabi?'

6.2 Possession

6.2.1 إضافة *idˤaafa 'construct state'*

The most frequent type of possessive structures is the so-called إضافة idˤaafa 'construct state,' where a bare nominal possessed is followed by a definite possessor (formed by the definite determiner or a proper name). In contrast with other Arabic dialects, especially those of North Africa, Emirati Arabic shows a strong preference for the use of the إضافة idˤaafa in expressing possession.

أنا بسألكم سؤال، انتو شفتو ملف حسين؟

ʔana ba-sʔal-kum suʔaal ʔənt-u tʃəf-tu malaff ħseen?
I will-I-ask.imperf-you.pl question you-pl see.perf-you.pl file Hosain
'I'll ask you a question, did you see Hussain's file?'

شوفي آمنة، إنتي خذي راي علي و نحن حاضرين

ʧuuf-i ʔaamna ʔənti xəð-i raaj ʕəlii w nəħən ħaaðˤr-iin.

see.imp-you.f Amna you.f take.imp-you.f opinion Ali and we present-we

'Look Amna, you take Ali's opinion, and we will help you.'

أسرار المدير كلها عندك

ʔasraar əl-mudiir kəl-ha ʕənd-ək.

secrets the-manager all-it with-you

'All the manager's secrets are with you.'

Construct states may be embedded inside one another, giving a nested structure in which the definite article is only found on the very last noun.

جمعية حقوق الإنسان

ʤamʕijja-t ħəquuq əl-ʔənsaan

association-f rights the-human

'The Human Rights Association'

The second property of إضافة idˤaafa is that the possessor and possessed must be adjacent. For example, an adjective cannot intervene between the two elements and has to appear at the end of إضافة idˤaafa.

أسرار المدير الكبيرة

ʔasraar əl-mudiir əl-kəbiira

secrets the-manager the-big

'the manager's big secrets'

The post-possessive position of the adjective creates ambiguity, which may be resolved by gender agreement with the head noun. Thus, in the previous examples, if we want the adjective to modify المدير əlmudiir 'the manager' and not الكبيرة ʔasraar 'secrets,' the masculine adjective الكبيرة əlkbiir 'big' is required. Consider also the following examples:

كتاب الطالبة الجديدة			كتاب الطالبة الجديد		
ktaab	ətˤ-tˤaalb-a	əl-jədiid-a	ktaab	ətˤ-tˤaalb-a	əl-jədiid
book	the-student-f	the-new-f	book	the-student-f	the-new
'the new female student's book'			'the (female) student's new book'		

Gender agreement between the feminine noun الطالبة ətˤtˤaalˤba 'the student' and the adjective الجديدة əljidiidah 'new' in the first example, or between the masculine noun كتاب ktaab 'book' and the adjective الجديد əljidiid 'new' in the second example, aids in disambiguating the interpretation. However, if both nouns in the possessive construction are of the same gender then the sentence remains ambiguous.

استعرت كتاب الطالب اليديد

ʔəstaʕar-t	ktaab	ətˤ-tˤaalˤəb	əl-jədiid.
refl.borrow.perf-I	book	the-student	the-new

'I borrowed the new (male) student's book.' or 'I borrowed the (male) student's new book.'

In this example, the adjective الجديد əljidiid 'new' may be interpreted as modifying either 'the student' or 'the book,' as both share the same gender value. A way to disambiguate the sentence would be to use the possessive particle مال maal (Section 6.2.3.1).

الكتاب مال الطالب اليديد

l-əktaab	maal	ətˤ-tˤaaləb	əl-jədiid
the book	poss	the-student	the-new

'the new (male) student's book'

الكتاب اليديد مال الطالب

l-əktaab	əl-jədiid	maal	ətˤ-tˤaaləb
the book	the-new	poss	the-student

'the (male) student's new book'

Finally, possessive structures exhibit word-like properties in that they form a single prosodic unit for the purpose of stress assignment. In addition, the feminine suffix ة- -t (Section 5.8.1.2) mediates between the possessor and the possessed.

المكتبة	في مكتبة الجامعة		
əl-maktəba	f	maktəba-t	əl-jaamʕa
the-library	in	library-f	the-university
'the library'	'in the university library'		

The possessive structure created by إضافة idˤaafa expresses a wide range of semantic relation between the possessor and the possessed (Table 6.1).

Table 6.1 Semantic relations expressed by the construct state

Body parts	عيون ميري الخضرا ʕjuun meeri l-xaðˤra eyes Mary the-green.f 'Mary's green eyes'	إيد أحمد ʔiid ʔaħmad arm Ahmad 'Ahmad's arm'
Familial relationship	ريل ميري rajəl meeri husband Mary 'Mary's husband'	عيال وبنات شيخة ʕjaal w banaat ʃeexa sons and daughters Sheikha 'Sheikha's sons and daughters'
Subordinate relation	رئيس/سكرتير ماري raʔiis/səkərteer meeri boss/secretary Mary 'Mary's boss/secretary'	أستاذ/طالب راشد ʔəstaað/tˤaaləb raaʃəd teacher/student Rashid 'Rashid's teacher/student'
Container	قلاس الماي glˤaasˤ əl-maaj glass the-water 'the glass of water'	علبة الحلاوة ʕəlba-t əl-ħalaawa box-f the-candy 'the box of candy'
Type/kind relation	نوعين الشيبس nooʕ-een əl-ʧəbs kind-du the-chips 'the two kinds of chips'	ماركة السيارة maarka-t əs-sajjaara brand-f the-car 'the car's brand'

(*Continued*)

Table 6.1 (Continued)

Intrinsic properties	حر الصيف ħar əsˤ-sˤeef heat the-summer 'the summer's heat'	طول ووزن علي tˤuul w wazn ʕəlii height and weight Ali 'Ali's height and weight'
Part-whole relation	مفتاح القفل məftaaħ əl-gəfel key the-lock 'the key lock'	ريل الطاولة riil ət-ˤtˤaawla leg the-table 'The table's leg'
Membership	فريق كوب بريانت faariiq koob brəjant team Kobe Bryant 'Kobe Bryant's team'	مدرسة مريم madrəsa-t marjam school-f Mariam 'Mariam's school'
Ownership	كتاب ميري ktaab meeri book Mary 'Mary's book'	بيت راشد beet raaʃəd house Raashid 'Rashid's house'
	أصول الحرب الأولية ʔəsˤuul əl-ħarb əl-ʔawwəlijjah origins the-war the-ancient 'the war's ancient origins'	تاريخ اليابان taariix əl-jaabaan history the-Japan 'Japan's history'
Psychological state	عصبية ميري ʕasˤsˤabijja-t meeri anger-f Mary 'Mary's anger'	زعل احمد zaʕal ʔaħmad sadness Ahmad 'Ahmad's sadness'
Degree	زيادة الاثنين بالمئة zijaada-t lə-θneen bə-l-ʔəmja rise-f the-two in-the-hundred 'the rise of 2%'	رطوبة العشرة بالمئة rətˤuuba-t əl-ʕaʃra bə-l-ʔəmja humidity-f the-ten in-the-hundred '10% humidity'

Age	بنت الخمسة عشر سنة bənt əl-xaməstˁaʕʃar səna girl the-fifteen year 'the girl of 15 years'	تاريخ مئة سنة taariix ʔəmjat səna history hundred year 'history of 100 years'
Event	عملية ميري ʕamalijja-t meeri surgery-f Mary 'Mary's surgery'	اغتيال الرئيس ʔəɣtijaal ər-raʔiis assassination the-president 'president's assassination'
	طباعة الورقة tˁəbaaʕa-t əl-wərga printing-f the-paper 'the paper's printing'	استهلاك المواطنين ʔəstəhlaak əl-mwaatˁniin consumption the-citizens 'the citizens' consumption'

6.2.2 إضافة idˁaafa in verb nominalizations (مَصْدَر masdars)

إضافة idˁaafa also allows the possessed derived from مَصْدَر masdars (Section 5.1.2.7). The possessor in this construction may be definite or indefinite.

تصليح السيارة ياخذ وقت

tasˁliiħ	əs-sajjaara	j-aaxəð	wagt.
fixing	the-car	he-take.imperf	time

'Fixing the car takes time.'

تدمير الأمّة يبدا بشبابها

tadmiir	əl-ʔummah	jə-bda	b-ʃabaab-ha.
destruction	the-nation	he-start.imperf	with-youth-her

'The nation's destruction starts with their youth.'

أكل تفاحة يومياً زين للصحة

ʔakəl	təffaaħa	kəl	joom	zeen	l-əsˤ-sˤəħħa.
eating	apple	every	day	good	for-the-health

'Eating an apple daily is good for health.'

متابعة أفلام الرعب ما منه فايدة

mtaabaʕat	ʔaflaam	ər-ruʕb	maa	mənn-ha	faajda.
watching	movies	the-horror	not	from-it	good

'Watching horror movies is no good.'

6.2.3 *Analytic possessive structure*

6.2.3.1 *The linking particle* مال *maal*

Possession may be additionally expressed with a preposition-like linking particle مال maal which stems from a nominal origin (lit. 'property,' 'possessions,' or 'money'). مال maal may be used independently and sandwiched between the possessor and the possessed. It may also be suffixed by the personal suffixes which denote the grammatical (e.g. gender and number) features of the possessor.

مال maal with the possessed which is masculine

مالي	maali	'mine'	مالها	maalha	'hers'
مالك	maalək	'yours'	مالنا	maalna	'ours'
مالج	maaləʧ	'yours (f)'	مالهم	maalhum	'theirs'
ماله	maalah	'his'			

مال maal with the possessed which is feminine

مالتي	maalti	'mine'	مالته	maaltah	'his'
مالتيه	malatja	'mine'	مالتها	maalatha	'hers'
مالتك	maalatk	'yours'	مالتنا	maalatna	'ours'
مالتج	maalaʧ	'yours (f)'	مالتهن	maalathən	'theirs (f)'
مالتكم	maalatkum	'yours (pl)'			

مال maal with the possessed which is plural

مالاتي/ماليلي	maaleeli/ maalaati	'mine/ (f)'	ماله/ماليله	maaleelah/ maalah	'his'
مالك	maalək	'yours'	مالها/ماليلها	maaleelha/ maalha	'hers'
مالج	maaləʧ	'yours (f)'	مالنا/ماليلنا	maaleelna/ maalna	'ours'
مالكم/ماليلكم	maaleelkom/ maalkum	'yours (pl)'	مالهم/ماليلهم	maaleelhum/ maalhum	'theirs'

The possessive structure formed by مال maal is usually predicative—it describes the property which is true of the subject.

يعني مب مالي

jaʕni mub maal-i.

mean not poss-me

'So, it's not mine.'

أخوي مفتاح ذكرني أنا ناسي هالدّبّاسة مالتي و لا مالتهم؟

ʔuxuu-j məftaaħ ðakkərn-i ʔana naasi h-ad-dabbaasa maal-t-i wəlla maal-at-hum?

brother-my Moftah remind-me I forget this-the-stapler poss-f-me or poss-f-them

'Brother Moftah, remind me, is this stapler mine or theirs?'

In some cases, the possessive structures formed by مال maal functions as an argument.

و تعطيه التلفون مالي

. . . uu t-aʕtˤii-h ət-təlfoon maal-i.

. . . and you-give.imperf-him the-phone poss-my

' . . . and give him my phone . . . '

مال maal is very productive with loanwords:

البرنامج مال التلفزيون مال الرياضة

əl-barnaaməʤ maal ət-talfəzoon maal ər-rijaaðˤa

the-program poss the-television poss the-sport

'the television sports program'

الامتحان مال الانجليزي

l-əmtəħaan maal l-əngəliizii
the-test poss the-English
'the English test'

The possessive structures formed by مال maal seem to be favored in cases where the structure is ambiguous. In the following example, the adjective 'big' unambiguously modifies the possessee 'house' because the particle مال maal separates it from the possessor:

البيت الكبير مال ربيعي

əl-beet əl-kəbiir maal rəbiiʕ-i
the-house the-big poss friend-my
'my friend's big house'

6.2.3.2 *The preposition حقّ ħagg 'for'*

The preposition حقّ ħagg 'for' may sometimes function as a possessive marker. The possessive structure generated functions as a predicate, as well as the possessive meaning, tends to be benefactive.

هالكتاب حقّ أحمد

ha-lə-ktaab ħagg ʔaħmad.
this-the-book for Ahmad
'This book is for Ahmad (e.g. as a result of transfer of ownership).'

يعني مب حقّك

jaʕni mub ħagg-ək.
mean not for-your
'So, it's not for you.'

Overall, the use of حقّ ħagg cannot function as a subject or an object in the sentence. For cases such as 'Ahmad's book' or 'Mariam's house,' the possessive structures generated by إضافة idˤaafa and مال maal should be used.

Moreover, حقّ ħagg mostly functions as a benefactive or purposive preposition (Section 5.5).

محمد حطها فالشنطة حقها

mħammad	ħatˤ-ha	f-əʃ-ʃantˤa	ħagg-ha.
Mohammed	put.imp-it	in-the-bag	for-her

'Mohammed, put it in the bag for her.'

أنا بشتريه حق عمري عندي فلوس

ʔana	ba-ʃtərii-h	ħagg	ʕəmr-i	ʕənd-i	fluus.
I	will-I-buy.imperf-it	for	self-my	with-me	money

'I will buy it for myself, I have money.'

يشتغل سوّاق حق الكلّية

jə-ʃtəɣəlˤ	sawwaag	ħagg	əl-kəlləjja.
he-work.imperf	driver	for	the-college

'He works as a driver for the college.'

6.2.4 *Possessive suffixation*

A common strategy for expressing possession is to suffix possessive affixes to the possessed (Section 5.8.2). The following lists the paradigm of available possessive suffixes, and some examples:

ـي	-i/j(a)	كتابي	ktaab-i	'my book'
ـك	-ak/-ək	كتابك	ktaab-ək	'your book'
ـج	-atʃ/-ətʃ	كتابج	ktaab-ətʃ	'your (f) book'
ـه	-a(h)	كتابه	ktaab-ah	'his book'
ـها	-ha/-aha	كتابها	ktaab-ha	'her book'
ـنا	-na/-ana	كتابنا	ktaab-na	'our book'
ـكم	-kum/-akum	كتابكم	ktaab-kum	'your (pl) book'
ـكن	-kən/-akən	كتابكن	ktaab-kən	'your (f.pl) book'
ـهم	-hum/-ahum	كتابهم	ktaab-hum	'their (m.pl) book'
ـهن	-hən/-ahən	كتابهن	ktaab-hən	'their (f.pl) book'

Possessive affixes mark the noun as definite and establish the definiteness agreement with their modifying adjectives (Sections 5.3 and 6.5).

6.3 Appositives

Appositives are noun phrases that immediately follow and modify or rename a noun phrase. Emirati Arabic uses appositives in the same way as other languages.

ربيعي علي سار من وقت

rbiiʕ-i	ʕəli	saar	mən	wagt.
friend-my	Ali	go.perf-he	in	time

'My friend Ali left early.'

كلبي ألفي عمره ثلاث سنوات

ʧalb-i	ʔəlfi	ʕəmr-a	θalaaθ	sana-waat.
dog-my	Alfie	age-his	three	year-f.pl

'My dog Alfie is three years old.'

نحن أهل الخليج نحب البرّ

nəħən	ʔahl	əl-xaliidʒ	n-ħəb	əl-barr.
we	people	the-gulf	we-love.imperf	the-desert

'We, the people of the Gulf, love the desert.'

The appositives may be restrictive or non-restrictive (Chapter 12), depending on the set of denotations of the head noun. For instance, the appositive أخوي ʔuxuuj 'my brother' in the following example suggests that Ali is the only brother the speaker has:

علي أخوي يَا الإجتماع

ʕəli	ʔəxuu-j	jaa	l-əʤtəmaaʕ
Ali	brother-my	come.perf-he	the-meeting

'Ali, my brother, came to the meeting.'

On the other hand, the appositive expression can be restrictive (Chapter 12). For instance, Ali in the following example functions to restrict the denotation of أخوي ʔuxuuj 'my brother' as the head noun, which further suggests that the speaker has more than one brother:

أخوي علي يَا الإجتماع

ʔuxuu-j	ʕəli	jaa	l-əʤtəmaaʕ.
brother-my	Ali	come.perf-he	the meeting

'My brother Ali came to the meeting.'

And, in the following, الأم lʔumm 'the mother' restricts the denotation of الشركة əʃʃərika 'the company':

الشركة الأم باعت المباني

əʃ-ʃərika l-ʔumm baaʕ-at əl-mabaanii.

the-company the-mother sell.perf-she the-building

'The mother company sold the building.'

In addition, proper names can serve as a restrictive appositive. For example:

الرئيس ترامب كلم الناس

ər-raʔiis tramb kallam ən-naas.

the-president Trump speak.perf-he the-people

'President Trump spoke to the people.'

الملكة فكتوريا عاشت قبل سنوات

əl-maləka fəktoorja ʕaaʃ-at gabəl sana-waat.

Queen Victoria live.perf-she before year-f.pl

'Queen Victoria lived many years ago.'

الأوبرا كاتس شافوها أكثر عن مية مليون واحد

əl-ʔoopəra kaats ʧaaf-oo-ha ʔakθar ʕan ʔəmjat maljoon waaħəd.

the-opera cats watch.perf-they-it more than hundred million one

'The opera *Cats* has been watched by more than 100 million people.'

Another usage of appositives is quantificational. In the following example, the quantifier does not restrict the denotation of the head noun—instead, it indicates the quantity (Section 5.6.5):

الناس كلهم قرّرو يسيرون من وقت.

ən-naas kəl-hum qarrər-aw j-siir-uun mən wagt.

the-people all-them decide.perf-they they-go.imperf-they in time

'The people, all of them, decided to leave early.

6.4 Nominal modifiers

A number of elements appear mainly postnominally but also sometimes in a prenominal position, functioning as modifiers of the head noun. We will examine each of these modificational phrases in the following subsections.

6.4.1 Adjectival phrases

In Emirati Arabic, as in other Arabic dialects, adjectives appear in a postnominal position.

شفت طالب ذكي

ʧəf-t	tˤaaləb	ðaki.
meet.perf-I	student	clever

'I met a clever student.'

شفت طالب انجليزي يديد ذكي

ʧəf-t	tˤaalˤəb	ʔəngəliizi	jdiid	ðaki.
meet.perf-I	student	English	new	clever

'I met a new, clever English student.'

There are no prenominal adjectives, and even non-predicative, attributive-only adjectives appear postnominally. All adjectives in the following examples are attributive in that they cannot appear as predicates (i.e. it is not possible to say, 'The engineer is electric' or 'The role is main'). In many other languages, such as the Romance languages, attributive-only adjectives appear in a prenominal position in languages with postnominal adjectives, but they clearly cannot in Emirati Arabic.

المدير الجديم

əl-mudiir	əl-dʒediim
the-director	the-old

'the former director'

الدور الرئيسي

əd-door	ər-raʔiisi
the-role	the-main

'the main role'

المجرم المتّهم

əl-mudʒrəm	əl-muttaham
the-criminal	the-alleged

'the alleged criminal'

مهندس كهربا

muhandəs	kahrəba
engineer	electrical

'electrical engineer'

An adjective can appear in a prenominal position only if it is in the superlative form (Section 5.3.5).

أذكى طالب		أطول بنت	
ʔa-ðka	tˤaalˤəb	ʔa-tˤwal	bənt
most-clever	student	most-tall	girl
'the cleverest student'		'the tallest girl'	

Quite often, attributive adjectives function as head nouns (cf. English 'the rich' and 'the impossible'). Given that adjectives agree with their head nouns with respect to number and gender, and that noun ellipsis is productive in Emirati Arabic (Section 16.3) when the relevant context facilitates the recovery of the elided noun, it may be difficult to distinguish between adjectives and nouns as distinct grammatical categories. Consider the following examples:

الأغنياء عطَوْ الفقارة فلوس

əl-ʔaɣnəja	ʕatˤ-aw	əl-fqaara	fluus.
the-rich.pl	give.perf-they	the-poor	money

'The rich offered money to the poor.'

الصغارية مرّات ما يحترمون الكبار

əsˤ-sˤɣaar-ijja	marraat	maa	jə-ħtarm-oon	lə-kbaar.
the-young-pl	sometimes	not	they-respect.imperf-they	the-elderly.pl

'The young sometimes have no respect for the old.'

الحلوين دايماً ينجحون في الحياة

əl-ħəlw-iin	daajman	jə-ndʒəħ-uun	fə-l-ħayaa.
the-beautiful-pl	always	they-succeed.imperf-they	in-the-life

'The beautiful always succeed in life.'

الناس دايماً يخافون من المجهول

ən-naas	daajman	j-xaaf-uun	mən	əl-madʒhuul.
the-people	always	they-fear.imperf-they	from	the-unknown

'People always fear the unknown.'

It remains unclear if these adjectives are de facto nouns or if they modify 'silent' (i.e. unpronounced) generic nouns such as 'person,' 'thing,' and so on.

6.4.2 *Participles in noun phrases*

The attributive function of adjectives in the formation of noun phrases may also be expressed by the use of active and passive participles (Sections 5.2 and 5.3.2). Both active and passive participles may function attributively.

طيارة ورقية طايرة

tˤajjaara	waragij-ja	tˤaajr-a
plane	paper-f	part.fly-f

'A flying kite'

الريال المار

ər-rajjaal	əl-maar
the-man	the-part.pass

'the passing man'

القطوة الشاردة

əl-gatˤwa	əʃ-ʃaard-a
the-cat	the-part.run.away-f

'the runaway cat'

الوردة الطايحة

əl-warda	ətˤ-tˤaajħ-a
the-flower	the-part.fall.down-f

'the fallen flower'

قلم مفرور

galam	ma-fruur
pen	part-pass.throw.perf

'a thrown pen'

بناية مكسّرة

bnaaja	m-kassar-a
building	part-pass.break.perf-f

'a destroyed building'

قميص مغسل

gəmiisˤ	m-ɣassal
shirt	part-pass.wash.perf

'a washed shirt'

دريشة مكسورة

dəriiʃa	ma-ksuur-a
window	part-pass.break.perf-f

'a broken window'

موظف مستقيل

muwaðˤðˤaf	mə-stəqiil
employee	part-pass.refl.resign.perf

'a resigned employee'

اقتصاد متدمر

əqtəsˤaad	mə-ddammər
economy	part-refl.destroy.perf

'a destroyed economy'

6.4.3 *Demonstratives*

Two types of demonstratives express distal properties, namely, هذي haaða 'this' for proximal entities, and هذاك haaðaak 'that' for distal entities (Section 5.8.4).

هالكتاب	هالبنت
h-al ktaab	h-al bənt
this-the book	this-the girl
'this book' (masculine)	'this girl' (feminine)

هاذيلا الكتب	هذيلا البنات
haaðeela əl-kətəb	haaðeela əl-banaat
these the-books	these the-girls
'these books'	'these girls'

هاذاك الكتاب	هاذيج البنت
haaðaak əl-ktaab	haaðiitʃ əl-bənt
that the-book	that the-girl
'that book'	'that girl'

هاذيلاك الكتب	هاذيلاك البنات
haaðeelak əl-kətəb	haaðeelak əl-banaat
those the-books	those the-girls
'those books'	'those girls'

The demonstrative is placed before or after the noun it modifies and is accompanied by a definite noun phrase prefixed with the determiner الـ əl- 'the.'

هذي الدريشة	الدريشة هذي
haaði əd-diriiʃa	əd-diriiʃa haaði
this the-window	the-window this
'this window'	'this window'

هالكتاب وايد حلو	الكتاب ها وايد حلو
h-al ktaab waajəd ħəlu.	lə-ktaab haa waajəd ħəlu.
this-the book very good	the-book this very good
'This book is very good.'	'This book is very good.'

هاي البنت مجتهدة
haaj əl-bənt məʤtahd-a.
this the-girl hardworking-f
'This girl is hardworking.'

البنت هاي مجتهدة
əl-bənt haaj məʤtahd-a.
the-girl this hardworking-f
'This girl is hardworking.'

هاذاك القميص مريح
haaðaak əl-qamiisˤ muriiħ.
that the-shirt comfortable
'That shirt is comfortable.'

القميص هاذاك مريح
əl-qamiisˤ haaðaak muriiħ.
the-shirt that comfortable
'That shirt is comfortable.'

هاذيج/هاييج البنت حلوة
haaðiiʧ/haajiiʧ əl-bənt ħəlw-a.
that.f the-girl beautiful-f
'That girl is beautiful.'

البنت هاذيج/هاييج حلوة
əl-bənt haaðiiʧ/haajiiʧ ħəlw-a.
the-girl that.f beautiful-f
'That girl is beautiful.'

The proximal demonstratives, هذا haaða 'this' and هذيلا haaðeela 'these,' can be contracted to become the prefix -ها ha-, although the non-contracted variant is also available.

هالكتاب/هذا الكتاب وايد ممتع
ha-l-əktaab/haaða-l-əktaab waajəd mumtəʕ.
this-the-book very interesting
'This book is very interesting.'

مابا هالكتب/هذيلا الكتب
maa-ba ha-l-kətəb/haðeela-əl-kətəb.
not-I-want.imperf these-the-books
'I don't want these books.'

توني اشتريت هالسيّارتين/هذيلا السّيارتين
taw-ni əʃtəree-t ha-s-sajjaart-een/haðeela-s-sajjaart-een.
just-me refl.buy.perf-I these-the-car-du
'I just bought these two cars.'

In contrast, it is not common for هذاك haaðaak 'that' to be contracted to a prefix. Occasionally, the contraction form هاك haak is heard, but it is usually understood as the expression 'take that thing.' The plural distal demonstrative هذيلاك haaðeelak 'those' is never contracted.

هذاك البيت مال أحمد/هاك البيت مال أحمد

haaðaak/haak	əl-beet	maal	ʔaħmad.
that	the-house	poss	Ahmad

'That house is Ahmad's.'

هذيلاك الطاولات مالاتي

haaðeelaak	ətˤ-tˤaawl-aat	maal-aat-i.
those	the-table-pl	poss-f.pl-me

'Those tables are mine.'

Demonstratives may also be used as deictic pronouns with no accompanying noun, in which case they refer either to an entity in the immediate environment in a deictic sense, or to a generic interpretation meaning 'person' or 'thing.'

ها/هذا ما منّه فايدة

haa/haaða	maa	mən-na	faajda.
this	not	from-him	use

'This (person/thing) is useless.'

هذا/ها عدو لكن هذاك ربيع

haaða/haa	ʕədu	laakən	haaðaak/ðaak	rbiiʕ.
this	enemy	but	that	friend

'This (person) is an enemy but that (person) is a friend.'

لألوان السّيارات لازم تختار يا هذا أو هذاك

l-ʔalwaan	əs-sajjaar-aat	laazəm	t-əxtaar	jaa
haaða/haa	ʔaw	haaðaak/ðaak.		
for-colors	the-car-f.pl	should	you-choose.imperf	either
this	or	that		

'For car colors you should either go with this or with that.'

Finally, in reference to events or utterances previously mentioned in the discourse, the proximal demonstrative هذا haaða, rather than the distal one, is used.

لا، إنت خطّطه/خطّطت هذا

laa,	ʔənt/ʔənta	xatˤtˤatˤ-t-a	/xatˤtˤatˤ-t	haaða.
no	you	arrange.perf-you-it	arrange.perf-you	this

'No, you arranged it/that (e.g. a meeting, a party).'

توافق عليه/على هذا؟

t-waafəg	ʕəleeh/ʕala	haaða?
you-agree	on-it/on	this

'Do you agree with that (e.g. we should leave early)?'

6.4.4 *Quantifiers*

Various quantificational elements may combine with the head noun. In non-partitive contexts these quantifiers precede the noun without the presence of the definiteness marker ال əl- 'the' (Section 5.6.5).

وايد طلّاب

waajəd	tˤəlˤlˤaab
many	students

'many students'

وايد كتب

waajəd	kətəb
a.lot	books

'a lot of books'

Negative quantification is not expressed at the noun phrase level; instead, the sentential negation configuration is used (Chapter 10).

ما شفت طلّاب في الصّف

maa	ʧəf-t	tˤəlˤlˤaab	f-əsˤ-sˤaff.
not	see.perf-I	students	in-the-classroom

'I saw no students in the classroom.'

6.4.5 *Numerals*

The cardinal numerals (Section 5.6.1) 'three' and above precede the noun they modify.

ثلاث أولاد

θalaaθ	awlaad
three	boys

'three boys'

سبع بناطلين

sabəʕ	bənaatˤl-iin
seven	trouser-pl

'seven (pairs of) trousers'

عشر ربايع
ʕashər rəbaayəʕ
ten friends
'ten friends'

Ordinal numerals (Section 5.6.2) also appear prenominally.

أوّل سيّارة	ثاني وجبة
ʔawwal sajjaara	θaani wadʒba
first car	second meal
'first car'	'second meal'

In most cases, the ordinal numeral appears before the cardinal numeral.

أوّل ثلاث سندويجات
ʔawwal θalaaθ sandəwiitʃ-aat
first three sandwich-f.pl
'first three sandwiches'

6.5 Agreement in the noun phrase

Most nominal modifiers agree with the head noun in number and gender, while adjectives also carry definiteness agreement. A definite noun is usually followed by a definite adjective carrying the same gender and number features as the noun it modifies.

شفت طالب ذكي	شفت الطّالب الذّكي
tʃəf-t tˤaalˤəb ðaki.	tʃəf-t ətˤ-tˤaalˤəb əð-ðaki.
meet.perf-I student clever	meet.perf-I the-student the-clever
'I met a clever (male) student.'	'I met the clever (male) student.'

شفت طالبة ذكية	شفت الطّالبة الذّكية
tʃəf-t tˤaalˤəb-a ðakijj-a.	tʃəf-t ətˤ-tˤaalˤəb-a əð-ðakijj-a.
meet.imperf-I student-f clever-f	meet.perf-I the-student-f the-clever-f
'I met a clever (female) student.'	'I met the clever (female) student.'

These examples exhibit gender and definiteness agreement on the adjective modifying the preceding noun. The following examples do the same for number agreement:

شفت ثلاث طلّاب أذكياء

ʧəf-t	θalaaθ	tˤəlˤlˤaab	ʔaðkija.
meet.perf-I	three	students	clever.pl

'I met three clever (male) students.'

شفت ثلاث طالبات ذكيّات

ʧəf-t	θalaaθ	tˤaalb-aat	ðakijj-aat.
meet.perf-I	three	student-f.pl	clever-f.pl

'I met three clever (female) students.'

However, there is significant variation in the patterns of agreement acceptable in the distribution of noun-adjective sequences in Emirati Arabic. The variation is subject to a number of parameters, most significantly whether the noun is animate or inanimate and whether it is marked as plural or dual in the context. The following presents all possible combinations that native speakers of Emirati Arabic accept in such contexts. Overall, gender agreement between the noun and adjective is agreed upon by all native speakers. In some cases (e.g. inanimate nouns), a feminine plural noun may be matched by a masculine plural adjectival agreement.

Animate masculine nouns

Singular	m.sg	دكتور ذكي	dəktoor ðaki	'smart professor'
Dual	m.pl	دكتورين اذكيا	dəktooreen ʔaðkija	'two smart professors'
Plural	m.pl	دكاترة اذكيا	dəkatra ʔaðkija	'smart professors'

Animate feminine nouns

Singular	f.sg	دكتورة ذكية	dəktoora ðakijja	'smart (f) professor'
Dual	f.pl	دكتورتين ذكيات	dəktoorteen ðakijjaat	'two smart (f.pl) professors'
Dual	m.pl	دكتورتين اذكيا	dəktoorteen ʔaðkija	'two smart (m.pl) professors'
Plural	f.pl	دكتورات ذكيات	dəktooraat ðakijjaat	'smart (f.pl) professors'

Inanimate masculine nouns

Singular	m.sg	كرسي كبير	kərsi kbiir	'big chair'
Dual	m.pl	كرسيين كبار	kərsijjeen kbaar	'two big chairs'
Plural	m.pl	كراسي كبار	karaasi kbaar	'big chairs'

Inanimate feminine nouns

Singular	f.sg	نظارة غالية	naðˤðˤaara ɣaalja	'expensive (pair of) glasses'
Dual	f.pl	نظارتين غاليات	naðˤðˤaarteen ɣaaljaat	'two pairs of expensive (f.pl) glasses'
Dual	m.pl	نظارتين غاليين	naðˤðˤaarteen ɣaaljiin	'two pairs of expensive (m.pl) glasses'
Plural	f.pl	نظارات غاليات	naðˤðˤaarat ɣaaljaat	'expensive (f.pl) glasses'
Plural	m.pl	نظارات غاليين	naðˤðˤaarat ɣaaljiin	'expensive (m.pl) glasses'

There is no dual form for adjectives—thus, when the noun is in the dual, the adjective appears with plural morphology.

الاستاذين اليداد
əl-ʔəstaað-een əl-jədaad
the-teacher-du the-new.pl
'the two new teachers'

الأساتذة اليداد
əl-ʔasaatða əl-jədaad
the-teacher.pl the-new.pl
'the new teachers'

القلمين الكبار
əl-galam-een əl-kbaar
the-pen-du the-big.pl
'the two big pens

الأقلام الكبار
l-aglaam əl-kbaar
the-pen.pl the-big.pl
'the big pens'

الشغالتين الطوال/الطويلات
əʃ-ʃaɣɣaal-t-een ətˤ-tˤəwaal/ətˤ-tˤəwiil-aat
the-maid-f-du the-tall.pl/the-tall-f.pl
'the two tall (female) maids'

الموظفتين اليداد/اليديدات
əl-mwaððˤˤaf-t-een əl-jədaad/əl-jədiid-aat
the-employee-f-du the-new.pl/the-new-f.pl
'the two new (female) employees'

الشغالات الطوال/الطويلات		الموظفات اليداد/اليديدات	
əʃ-ʃaɣɣaal-aat	ətˤ-tˤəwaal/ ətˤ-tˤəwiil-aat	əl-mwaðˤðˤəf-aat	əl-jədaad/ əl-jədiid-aat
the-maid-f.pl	the-tall.pl/the-tall-f.pl	the-employee-f.pl	the-new.pl/ the-new-f.pl
'the tall (female) maids'		'the new (female) employees'	

هالكتب اليديدة		هالقمصان الغالية	
ha-l-kətəb	əl-jədiid-a	ha-l-gəmsˤaan	əl-ɣaalj-a
these-the-books	the-new-f	these-the-shirts	the-expensive-f
'these new books'		'these expensive shirts'	

Feminine animate nouns require feminine singular adjectives when they are singular. If they are dual or plural, both the feminine plural and masculine plural adjectives may be used in free variation. Some feminine animate nouns, such as حرمة ħərma 'woman' and بنت bənt 'girl,' favor gender agreement with the adjective (i.e. feminine). Feminine inanimate nouns follow the same pattern as their animate counterparts.

المساطر الطويلات/الطوال		الغراش الكبار	
əl-masˤaatˤər	ətˤ-tˤwiil-aat/ ətˤ-tˤwaal	lə-ɣraaʃ	əl-kbaar
this-the-rulers.f	the-long-f.pl/ the-long.m.pl	the-bottles.f	the-big.m.pl
'these long rulers'		'the big bottles'	

الغرشتين الكبار		الأقلام الملونة	
l-ɣarʃət-een	əl-kbaar	l-aglaam	əl-mlawwən-a
the-bottle-f.du	the-big.m.pl	the-pens	the-colored-f
'the two big bottles'		'the colored pens'	

6.6 Demonstratives

In general, demonstratives agree with the head noun in number and gender. The only exception is the same demonstrative هاذيلا haaðeel 'these' is used, regardless of the gender of the head noun.

هذا الطّالب
haaða   ətˤ-tˤaalˤəb
this   the-student
'this (male) student'

هاذي الطّالبة
haaði   ətˤ-tˤaalˤb-a
this.f   the-student-f
'this (female) student'

هاذيلا/هاييل الطّلاب
haaðeela/hajeel   ətˤ-tˤəlˤlˤaab
these   the-students
'these (male) students'

هاذيلا/هاييل الطّالبات
haaðeel/hajeel   ətˤ-tˤaalˤb-aat
these   the-student-f.pl
'these (female) students'

هاذاك الطّالب
haaða/ðaak   ətˤ-tˤaalˤəb
that   the-student
'that (male) student'

هاذيج/ذيج الطّالبة
haaðiitʃ/ðiitʃ   ətˤ-tˤaalˤb-a
that.f   the-student-f
'that (female) student'

هاذيلاك/ذيلاك/هايلاك الطّلاب
haaðeelaak/ðeelak/hajeelaak
ətˤ-tˤelˤlˤaab
those
the students
'those (male) students'

هاذيلاج/ذيلاك/هايلاك الطّالبات
haaðeelaa-tʃ/ðeelak/hajeelaak
ətˤ-tˤaalˤəb-aat
those-f
the-student-f.pl
'those (female) students'

The cardinal numerals واحد waaħəd 'one' and اثنين ʔəθneen 'two' show gender agreement with the noun they modify and mainly appear following the modified noun, much like adjectives (Section 5.6.1) (an 'unmarked' noun or adjective is by default masculine).

طالب واحد
tˤaalˤəb   waaħəd
student   one
'one (male) student'

طالبة واحدة
tˤaalˤəb-a   wəħd-a
student-f   one-f
'one (female) student'

طالبين اثنين
tˤaalˤb-een   ʔəθneen
student-du   two
'two (male) students'

طالبتين ثنتين
tˤaalˤəb-t-een   θən-t-een
student-f-du   two-f-du
'two (female) students'

The numerals 'three' to 'nine' in attributive use always appear before the noun they modify. There is no gender agreement between the plural noun (regardless of its gender) and the numeral. The numeral always appears in the unmarked (i.e. masculine) form.

ثلاث طلاب
θalaaθ tˁəlˁlˁaab
three students
'three students'

أربع بناطلين
ʔarbaʕ bənaatˁlˁ-iin
four trouser-pl
'four (pairs of) trousers'

ثلاث طالبات
θalaatˁ tˁaalˁb-aat
three student-f.pl
'three (female) students'

أربع سيارات/سيايير
ʔarbaʕ sajjaar-aat/səjaajiir
four car-f.pl/cars
'four cars'

خمس دكاترة
xams dəkaatra
five doctors
'five (male) doctors'

خمس دكتورات
xams dəktoor-aat
five doctor-f.pl
'five (female) doctors'

ست مدرا
sətt mudara
six managers
'six managers'

ست مديرات
sətt mudiir-aat
six manager-f.pl
'six (female) managers'

سبع عمال كبار
sabəʕ ʕəmmaalkbaar
seven workers senior.pl
'seven senior workers'

سبع عاملات كبار/كبيرات
sabəʕ ʕaaməl-aat kbaar/kəbiir-aat
seven worker-f.pl senior.pl/senior-f.pl
'seven (female) senior workers'

تسع كتب يداد/يديدة
təsəʕ kətəb jdaad/jidiid-a
nine books new.pl/new-f
'nine new books'

تسع طاولات يداد/يديدة
təsəʕ tˁaawl-aat jdaad/jdiid-a
nine table-f.pl new.pl/new-f
'nine new tables'

The use of an unmarked masculine gender for the numeral also appears in elliptical contexts (Section 16.3).

أمس، خذيت خمس سياير يديدة، بس بعت ثلاث.

ʔams	xaðee-t	xams	sjaajiir	jdiid-a	bas	bəʕ-t	θalaaθ
yesterday	buy.perf-I	five	cars	new-f.pl	but	sell.perf-I	three

'I bought five new cars yesterday, but I sold three.'

Even in questions where the question word refers to feminine nouns, the numerical answer is masculine.

كم سيّارة اشتريت؟

kam	sajjaara	ʃtəree-t?
how.many	car	refl.buy.perf-you

'How many cars did you buy?'

ثلاث سياير

θalaaθ	səjaajiir
three	car.f.pl

'Three cars.'

For a detailed discussion of numerals, see Section 5.6.

6.7 Word order in the noun phrase

Emirati Arabic presents a relatively strict order of nominal modifiers when more than one is present within the noun phrase. However, this does not mean that only one order is permitted—there is in fact some flexibility in possible word orders. This is especially the case with adjectival modifiers, as the following examples show (Section 5.3):

وردة حلوة صغيرة

warda	ħəlwa	sˤɣiira
flower	beautiful	small

'a beautiful small flower'

وردة صغيرة حلوة

warda	sˤɣiira	ħəlwa
flower	small	beautiful

'a beautiful small flower'

The linear order of adjectives belonging to the same conceptual field is flexible. For instance, the following examples are acceptable and have the same meaning (Chapter 11):

كتاب انجليزي غالي يديد ممتع

ktaab	ʔəngəliizi	ɣaali	jdiid	mumtəʕ.
book	English	expensive	new	interesting

كتاب انجليزي ممتع غالي يديد

ktaab	ʔəngəliizi	mumtəʕ	ɣaali	jdiid.
book	English	interesting	expensive	new

كتاب انجليزي ممتع يديد غالي

ktaab ʔəngəliizi mumtəʕ jdiid ɣaali.

book English interesting new expensive

'an interesting, expensive, new, English book'

سيارة حمرة كبيرة قديمة معفنة

sajjara ħamra kbiira dʒədiima mʕafna.

car red big old rotten

سيارة حمرة قديمة كبيرة معفنة

səjjara ħamra dʒədiima kbiira mʕafna.

car red old big rotten

'a rotten, big, old, red car'

When additional modifiers are included in the noun phrase, the preferred order of modifiers seems to be:

Demonstrative—Quantifier/Numeral—Determiner—Noun—Possessive—Adjective—Prepositional Phrase—Relative Clause

This is evident in the following noun phrase:

هالثلاث سيايير اليداد من دبي، إللي شفتهم أمس

ha-θ-θalaaθ səjaajiir əl-jədaad mən dbaɪ ʔəlli ʧəf-t-hum ʔams

these-the-three the-cars the-new.pl from Dubai that see.perf-I-them yesterday

'These three new cars from Dubai that I saw yesterday'

A certain flexibility is allowed, for example, in the position of the demonstrative and the numeral, which can also appear postnominally.

هالسيايير الثلاث اليداد من دبي، إللي شفتهم أمس

ha-s-səjaajiir əθ-θalaaθ əl-jədaad mən dbaɪ ʔəlli ʧəfə-t-hum ʔams.

these-the-cars the-three the-new from Dubai that see.perf-I-them yesterday

'These three new cars from Dubai that I saw yesterday'

Further reading

General grammatical descriptions of the noun phrase structure and distribution in Gulf Arabic are in Holes (1984, 1990) and Qafisheh (1977); the latter of these is based on the dialect of the Emirate of Abu Dhabi. Brustad (2000) has an extensive discussion on definiteness and possession issues with examples from the closely related dialect of Kuwaiti Arabic.

Chapter 7

The verb phrase

The structure of verb phrases stems from how various argument structures are grammaticalized at the syntactic level. Argument structures project the subject-predicate relation, namely, how the sentential subject is involved in the proposition set out by the predicate. The predicate of a proposition describes the properties or what holds true for the subject. In Emirati Arabic, the predicate may be realized by the main verb or by other grammatical categories such as adjectives and prepositions, as long as the subject-predicate relation can be properly interpreted.

7.1 The copular structure

Copular structures express the predicative properties of the subject. In Emirati Arabic, the copula كان kaan (cf. English 'be') is not overtly expressed in the imperfective aspect (Section 8.2). The predicate of the copular structures may express the individual-level property or the identity of the subject.

أحمد مجتهد/لغوي

ʔaħmad	mədʒtəhəd/ləɣawi.
Ahmad	hardworking/linguist

'Ahmad is hardworking/(a) linguist.'

On the other hand, copulas are overtly expressed by inflecting كان kaan with the perfective aspect and the future imperfective aspect (Chapters 8 and 9).

أحمد كان مجتهد/لغوي

ʔaħmad	kaan	mədʒtəhəd/ləɣawi.
Ahmad	be.perf-he	hardworking/linguist

'Ahmad was hardworking/(a) linguist.'

أحمد بيكون طيار

ʔaħmad ba-j-kuun tˤajjaar.
Ahmad will-he-be.imperf pilot
'Ahmad will be a pilot.'

The copula can also be used in elliptical structures (Chapter 16).

أنا مب مدرّس، بس كنت

ʔana mub mudarrəs bas kənt.
I not teacher but be.perf-I
'I am not a teacher, but I was.'

أنا مب مدرّس، بس بكون

ʔana mub mudarrəs bas b-a-kuun.
I not teacher but will-I-be.imperf
'I am not a teacher, but I will be.'

Note that كان kaan in the imperfective aspect is not realized even in this elliptical structure. Instead, native speakers prefer repeating the predicate.

ما كنت استاذ قبل بس الحين انا استاذ

maa kənt ʔəstaað gabəl bas əl-ħiin ʔana ʔəstaað.
not be.perf-I teacher before but the-now I teacher
'I was not a teacher before, but now I am a teacher.'

In addition to كان kaan, the subject pronoun (Section 5.8.1.1) may function as a copula in identificational and specificational sentences. The copular pronoun agrees in number and gender with the sentence subject.

أحمد هو الأستاذ اللي كنت أتكلم عنه

ʔaħmad huu l-əstaað ʔəlli kən-t ʔa-t-kallam ʕan-na.
Ahmad he the-teacher that be.perf-I.f I-refl-caus.talk.imperf about-him
'Ahmad is the teacher I was talking about.'

أحمد هو الطالب الذكي فكلاسنا

ʔaħmad	huu	ətˤ-tˤaalˤəb	əð-ðaki	fə-klaas-na.
Ahmad	he	the-student	the-smart	in-class-our

'Ahmad is the smart student in our class.'

نورا هي العضوة اللطيفة مالت النادي

nuura	hii	l-ʕəðˤw-a	əl-latˤiif-a	maal-at	ən-naadi.
Nora	she	the-member-f	the-cute-f	poss-f	the-club

'Nora is that cute member of the club.'

أحسن لاعب كورة فالعالم هو ميسي

ʔa-ħsan	laaʕəb	kuura	f-əl-ʕaalam	huu	mesi
most-good	player	ball	in-the-world	he	Messi

'The best footballer in the world is Messi.'

مريم هي اللي كانت تدرس فالمدرسة

Marjam	hii	ʔəlli	kan-at	əd-darrəs	fə-l-mədərsa.
Mariam	she	that	be.perf-she	she-caus.teach	in-the-school

'Mariam was the teacher at school.'

7.2 State verbs

State (or stative) verbs are non-action verbs ascribing a 'state of being' to their sentence subject. The following tables show some typical members of each class of verbs. The 'base' verbal form is the third-person singular masculine in the perfective, as it is how the bare consonantal root is pronounced when the consonants are concatenated (Sections 5.2 and 8.4).

وافق	waafaq	'agreed'	قصد	qəsˤad	'meant'
رفض	rəfaðˤ	'refused'	ملك	məlak	'owned'
كلّف	kallaf	'cost'	حط	ħatˤtˤ	'included'

الهدية ايي داخلها تلفون و كمبيوتر

əl-hadiija	ə-jji	daaxəl-ha	təlfuun	w	kambjuutar.
the-gift	it-come.imperf	inside-it.f	phone	and	computer

'This gift contains (i.e. has inside) a phone and a computer.'

المشروع بكبره بيكلف مليون درهم

əl-maʃruuʕ b-kəbr-ah ba-j-kalləf məljoon dərham.
the-project with-hugeness-its will-it-cost.imperf million Dirham
'The entire project will cost one million Dirhams.'

وايد علماء يحسون انه اينشتاين يستاهل جايزة نوبل على نظرية النسبية

waajəd ʕəlama jə-ħəss-uun ʔənnah ʔajnəʃtaajn jə-staahəl ʤaajjza-t noobəl ʕala naðarijja-t ən-nəsbəjja.
many scientists they-feel.imperf-they that Einstein he-deserve.imperf prize-f Nobel on theory-f the-relativity
'Many scientists agree that Einstein deserves the Nobel Prize for the theory of relativity.'

أحمد رافض يفضح سر علي

ʔaħmad raafəðʕ jə-fðʕaħ sərr ʕəli.
Ahmad refuse.perf-he he-expose.imperf secret Ali
'Ahmad refused to disclose Ali's secret.'

7.3 Experiencer verbs

The subjects (or sometimes objects, e.g. 'frighten' and 'annoy') of experiencer verbs are non-actional experiencers of the verbal event (Table 7.1).

شيخة تحب علم الصوتيات لكن تكره علم النحو

ʃeexa t-ħəbb ʕəlm əsʕ-sʕootijj-aat laakən tə-krah ʕəlm ən-naħu.
Shaikha she-like.imperf science the-sound-f.pl but she-hate.imperf science the-grammar
'Shaikha likes phonetics but hates syntax.'

Table 7.1 Experiencer verbs

خاف	xaaf	'was afraid'	سمع	səmaʕ	'heard'
حب	ħabb	'liked'	زاغ	zaaɣ	'feared/was scared'
كره	kərah	'hated'	خوّف	xawwaf	'frightened'
شاف	ʧaaf	'looked'	فرح	fərah	'became happy'
حاتى	ħaata	'worried'	حس	ħass	'felt'

موزة كانت تحاتي مريم ماتوصل من وقت

mooza kaan-at t-ħaat-ii marjam maa-t-uusˤalˤ
mən wagt.
Moza be.perf-she she-worry.imperf-she Mariam not-she-reach.imperf
from time
'Moza worried that Mariam might not arrive on time.'

الطلاب يحسون ان الامتحان وايد صعب

ət-tˤəlˤlˤaab jə-ħəss-uun ʔənna l-əmtəħaan waajəd sˤaʕab.
the-students they-feel.imperf-they that the-test a.lot hard
'The students feel that the exam is too difficult.'

7.4 Unergative verbs

There are at least two types of intransitive verbs (i.e. verbs without direct objects) depending on the type of argument structure. One subtype are the unergative verbs (Table 7.2), for which the sentence subject (its only argument) is a semantic agent who initiates the action (defined by the unergative verb).

كانت تركض لمدة ساعة

kaan-at tə-rkəðˤ l-məddat saaʕa.
be.perf-she she-run.imperf for-duration hour
'She has been jogging for an hour.'

شيخة غنت في المسرح البارحة فالليل

ʃeexa ɣann-at f-əl-masraħ əl-baarħa f-əl-leel.
Sheikha sing.perf-she in-the-auditorium the-yesterday in-the-night
'Sheikha sang in the auditorium last night.'

Table 7.2 Unergative verbs

رقص	rəgasˤ	'danced'	رقد	rəgad	'slept'
غنى	ɣanna	'sang'	ربع	rəbaʕ	'ran'
ضحك	ðˤəħak	'laughed'	ركض	rəkəðˤ	'ran'
نام	naam	'slept'	بكى	bəka	'cried'

7.5 Unaccusative verbs

Another type of intransitive verb are the unaccusative verbs (Table 7.3), for which the sentence subject semantically denotes a person or entity which undergoes a verbal action (defined by the unaccusative verb). In the following, the subject is not the initiator, but the 'undergoer' of the verbal event:

Table 7.3 Unaccusative verbs

ذاب	ðaab	'melt'	نزل	nəzal	'decreased'
غرق	ɣərag	'sank'	كسر	kəsar	'broke'
طاح	tˤaaħ	'fell'	كبر	kəbar	'grew'
سكّر	sakkar	'closed'	فتح	fətaħ	'opened'
جمد	ʤəmad	'froze'	رجع	rəʤaʕ	'got back'

الثلج يذوب أسرع تحت الشمس

əθ-θalʤ j-ðuub ʔa-sraʕ taħt əʃ-ʃams.
the-ice it-melt.imperf more-fast under the-sun
'Ice melts faster under the sun.'

المحل بيسكر عقب نص ساعة

əl-maħal bə-j-sakkər ʕəgb nəsˤ saaʕa.
the-shop will-it-close.imperf after half hour
'The store will close in half an hour.'

7.6 Ditransitive verbs

Ditransitive verbs take two objects—a direct object and an indirect object. In many cases, the indirect object precedes the direct object in double-object constructions. Table 7.4 contains verbs which are ditransitive by nature (e.g. 'give' and 'send'), and verbs which have the capacity of selecting two objects (e.g. 'write' and 'teach').

شما عطت حصة كتابها

ʃamma ʕatˤa-t ħəsˤsˤa ktaab-ha.
Shamma give.perf-she Hessa book-her
'Shamma gave Hessa her book.'

Table 7.4 Ditransitive verbs

عطى	ʕatˤa	'gave'	درّس	darras	'taught'
طرّش	tˤarraʃ	'sent'	علّم	ʕallam	'taught'
بعث	baʕaθ	'sent'	سلّف	sallaf	'lent'
رد	radd	'returned'	طلب	tˤəlab	'ordered'
سأل	səʔal	'asked'	خذ	xað	'took'
كتب	kətab	'wrote'	سلّم	sallam	'greeted/ handed/ conveyed'
سرق	sarag	'stole'	كلّف	kallaf	'assigned'

الاستاذ سأل حمدان سؤال ما رام يجاوب عليه

l-əstaað saʔal ħamdaan suʔaal maa raam j-ʤaawəb ʕalee-h.

the-teacher ask.perf-he Hamdan question not can.perf-he he-answer.imperf on-it

'The teacher asked Hamdan a question he could not answer.'

عيسى سلّف يوسف عشر آلاف درهم

ʕiisa sallaf juusəf ʕaʃər-t-aalaaf dərham.

Eisa caus.lend.perf-he Yousif ten-f-thousand Dirham

'Eisa lent Yousif ten thousand Dirhams.'

سارة درّست اختها الصغيرة رياضيات

saara darrəs-at ʔəxət-ha əsˤ-sˤəɣiir-a rijaaðˤijjaat.

Sara teach.perf-she sister-her the-little-f mathematics

'Sara taught her little sister mathematics.'

Some path-denoting verbs require a preposition to mark the indirect object.

أحمد توه كتب للشركة رسالة استقالته

ʔaħmad tawa-h kətab l-əʃ-ʃarəka rəsaala-t ʔəstəqaalt-ah.

Ahmad just-him write.perf-he to-the-company letter-f resignation-his

'Ahmad just wrote his resignation letter to the company.'

علي طرش حق موزة هدية يوم ميلادها

ʕəli tˤarraʃ ħag mooza hadijja-t joom-miilaad-ha.

Ali caus.send.perf-he to Moza gift-f joom-birth-her

'Ali sent (to) Moza her birthday gift.'

For verbs such as طرش tˤarraʃ 'sent,' the indirect object can also follow the direct object (Section 11.3).

علي توه طرش هدية يوم ميلاد موزة

ʕəli taww-a tˤarraʃ hadijja-t joom-miilaad muuza.

Ali just-him caus.send.perf-he gift-f joom-birth Moza

'Ali just sent Moza a birthday gift.'

7.7 Existential and possessive predicates

The expression of existential and possessive constructions is formed by the prepositions في fii 'in,' عند ʕənd 'with,' and -ل li- 'to,' which entails an ownership relation between the subject and the object (Section 5.5). These existential prepositions may take an object pronoun which is anaphoric to the subject's reference.

أحمد عنده مرسيدس، والشهر الياي بيكون عنده بي أم دبليو

ʔaħmad ʕend-ah marsiidis, w əʃ-ʃahr əl-jaaj ba-j-kuun ʕend-ah BMW.

Ahmad with-him Mercedes and the-month the-coming will-he-be.imperf with-him BMW

'Ahmad has a Mercedes and will have a BMW next month.'

الكبت فيه ملابس للشتا

əl-kabat fii-h malaabəs l-əʃ-ʃətaa.

the-closet in-it clothes for-the-winter

'The closet contains (lit. has in it) winter clothes.'

هالشنطه لج

ha-ʃ-ʃantˤa l-əʧ.

this-the-bag for-you.f

'This bag is for you (f).'

Since they are grammatically prepositions, they are unable to host aspectual properties as other verbs do. To express further temporal specification for the existential/possessive predicates, the copular verb كان kaan (with the particular aspect) is used (Section 7.11 and Chapter 8).

كان عندي سلحفاة بس ماتت

kaan	ʕənd-ii	səlħəfaah	bas	mat-at.
be.perf-I	with-me	turtle	but	die.perf-it.f

'I had a turtle but it passed away.'

المفتاح كان عند أحمد

əl-məftaaħ	kaan	ʕənd	ʔaħmad.
the-key	be.perf-it	with	Ahmad

'The key was with Ahmad.'

أمي كانت عند الحريم

ʔumm-i	kaan-at	ʕənd	əl-ħariim.
mother-my	was.perf-she	with	the-women

'My mom was with the women.'

كان في موز فالثلاجة

kaan	fii	mooz	f-əθ-θallaadʒah.
be.perf-it	there.is	banana	in-the-fridge

'There was a banana in the fridge.'

هالمفتاح كان لج

hal-məftaaħ	kaan	l-ətʃ.
this-key	be.perf-it	for-you.f

'This key was for you.'

7.8 Raising predicates

In the study of linguistics (especially syntax), there exists a class of predicates which establish a special relation between the grammatical structure and the argument (i.e. logical) structure. Semantically, verbs such as English 'seem' and 'appear,' and adjectives such as 'likely' require a clause as their internal argument and do not have an external argument (i.e. semantic subject). However, at the grammatical level, these verbs require a grammatical subject (e.g. 'John always seems to offend everyone' and 'His performance is likely to be the best one'). These verbs are called *raising verbs* since there is an impression that the grammatical subject 'raises' from a lower position at the underlying level (e.g. (always seems John to offend everyone) → (John always seems __ to offend everyone)).

In Emirati Arabic, the class of raising verbs is extremely limited, compared with, say, MSA). The best example of a raising verb is كان kaan which expresses an aspectual meaning of 'be about to' (Chapter 8) in complex predicate structures (Section 7.11). In the following examples, the subject may be sandwiched between كان kaan and the main verb, or it may surface at the sentence-initial position by raising.

كانوا بيضيعون في البر

kan-aw	ba-j-ðˤiiʕ-uun	f-əl-barr.
be.perf-they	will-they-lost.imperf-they	in-the-desert

'They were about to get lost in the desert.'

(السماء) كانت (السماء) بتمطر

(əs-səma)	kaan-at	(əs-səma)	ba-təmtˤtˤər.
the-sky	be.perf-it.f	the-sky	will-it.rain.imperf

'The sky was about to rain.'

الوقت كان جريب بيخلص

əl-wagt	kaan	ʤriib	ba-j-xalləsˤ.
the-time	be.perf-it	soon	will-it-end.imperf

'The time was about to end.'

That the grammatical subject stems from a lower position is evident in the following example in which the subject and the main verb forms an idiomatic expression:

(لسانج) كان (لسانج) بينربط

(əlsaan-əʧ)	kaan	(əlsaan-əʧ)	ba-jə-n-rəbətˤ.
tongue.f-your	be.perf-it	tongue.f-your	will-it-pass-tie.imperf

'Your tongue was about to be tied (tongue-tied = speechless).'

The English raising verb 'seem' cannot be directly expressed by any verb in Emirati Arabic. Alternatively, the modal adverb شكل ʃakəl (cf. English 'apparently' and 'seemingly') may serve a similar function (Section 5.4). The following examples show that the subject may immediately precede or follow شكل ʃakəl without any meaning change. شكل ʃakəl is always suffixed by the object pronoun which refers to the identity of the subject.

(مريم) شكلها (مريم) مستانسة على درجة الامتحان

(marjam) ʃakəl-ha (marjam) məstans-a ʕala daradʒat l-əmtəħan.

Mariam apparently-her Mariam happy-f on score the-exam

'Mariam seems happy with the exam score.'

(الطلاب) شكلهم (الطلاب) مستانسين ع الفلم

(ətˤ-tˤəlˤlˤaab) ʃakəl-hum (ətˤ-tˤəlˤlˤaab) məstaans-iin ʕa-l-fələm.

the-students apparently-them the-students happy-pl on-the-movie

'The students seem to enjoy the movie.'

(الغدا) شكله (الغدا) حلو اليوم

(əl-ɣədaa) ʃakl-ah (əl-ɣədaa) ħəlu əl-joom.

the-lunch apparently-it the-lunch good the-today

'It seems that lunch is good today.'

The claim that شكل ʃakəl serves a function similar to a raising verb is indicated in the following example which consists of an idiom chunk. In Emirati Arabic (and MSA), the sentence إلسانه إنربط əlsaanah ənrəbatˤ expresses an idiomatic meaning 'speechless.' The idiomatic meaning remains intact even if إلسانه əlsaanah 'his tongue' is separated from إنربط ənrəbatˤ 'got tied' by the modal adverb شكل ʃakəl. One explanation for this is that the sentence-initial position of the subject is the result of raising from a 'lower' position.

(إلسانه) شكله (إلسانه) إنربط

(əlsaan-ah) ʃakl-ah (əlsaan-ah) ənrəbatˤ

tongue-his apparently-him tongue-his refl.tie.perf-it

'He seems to be speechless.' (lit. 'His tongue seems to be tied.')

شكل ʃakəl is also used in weather verb expressions, with the third-person singular possessive pronoun suffix ـها -haa.

شكلها بتمطر

ʃakəl-ha b-tə-mtˤtˤər.

apparently-it.f will-it.rain.imperf

'It seems (that) it's going to rain.'

Modal adjectives (Section 5.3) and verbs such as طلع tˤəlaʕ 'turned out' also serve the function of raising predicates.

التذاكر أغلب الظن بتكون غالية

ət-təθaakər ʔaɣlab əðˤ-ðˤan ba-t-kuun ɣaalj-a.

the-tickets most the-speculation will-they-be.imperf expensive-f

'Tickets are likely to become expensive.'

أحمد أكيد بيفوز

ʔaħmad ʔakiid ba-j-fuuz.

Ahmad sure will-he-win.imperf

'Ahmad is sure to win.'

النظرية طلعت غلط

ən-naðˤarijja tˤəlʕʕ-at ɣalatˤ.

the-hypothesis come.out.perf-it.f wrong

'The hypothesis turns out to be wrong.'

7.9 Control verbs

Control verbs (Table 7.5) differ from raising verbs in that their argument structure consists of two arguments. The external argument is the sentential subject of the sentence, and the internal argument is an embedded clause which does not have a realized subject. In control structures, the sentence subject controls the identity of the subject of the embedded clause. For instance, in English control structures such as 'John wants to join the party,' 'John' as the subject of 'want' also controls the subject of the embedded clause 'to join the party'—that is, 'John' is the person who wants and who joins the party.

Control structures have two types: subject control and object control. For subject control, the subject of the embedded clause is

Table 7.5 Control verbs

يبا	jəba	'wants'	خايف	xaajəf	'was afraid'
حب	ħabb	'liked'	اتجنب	ətʤannab	'avoided'
تمنى	ətmanna	'hoped'	قدر	gədar	'was able'
وعد	waʕad	'promised'	احتاي	əħtaai	'needed'
حاول	ħaawal	'tried'	غصب	ɣəsˤab	'forced'
وافق	waafaq	'agreed'	توقع	twaqqaʕ	'expected'
قنع	qənaʕ	'convinced'			

controlled by the subject of the control verb, e.g. verbs such as يبا jəba 'wants,' حب ħabb 'liked,' and حاول ħaawal 'tried.' Note that the embedded verb of subject control structures is in the imperfective aspect (Section 8.2).

أنا بس أحاول اساعدك

ʔana bas a-ħaawəl a-saaʕd-ək.

I only I-try.imperf I-help.imperf-you

'I am just trying to help you.'

الدولتين اتفقوا يصلحون علاقتهم

əd-doowlt-een ətafq-aw jə-sˤalħ-uun ʕəlaaqat-hum.

the-country-du agree.perf-they they-reconcile.imperf-they relation-their

'The two countries agree to reconcile their relationship.'

أغلب الناس يبون يشتغلون في المدن الكبيرة

ʔaɣlab ən-naas jə-b-oon jə-ʃtaɣl-oon f əl-məden əl-kbiir-a.

most the-people they-want.imperf-they they-work.imperf-they in the-cities the-big-f

'Most people want to work in big cities.'

For subject control verbs that select a direct object, the use of the complementizer انه ʔənnah 'that' before the embedded verb is preferred (it may be omitted).

أحمد وعد علي (انه) يصلح الكمبيوتر البارحة

ʔaħmad weʕad ʕəli (ʔənnah) j-sˤalleħ
əl-kəmbjuutar ʔams f-əl-leel.
Ahmad promise.perf-he Ali that he-fix.imperf
the-computer yesterday in-the-night
'Ahmad promised Ali to fix the computer last night.'

For object control, the subject of the embedded clause is controlled by the object of the main clause, e.g. verbs such as قنع qenaʕ '(he) convinced.' The embedded clause of object control verbs is identical to that of subject control verbs, i.e. the embedded verb is in the imperfective aspect (Section 8.2). In these cases, the complementizer انه ʔənnah 'that' may still be used, although it is not favored by native speakers.

مريم قنعت ابوها (انه) يخليها تدرس برع

marjam qenʕ-at ʔəbuu-ha (ʔənnah) j-xallii-ha
tə-drəs barraʕ.
Mariam convince.perf-she father-her that he-let.imperf-her
she-study.imperf outside
'Mariam convinced her father to let her study abroad.'

البروفسور غصب الطلاب (انهم) يسلمون الشغل على نهاية اليوم

əl-brofəsoor ɣəsˤab ət-tˤəlˤlˤaab (ʔen-hum)
jə-salm-uun əʃ-ʃəɣəl ʕa nəhaaja-t əl-joom.
the-professor force.perf-he the-student.pl that-them
they-submit.imperf-they the-work on end-f the-today
'That professor forced the students to submit assignments by the end of tonight.'

7.10 Reflexive verbs

Reflexive verbs (Table 7.6) are verbs whose object is identical to the subject, e.g. English 'John shampooed himself.' Sometimes the meaning of the reflexive verb is so salient that its object (which is usually a reflexive pronoun) (Section 5.8.3) is not necessarily realized, e.g. 'John shaved.' In Emirati Arabic, the reflexive verb may be expressed by prefixing -تـ tə- to the verbal stem with a geminate consonant, resulting in Form V verbs (Section 5.2.7).

Table 7.6 Reflexive verbs

وقّف	waggaf	'stopped s.o/s.th'	توقف	twaggaf	'stopped oneself'
وصّخ	wasˁsˁax	'dirtied s.o/s.th'	توّصخ	twasˁsˁax	'dirtied oneself'
كبّر	kabbar	'made s.o/s.th big'	تكّبر	tkabbar	'got arrogant'
غسّل	ɣassal	'washed s.o/s.th'	تغّسل	tɣassal	'washed oneself'

هند تعودت تشرب جاهي كل يوم

hend t-ʕawwəd-at t-ʃrab ʧaahi kəl joom.

Hind refl-accustom.perf-she she-drink.imperf tea every day

'Hind is used to drinking tea every day.'

منى تكبرت عقب ما حصلت وظيفة

muna t-kabbər-at ʕəgəb maa ħasˁsˁəl-at waðˁiifa.

Muna refl-arrogant.perf-she after that find.perf-she job

'Muna got arrogant after she found a job.'

تلفوني طاح فالوصاخة وتوصخ

talfon-i tˁaaħ f-əl-wəsˁaaxa w-t-wasˁsˁax.

phone-my fall.perf-it in-the-dirt and-refl-dirty.perf-it

'My phone fell in the dirt and got dirty.'

7.11 Complex predicates

Complex predicates (Table 7.7) are formed by two (or more) adjacent verbs which share the same subject and subject agreement. Depending on the intended semantics, the verbs of complex predicates may bear the same or distinct aspect (Chapter 8). Complex predicates can express two temporal events, for instance:

In Emirati Arabic, it is possible to construct two successive events by concatenating two predicates without the mediation of a coordinator (Chapter 15). Some grammarians may consider the following sentence as an example of serial verb

Table 7.7 Common verbs used in complex predicates

خلص	xalˤlˤasˤ	'finished'
بدا	bəda	'started'
كان	kaan	'was'
قعد	gaʕad	'sat' (in progressives)
يلس	jəlas	'sat' (in progressives)

construction or verb serialization (as observed in numerous African languages):

حسين قام (و) حرّك الكرسي

ħseen	gaam	(w)	ħarrak	əl-kərsi.
Husain	stand.perf-he	and	move.perf-he	the-chair

'Husain stood (and) moved the chair.'

In other cases, the complex predicates represent a single event. An asymmetry normally exists in the sense that the first predicate usually expresses a more grammatical (e.g. aspectual) function, whereas the second predicate expresses the main verbal event. In the formation of complex predicates, verbs such as راح raaħ '(he) went' and بدا bəda '(he) started' lose their original lexical meanings (Chapter 8).

علي راح يشتغل على البروجكت ماله

ʕəli	raaħ	jə-ʃtəɣəl	ʕ-al-brodʒəkt	maal-ah.
Ali	go.perf-he	he-work.imperf	on-the-project	poss-him

'Ali went to work on his project.'

خل نكمل ندرس

xal	n-kamməl	nə-drəs.
let's	we-continue.imperf	we-study.imperf

'Let's continue to study.'

ريم بدت تدرس حق الميدتيرم

riim	bəd-at	tə-drəs	ħagg	əl-mədteerm.
Reem	start.perf-she	she-study.imperf	for	the-midterm

'Reem started to study for the midterm.'

أمي كانت تزرع النخل برع

ʔumm-i	kaan-at	tə-zraʕ	ən-naxəl	barraʕ.
mother-my	be.perf-she	she-plant.imperf	the-palm.trees	outside

'My mother was planting palm trees outside.'

بكون يالس أدرس

ba-kuun	jaaləs	ʔa-drəs.
will-I-be.imperf	part.sit	I-study.imperf

'I will be studying.'

يالس يتحرطم

jaaləs	jə-t-ħartˤam.
part.sit	he-refl-complain.imperf

'He kept complaining.'

7.12 Causative verbs

Causative verbs (Table 7.8) are verbs whose subject is the causer or initiator of a verbal event. In most cases the subject is agentive in the sense that he/she is directly involved in the event (e.g. English 'John killed Peter' means John initiated actions which caused Peter to die). In Emirati Arabic, causative verbs may be

Table 7.8 Causative verbs

سمع	səmaʕ	'heard'	سمّع	sammaʕ	'made s.o hear'
كل	kal	'ate'	أكّل	ʔakkal	'fed'
طلع	tˤəlaʕ	'went out'	طلّع	tˤallaʕ	'took/brought s.o out'
نزل	nəzal	'descended'	نزّل	nazzal	'made s.th/s.o descend'
طاح	tˤaaħ	'fell'	طيّح	tˤajjaħ	'made s.th/s.o fall'
مشى	məʃa	'walked'	مشّى	maʃʃa	'took s.o for a walk'
ضحك	ðˤəħak	'laughed'	ضحّك	ðˤaħħak	'made s.o laugh'

derived by geminating (i.e. lengthening) the second consonant of the root (Sections 5.2.5 and 5.2.7). In causative structures, the causee follows the causative verb. The causative verb agrees with the sentential subject (i.e. the causer) in terms of number and gender; it does not agree with the causee.

الكوميديا تضحّك أحمد

əl-koomiidja	t-ðˁaħħ-ək	ʔaħmad.
the-comedy	it-refl-caus.laugh.perf-it	Ahmad

'Comedy makes Ahmad laugh.'

شفت القرار اللي طلعوه؟

ʧəft	əl-qaraar	ʔəlli	tˁalˁlˁaʕ-ooh?
see.perf-you	the-decree	that	caus.bring.out.perf-they

'Have you seen the decree they announced?'

أ: أكّلتي السمج اليوم؟

ʔakkal-ti	əs-semaʧ	əl-joom?
caus.feed.perf-you.f	the-fish	the-today

'Have you fed the fish (lit. caused it to eat) today?'

ب: هيه أكّلتهم من شوي

heeh	ʔakkal-t-hum	mən ʃwaj
yes	caus.feed.perf-I.f-them	from little

'Yes, I fed them a while ago.'

7.13 Passive verbs

Passive constructions may be formed by the Form VII passivized verbs (Section 5.2.9).

اللوحة نرسمت أمس لان فاطمة كانت فاضية

əl-looħa	n-rəsma-t	ʔams	lanna	faatˁma
kaan-at	faadˁ-ja.			
the-picture	pass-draw.perf-f	yesterday	because	fatima
be.perf-she	free-f			

'The picture was painted yesterday because Fatima was free.'

الدريشة انكسرت بسبة احمد

əd-dəriiʃa	n-kasra-t	b-səbba-t	ʔaħmad.
the-window	pass-break.perf-f	by-reason-f	Ahmad

'The window was broken because of Ahmad.'

خالد انسحب من المدرسة عشان شطانته

xaaləd ən-səħab mən əl-madrəsa ʕaʃaan ʃatˤaan-ta.

Khalid pass-withdraw.perf from the-school because naughtiness-his

'Khalid was removed from school because of his naughtiness.'

For the passivized ditransitive verbs, the indirect object linearly follows the verb without any preposition.

التقرير انعطى أحمد من سالم

ət-taqriir	n-ʕətˤa	ʔaħmad	mən	saaləm.
the-report	pass-give.perf	ahmad	from	Salim

'The report was given (to) Ahmad by Salim.'

المعاش انرسل من الشركة لموظفينها

l-maʕaaʃ	n-rəsal	mən	əʃ-ʃarika	l-muwadˤaf-iin-ha.
the-salary	pass-send.perf	from	the-company	to-employee-pl-its

'The salary was sent from the company to its staff.'

Another type of passive verb is formed by some Form VI verbs (Section 5.2.8) which express reciprocality and a mediopassive voice. These are also called *pseudopassives* (Holes, 1990, p. 181). Compared with the passive sentences created by Form VII, the semantic relation between the grammatical object (although it assumes the role of the action doer or event initiator) and Form VI verbs in pseudopassives is less direct. In the following first example, the stranger did not necessarily hit or bump Rashid on purpose, although Rashid was injured as a result of physical contact. In the second example, the traffic jam is an event which indirectly caused Ahmad to become nervous.

راشد تصاوب من حد غريب

raʃəd	t-sˤaawab	mən	ħad	ɣariib
Rashid	refl-injure.perf-he	from	someone	stranger

'Rashid got (was) injured by some stranger.'

حمد تنرفز من زحمة الشارع

ħamad	t-narfaz	mən	zaħmat	əʃ-ʃaarəʕ.
hamad	refl-nervous.perf	from	crowd	the-street

'Ahmad became nervous by (because of) the traffic jam.'

7.14 Complement-taking verbs

A number of verbs may take a clause as their internal argument. Depending on the grammatical and semantic properties of the complement-taking verbs (Table 7.9), some embedded clauses (i.e. the clauses selected by these verbs) are complete in the sense that they are full sentences themselves. 'Impoverished' embedded clauses, on the contrary, are clauses that are not grammatically independent. Most impoverished embedded clauses do not have an independent embedded subject, and their temporal orientation depends on the time reference of the main predicate (i.e. the complement-taking verb).

7.14.1 *Impoverished embedded clauses*

The impoverished embedded clause always contains an embedded verb in the imperfective aspect. Since it is impoverished, the temporal orientation of the embedded clause is determined by the main predicate. For instance, in the following example, since the main predicate طلب 'asked' is a perfective verb, the embedded clause (which consists of an imperfective verb) is also interpreted

Table 7.9 Complement-taking verbs

سأل	saʔal	'asked'	بلّغ	ballaɣ	'reported'
بغى	baɣa	'wanted'	فكّر	fakkar	'thought'
ندم	nədam	'regretted'	تمنّى	tmanna	'wished'
تذكّر	tðakkar	'remembered'	حاول	ħaawal	'tried'
قال	gaal	'said'	صدّق/آمن	sˁaddag/ ʔaaman	'believed'
عرف	ʕaraf	'knew'	ظن	ðˁan	'guessed'
سمع	səmaʕ	'heard'	سأل	saʔal	'asked'
حس	ħas	'felt'	روّح	rawwaħ	'left'

as a complete event. The subject of the embedded clause is also the subject of the main clause.

كارن طلبت تقابل الدكتور

kaarən tˤəlba-t t-gaabəl əd-dəktoor.
Karen request.perf-she she-meet.imperf the-doctor
'Karen asked to see the doctor.'

أبا أستقيل الشهر الياي

ʔa-ba ʔa-stəqiil əʃ-ʃahar əl-jaaj.
I-want.imperf I-resign.imperf the-month the-next
'I want to resign next month.'

The main predicate can also take an object. In some cases, the embedded subject is the object of the main predicate, as the following example shows:

شيخة طلبت منها تروح

ʃeexa tˤəlba-t mən-ha t-rawwəħ.
Shaikha request.perf-she from-her she-caus.leave.imperf
'Shaikha requested her to leave.'

7.14.2 *Complete embedded clauses*

Verbs of saying and verbs which describe the speaker's mental state may select a complete embedded clause. These embedded clauses are always marked by the complementizer انه ʔənn(ah) 'that' (Section 5.7.1).

أحمد توه قال انه بيحضر الحفلة الليلة

ʔaħmad taww-a gaal ʔənn-ah ba-jə-ħðˤar
l-ħafla əl-leela.
Ahmad just-him say.perf-he that-him will-he-attend.imperf
the-party the-night
'Ahmad just said that he will join the party tonight.'

سارة تذكرت انها خلّت كتبها فالبيت

saara t-ðakkər-at ʔən-ha xalla-t
kətəb-ha f-əl-beet.
Sarah refl-caus.remember.perf-she that-her leave.perf-she
book.pl-her in-the-home
'Sarah remembered that she left her books at home.'

راشد حس انه سوّى غلطة كبيرة فالشغل

raaʃəd ħass ʔənn-a sawwa ɣaltˤa kbiir-a f-əʃ-ʃəɣəl.

Rashid feel.perf-he that-him make.perf-he mistake big-f in-the-work

'Rashid felt that he made a big mistake in work.'

7.14.3 *Interrogative embedded clauses*

Verbs of interrogatives and verbs of knowing always select an interrogative embedded clause.

مريم نست وين حطت الكتب

marjam nəsa-t ween ħatˤtˤa-t l-kətəb.

Mariam forget.perf-she where put.perf-she the-book.pl

'Mariam forgot where she put the books.'

العلماء عرفوا وين ومتى بدا انتشار هالفيروس

l-ʕulamaaʔ ʕərf-aw ween w məta bəda ntəʃaar h-al-fajruus.

the-scientists know.perf-they where and when start.perf-it outbreak this-the-virus

'Scientists knew where and when the virus outbreak happened.'

Further reading

For the research on raising predicates in MSA, see Haddad (2012); and on control predicates, see Arad Greshler et al. (2017). For the study of embedded clauses in MSA, consult Fassi Fehri (1993, 2012), Persson (2002), and Aoun et al. (2010). For a discussion of verb categorization in various Arabic dialects, see Brustad (2000).

Chapter 8

Aspect

Linguistic scholars and students interested in Arabic are occasionally puzzled by the distinction between tense and aspect in grammaticalizing temporal events. Tense is generally used to grammaticalize the time of events related to other times (usually the speech time), whereas grammatical aspect concerns various viewpoints toward the temporal events, signaling whether the event has started, is ongoing, or has been completed. Another type of aspect, namely lexical aspect (or *aktionsart*, lit. 'kind of action' in German), is inherent to the lexical semantics of the verb and indicates the internal constituency of the temporal events. A verb may be classified as denoting a state (e.g. 'know' and 'hate'), activity (e.g. 'run' and 'write'), achievement (e.g. 'arrive' and 'win'), and accomplishment (e.g. 'build a house' and 'bake a cake'). In Emirati Arabic morphology, a verb may be inflected with perfective (Section 8.1) or imperfective (Section 8.2) aspect. In addition, the participle (Section 5.3.2) of the verb can indicate a progressive and a complete event. Each aspect (including the participle which is considered as a type of verbal aspect) must further indicate the grammatical properties of the sentential subject with respect to person (always the third), number, and gender. The combination between grammatical aspect (which is morphologically realized) and lexical aspect (which is semantically inherent) creates an intricate system of various event types.

8.1 The perfective aspect

The perfective aspect expresses a complete event, action, or state of affairs. In all cases, events expressed by the perfective aspect must be completed in their entirety. The following examples imply that the action of building a house or eating breakfast is accomplished, i.e. no building or eating is ongoing at the time of utterance:

أحمد بنى بيت عدال الواحة

ʔaħmad bənaa beet ʕəddaal əl-waaħa.

Ahmad build.perf-he house next the-oasis

'Ahmad (has) built a house next to the oasis.' (Building is completed at the speech time)

أحمد تريّق

ʔaħmad t-rajjag.

Ahmad refl-eat.breakfast.perf-he

'Ahmad has eaten breakfast.' (Breakfast is finished)

The perfective aspect is also widely used to express historical events which, by nature, must have been completed.

أمريكا سحبت قواتها من الفيتنام فسنة ألف وتسعمية وثلاث وسبعين

ʔamriikaa səħb-at quwwaat-haa mən əl-veetnam f-sənat ʔalf w-təsʕəmjja w-θalaaθ w-sabʕiin.

America withdraw.perf-it.f troops-it.f from the-Vietnam in-year thousand and-nine.hundred and-three and-seventy

'US withdrew its troops from Vietnam in 1973.'

الأرجنتين هزمت إنجلترا فكاس العالم فألف وتسعمية وست وثمانين

l-arʤantiin həzm-at ʔəngaltra f-kaas əl-ʕaalam f-ʔalf w-təsʕəmjja w-sətta w-θəmaaniin.

the-Argentina defeat.perf-it.f England in-cup the-world in-thousand and-nine.hundred and-six and-eighty

'Argentina defeated England in the 1986 World Cup.'

الصين بنت سور الصين العظيم من قبل ألفين سنة

ʔəsˤ-sˤiin bən-at suur əsˤ-sˤiin əl-ʕaðˤiim mən gabəl ʔalf-een səna.

the-china build.perf-it.f wall the-china the-great from before thousand-du year

'China built the Great Wall more than 2000 years ago.'

The use of perfect aspect can also express a 'pluperfect' event, i.e. events which are anterior to another past event (cf. English past perfect). The pluperfect nature of the perfective aspect is always supported by a subordinate clause, e.g. the clause formed by قبل

gabəl 'before' (Section 14.1.2), which establishes a reference time itself. The pluperfect reading is not formally (i.e. morphologically) expressed but inferred by the speaker/hearer. Emirati speakers may infer the imperfective verb (e.g. يوصل joosˤal '(he) comes') within the subordinate clause as indicating a past event, and the perfective verb (e.g. روّح raawaaħ '(he) left') as expressing a 'past-in-the-past' meaning. The speaker may also maintain the original time of reference; the pluperfect meaning then disappears.

أحمد روح قبل لا يوصل علي

ʔaħmad rawwa-ħ gabəl laa j-uusˤal ʕəli.
Ahmad leave.perf-he before that he-come.imperf ali
'Ahmad had left before Ali came.'

القاتل ذبح الرئيس قبل لا تكتشف الشرطة خطته

əl-gaatəl ðəbaħ ər-raʔiis gabel laa tə-ktəʃəf əʃ-ʃərtˤa xətˤtˤəta-h.
the-assassin kill.perf-he the-president before not she-refl.discover.imperf the-police plot-his
'The assassin had killed the president before the police discovered his plot.' (or 'The assassin kills the president before the police discovers his plot.')

نورة خلصت الواجب قبل لا نتلاقى

nuura xalˤlˤəsˤ-at əl-waadʒeb gabəl laa nə-tlaaga.
Noora finish.perf-she the-homework before not we-meet.imperf
'Noora had finished the homework before we met.' (or 'Noora finished the homework before we meet.')

The perfective aspect, if embedded in the conditional clause, can express a counterfactual reading. Note that the main clause may contain the modal auxiliary جان ʧaan 'would' (Section 9.2, 9.8) with a perfective verb.

لو أحمد درس عدل جان نجح فالامتحان

loo ʔaħmad dəras ʕadel ʧaan nədʒaħ f-əl-ʔəmtəħaan.
If Ahmad study.perf-he proper would pass.perf-he in-the-exam
'If Ahmad (had) studied properly, he would have passed the examination.'

لو علي شرى السيارة الاسبوع اللي طاف جان سقناها للعين

loo ʕəli ʃara əs-sajjaara l-esbuuʕ ʔəlli tˤaaf tʃaan səg-naa-ha l-əl-ʕeen.

if Ali buy.perf-he the-car the-week that pass.perf-it would drive.perf-we-it to-Al Ain

'If Ali (had) bought the car last week, we could have driven (it) to Al Ain.'

For future counterfactual conditionals, given that the irrealis event has not happened at the speech time, an imperfective verb may still be used in the main clause.

لو أحمد يدرس عدل الحين، بينجح فامتحان الاسبوع الياي

loo ʔaħmad jə-drəs ʕadəl əl-ħiin ba-jə-ndʒaħ f-əl-əmtəħaan əl-əsbooʕ əl-jaaj.

if Ahmad he-study.imperf proper the-now will-he-pass.imperf in-the-examination the-week the-next

'If Ahmad (had) studied properly now, he should pass the examination next week.'

Morphologically, perfective aspect is realized on the verbal stem (Section 5.2), which also contains information about the sentential subject with respect to its person, number, and gender. For transitive verbs (Chapter 7), which require an object pronoun, the object pronoun suffix (sometimes called the clitic) may be attached to the perfective verbal stem, especially if the reference of the pronoun is not explicitly mentioned but discourse-salient. The object pronoun suffix must follow the subject pronoun agreement (see Section 5.2).

8.2 The imperfective aspect

The imperfective aspect is always used to express any generic (e.g. individual-level) statement. For example:

الدكاترة يحبون يسوون بحوث

əd-dəkaatra j-ħəbb-uun j-saww-uun bħuuθ.

the-professors they-love.imperf-they they-do.imperf-they research

'Professors (usually) love doing research.'

دايرة الجوازات تدقق عهوية اللاجئين اليدّد

daajrat	əl-ʤawaazaat	ət-daqqəq	ʕa-həwijj-jat
əl-laaʤʔ-iin	əl-jəddad.		
department	the-immigration	it.f-caus.inspect.imperf	on-identity-f
the-immigrants	the-new.pl		

'The Immigration Department inspects the new immigrants' identities.'

Statements about the natural world must be expressed by the imperfective aspect. For example:

الأرض تدور حول الشمس

əl-ʔarðˤ	ət-duur	ħool	əʃ-ʃams.
the-Earth	it.f-rotate.imperf	around	the-sun

'The Earth rotates around the sun.'

الطيور تقدر تطير

ətˤ-tˤjuur	tə-gdar	ətˤ-tˤiir.
the-birds	they-can.imperf	they-fly.imperf

'Birds can fly.'

الماي يغلي فدرجة حرارة مئة

əl-maaj	jə-ɣli	f-daraʤa-t	ħaraara-t	ʔəmja.
the-water	it-boil.imperf	in-degree-f	heat-f	hundred

'Water boils at 100 degrees.'

Generic statements which refer to other times (e.g. future) can be expressed by the imperfective aspect. In such cases, the use of a future modal marker بـ b- 'will' (Section 5.2.14 and Chapter 7) may be used. Whether the future marker in conditional clauses is optional depends on the context. In the presence of adverbs such as دوم doom 'always,' native speakers appear to deprecate the use of the future marker. On the other hand, without any adverbial modification, the future marker is completely optional.

لو حطيت شمعة تحت الشمس بتذوب

loo	ħatˤtˤee-t	ʃamʕa	taħt	əʃ-ʃams	(ba-)t-ðuub.
if	put.perf-you	candle	under	the-sun	will-it.f-melt.imperf

'If you put a candle under the sun, it will melt.'

مساعد البروفسور دوم يترقى عقب ست سنوات تدريس

musaaʕəd lə-brofəsoor doom jə-traqqa ʕəgəb sət sanaw-aat ta-driis.

assistant the-professor always he-promote.imperf after six year-f.pl part-teach

'Assistant professors (will) always be promoted after six years of teaching.'

The imperfective aspect also expresses episodic events and situations. For events which happen during the speech time, the use of an imperfective aspect is felicitous if the main verb is preceded by the progressive aspect marker قاعد gaʕəd/يالس jaləs (lit. 'sitting') (Section 7.11). Emirati speakers strongly prefer the use of قاعد gaʕəd/يالس jaləs 'sitting' as a grammaticalized aspectual marker to express an ongoing action, and its absence is considered as unnatural.

أحمد قاعد يرقد، لا تزعجه

ʔaħmad gaaʕəd jə-rgəd laa tə-zʕəʤ-ah.

Ahmad part.sit he-sleep.imperf not you-disturb.imperf-him

'Ahmad is sleeping. Don't disturb him.'

أحمد يلس يرسم وياهم ، وايد مركّز

ʔaħmad jəlas jə-rsəm wijjaa-hum waajd m-rakkəz.

Ahmad part.sit he-draw.imperf with.them very part-focus

'Ahmad is drawing a picture. He is very focused.'

However, if the grammatical context of the present time is salient (e.g. with the word الحين əlħiin 'now'), the use of قاعد gaaʕəd/يالس jaaləs is optional and the use of a bare imperfective aspect is acceptable.

أحمد يرسم الحين، وايد مركّز

ʔaħmad jə-rsəm əl-ħiin waajəd m-rakkəz.

Ahmad he-draw.imperf the-now very part-focus

'Ahmad is drawing a picture now. He is very focused.'

موزة تمتحن الحين. بتكون فالبيت عقب ساعتين

mooza tə-mtəħən əl-ħiin bə-t-kuun f-əl-beet ʕəgəb saaʕ-teen.
Moza she-refl.examine.imperf the-now will-she-be.imperf at-the-home after hour-du
'Moza is taking the examination now. She will be home after two hours.'

The imperfective aspect may also express past or future episodic events. However, for past events, the imperfective main verb must be preceded by the perfective verb كان kaan 'was' (or its inflected form). Compared with the use of the perfective aspect, the combination of كان kaan and the imperfective verb expresses a past continuous event. The combination is considered as natural without the use of قاعد gaaʕəd/يالس jaaləs. On the other hand, the addition of قاعد gaʕəd/يالس jaləs (e.g. كانت قاعده تطبخ kanat gaaʕda tatˤbax '(she) was cooking') is considered by many to be clumsy.

فاطمة كانت تطبخ هني أمس فنفس هالوقت

faatˤma kaan-at tə-tˤbax hnii ʔams f-nafs ha-l-wagt.
Fatima be.perf-she she-cook.imperf here yesterday in-same this-the-time
'Same time yesterday, Fatima was cooking here.'

The imperfective aspect, if preceded by the future marker بـ b-, may express various future events. The exact nature of the verbal aspect depends upon the semantics of the main verb, especially its lexical aspect. It can express a future state (cf. simple future tense in English) or a future progressive event.

أحمد بيسافر أمريكا

ʔaħmad ba-j-saafər ʔamriikaa.
Ahmad will-he-travel.imperf America
'Ahmad will travel to America.'

شمسة بتدرس لغويات فهارفرد السنة الياية

ʃamsa b-tə-drəs luɣawijjaat f-haarfard əs-səna əl-jaaj-ja.
Shamsa will-she-study.imperf linguistics in-Harvard the-year the-coming-f
'Shamsa will study linguistics at Harvard next year.'

موزة بتبيع عبي فالسوق الأحد الياي

mooza bə-t-biiʕ ʕəbi f-es-suug əl-ʔaħad əl-jaaj.

Moza will-she-sell.imperf abaya.pl in-the-souq the-Sunday the-coming

'Next Sunday, Moza will be selling abaya in the souq.'

فاطمة بتشتغل فمدرسة السنة الياية

faatˤma b-tə-ʃtəɣəl f-madrəsa əs-səna əl-jaaj-ja.

Fatima will-she-work.imperf in-school the-year the-coming-f

'Fatima will be working in school next year.'

The imperfective verb is commonly used in control structures formed by control predicates such as بغى baɣa 'wanted' and قرر qarrar 'decided' (Section 7.9).

أحمد كان يبا يسافر أمريكا

ʔaħmad kaan jə-baa j-saafər ʔamriikaa.

Ahmad be.perf-he he-want.imperf he-travel.imperf America

'Ahmad (had) wanted to travel to America.'

ريم قررت تدرس ماستر فجامعة الإمارات

riim qarrəra-t tə-drəs maastar f-ʤaamʕa-t l-əmaara-at.

Reem caus.decide.perf-she she-study.imperf master at-university-f the-Emirate-pl

'Reem decided to study for a master's degree at UAE University.'

علي حاول يتواصل ويا محمد لاسبوع، بس ماقدر يوصله

ʕəli ħaawal jə-twaasˤal wijja mħammad l-sbuuʕ bas maa gədar j-uusˤala-h.

Ali try.perf-he he-refl.contact.imperf with Mohammed for-week but not can.perf-he he-find.imperf-him

'Ali tried to contact Mohammed for a week, but he could not find him.'

Depending on the intended meaning, raising structures (e.g. شكل ʃakəl 'apparently' or 'seemingly') (Section 7.8) may allow embedded clauses formed by the imperfective aspect. For instance, the following examples show that the embedded clause is an irrealis event which is felicitously expressed by the imperfective verb (Chapter 9):

الفريق شكلة بيفوز فالمباراة
əl-fariiq ʃakl-ah ba-j-fuuz fə-l-mbaaraa.
the-team apparently-it will-it-win.imperf in-the-match
'It seems the team will win (in) the match.'

The use of the perfective aspect in raising structures is equally grammatical (Section 7.8).

موزة شكلها فتحت مطعم اماراتي فبوظبي
mooza ʃakəl-ha fətħa-t mat^{ʕ}ʕam əmaaraati f-buð^{ʕ}abi.
Moza apparently-her open-she.perf restaurant Emirati in-Abu.Dhabi
'Moza seems to have opened an Emirati restaurant in Abu Dhabi.'

شكلها جامعتنا فازت بالجايزة
ʃakəl-ha dʒaamʕat-naa faaz-at b-əl-dʒaajza.
apparently-it.f university-our win.perf-it.f with-the-award
'Our university seems to have won the award.'

Imperfective verb stems are marked for subject agreement. The subject agreement always contains prefixal part to the imperfective verb stem (Section 5.2), e.g. يقرا jəgra 'he reads' and تقرا təgra 'she reads.' Some person features (e.g. third-person plural) require a suffixal part. For details refer to Section 5.2.

8.3 Participles

Emirati Arabic allows the use of participles to express a complete event/action in the past (cf. past perfect) and the future (cf. future perfect). The participle is always used with the copular verb كان kaan 'be' (Section 7.1), forming complex predicates (Section 7.11).

نورة كانت راقدة خمس ساعات قبل لانتلاقى
nuura kaan-at raagd-a xams saaʕaat gabəl laa nə-tlaaga.
Noora be.perf-she part.sleep-f five hours before that we-meet.imperf
'Noora had slept for five hours before we met.'

نورة كانت مسوية تمارين يوم تلاقينا

nuura kaan-at m-sawij-a tamaar-iin joom t-laag-eena.
Noora be.perf-she part-do-f exercise-pl day refl-meet.perf-we
'Noora had done (i.e. had finished doing) exercises when we met.'

الشركة بتكون بانية بيت السنة اليابة

əʃ-ʃərka bə-t-kuun baanj-a beet əs-səna əl-jaajja.
the-company will-it-be.imperf part.build-f house the-year the-coming
'The company will have built a house next year.'

الشركة بتكون مخلصة بنى السنة اليابة

əʃ-ʃərka bə-t-kuun m-xalsˤ-a bənaa əs-səna əl-jaajja.
the-company will-it-be.imperf part-finish-f part.build the-year the-coming
'The company will have finished building a house next year.'

عهود بتكون متخرجة الفصل الياي

ʕəhuud b-ət-kuun mə-txarʤ-a əl-fasˤl əl-jaaj.
Uhood will-she-be.imperf part-refl.graduate-f the-semester the-coming
'Uhood will have graduated next semester.'

In other cases, the existence of a bare participle may express a present ongoing event.

سارة راقدة، لاتزعجونها

Saara raagd-a, laa tə-zʕəʤ-uun-ha.
Sarah part.sleep-f don't you.f-disturb.imperf-you.f-her
'Sarah is sleeping. Do not disturb her!'

هند مسافرة مكة

hənd m-saafr-a makka.
Hind part-traval-f Mecca
'Hind is traveling to Mecca.' (i.e. Hind is in the process of traveling to Mecca. She may be en route, or is already in Mecca traveling.)

The form of active/passive participle is based on the imperfective verb stem and depends on the verb form (Section 5.2).

8.4 Lexical aspect

As mentioned before, event semantics arise by combining grammatical aspect (perfective or imperfective) with the lexical semantics of verbs. Overall, a verb can be aspectually classified as a state, activity, achievement, or accomplishment. The lexical aspect of a verb is also known as its aktionsart.

8.4.1 *State verbs*

State (or stative) verbs describe the state of being of the sentence subject. When the state verb is imperfective, it is understood that the subject is in the particular state of being at the utterance time and thereafter.

أحمد يعرف نتيجة الامتحان

ʔaħmad jə-ʕarf natiidʒ-at lə-mtiħaan.
Ahmad he-know.imperf result-f the-examination
'Ahmad (just) knows the examination result.'

فاطمة تفهم صعوبة السؤال

faatˤma tə-fham sˤʕuuba-t əs-suʔaal.
fatima she-understand.imperf difficulty-f the-question
'Fatima understands the difficulty of the question.'

مريم بعدها تحيد طفولتها

marjam baʕad-haa t-ħiid tˤəfuulat-ha.
Mariam still-her she-remember.imperf childhood-her
'Mariam still remembers her childhood.'

On the other hand, the use of perfective aspect with stative verbs entails the subject to have been in a particular state of being in the past. Because of the lexical semantics of state verbs (Table 8.1), native speakers may infer that the past state of being is extended to present (and possibly future) time (Section 7.2).

Table 8.1 Stative verbs

عَيَب	ʕəjab	'liked'	عرف	ʕəraf	'knew'
حب	ħab	'loved'	استوعب	(ə)stawʕab	'realized'
كره	karah	'hated'	افترض	(ə)ftəraðˤ	'supposed'
بغى	bəɣaa	'wanted'	فهم	fəham	'understood'
احتاج	(ʔ)əħtaaj	'needed'	صدّق	sˤaddag	'believed'
فضل	faðˤðˤal	'preferred'	ذكر	ðəkar	'remembered'
وافق	waafag	'agreed'	استغرب	(ə)staɣrab	'confused'

8.4.2 Activity verbs

The subject of the activity verb initiates an observable action. If the activity verb is perfective, the verbal action has been completed by the time of utterance. Distinctions may be drawn about whether the verb depicts a complete action in its entirety (by using the perfective form on the main verb) or a past progressive action (by using the perfective form on the auxiliary verb كان kaan 'was').

علي ركض ساعة الليلة اللي طافت

ʕəli	rəkaðˤ	saaʕa	əl-leela	ʔəlli	tˤaafa-t.
Ali	run.perf-he	hour	the-night	that	pass.perf-it.f

'Ali ran for an hour last night.'

The 'completeness' of an activity ('boundedness' or 'delimitedness' in linguistic terms, i.e. whether the event has a definite endpoint in time) also depends on whether the semantic feature of the direct object. For activity verbs (Table 8.2) that take a specific (i.e. bounded, delimited) object, the event becomes bounded.

شيخة غنت غنية يديدة الليلة اللي طافت

ʃeexa	ɣanna-t	əɣnijja	jdiid-a	əl-leela	ʔəlli	tˤaafa-t.
Shaikha	sing.perf-she	song	new-f	the-night	that	pass.perf-it.f

'Shaikha sang a new song last night.'

In contrast, if the direct object is indefinite (nonspecific), the event may be interpreted as unbounded.

Table 8.2 Activity verbs

مشى	məʃa	'walked'	رقد	rəgad	'slept'
سبح	səbaħ	'swam'	حلم	ħəlam	'dreamed'
طار	tˁaar	'flew'	رمس	rəmas	'spoke'
لوّن	lawwan	'colored'	غنى	ɣanna	'sang'
كتب	kətab	'wrote'	ربع	rəbaʕ	'ran'
كل	kall	'ate'	شاف	ʧaaf	'watched'
شخر	ʃaxxar	'snored'	طلب	tˁəlˁab	'sought'
تنفس	tnaffas	'breathed'	قعد	gəʕad	'sat'

شيخة تقرا كتب طول الصبح فالمكتبة

ʃeexa tə-gra kətəb tˁuul əsˁ-sˁəbħ f-əl-maktəba.
Shaikha she-read.imperf books all the-morning in-the-library
'Shaikha reads books in the library the whole morning (every morning).'

For intransitive activity verbs which do not take any object, the verbal event is interpreted as unbounded.

الببغا كان يغني طول اليوم

əl-babbaɣaa kaan j-ɣannii tˁuul əl-joom.
the-parrot be.perf-it it-sing.imperf whole the-today
'The parrot was singing the entire day.'

8.4.3 Achievement verbs

Achievement verbs are semantically instantaneous in the sense that they possess no inherent time interval (i.e. not durative), and thus cannot be modified by durative adverbial expressions (e.g. 'for an hour'). Achievement verbs are always perfective, and the use of an imperfective stem is considered infelicitous (Table 8.3).

فاطمة وصلت الصف

faatˁma wəsˁlˁa-t əsˁ-sˁaff.
Fatima arrive.perf-she the-class
'Fatima has arrived at the class.'

Table 8.3 Achievement verbs

وصل	wəsˤal	'arrived'	نجح	nədʒaħ	'succeeded'
فاز	faaz	'won'	مر	marr	'passed'
خسر	xəsar	'lost'	لقى	ləga	'found'
مات	maat	'died'			

عهود توها نجحت فالامتحان النهائي

ʕəhuud taw-ha nədʒħa-t f-əl-əmtəħaan ən-nəhaaʔii.

Uhood just-her pass.perf-she in-the-examination the-final

'Uhood just passed the final examination.'

8.4.4 Accomplishment verbs

Accomplishment verbs (Table 8.4) always involve an observable verbal action (cf. activity verbs) which contains an endpoint. Similar to activity verbs, accomplishment verbs may be modified by temporal expressions, such as 'for an hour,' which indicate the event duration. However, accomplishment verbs may also be modified by expressions such as 'in an hour,' which suggests the event's endpoint. Events expressed by accomplishment verbs are cumulative and may be quantized by adverbial expressions such as 'almost,' whereas activity verbs cannot. In terms of argument structure (Chapter 7), accomplishment verbs always select a direct object, e.g. ذبح ðəbaħ 'killed' and لوّن lawwan 'painted.' If the accomplishment verb is imperfective, the verbal event is interpreted as cumulative without reaching the endpoint.

Table 8.4 Accomplishment verbs

كسر	kəsar	'broke s.o'
ذبح	ðəbaħ	'killed s.o'
غيّر	ɣajjar	'changed s.th'
بنى	bəna	'built s.th'
لوّن صورة	lawwan	'painted s.th'

الحكومة قاعدة تبني نفق ثاني عسب تحل مشكلة الزحمة

əl-ħukuuma gaaʕd-a tə-bni nafaq θaani ʕasab
t-ħəll məʃkəl-at əz-zaħma.
the-government part.sit-f it-build.imperf tunnel another in.order.to
it-solve.imperf problem-f the-traffic
'The government is building another tunnel to solve traffic problems.'
(The tunnel is not finished yet.)

شمة اطالع فلم فالسينما. الفلم بيخلص عقب ساعتين

ʃamma ətˤ-tˤaaləʕfəlm f-əs-seenəma. əl-fələm
bi-j- xalˤlˤəsˤ ʕəgub saaʕ-teen.
Shamma she-watch.imperf movie in-the-theater the-movie
will-it-finish.imperf after hour-du
'Shamma is watching a movie in the theater. The movie will finish in two hours.'

If the accomplishment verb is perfective, the endpoint of the verbal event has been reached. For example:

علي بدل ثلاث تواير لكنه ماقدر يبدل آخر واحد لانه المحل سكر

ʕəli baddal θalaaθ təwaajər laakənn-ah maa-gədar
j-baddəl ʔaaxər waaħəd lanna l-maħal sakkar.
Ali change.perf-he three tires but-him not-can.imperf
he-change.imperf the-last one because the-shop close.perf-it
'Ali has (already) changed three tires, but he could not change the last one because the shop closed.'

هالشركة الصينية طردت مية عامل عسبت مشكلة الفلوس

h-aʃ-ʃarəka əsˤ-sˤiiniij-ja tˤərd-at əmj-at
ʕaaməl ʕ-asəbb-at məʃkəl-at lə-fluus.
this-the-company the-Chinese-f fire.perf-it.f 100-f
employee on-reason-f problem-f the-money
'This Chinese company has fired 100 employees because of financial problems.'

8.5 Grammatical aspect

Aspect may also be indicated grammatically, especially by using complex predicates (Section 7.11). In the expression of grammatical aspect, the first verb of the complex predicate is grammaticalized and encodes the aspectuality of the main verb. Various aspectual meanings may be generated.

8.5.1 Continuative

The continuative aspect expresses that a verbal action or state of affairs is still ongoing. In some cases, it expresses the state/property of the subject (e.g. 'John is working' suggests that John is no longer a student).

أحمد تم يسوي الكيك

ʔaħmad tamm j-sawwi əl-keek.
Ahmad keep.perf-he he-make.imperf the-cake
'Ahmad continued making the cake.'

موزة تمت تغني طول الليل

Mooza tamm-at t-ɣanii tˁuul əl-leel
moza keep.perf-she she-sing.imperf whole the-night
'Moza continued singing for the whole night.'

8.5.2 Progressive

The progressive aspect mainly describes an ongoing event. It may be expressed by the grammaticalized verb قاعد gaaʕəd 'sitting.'

راشد قاعد يكتب الرسالة

raaʃəd gaaʕəd jə-ktəb ər-rəsaala.
Rashid part.sit he-write.imperf the-letter
'Rashid is writing the letter.'

علي كان قاعد يشوف التلفزيون يوم ابوه رد البيت

ʕəli kaan gaaʕəd j-ʧuuf əl-təlfəzjuun joom ʔəbuu-h rad əl-beet
Ali be.perf-he part.sit he-see.imperf the-TV when father-his return.perf-he the-home
'Ali was watching TV when his father came back home.'

It is also possible to use the prepositional expression في عز fi ʕəz 'in the process of' to express the progressive aspect. Note that

في عز fi ʕəz may be followed by a noun or verbal noun, not by an aspectual verb.

وعاني وانا في عز رقادي عسب نتغدى

wəʕʕaa-ni w-ana f-ʕəz rgaad-i ʕasab nə-tɣadda

caus.wake.perf-he-me and-me in-middle sleep-my in.order.to we-refl.have.lunch.imperf

'He woke me up in the middle of my sleep to have lunch.'

8.5.3 *Inceptive*

The inceptive aspect describes the beginning of an action or event. For example:

قام ياكل بإيده الحين

gaam jaa-akəl b-ʔiid-a əl-ħiin.

start.perf-he he-eat.imperf with-hand-his the-now

'He has started eating with his hands now.'

بدا يلعب كورة من عشر سنوات ومن سنة صار محترف

bəda jə-lʕab koora mən ʕaʃər sana-waat w-mən səna sˤaar mə-ħtərəf

begin.perf-he he-play.imperf ball from ten year-f.pl and-from one-year become part-refl.professional

'He started to play football ten years ago and became a professional one year ago.'

8.5.4 *Prospective*

The prospective aspect describes an event that is realized after the reference time/event. A prospective event is mostly irrealis and expressed by the imperfective aspect.

يه ياخذ شنطته

ja j-aaxəð ʃantˤət-a.

come.perf-he he-take.imperf bag-his

'He came to take his bag.'

راح يلعب في الحجرة بروحه

raaħ jə-lʕab fəl-ħədʒra b-ruuħ-ah
go.perf-he he-play.imperf in-room with-soul-his
'He went to play in the room by himself.'

The adverb تو taw 'just,' which combines with the irrealis modality marker b-, also expresses the prospective aspect.

وصلنا القاعة يوم الاحتفال كان توه بيبدا

wəsˤalˤ-na l-qaaʕa joom əl-əħtəfaal kaan taww-ah ba-jə-bda
arrive.perf-we the-hall when the-ceremony be.perf-it just-it will-it-begin.imperf
'We arrived at the hall just as the ceremony was about to begin.'

It is also possible to express the prospective aspect by the subordinator عشان ʕʃaan 'in order to' (Chapter 14).

دقيت على محمد عشان أسأله بس ما رد

daggee-t ʕala mħammad ʕaʃaan ʔa-sʔal-ah bas maa rad
call.perf-I on Mohammed in.order.to I-ask.imperf-him but not answer.perf-he
'I called Mohammed to ask him but he did not answer.'

8.5.5 Terminative

The terminative aspect signals that an event or situation is completed or accomplished. For example:

خلص دراسة حق الامتحان

xalˤlˤasˤ dəraas-a ħag l-əmtəħaan.
finish.perf-he part.study-f for the-exam
'He finished studying for the exam.'

نوف وقفت تاكل عقب الساعة سبع فالليل

noof waggəf-at t-aakəl ʕəgəb əs-saaʕa sabəʕ f-əl-leel.
Nouf caus.stop.perf-she she-eat.imperf after hour seven in-the-night
'Nouf stopped eating after 7pm.'

One can also express the recent completion of an event by the adverb تو taw 'just.' This adverb is compatible with the two lexical aspects and participles.

أمي توها مخبرتني

ʔumm-i taw-ha m-xabbər-tə-nni
mom-my just-her part-caus.tell-f-me
'My mom has just told me.'

توني سرت بيت عمي، محد كان موجود

taw-ni sər-t beet ʕamm-i ma-ħħad kaan ma-wʤuud
just-me go.perf-I house uncle-my no-one be.perf-he part-exist
'I've just been to my uncle's house, no one was there.'

توها تعرف ان محمد تخرج

taw-ha t-ʕarf ʔənna mħammad t-xarraʤ
just-her she-know.imperf that Mohammed refl-caus.graduate.perf-he
'She just knows that Mohammed graduated.'

Another adverb which serves a similar function is ʧəd جد 'already,' which is compatible with the perfective aspect and participles.

وصل البيت وجدني ظاهر وخالص

wəsˤalˤ əl-beet w ʧəd-ni ðˤaahər w-xaaləsˤ.
arrive.perf-he the-house and already-me part.leave and-part-finish
'He arrived at the house while I had already left.'

وصل البيت وجدني ظهرت وخلصت

wəsˤalˤ əl-beet w ʧəd-nii ðˤəhar-t w-xllasˤ-t.
arrive.perf-he the-house and already-me leave.perf-I and-finish.perf-I
'He arrived at the house and I had already left.'

8.5.6 *Habitual*

The copula كان kaan, in the formation of complex predicates (Section 7.11), may serve to express the habitual aspect. For example:

كان يحل الواجبات حقها

kaan	j-ħəll	əl-waadʒəb-aat	ħag-ha.
be.perf-he	he-solve.imperf	the-homework-f.pl	for-her

'He used to do the homework for her.'

كنتي متعودة تلعبين ويانا

kən-t-i	mə-tʕawd-a	tə-lʕəb-iin	wijjaa-naa.
be.perf-you-f	part-refl.used.to-f	you.f-play.imperf-you.f	with-us

'You used to play with us.'

Further reading

For the detailed study of the grammaticalization in Emirati Arabic and the usage of يالس jaalas 'sit' as a grammaticalized progressive aspectual marker, see Jarad (2015, 2017). Aspect in the related Kuwaiti Arabic variety is discussed in Al-Najjar (1984). Persson (2008a) examines the future/irrealis marker بـ b- 'will' in Gulf Arabic, while Persson (2008b) surveys several modal and aspectual markers in Gulf Arabic. On the aspectual system in MSA and other Arabic dialects, see Eisele (1990), Brustad (2000), Fassi Fehri (2012), and Ouali (2017), and Mughazy (2005) for lexical aspect in Egyptian Arabic. For a linguistic discussion of the aspectuality of events and objects, refer to Krifka (1992), Tenny (1992), and Verkuyl (1993), among many others.

Chapter 9

Mood and modality

The issue of modality is concerned with how the speaker expresses *possible world semantics* regarding the necessity (deontic modality, Section 9.1), possibility (epistemic modality, Section 9.2), and capacity (dynamic modality, Section 9.3) of the state of affairs. Speakers may also indicate the source of information—whether their statements are based on direct or indirect evidence (evidential modality, Section 9.6). Languages further grammaticalize particular types of modality, e.g. imperatives (Section 9.7).

9.1 Deontic modality

Deontic modality expresses necessity, obligation, and other external conditions imposed on the subject of the sentence. These conditions are established by the speaker or other forms of authority such as laws and regulations. In Emirati Arabic, this function may be expressed by the use of modal auxiliaries (Table 9.1).

Table 9.1 Deontic modal auxiliaries

لازم	laazəm	'must' (strong necessity)
ضروري	ðˤaruurii	'must/should' (mild-strong necessity)
المفروض	(əl)mafruuðˤ	'should' (mild necessity)
ممكن	mumkən	'can' (permission)
روم	ruum	'can' (permission)

ما أريد أدرس بس لازم لأنه عليه امتحان

maa-riid ʔa-drəs bas laazəm lanna ʕala-jja əmtəħaan.

not-I-want.imperf I-study.imperf but necessary because on-me exam

'I don't want to study but I have to because I have an exam.'

الطلاب لازم يدرسون زين عشان يدخلون الجامعة

ətˤ-tˤəlˤlˤaab laazəm jə-drəs-uun zeen ʕaʃaan jə-dxəl-uun l-ʤaamʕa

the-students must they-study.imperf-they well in.order.to they-enter.imperf-they the-university

'Students must study hard to get into universities.'

ضروري أدرس

ðˤaruuri ʔa-drəs.

must I-study.imperf

'I must study.'

المفروض ادرس قبل لا سير السوق

əlmafruuðˤ ʔa-drəs gabəl laa-siir əs-suug.

should I-study.imperf before that-I-go.imperf the-market

'I should study before going to the market.'

ممكن اخذ قلمج؟

mumkən ʔaa-xəð galam-ʧ?

can I-take.imperf pen-your.f

'Can I take your pen?'

Some modal auxiliaries, e.g. روم ruum 'can,' may be inflected, depending on the sentence subject.

ما روم أيي

maa-ruum ʔajj-i.

not-I-can.imperf I-come.imperf

'I can't come.'

ما تروم تيي

maa-t-ruum ət-jii.

not-she-can.imperf she-come.imperf

'She can't come.'

ما يروم أيي

maa-j-ruum ʔə-jj-i.

not-he-can.imperf he-come.imperf

'He can't come.'

Modal auxiliaries always linearly precede the main verb, which is inflected for person, number, and gender in agreement with the sentence subject. However, most modal auxiliaries are never inflected in this context (cf. English 'must'). Moreover, the modal auxiliaries and the main verb may be separated by the sentence subject, but the location of the sentence subject is not entirely optional. If the sentence subject is sentence-initial, the sentence is always interpreted as a statement. In contrast, if the subject is positioned between the modal auxiliary and the main verb, the sentence may be interpreted as a statement or a question. Native speakers usually prefer a question reading if the modal is sentence-initial.

(علي) لازم (علي) يدرس للامتحان

(ʕəli)	laazəm	(ʕəli)	jə-drəs	l-əl-əmtəħaan.
Ali	must	Ali	he-study.imperf	for-the-exam

'Ali must study for the exam.' (or 'Must Ali study for the exam?')

(علي) ضروري (علي) يدرس

(ʕəli)	ðˤaruuri	(ʕəli)	jə-drəs.
Ali	must	Ali	he-study.imperf

'Ali must study.' (or 'Must Ali study?')

(شما) ممكن (شما) تحضر الحفلة الليلة؟

(ʃamma)	mumkən	(ʃamma)	tə-ħðˤar	əl-ħafla	əl-leela
Shamma	can	Shamma	she-join.imperf	the-party	the-tonight

'Shamma can join the party tonight' (or 'Can Shamma join the party tonight?')

For the modal auxiliary المفروض əlmafruuðˤ 'should,' the containing sentence is almost always interpreted as a statement, regardless of the position of the subject.

(علي) المفروض (علي) يدرس للامتحان

(ʕəli)	əlmafruuðˤ	(ʕəli)	jə-drəs	l-əl-əmtəħaan.
Ali	should	Ali	he-study.imperf	for-the-exam

'Ali should study for the exam.'

(سالم) المفروض (سالم) يروح ويانا
(Saaləm) əlmafruuðˤ (Saaləm) j-ruuħ wəjjaa-na.
Salim should Salim he-go.imperf with-us
'Salim should go with us.'

Some deontic modal auxiliaries (except ممكن mumkən 'can' and لازم laazəm 'must') function as the predicate of a sentence, hence modal adjectives. In this situation, the modal adjectives may be inflected for person, number, and gender (Section 6.5).

المدرسة ضرورية للأطفال
əl-madrəsa ðˤaruurijj-a le-l-ʔatˤfaal.
the-school necessary-f for-the-kids
'School is necessary for kids.'

أكل تفاحة فاليوم ضروري لصحتج
ʔakəl təffaaħa f-əl-joom ðˤaruuri l-sˤeħħa-ʧ.
eating apple in-the-today necessary for-health-your.f
'Eating an apple a day is necessary for your health.'

السيارات ضرورية للحياة الحديثة
əs-sajjaar-aat ðˤaruurijj-a le-l-ħajaa əl-ħadiiθa.
the-car-f.pl necessary-f.pl for-the-life the-modern
'Cars are necessary for modern life.'

اللاعبين الأجانب ضروريين لدورينا
əl-laaʕəb-iin əl-ʔaʤaanəb ðˤaruurijj-iin lə-dawrii-na.
the-player-pl the-foreign necessary-pl for-league-our
'The foreign players are necessary for our league.'

الصلاة كانت مفروضة
əsˤ-sˤalaah kaan-at mafruuðˤ-a.
the-prayer be.perf-it.f mandatory-f
'The prayer was mandatory.'

Some modal adjectives function attributively. In this case, they agree with the head noun they modify.

الصلاة المفروضة
əsˤ-sˤalaa əlmafruuðˤ-a.
the-prayer mandatory-f
'the mandatory prayer'

The modal adjective may also be followed by an embedded clause (Section 7.14). In these cases, the modal adjective agrees with the pleonastic pronoun, which is the third-person singular (cf. English 'it'). In such cases, the modal adjective may be separated with the embedded clause by the complementizer ان ʔənn(ah) 'that' (Section 5.7.1).

ضروري انه يدرس
ðˤaruuri ʔənn-ah jə-drəs.
necessary that-him he-study.imperf
'(It is) necessary that he studies.'

المفروض انه سالم يروح ويانا
(əl)mafruuðˤ ʔənna saaləm j-ruuħ wəjjaa-na.
necessary that Salim he-go.imperf with-us
'(It is) necessary that Salim goes with us.'

The sentence subject may precede or follow the modal adjective, showing that the modal adjective functions as a raising predicate (Section 7.8).

موزة المفروض إنها تاخذ توفل عشان تدرس في أمريكا
mooza (ʔəl)mafruuðˤ ʔən-ha t-aaxəð toofəl ʕaʃaan tə-drəs f-amriika
Moza necessary that-her she-take.imperf TOFEL in.order.to she-study.imperf in-America
'It is necessary that Moza takes the TOEFL exam to study in the US.'

Modal adjectives may be preceded by the negative marker, which directly reflects the scope relation. The following examples show that the predicative negation marker مب mub (or var. مش məʃ) 'not' may be used (Section 10.2):

مب ضروري ادرس
mub ðˤaruuri ʔa-drəs.
not necessary I-study.imperf
'It is not necessary that I study.'

مب المفروض تخبرين أمج كل شي

mub (əl)mafruuð^{ʕ} t-xabr-iin ʔummə-ʧ kəl ʃaj.

not necessary you.f-tell.imperf-you.f mother-your every thing

'It is not necessary that you tell your mother everything.'

مب لازم تداومين اليوم

mub laazəm t-daawm-iin əl-joom.

not obligatory you.f-go.work.imperf-you.f the-today

'You don't have to go to work today.' (lit. It is not necessary (that) you go to work today.)

مش ممكن تساعدينها فالامتحان

məʃ mumkən t-saaʕd-iin-haa f-əl-əmtəħaan.

not possible you.f-help.imperf-you.f-her in-the-exam

'You cannot help her in the exam.' (lit. It is not possible for you to help her in the exam.)

In contrast, to indicate that the negation receives a narrow scope with the modal adjective (cf. English 'must not,' and 'should not'), the verbal negative marker ما maa is used (Section 10.1). In most cases, the complementizer ان ʔənn 'that' is added right after the modal adjectives, although native speakers will consider it as clumsy. ان ʔənn cannot be added after laazəm لازم 'must.'

لازم ما تكتبين واجبج متأخر

laazəm maa tə-ktəb-iin waaʤəb-ʧ mə-ttaxxər.

must not you.f-write.imperf-you.f homework-your.f part-refl.late

'You must not write your homework late.'

لازم ما تنسين تحلين الواجب

laazəm maa t-əns-een t-ħəll-iin əl-waaʤəb.

must not you-forget.imperf-you.f you.f-solve.imperf-you.f the-homework

'You must not forget to solve your homework.'

ضروري ما تغيبين باجر

ð^{ʕ}aruuri maa t-ɣiib-iin baaʧər.

necessary not you.f-absent.imperf-you.f tomorrow

'You should not be absent tomorrow.' (lit. It's necessary that you are not absent tomorrow.)

المفروض ما تتأخرين عالدوام
(əl)mafruuðˤ maa tə-ttaxxər-een ʕa-d-dəwaam.
should not you.f-refl.late.imperf-you.f on-the-work
'You should not be late for work.'

المفروض ما تاكل أكل مش صحي
əlmafruuðˤ maa ta-akəl ʔakəl məʃ sˤəħħi.
should not you-eat.imperf food not healthy
'You should not eat unhealthy food.'

ممكن ما تخبرين حد عن الامتحان؟
mumkən maa t-xabr-iin ħadd ʕan l-əmtəħaan?
can not you.f-tell.imperf-you.f person about the-exam
'Can you not tell anybody about the exam?'

ممكن ما تتكلم وإنا على التلفون؟
mumkən maa t-ətkallam w-ʔana ʕ-at-taləfoon?
can not you-refl.talk.imperf and-I on-the-phone
'Can you not talk when I am on the phone?'

مسموح ما تحضرون باجر
ma-smuuħ maa t-əħðˤər-uun baatʃər.
part-pass.allow not you.pl-present.imperf-you.pl tomorrow
'You are allowed to not be present tomorrow.' (lit. It's allowed that you don't come tomorrow.)

اليهال اللي أقل عن الثاني عشرسنة ما يرومون يتسبحون فالمسبح
ə-ljahhaal ʔəlli ʔaqal ʕan θnaʕʃar səna maa j-ruum-uun jə-tsabbəħ-oon fə-l-masbaħ.
the-children that less than twelve year not they-can.imperf-they they-swim.imperf-they in-the-pool
'Children under 12 years cannot swim in the pool.'

9.2 Epistemic modality

Epistemic modality refers to the speaker's attitude toward the truth and possibility of the state of affairs or an event. This covers a wide range of expressions, including statements of fact, affirmation, speculation, prediction, deduction, induction, doubt, and falsity. Some deontic modal auxiliaries, such as لازم laazəm 'must' and مستحيل mustaħiil 'impossible,' also express the epistemic interpretation, depending on the context. Table 9.2 is a summary of some Emirati Arabic epistemic modal auxiliaries:

Table 9.2 Epistemic modal auxiliaries

لازم	laazəm	'must'	طبيعي	tˤabiiʕi	'normal'
عادي	ʕaadi	'may'	مستحيل	mustaħiil	'impossible'
جان	ʧaan	'would'	لابد	laabəd	'must'
يمكن	jəmkən	'may'	احتمال	əħtəmaal	'probably'

Similar to the case in deontic modality (Section 9.1), the form of epistemic modal auxiliary is invariant when followed by the main verb. For example:

مستحيل أنسى الدكتور سالم

mustaħiil ʔa-nsa əd-dəktoor saaləm.

impossible I-forget.imperf the-doctor Salem

'I can never forget Dr. Salem.' (lit. It is impossible that I forget Dr. Salem.)

عادي تدرسين قبل

ʕaadi tə-drəs-iin gabəl.

may you.f-study.imperf-you.f before

'You may study before.' (lit. (It is) possible (that) you study before.)

عادي ما تداومين اليوم؟

ʕaadi maa t-ddawm-iin əl-joom?

may not you.f-work.imperf-you.f the-today?

'May you not go to work today?' (lit. Is it possible that you do not work today?)

طبيعي تنجحين اذا درستي

tˤabiiʕi t-əndʒəħ-iin ʔəða daras-t-i.

normal you.f-succeed.imperf-you.f if study.perf-you-f

'You would succeed if you had studied.' (lit. (It is) normal (that) you succeed if you have studied.)

يمكن أدرس قبل ماسير السوق
jəmkən ʔa-drəs gabəl maa-siir əs-suug.
may I-study.imperf before that-I.go.imperf the-market
'I might study before going to the market.'

جان درستي لغويات لو تحبين اللغات الأجنبية
ʧaan daras-ti luɣawiijjaat law t-ħəbb-iin əl-luɣ-aat əl-ʔadʒnabi-jja.
could study.perf-you.f linguistics if you.f-love.imperf-you.f the-language-f.pl the-foreign-f
'You could have studied linguistics if you loved foreign languages.'

الجو مغيم الحين. لابد بيطيح مطر بعدين.
əl-dʒaw mɣajjəm əl-ħiin laabəd bə-j-tˤiiħ mətˤar baʕdeen.
the-weather cloudy the-now must will-it-fall.imperf rain later
'The weather is cloudy now. It must rain later.'

كالعادة الساعة 9. علي المفروض يكون فالبيت الحين
kəl ʕaad-ha əs-saaʕa təssəʕ. ʕəli əlmafruuðˤ jə-kuun fə-l-beet əl-ħiin.
all already-it the-clock nine Ali should he-be.imperf in-the-house the-now
'It is already 9pm. Ali should be home by now.'

الصين يمكن يزيدون ضريبة الدخل السنة الياية
əsˤ-sˤiin jəmkən j-ziid-uun ðˤariiba-t əd-daxəl əs-səna əl-jaaj-ja.
the-China may they-increase.imperf-they tax-f the-income the-year the-next-f
'China may increase income tax next year.'

احتمال أسير السينما باجر
əħtəmaal ʔa-siir əs-seenəma baaʧər.
probable I-go.imperf the-cinema tomorrow
'I probably will go to the cinema tomorrow.'

9.3 Dynamic modality

Dynamic modality expresses the subject's inherent capability to instantiate a particular state of affairs or realize a verbal event. Some modals, for instance, *mumkin* 'can,' are used with both deontic and dynamic modal interpretations, depending on the context (cf. English 'I can go to the party tonight' (deontic) vs. 'I can drive' (dynamic)). In addition to modal auxiliaries, Emirati Arabic may express dynamic modality by verbs of knowing and modal adjectives which signal the inherent capability of the subject (Table 9.3).

علي يعرف يتكلم صيني

ʕəli jə-ʕarf jə-tkallam sˤiini.

Ali he-know.imperf he-refl.speak.imperf Chinese

'Ali knows (how) to speak Chinese.'

موزه تروم ترمس فرنسي

mooza t-ruum tə-rməs faransi.

Moza she-can.imperf she-speak.imperf French

'Moza can speak French.'

طلاب اللغويات يرومون يشتغلون مدرسين انجليزي

tˤəlˤlˤaab əl-luɣawijj-aat j-ruum-uun jə-ʃtaɣl-oon mudarris-iin ʔingliizii.

student.pl the-linguistics-f they-can.imperf-they they-work.imperf-they teacher-pl English

'Linguistic students can work as English teachers.'

Table 9.3 Dynamic modal verbs and adjectives

Verbs of knowing			Modal adjectives		
عرف	ʕəraf	'know'	زين	zeen	'good (at)'
فهم	faham	'understand'	ممتاز	mumtaaz	'excellent (in)'
روم	ruum	'can'	ضعيف	ðˤəʕiif	'weak (in)'

شيخه فهمت كيف تحل هاي المعادلة الصعبة

ʃeexa fəhm-at keef t-ħəll haajj əl-muʕaadala esˤ-sˤaʕba.

Shaikha understand.perf-she how she-answer.imperf this the-equation the-difficult

'Shaikha understood how to solve this difficult equation.'

كل العمال تعلموا كيف يشغلون هالمكينة

kəl əl-ʕəmmaal tʕaləm-aw keef j-ʃaɣl-uun ha-l-məkiina.

all the-worker.pl learn.perf-they how they-run.imperf-they this-machine

'All of the workers have learned how to run this machine.'

Dynamic modal adjectives behave like other adjectives, which can be inflected for the subject's number and gender.

مريم وايد زينه فالرياضيات

marjam	waajəd	zeen-ah	f-ər-rijaaðˤijjaat.
Mariam	very	good-f	in-the-math

'Mariam is very good at math.'

علي كان ممتاز فالصيني

ʕəli	kaan	mumtaaz	f-əsˤ-sˤiini.
Ali	be.perf-he	excellent	in-the-Chinese

'Ali was excellent in Chinese (language).'

الطلاب كلهم ضعاف فالمنطق

ətˤ-tˤəlˤlˤaab	kəl-hum	ðˤʕaaf	f-əl-mantˤəq.
the-student.pl	all-them	weak.pl	in-the-logic

'The students are all weak in logic.'

For the type of dynamic modality in which the subject's ability to perform a particular action is licensed by the situation (such as صعب sˤaʕeb 'difficult' and سهل sahəl 'easy'), the dynamic modal adjective has to precede the verb. The adjectives are morphologically unmarked (i.e. the default third-person singular masculine). They may also be followed by the complementizer ان in 'that' (Section 5.7).

صعب انها تفوز فالمباراة

sˤaʕb ʔən-haa t-fuuz f-əl-əmbaaraa.

difficult that-her she-win.imperf in-the-match

'(It is) difficult (for) her to win the match.' (lit. It is difficult that she wins the match.)

كان سهل على أحمد انه ينجح فامتحان السواقة، لانه ما كان شيء سيايير فالشارع

kaan sahəl ʕala ʔaħmad ʔənn-ah jə-ndʒaħ f-əmtəħaan əs-swaagah laʔann-ah maa kaan ʃajj səjaajiir f-əʃ-ʃaarəʕ.

be.perf-it easy on Ahmad that-him he-pass.imperf in-exam the-driving because-it no be.perf-it there cars in-the-street

'It was easy for Ahmad to pass the driving test, because there were no cars on the street.'

كان سهل عأحمد انه ينجح ف امتحان السواقة، لانه تدرب لمدة سنة.

kaan sahəl ʕa ʔaħmad ʔənn-ah jə-ndʒaħ f-əmtəħaan əs-swaagah laʔann-ah t-darrab lə-muddat sənah.

be.perf-it easy on Ahmad that-him he-succeed.imperf in-exam the-driving because-he refl-caus.practice.perf-he for-period year

'It was easy for Ahmad to pass the driving test, because he practiced for a year.'

If the adjective is immediately followed by the verb, the sentence subject position can vary.

(فاطمة) صعب تفوز (فاطمة) فالمباراة

(faatˤma) sˤaʕəb t-fuuz (faatˤma) f-əl-əmbaaraa.

(Fatima) difficult she-win.imperf (Fatima) in-the-match

'(It is) difficult (for) Fatima to win the match.' (lit. 'Fatima is difficult to win the match.')

9.4 Modal adverbs

The meaning of modality may be readily expressed by the use of modal adverbs which are always positioned sentence-initially. See Table 9.4.

Table 9.4 Modal adverbs

يمكن	jəmkən	'maybe'	أكيد	ʔakiid	'surely'
احتمال	əħtəmaal	'probably'	أونه	ʔawannah	'supposedly'

يمكن انه مسافر
jəmkən ʔənn-ah m-saafər.
maybe that-him part-travel
'Maybe he is traveling.'

اكيد انه مسافر
ʔakiid ʔənn-ah m-saafər.
surely that-him part-travel
'Surely he is traveling.'

احتمال نيوتن أعظم عالم فالتاريخ
əħtəmaal njuutən ʔa-ʕðˤam ʕaaləm f-ət-taariix.
probably Newton most-great scientist in-the-history
'Newton is probably the greatest scientist in history.'

احتمال الحكومة ترجع الضرايب للمواطنين
əħtəmaal əl-ħukuuma t-radʒdʒəʕ əðˤ-ðˤaraajəb l-əl-məwaatˤn-iin.
probably the-government she-caus.return.imperf the-taxes to-the-citizen-pl
'The government will probably return tax to the citizens.'

احتمال ها اصعب شغلة
əħtəmaal haa ʔa-sˤʕab ʃəɣla.
probably this most-hard job
'This is probably the most difficult job.'

احتمال هالسكين هي سلاح الجريمة
əħtəmaal ha-s-sətʃiin hii slaaħ əl-dʒariima.
probably this-the-knife she weapon the-crime
'This knife is probably the murder weapon.'

أونه محد كان فالبيت يوم دقيت الباب

ʔawanna maħħad kaan fə-l-beet joom daggee-t əl-baab.

Supposedly no.one be.perf-he in-the-house when knock.perf-I the-door

'Supposedly no one was home when I knocked on the door.'

For all these modal adverbs, it is possible to insert the complementizer ان in (var. en-) 'that' (Section 5.7) without any change of meaning. For instance:

احتمال انه راقد

əħtəmaal ʔənn-ah raagəd.

probably that-him part.sleep

'Probably (that) he is sleeping.'

It is also possible to express modal adverbial meaning by prepositional phrases such as 'without doubt' and 'with intention.'

بدون شك، الاجتهاد والنجاح مترابطات

bəduun ʃak əl-əʤtəhaad w ən-naʤaaħ mə-t-raabtˤ-aat.

without doubt the-refl.hard.work and the-success part-pass-relate.perf-they.f

'Undoubtedly (= without doubt), hard work and success are related.'

دعم سيارتي بالعمد

daʕam sajjaart-i b-əl-ʕamd.

hit.perf-he car-my with-the-intention

'He hit my car intentionally.'

واضح هالمشكلة كانت من دون قصد.

waaðˤəħ ha-l-məʃkəla kaan-at mən-duun qasˤd.

clearly this-the-problem be.perf-it.f with-no intention

'This problem was clearly without intention.'

Modal adverbs can be preverbal without any change of meaning. For example:

(يمكن) فاطمة (يمكن) تسير السوق

(jəmkən) faatˤma (jəmken) t-siir əs-suug.
maybe Fatima maybe she-go.imperf the-market
'Fatima might go to the market.'

(أكيد) الشركة (أكيد) بتفتح فرع فالصين

(ʔakiid) əʃ-ʃərka (ʔakiid) ba-tə-ftaħ farʕ f-əsˤ-sˤiin.
certainly the-company certainly will-it.f-open.imperf branch in-the-China
'Certainly, the company will open a branch in China.'

9.5 Verbs expressing modality

In addition to the use of modal auxiliaries/adjectives, a small number of verbs express the meaning of modality (Table 9.5). Some modal verbs (e.g. يرومون jərumuun '(they) can') agree in gender and number with the sentence subject, whereas others are verbal participles (Section 5.3.2). Verbs of modality may select an

Table 9.5 Verbs expressing modality

توقع	twaqqaʕ	'expected'	قدر	gədar	'can/was able'
سمح	səmaħ	'allowed'	حبس	ħəbas	'arrested'
عرف	ʕəraf	'knew'	قصد	gəsˤad	'intended'
بغا	bəɣa	'wanted'	تمنى	tmanna	'wished'
تأمّل	tʔammal	'hoped'	وافق	waafag	'agreed'
تضارب	tðˤaarab	'disagreed'	انطلب	ntˤəlˤab	'was required'
احتاي	əħtaaj	'needed'	تحدى	tħadda	'dared'
صدق	sˤaddag	'believed'	وثق	wəθag	'trusted'
ظن	ðˤann	'guessed'	منع	mənaʕ	'forbade'
مستعد	məstəʕədd	'willing to'	مسك	məsak	'caught'
طلب	tˤəlab	'demanded'	ترك	tərak	'left'
حاول	ħaawal	'tried'	صب	sˤabb	'poured'

impoverished or a complete embedded clause formed by the complementizer انه ʔənn(ah) 'that' (Section 5.7, 7.14).

متوقعة أنجح

mə-t-waqʕ-a ʔa-ndʒaħ.

part-refl-expect-f I-succeed.imperf

'I am expecting to succeed.'

متوقعه الطالبات ما بيتأخرن عن الامتحان

mə-t-waqʕ-a ətˤ-tˤaalˤb-aat maa b-jə-ttaxxər-an ʕan l-əmtəħaan.

part-refl-expect-f the-student-f.pl not will-they.f-refl.late.imperf-they.f from the-exam

'I am expecting (that) the students will not be late for the exam.'

(روسيا) معروف (روسيا) قوية

(ruusjaa) ma-ʕruuf (ruusjaa) gəwijj-a.

Russia part-pass.know.perf Russia strong-f

'Russia is known to be strong.'

معروف عن روسيا أنها قوية

ma-ʕruuf ʕan ruusjaa ʔənn-ha gəwijj-a.

part-pass.know.perf about Russia that-it.f strong-f

'It's known about Russia that it is strong.'

الطلاب مب مسموح لهم يلعبون فالصف

ətˤ-tˤelˤlˤaab mub ma-smuuħ əl-hum jə-lʕəb-uun fə-sˤ-sˤaf.

the-student.pl not part-pass.allow.perf for-them they-play.imperf-they in-the-classroom

'The students cannot play in the classroom.'

مب مسموح للطلاب انهم يلعبون فالصف

mub ma-smuuħ l-ətˤ-tˤəlˤlˤaab ʔən-hum jə-leʕəb-uun fə-sˤ-sˤaf.

not part-pass.allow.perf for-the-student.pl that-them they-play.imperf-they in-the-classroom

'The students cannot play in the classroom.' (lit. (It is) not allowed for the students to play in the classroom.)

9.6 Evidential modality

Evidential modality indicates the evidence the speaker has for its factual status (Palmer, 2001, p. 8). Evidentiality is always discussed within the epistemic system (Section 9.2). For instance, the sentence 'Ali must be sick' expresses the speaker's judgment about the possibility that Ali is sick (which is high). The speaker's epistemic judgment stems from various sources of direct or indirect evidence. Some languages express grammatical differences between epistemic and evidential modality, whereas others simply merge the two. The two types of modality may also be distinguished by the use of adverbs, e.g. 'perhaps' (epistemic) vs. 'clearly/apparently' (evidential).

أونه جون كان يغني

ʔawanna	ʤoon	kaan	j-ɣanni.
allegedly	john	be.perf-he	he-sing.imperf

'John was allegedly singing.' (or 'John allegedly sang.')

واضح انه جون كان يغني

waaðˤəħ	(ʔənnah)	ʤoon	kaan	j-ɣanni.
clear	(that)	John	be.perf-he	he-sing.imperf

'John was clearly singing.'

أونه علي رسب فامتحان السواقة

ʔawanna	ʕəli	rəsab	f-əmtəħaan	əs-swaaga.
allegedly	Ali	fail.perf-he	in-test	the-driving

'Ali allegedly failed the driving test.'

Interestingly, these evidential modal adverbs may be used independently as question words. In the following example, the use of اونه ʔawanna 'allegedly' as a short question can express a sarcastic tone:

أ: موزة أونه تدرس فامريكا

mooza	ʔawanna	tə-drəs	f-amriika.
Moza	allegedly	she-study.imperf	in-America

A: 'Moza is allegedly studying in America.'

ب: أونه
ʔawanna?
allegedly
B: 'Really?'

In addition to modal adverbs, evidential modality may be expressed by modal adverbs such as شكل ʃakəl 'apparently/seemingly' (Section 7.8).

شكله يطيح مطر
ʃakl-ah j-tˤiiħ mətˤar.
apparently-it it-fall.imperf rain
'It seems to be raining.'

Evidentials can also be indicated by reportive verbs such as قول guul 'say.'

علي يقول انه نجح فامتحان السواقة
ʕəli j-guul ʔənn-ah nədʒ-aħ f-əmtəħaan əs-səwaaga.
Ali he-say.imperf that-him pass.perf-he in-test the-driving
'Ali says that he passed the driving test.'

Hearsay evidentials may only be expressed by the corresponding matrix verb, e.g. سمع semaʕ 'hear.'

سمعت انه موزة سارت تدرس ف أمريكا، بس مب متأكدة
səmaʕ-t ʔənnah mooza tə-drəs f-amriika bas mub mə-ttakd-ah.
hear.perf-I that Moza she-study.imperf in-America but not part-refl.sure-I.f
'I heard that Moza went to study in the US, but I am not sure.'

9.7 Imperatives

Imperatives are directives which describe the speaker's request (cf. 'Please come!'), order (cf. 'Drop the gun!'), and prohibition (cf.

'Don't leave the classroom without my permission!'). In Emirati Arabic, imperative verbs are indicated by a specialized, 'truncated' form (Section 5.2). As is evident in other languages, imperative sentences do not usually contain an overt subject 'you.'

اطلع برا	
ʔətˤlˤaʕ	barraa.
get.imp	out
'Get out!'	

دق للشرطة	
dəg	l-əʃ-ʃərtˤa.
call.imp	to-the-police
'Call the police!'	

The imperative verb may be inflected, depending on the addressee. The following examples indicate morphological variation regarding the form of the imperative verb. Some Emirati speakers may append the clitic /ʔə-/ to the imperative verb. Overall, the unmarked form without /ʔə-/ is accepted by all Emirati speakers (Section 5.2.15).

كتبي/أكتبي اسمج

kətb-i/(ʔə-)ktəb-i	ʔəsmə-ʧ.
write.imp-f	name-your.f

'(To a female) Write down your name!'

أكتب الواجب

(ʔə-)ktəb	əl-waadʒəb.
write.imp	the-homework

'(To a male) Write down the homework!'

كتبوا/أكتبوا/كل شيء

kətb-u/(ʔə-)ktəb-uu	kəl	ʃajj.
write.imp-you.pl	every	thing

'(To a group) Write down everything!'

سير يسار وانتي سيري يمين

siir	jəsaar	w-ənti	siir-i	jəmiin.
go.imp	left	and-you.f	go.imp-you.f	right

'(to the boy) Go left!' and '(to the girl) You go right!'

Negative imperatives are expressed by adding لا laa in front of the imperative sentence (Section 10.3). Note that the negative imperative verb is in the declarative.

لا تتكلمون فالصف

laa tə-t-kalləm-oon f-əsˤ-sˤaf.
no you.pl-refl.talk.imperf-you.pl in-the-classroom
'Don't talk in the classroom!'

لا تيي البيت متأخر

laa (ʔə)t-jii əl-beet məttaxxər.
no you-come.imperf the-home part-refl.late
'Don't come home late!'

Reporting an order or a request may also be expressed by verbs of ordering. Note that the verb in the embedded clause is in the declarative form.

أحمد طلب من ربعه انه يكلم للشرطة

ʔaħmad tˤalˤab mən rabʕ-a ʔənna j-kalləm əʃ-ʃertˤa.
Ahmad order.perf-he from friends-his that he-talk.imperf the-police
'Ahmad asked his friends to call the police.'

الدكتور طلب من الطلاب انهم ما يتأخرون

əd-dəktoor tˤalˤab mən ətˤ-tˤəlˤlˤaab ʔən-hum maa jə-ttaxxər-uun.
the-doctor order.perf-he from the-student.pl that-them not they-refl.late.imperf-they
'The doctor ordered the students not to be late.'

9.8 Counterfactuals

The aforementioned sections essentially address the realis-irrealis distinction, i.e. whether the proposition is factual (realis) or non-factual (irrealis). Irrealis modality manifests on a continuum in the sense that the speaker may project various types of modality towards the truth of the proposition. For instance, while 'Susan should win the competition' and 'Susan may win the competition' are both irrealis (i.e. neither is factually true), they differ in the likelihood the proposition will be true. On the other hand, for the expressions of non-factual statements, in addition to the use of negation (Chapter 10), counterfactuals may be used. Emirati

Arabic counterfactuals require the use of perfective in the conditional (antecedent) clause. For the main (consequent) clause, the modal auxiliary جان ʧaan 'would' is obligatory, without which the sentence would be ungrammatical. In general, native speakers interpret counterfactual conditionals as expressing a past irrealis event (which therefore can never be real), i.e. past counterfactuals.

لو احمد درس زين، جان نجح فالامتحان

loo	ʔaħmad	daras	zeen	ʧaan	nədʒ-aħ	f-əl-əmtəħaan.
if	Ahmad	study.perf-he	well	would	pass.perf-he	in-the-exam

'If Ahmad had studied hard (= he never studied), he should have passed the exam (= he failed).'

.لو فزت بالفلوس أمس، جان الحين عندك سيارة

loo	fəzt	b-əl-fluus	ʔams	ʧaan	əl-ħiin
ʕənd-ək		sajjaara.			
if	win.perf-you	with-the-money	yesterday	would	the-now
with-you		car			

'If you had won the money yesterday (= you did not), you should have owned a car by now (= you don't own a car).'

For past counterfactuals which do not have a consequent clause, the verb of the counterfactual clause consists of the perfective auxiliary كان kaan 'be,' followed by the imperfective verb.

ياليت كنت أعرف الأجابة

jalee-t	kənt	ʔa-ʕarf	əl-ədʒaaba.
wish.perf-I	be.perf-I	I-know.imperf	the-answer

'I wished I had known the answer.' (= I did not know the answer)

لو أحمد كان يعرف الجواب بس

loo	ʔaħmad	kaan	jə-ʕarf	əl-dʒawaab	bas.
if	Ahmad	be.perf-he	he-know.imperf	the-answer	only

'If only Ahmad had known the answer!' (= Ahmad did not know the answer)

On the other hand, if the contrary-to-fact event or action refers to the present time (present counterfactuals), the conditional clause consists of the auxiliary kaan, where the consequent clause is expressed by the future modal marker بـ b- with an imperfective verb (Section 8.2). In such cases, the future is interpreted as a hypothetical instead of as a counterfactual.

بتتقاعد السنة اليايه لو مريم كان عندها فلوس كفايه

b-tə-t-qaaʕad	əs-səna	əl-jaajja	loo	marjam
kaan	ʕənd-ha	fluus	kfaaja.	
will-she-refl.retire.imperf	the-year	the-coming	if	Mariam
be.perf-she	with-her	money	enough	

'If Mariam had enough money (= Mariam does not have enough money now), she would retire next year (= she is unlikely to retire next year).'

إذا تبعت الخطوات ، بتشوف الطريقة الصح عشان تحل المسألة.

ʔəða	təbaʕ-t	əl-xətˤw-aat	bə-tʧuuf	ətˤ-tˤariiqa
əsˤ-sˤaħ		ʕaʃaan	t-ħəll	əl-masʔala.
if	follow.perf-you	the-step-f.pl	will-you-see.imperf	the-method
the-correct		in.order.to	you-solve.imperf	the-problem

'If you followed the instructions (you still don't follow them, but you can), you should find the correct method to solve the problem.'

إذا جون يا، بنسير نتعشا

ʔəða	ʤoon	jaa	bə-n-siir	nə-tʕaʃʃaa.
if	John	come.perf-he	will-we-go.imperf	we-refl.dine.imperf

'If John came (= he has not come, but he may later), we will go and have dinner.'

9.9 Hortatives

Hortatives are another type of irrealis modality which encodes the speaker's suggestion, encouragement, or discouragement of a particular action or event. In Emirati Arabic, the sentence-initial particle يلا jalˤlˤa 'let's' may be followed by a simple sentence (expressed in the imperfective) to express the speaker's suggestion. In this case, the subject must be plural inclusive of the speaker (cf. English 'let's'). Linguists term this structure as *cohortative*, in which the encouragement is mutual (i.e. inclusive of the speaker).

يلا نجرب هذا المطعم بعدين نخبر أحمد عنه

jalˤlˤa n-dʒarrəb haaða əl-matˤʕam baʕdeen n-xabbər ʔaħmad ʕann-ah.
let's we-caus.try.imperf this the-restaurant then we-caus.tell.imperf Ahmad about-it
'Let's try this restaurant and tell Ahmad about it.'

On the other hand, the verb خل xal 'let' is used with the other persons. Depending on the grammarian's theoretical orientation, the terms inhortative, dehortative, exhortative, or suggestive are applied.

خلني اخلص هالمحادثة وبعدين بدقلك

xal-ni ʔa-xalˤlˤəsˤ ha-l-muħaadaθa w-baʕdeen ba-dəg-l-ək.
let.imp-me I-finish.imperf this-the-conversation and-then will-I-call.imperf-to-you
'Let me finish this phone call and I will call you back.'

خليه يروح الحين، ولا تراه ما بيلحق عالباص

xall-ii-h j-ruuħ əl-ħiin wəlla tara-ah maa b-jə-lħag ʕa-l-baasˤ.
let.you-imp-him he-leave.imperf the-now or by.the.way-him not will-he-catch.imperf on-the-bus
'Let him leave now, otherwise he cannot catch the bus.'

خلنا لا ندخل داخل، أنا متروعه

(xal-na) laa nə-dxəl daaxəl ʔana mə-trawʕ-a.
(let-us) no we-enter.imperf inside I part.refl.scared-f
'Let's not go inside, I'm scared!'

9.10 Optatives

Optatives are usually conventional or formulaic expressions a speaker uses to convey wishes to the addressee. They may be periphrastically expressed by the verb أتمنى ʔatmanna 'I wish,' followed by an embedded clause (in the imperfective).

أتمنى انك تكون قوي وبصحة زينه

ʔa-tmanna ʔənn-ək t-kuun gəwi w-b-sˤəħħa zeen-a.
I-refl.wish.imperf that-you you-be.imperf strong and-with-health good-f
'I wish that you are strong and healthy.'

Table 9.6 Optative constructions

الله يبارك فيك ʔalˤlˤah j-baarək fii-k. God he-bless.imperf in-you 'May God bless you.'	الله يرحمه ʔalˤlˤah jə-rħam-ah. God he-mercy.imperf-him 'May God have mercy on him.'
الله يحفظه ʔalˤlˤah jə-ħfaðˤ-ah. God he-preserve.imperf-him 'May God preserve him.'	الله يساعدك ʔalˤlˤah j-saaʕd-ək. God he-help.imperf-you 'May God help you.'
الله يطول بعمرك ʔalˤlˤah j-tˤawwəl b-ʕəmr-ək. God he-refl.lengthen.imperf with-age-your 'May God lengthen your life.'	الله يسلمك ʔalˤlˤah j-salm-ək. God he-refl.keep.safe.imperf-you 'May God keep you safe.'

أتمنى كل امنياتك تتحقق

ʔa-tmanna kəl ʔumnija-at-ək tə-tħaggag.

I-refl.wish.imperf all wish-pl-your they-refl.come.true.imperf

'I wish that all your wishes will come true.'

Some optative constructions (Table 9.6) are more formulaic, similar to English 'God bless you!' In such cases, the sentence-initial sacred expression الله ʔalˤlˤah 'God' is used, followed by the embedded clause. The verb of the embedded clause is in the imperfective.

Further reading

The study of the modality system of Arabic dialects is scanty. For a detailed discussion of the use of future modal marker بـ b- and other future markers in Gulf Arabic, see Persson (2008a). For the study of the modality system in MSA, see Bahloul (1994). Palmer (2001) is a useful linguistic introduction to the study of modality. For a model-theoretic approach to modality, consult Portner (2009).

Chapter 10

Negation

Negation is a language-universal phenomenon in which an operator renders a proposition false. In language, negation is always realized as a particular word or morpheme which applies to predicates and reverses their truth values. Negation may receive a further semantic function in the domain of modality, for instance, in expressing irrealis propositions (Chapter 9). It may also be used pragmatically as a speech act for rejection or refusal.

In Emirati Arabic, negative markers apply to predicates which consist of various grammatical categories. Negation may also be used to form negative imperatives (Section 9.7).

10.1 Verbal negation

ما maa 'not'

The negative marker ما maa 'not' always precedes the verb and negates the corresponding proposition. The interjection لا laa 'no' functions as a negative answer.

رحتي البيت؟ لا ما رحت

rəħt-i	əl-beet?	laa	maa	rəħt.
go.perf-you.f	the-home	no	not	go.perf-I

'Did you go home? No, I didn't go.'

تبين سناك؟ لا ما ابا سناك

t-əb-een	snaak?	laa	maa-ʔa-ba	snaak.
you.f-want.imperf-you.f	snack	no	not-I-want.imperf	snack

'Do you want a snack? No, I don't want a snack.'

The same negative marker is used regardless of the aspect (Chapter 8) of the verb forms. For example:

ما شربت الماي

maa	ʃərab-t	əl-maaj.
not	drink.perf-I	the-water

'I did not drink the water.'

ما بروح البيت

maa	ba-ruuħ	əl-beet.
not	will-I-go.imperf	the-home

'I will not go home.'

ما بخبرها عن السالفة

maa	b-a-xabbər-ha	ʕan	əs-saalf-a.
not	will-I-refl.tell.imperf-her	about	the-topic-f

'I will not tell her about the topic.'

ليش ما تاخذين بريك

leeʃ	maa	ta-axð-iin	breek.
why	not	you.f-take.imperf-you.f	break

'Why don't you take a break?

ما maa may also be used with complex predicate constructions (Section 7.11).

ما أتحمل أشوفها مضايقة

maa	ʔa-t-ħammal	ʔa-ʃuuf-ha	məðˁðˁaajʤ-a.
not	I-refl-caus.bear.imperf	I-see.imperf-her	part-refl.upset-f

'I can't bear to see her upset.'

ما يبا ياكل

maa	j-əba	j-aakəl.
not	he-want.imperf	he-eat.imperf

'He does not want to eat.'

ما أقدر أطلع

maa	ʔa-gdar	ʔa-tˁlaʕ.
not	I-able.imperf	I-go.out.imperf

'I cannot go out.'

ما تروم تغلبني

maa	t-ruum	t-əɣləb-ni.
not	you-can.imperf	you-beat.imperf-me

'You can't beat me.'

In addition, ما maa can negate existential expressions formed by في fii 'at,' ʃaj 'thing,' حصل ħasˤal 'get,' and عند ʕənd 'with' (Sections 5.2 and 7.1).

ما في كتب زيادة

maa	fi	kətəb	zjaada.
not	there.is	books	extra

'There are no extra books.'

ما عندها فواكه

maa	ʕənd-ha	fawaakəh.
not	with-her	fruits

'She does not have any fruit.'

ما حصلت الهوية

maa	ħasˤsˤəl-at	əl-həwəjja.
not	find.imperf-she	the-ID

'She didn't find the ID.'

10.2 Non-verbal predicate negation

مب mub (var. هب həb) 'not'

Another common negative marker مب mub (var. هب həb) 'not' immediately precedes other non-verbal predicates such as nouns (Section 5.1), adjectives (Section 5.3), prepositions (Section 5.5), participles (Section 5.3.2), comparatives (Section 5.3.4), and superlatives (Section 5.3.5). For Emirati Arabic speakers with a Bedouin origin, the alternative word هب həb may be used. Another phonological variant, مش məʃ (borrowed from Egyptian Arabic), is sometimes heard.

مب سستر

mub	səstar
not	nurse

'not a nurse'

هذي مب سعادة

haað-i	mub	saʕaada.
this-f	not	happiness

'This is not happiness.'

مب وقته تتحرطمين

mub	wagt-a	t-əthartˤəm-een.
not	time-it	you.f-refl.complain.imperf-you.f

'It's not the time for you to complain.'

لحم الخنزير مب حلال

laħam	əl-xənziir	mub	ħalaal.
meat	the-pork	not	halal

'Pork is not halal.'

الشارجة هب خالية

əl-ʃaarʤa	həb	xaalj-a.
the-Sharjah	not	empty-f

'Sharjah is not empty.'

مب لازم تسير البحر

mub	laazəm	t-siir	əl-baħar.
not	necessary	you-go.imperf	the-beach

'It is not necessary for you to go to the beach.'

مب يالسة أسمع شي

mub	jaals-a	ʔa-smaʕ	ʃaj.
not	part.sit-f	I-hear.imperf	thing

'I am not hearing anything.'

مب قاعدة أقرا شي

mub	gaaʕd-a	ʔa-gra	ʃaj.
not	part.sit-f	I-read.imperf	thing

'I am not reading anything.'

الكتاب مب لهالدرجة حلو

əl-ktaab	mub	lə-ha-d-daraʤa	ħəlu.
the-book	not	to-this-the-degree	beautiful

'The book is not that good.'

مب بالمقص تقصينه ها

mub	b-əl-məgasˤ	t-gəsˤsˤ-iin-ah	haa.
not	with-the-scissors	you.f-cut.imperf-you.f-it	this

'You don't cut this with the scissors.'

هاي مب أحلى عنها

haaj	mub	ʔa-ħla	ʕan-ha.
this.f	not	more-beautiful	than-her

'She is not more beautiful than her.'

هذا الولد مب أطول منه

haaða	əl-walad	mub	ʔa-tˤwal	mən-nah.
this	the-boy	not	more-tall	than-him

'This boy is not taller than him.'

مب أكبر شي

mub	ʔa-kbar	ʃaj
not	most-big	thing

'not the biggest thing'

هذا اللون مب أغمج شي

haaða	əl-loon	mub	ʔa-ɣmadʒ	ʃaj.
this	the-color	not	most-dark	thing

'This color is not the darkest.'

هذا مب أضخم برج

haað-a	mub	ʔa-ðˤxam	bərdʒ.
this-m	not	most-large	tower

'This is not the largest tower.'

عدم ʕadam 'lack'

A less common negator which only negates nouns is عدم ʕadam 'lack.' It is borrowed from MSA and is used mostly by highly educated people.

عدم الثقة مشكلة كبيرة

ʕadam	əθ-θəqa	məʃkəl-a	kbiir-a.
lack	the-confidence	issue-f	big-f

'Lack of confidence is a big issue.'

عدم الرضى سبب المشاكل

ʕadam ər-rəðˤa səbab əl-məʃaakəl.

lack the-content reason the-problems

'The lack of contentment is the reason for the problems.'

المشكلة في عدم التركيز

əl-məʃkəla fi ʕadam ət-tarkiiz.

the-problem in lack the-focus

'The problem is in the lack of focus.'

10.3 The negative particle لا laa 'no'

The negative particle لا laa 'no' is most commonly used as a response to polar (yes-no) questions (Section 13.1).

تتمرنين إنتي بانتظام؟ لا، أنا وايد كسولة

tə-t-marrən-een ʔənt-i b-əntəðˤaam? laa, ʔana waajəd kasuul-ah

you-refl-train.imperf-you.f you-f by-refl.regular no, I a.lot lazy-f

'Do you exercise regularly?' 'No, I am very lazy.'

If the polar question contains a negation, the use of لا laa 'no' is to agree with the supposed (negative) answer by the questioner (Chapter 17).

إنت ما تشتغل الحين؟ لا، أنا توني متقاعد

ʔənta ma t-əʃtəɣəl əl-ħiin? laa, ʔana taw-ni mə-tqaaʕəd.

you not you-work.imperf now no I just-me part-refl.retire

'Do you not work anymore?' 'No, I have just retired.'

In addition to being a negative answer, it may also be used to correct the previous sentence in discourse.

أنا رايحة الدكان الحين . . . لا بروح السوق أول

ʔana raajħ-a əd-dəkkaan əl-ħiin. . . laa, b-a-ruuħ əs-suug ʔawwal

I part.go-f the-grocery the-now no will-I-go.imperf the-market first

'I will go to the grocery now . . . no, I shall go to the market first.'

It is also possible to place لا laa 'no' sentence-finally to negate its preceding discourse-salient proposition or entity. In the following example, the negation applies to its object الحليب alħəliib 'milk':

أحب الكوفي بس الحليب لا

ʔa-ħəb	əl-koofii	bas	əl-ħəliib	laa
I-like.imperf	the-coffee	but	the-milk	no

'I like coffee but (for) milk no.'

10.4 The negative prefix -لا laa- 'not' and -غير ɣeer- 'non-'

In more formal conversations in Emirati Arabic, it is not unusual to use the negative prefix -لا laa- 'not' and -غير ɣeer- 'non-' and form negative adjectives and nouns. This type of morphological affixation is borrowed from MSA.

غير لايق	ɣeer laajəg	'non-fitting'	غير مدخن	ɣeer mudaxxin	'non-smoker'
لامحدود	laamaħduud	'unlimited'	غير مسؤول	ɣeer masʔuul	'irresponsible'
لاأخلاقي	laaʔaxlaaqi	'immoral'	غيرمنتهي	ɣeer məntəhi	'never-ending'
غير تقليدي	ɣeer taqliidi	'unconventional'	لايصدق	laa jsˤaddag	'unbelievable'
غير واقعي	ɣeer waaqəʕi	'unrealistic'	لانهائي	laa nəhaaʔi	'infinite'
غير قابل للتجديد	ɣeer qaabəl l-ət-tajdiid	'non-renewable'	لامعقول	laa maʕguul	'unreasonable'

10.5 Negative imperatives

Negative imperatives are formed by the negative marker لا laa 'don't' and a declarative sentence with a second-person agreement on the verb.

لا تلعب بالماي

laa	tə-lʕab	b-əl-maaj.
don't	you-play.imperf	with-the-water

'Don't play with water.'

لا تتريون لين ما أوصل

la tə-trajj-oon leen maa ʔa-wsˤal.

don't they-wait.imperf-they until that I-arrive.imperf

'Don't wait until I arrive.'

لا تسلمين المشروع متأخر

laa t-salm-iin əl-maʃruuʕ məttaxxər/mətʔaxxər.

don't you.f-submit.imperf-you.f the-assignment part-refl.late

'Don't submit the assignment late.'

10.6 Negative coordination

... ولا ... لا laa ... wala ... 'neither ... nor ...'

Coordinations of negative statements are expressed by the coordinator و wa 'and,' which connects two negative sentences, i.e. ... ولا ... لا laa ... wala ... 'neither ... nor' (Section 15.13.3).

لا تاكل ولا تشرب

la t-aakəl w-la tə-ʃrab.

don't you-eat.imperf and-not you-drink.imperf

'Don't eat or drink.'

لا شفت ولا سمعت

laa ʃəf-t wa-la səmaʕ-t.

not see.perf-I and-not hear.perf-I

'I neither saw nor heard.'

لا شغلة ولا مشغلة

laa ʃəɣəla wa-la ma-ʃɣala.

not work and-not part-occupancy

'No work or occupancy' (used to describe someone who has nothing to do)

لا حيا ولا مستحى

laa ħəja wa-la mə-staħa.

not shyness and-not part-pass.shame

'No shyness or shame' (used to describe a disrespectful person)

The coordinator بس bas or لكن laakən 'but' is used to combine two negative statements. Note that the negative markers may vary.

هو هب غالي لكن ما يسوى

huu həb ɣaali laakən maa jə-swaa.
it not expensive but not it-worth.imperf
'It is not expensive, but it's not worth it.'

ممكن ما تهذربين بس لا اتمين ساكته

mumkən maa t-haðrəb-iin bas laa
ət-təmm-een saakt-a
can not you.f-talk.much.imperf-you.f but don't
you.f-stay.imperf-you.f quiet.f
'You can stop talking nonsense, but don't be quiet.'

هو مب وايد حلو بس مب عنقاش

huu mub waajəd ħəlu bas mub ʕangaaʃ.
it not very beautiful but not old-fashioned
'It is not very beautiful but not old-fashioned.'

ما ذاكرت في البيت بس ما لعبت

maa ðaakar-t f-əl-beet bas maa ləʕab-t.
not study.perf-I in-the-house but not play.perf-I
'I did not study at home but I didn't play (either).'

لا تكتمين فقلبج بس لا تصارخين

laa tə-ktəm-iin f-galb-əʧ bas laa
t-sˤaarx-iin.
don't you.f-keep.imperf-you.f in-heart-your.f but don't
you.f-shout.imperf-you.f
'Don't keep it to yourself but don't shout (either).'

10.7 Negation in ellipsis

The negative marker is productively used in various elliptical structures (Chapter 16). The coordinator بس bas 'but' is optional in some cases (Section 15.6).

أحمد يقدر يرمس فرنسي وألماني، بس مب ايطالي

ʔaħmad jə-gdar jə-rməs faransi w ʔalmaani, bas mub ʔiitˤaalii.

Ahmad he-can.imperf he-speak.imperf French and German but not Italian

'Ahmad can speak French and German, but not Italian.'

جامعة الإمارات في العين، مب في دبي

ʤaamʕa-t əl-əmaaraat fə-l-ʕeen, mub fə-dbaɪ.

university-f the-Emirates in-Al Ain not in-Dubai

'UAEU is in Al Ain, not in Dubai.'

السياسيين يحبون يتناقشون عن التجارة، مب (عن) الاحتباس الحراري

əs-səjaasijji-in jə-ħəbb-uun jə-tnaaqəʃ-oon ʕan ət-təʤaara, mub (ʕan) l-əħtəbaas əl-ħaraari.

the-politician-pl they-love.imperf-they they-refl.discuss.imperf-they about the-trade not about the-retention the-thermal

'Politicians love discussing trades, not global warming.'

The elliptical clause formed by the negative marker may intervene in the main clause without any meaning change. For instance:

ميرة مب مريم كتبت هالكتاب

miira mub marjam kətb-at ha-lə-ktaab.

Meera not Mariam write.perf-she this-the-book

'Meera, not Mariam, wrote this book!'

ميرة كتبت هالكتاب، مب مريم

miira kətb-at ha-lə-ktaab, mub marjam.

Meera write.perf-she this-the-book not Mariam

'Meera wrote this book, not Mariam.'

10.8 Negative polarity items

Negative polarity items (NPIs) describe the lack of even the least quantity, extent, or degree of the meaning they modify. NPIs are licensed in negative contexts, although they are also found in questions (Chapter 13) and conditionals (Section 14.4). In Emirati Arabic, most NPIs also exist in positive contexts, and in such cases an existential interpretation is possible. NPIs may assume various categories, e.g. nouns, adverbs, and auxiliaries.

10.8.1 *Nominal NPIs*

10.8.1.1 *حد ħad '(any)one'*

The 'person' NPIs is حد ħad '(any)one.' Its meaning is non-referential and may be positive (cf. English 'someone/somebody') (Section 6.1) or negative (cf. English 'anyone/anybody' and 'no one/nobody'), depending on the sentence. As an NPI, حد ħad needs to be licensed by a preverbal negative marker ما maa. When حد ħad 'one' combines with ما maa, they form a single lexical item, محد maħħad 'no one,' which functions as negative concord (Section 10.9). محد maħħad only functions as a subject, and never appears at the object position.

ما أعرف حد

maa	ʔa-ʕarf	ħad.
not	I-know.imperf	one

'I don't know anyone.'

محد سوالهم سالفة

ma-ħħad	sawwaa-l-hum	saalfa.
no-one	make.perf-he-for-them	attention

'No one gave them any attention.'

رحت البيت و محد هناك

rəħ-t	əl-beet	w	ma-ħħad	hnaak.
go.perf-I	the-house	and	no-one	there

'I went home, and no one was there.'

NPIs may be licensed in the context of questions (Chapter 13) and conditionals (Chapter 14). Both حد ħad and محد maħħad as subject NPIs are grammatical in the following structures. Note that محد maħħad itself bears no negative meaning.

محد شاف كتابي؟

ma-ħħad	ʃaaf	əktaab-i?
no-one	see.perf-he	book-my

'Has anyone seen my book?'

محد بيروح وياي المول؟

ma-ħħad ba-j-ruuħ wəjjaa-ja əl-mool.

no-one will-he-go.imperf with-me the-mall

'Will anyone go to the mall with me?'

لو أحمد بيتلاقى ويا أي حد اليوم، بيخبر كل حد

loo ʔaħmad ba-jə-tlaaga wəja ʔaj ħad əl-joom, ba-j-xabbər kəl ħad

if Ahmad will-he-meet.up.imperf with any one the-today will-he-refl.tell.imperf every one

'If Ahmad meets anyone today he will let everyone know.'

On the other hand, in the context of existential structures (Section 7.7), حد ħad may function as a positive or negative polarity item, depending on the grammatical context. For instance, the following question licenses an NPI interpretation for حد ħad. Note that محد maħħad cannot be used in the same structure.

في حد بيي وياي اليوم؟

fii ħad bi-jji wəjja-ja əl-joom?

there.is one will-he.come.imperf with-me the-today

'Is there anyone who will come with me today?'

10.8.1.2 شي ʃaj '(any)thing'

The bare noun شي ʃaj 'thing' functions as an NPI with the preverbal negative marker ما maa, similar to حد ħad 'person.'

ما سويت شي بخصوص الدرجة

maa saww-eet ʃaj be-xsˤuusˤ əd-daradʒa.

not do.perf-I thing with-regard the-grade

'I have not done anything regarding the grade.'

رحت الحديقة و ما شفت شي

rəħ-t əl-ħadiiqa w maa ʃəf-t ʃaj.

go.perf-I the-garden and not see.perf-I thing

'I went to the garden and I did not see anything.'

As a subject NPI, ما maa and شي ʃaj are adjacent to each other, while not forming a single lexical item (cf. محد maħħad 'no one').

Similar to محد maħħad, ما شي maa ʃaj 'nothing' cannot be used as an object NPI.

مافي شي فالبيت

maa fi ʃaj f-əl-beet.
not there.is thing in-the-house
'There is nothing in the house.'

In many other cases, ما maa and شي ʃaj may be separated by other lexical items, e.g. في 'in' or verbs such as يستوي jəstəwi 'happens.'

ما يستوي شي فهاذي المدينة

maa jə-stəwi ʃaj f-haaði əl-madiina.
not it-refl.happen.imperf thing in-this the-city
'Nothing happens in this city.'

ما في شي يستوي فهذي المدينة

maa fi ʃaj jə-stəwi f-haaði əl-madiina.
not in thing it-refl.happen.imperf in-this the-city
'Nothing happens in this city.'

مافي شي فهذا الكرتون

maa fi ʃaj f-haaða l-kartoon.
not in thing in-this the-box
'There's nothing in this box.'

مافي شي يديد عن هذي النظرية

maa fi ʃaj jdiid ʕan haaði ən-naðˤarijja.
not in thing new about this the-theory
'There's nothing new about this theory.'

A distinctive feature of شي ʃaj is that, as a subject, it seems to undergo grammaticalization and its lexical meaning of 'thing' is depleted, resulting in an existential marker. This is salient when the type of thing needs to be specified in the sentence. In the following examples, the particle is interpreted as an existential item, similar to fii 'in' in existential constructions (Section 7.7):

ما شي قلم على الطاولة

maa	ʃaj	galam	ʕala	ətˤ-tˤaawla.
not	there.is	pen	on	the-table

'There is no pen on the table.'

شي كتاب في المكتب؟

ʃaj	ktaab	f-əl-maktab?
there.is	book	in-the-office

'Is there any book in the office?'

The claim that شي ʃaj 'thing' is a grammaticalized existential marker may be further verified by its co-occurrence restriction with the existential predicate في fii 'in' (Section 7.7). The combination في شي كتاب fii ʃaj ktaab (or with other nouns) is ungrammatical in Emirati Arabic, showing that the existential construction is formed by either شي ʃaj or في fii, but not both.

10.8.1.3 أي *ʔaj 'any'*

In addition to bare nouns, NPIs may be expressed by adding an indefinite determiner أي ʔaj 'any' to any noun (Section 6.1). While the use of أي ʔaj as an NPI determiner is optional, its usage may have a semantic contribution. Native speakers feel that أي ʔaj is more 'expressive' than the use of bare nouns in expressing negative entities. Moreover, أي ʔaj is more likely used in episodic sentences, namely, the absence of an entity in a particular situation. In contrast, expressions of negative generic statements favor the use of bare nouns as NPIs.

ما شفت أي حد يلعب برع

maa	ʃəf-t	ʔaj	ħad	jə-lʕab	barraʕ.
not	see.perf-I	any	one	he-play.imperf	outside

'I have not seen anyone playing outside.'

أحمد ما اشترى أي سيارة

ʔaħmad	maa	ʔəʃtəra	ʔaj	sajjaara.
Ahmad	not	refl.buy.perf-he	any	car

'Ahmad has not bought any car.'

رحت السوق بس ما دخلت أي محل

rəħ-t	əs-suug	bas	maa	dəxal-t	ʔaj	maħal.
go.perf-I	the-mall	but	not	enter.perf-I	any	store

'I went to the mall, but I did not enter any store.'

ما أعرف أي حد

maa	ʔa-ʕarf	ʔaj	ħad.
not	I-know.imperf	any	one

'I don't know anyone.'

لا تكلم أي حد

laa	t-kalləm	ʔaj	ħad.
don't	you-talk.imperf	any	one

'Don't talk to anyone.'

راشد ما كان يعرف أي حد منهم قبل

raaʃəd	maa	kaan	jə-ʕarf	ʔaj	ħad	mən-hum	gabəl.
Rashid	not	be.perf-he	he-know.imperf	any	one	from-them	before

'Rashid did not know any of them before.'

أي ʔaj can also be used with negative verbs such as رفض rəfaðˤ 'refused.'

موزة رفضت تجاوب على أي سؤال

mooza	rəfðˤa-t	t-ʤaawəb	ʕala	ʔaj	səʔaal.
Moza	refuse.perf-she	she-answer.imperf	on	any	question

'Moza refused to answer any questions.'

10.8.2 Grammaticalized NPIs

There is a class of aspectual verbs such as 'become' (e.g. استوى ʔəstəwa, صار sˤaar) and 'begin' (قام gaam) (Section 7.9) which are further grammaticalized to function as NPIs in negative contexts. These grammaticalized NPIs are inflected with pronominal suffixes and are always in the perfective aspect. The order between this type of NPI and the negative marker is variable. The grammaticalized verb استوى ʔəstəwa 'become' always precedes the negative marker ما maa 'not,' whereas صار sˤaar 'become' and قام

gaam 'begin' may precede or follow the negative marker without any meaning change. The subject position is flexible in that it may immediately precede or follow the verb (indicated by the parentheses). If the subject is sentence-final, it expresses an afterthought (Section 11.4.1).

10.8.2.1 استوى *ʔəstəwa and* صار *sˤaar 'become'*

استويت ماحب العصير

(ʔə)stəwee-t ma-a-ħəbb əl-ʕasˤiir.
become.perf-I not-I-like.imperf the-juice
'I don't like juice anymore.'

(ابراهيم) استوى (ابراهيم) ما يسمع موسيقى

(braahiim) ʔəstəwa (braahiim) maa j-əsmaʕ musiiqa.
Ibrahim become.perf-he Ibrahim not he-listen.imperf music
'Ibrahim doesn't listen to music anymore.'

(مريم) استوت (مريم) ما تسير المكتبة (مريم)

(marjam) ʔəstəwa-t (marjam) maa t-siir əl-maktəba (marjam).
Mariam become.perf-she Mariam not she-go.imperf the-library Mariam
'Mariam doesn't go to the library anymore.'

(الجيران) صاروا (الجيران) ما ايبونّا (الجيران)

(l-jiiraan) sˤaar-aw (l-jiiraan) maa ʔəj-juu-n-na (l-jiiraan).
the-neighbors become.perf-they the-neighbors not they-come.imperf-they-us the-neighbors
'The neighbors don't visit us anymore.' (or 'The neighbors ceased to visit us.')

صرت ما أفهم شي

sˤər-t maa ʔa-fham ʃaj.
become.perf-I not I-understand.imperf thing
'I don't understand anything anymore.'

10.8.2.2 قام *gaam 'begin'*

(العيال) ما قاموا (العيال) يلعبون شرات قبل

(lə-ʕjaal) maa gaam-aw (lə-ʕjaal) jə-lʕəb-uun ʃaraat gabəl.

the-boys not begin.perf-they the-boys they-play.imperf-they like before

'The boys do not play as they did before.'

(أحمد) ما قام يخليهم (أحمد) يلعبون

(ʔaħmad) maa gaam j-xallii-hum (ʔaħmad) jə-lʕəb-uun.

Ahmad not begin.perf-he he-let.imperf-them Ahmad they-play.imperf-they

'He doesn't let them play anymore.'

ما قمت أكتب قصايد

maa gəm-t ʔa-ktəb gəsˤaajəd.

not begin.perf-I I-write.imperf poem.pl

'I don't write poems anymore.'

10.8.3 Strong NPIs

These are a list of expressions which appear mostly in negative contexts. In English, expressions such as 'not lift a finger' and 'not give a damn' are typical examples of strong NPIs. Strong NPIs in Emirati Arabic include the following:

ما صرف فلس

maa sˤəraf fəls.

not spend.perf-he fils

'He did not spend a fils.'

ما شرب قطرة

maa ʃərab gatˤra.

not drink.perf-he sip

'He did not drink a sip.'

ما غمّض عين ليلة الحادث

maa ɣammaðˁ ʕeen leela-t əl-ħaadəθ.

not caus.blink.perf-he eye night-f the-accident

'He did not blink an eye on the night of the accident.'

Some NPIs such as من متى mən məta 'since when' and من سنة يدّي mən sənat jaddi 'from grandpa's age' also appear in positive contexts, although native speakers prefer their use as an NPI.

(من متى) ما قريت كتاب (من متى)

(mən məta) maa gəree-t ktaab (mən məta).

since when not read.perf-I.f book since when

'I have not read a book in ages.'

ما قريت كتاب من سنة يدّي

maa garee-t ktaab mən səna-t jad-di.

not read.perf-I book from year-f grandpa-my

'I have not read a book since the age of grandpa (i.e. a very long time).'

10.8.4 Adverb NPIs

10.8.4.1 عمر ʕəmər 'ever'

The adverb NPI عمر ʕəmər 'ever' (which can be suffixed by object pronouns) is immediately followed by the negative marker.

عمري ما راح أسمح لهالشي يصير

ʕəmr-i maa raaħ ʔa-smaħ l-ha-ʃ-ʃaj
jə-sˁiir.

ever-me not go.imperf-I I-let.imperf to-this-the-thing
it-happen.imperf

'I will never let this happen.'

أنا عمري ما بسامحه

ʔana ʕəmr-i maa b-a-saamħ-a.

I ever-me not will-I-forgive.imperf-him

'I will never forgive him.'

عمري ما شفت حد زطي شراته

ʕəmr-i maa ʧəf-t ħad zətˤtˤi ʃaraat-a.

ever-me not see.perf-I one stingy as-him

'I have never seen anyone as stingy as him.'

The sentence subject can exist in various positions (Chapter 11).

(عايشه) عمرها (عايشة) ما كذبت على حد (عايشة)

(ʕaajʃa) ʕəmər-ha (ʕaajʃa) maa ʧaðəəb-at (ʕaajʃa) ʕala ħad (ʕaajʃa).

Aisha ever-her Aisha not caus.lie.perf-she Aisha on one Aisha

'Aisha has never lied to anyone.'

The NPI usage of عمر ʕəmər should be distinguished from عمر ʕəmər as a noun, which may be used in positive contexts, such as the following:

طول عمري وأنا أحب هالمكان

tˤuul ʕəmr-i w-ʔana ʔa-ħəb ha-l-məkaan.

all life-my and-I I-love.imperf this-the-place

I have loved this place all my life.

طول عمرها وهي ذكية

tˤuul ʕəmər-ha w-hii ðakij-ja.

All life-her and-she smart-f

'She has been smart all her life.'

10.8.4.2 جد *ʧəd 'ever'*

The adverb NPI جد ʧəd (var. gad) 'ever' is used in positive and negative polarity contexts. As an NPI, جد ʧəd typically precedes the negative marker or appears in the contexts of questions (Chapter 13). Note that جد ʧəd 'ever' is not a negative concord (Section 10.9) and cannot be used as a fragment answer without a negative marker.

جدساير أوروبا؟

ʧəd saajər ʔoorobba.

ever go.perf-you Europe

'Have you ever been to Europe?'

لا ما جد سرت

laa	maa	ʧəd	sər-t.
no	not	ever	go.perf-I

'No, I never went.'

ما جد سمعنا هالرمسة من قبل

maa	ʧəd	səmaʕ-na	ha-r-ramsa	mən	gabəl.
not	ever	hear.perf-we	this-the-speech	from	before

'We have never heard about this before.'

علي سافر وايد بس ما جد راح لندن

ʕəli	saafar	waajəd	bas	maa	ʧəd	raaħ	landan.
Ali	travel.perf-he	a.lot	but	not	ever	go.perf-he	London

'Ali has traveled a lot but he has never been to London.'

As a positive polarity item, جد ʧəd 'ever' may be interpreted as a marker of modality, i.e. it signals the speaker's confirmation of the truth of the sentence (cf. English 'certainly' and 'definitely') (Chapter 9).

هيه جد ساير، مرة سرنا سويسرا

heeh	ʧəd	saajər	marra	sər-na	sweesra.
yes	ever	go.perf-I	once	go.perf-we	Switzerland

'Yes I certainly have. We went to Switzerland once.'

جد تكلمنا فالموضوع قبل

ʧəd	t-kallam-na	f-əl-mawðˤuuʕ	gabəl.
ever	refl-caus.talk.perf-we	on-the-subject	before

'We have (certainly) talked on the subject before.'

10.8.4.3 حتى *ħatta 'even'*

In theory-neutral descriptions, the sentence marked by حتى ħatta 'even' presupposes that the realization of the event is least likely to happen (yet it happens). For instance, 'even John came' asserts that John did come and presupposes that it was the least possible event (compared with, for example, 'Mary came' and 'Peter came'). In Emirati Arabic, the adverb حتى ħatta 'even' assumes a similar function. It is used in positive and negative sentences.

سارة حتى سطر ما قرت

Saara	ħatta	sat^ʕər	maa	gər-at.
Sara	even	line	not	read.perf-she

'Sara did not even read a line.'

محد سار العزيمة. حتى أحمد ما سار

ma-ħħad	saar	əl-ʕəziima.	ħatta	ʔaħmad	maa	saar.
no-one	go.perf-he	the-gathering	even	Ahmad	not	go.perf-he

'No one went to the gathering. Even Ahmad did not go.'

حتى ħatta 'even' cannot be used in elliptical structures (Chapter 16). The following short conversation shows that it has to be followed by a full sentence:

ما سويت الواجب

maa	sawwee-t	əl-waadʒəb.
not	do.perf-I	the-homework

'I didn't do the homework.'

حتى أنا ما سويته

ħatta	ʔana	maa	sawwee-t-a.
even	I	not	do.perf-I-it

'Even I didn't do it.'

حتى ħatta 'even' can be idiomatic, which serves to induce further pragmatic effects.

حتى الحمار بيفهم

ħattạ-lə-ħmaar	ba-jə-fham.
even-the-donkey	will-he-understand.imperf

'Even a donkey would get it.'

حتى النملة تقدر تشله

ħatta	ən-namla	tə-gdar	t-ʃəll-ah.
even	the-ant	she-can.imperf	she-carry.imperf-it

'Even an ant can carry it.'

10.9 Negative concord

Negative concord (NC) occurs when more than one negative item is found in the sentence, yet these negative items neither magnify nor cancel out the negative meaning, i.e. only a single negative meaning is expressed. For NC, some negative items are semantically independent in the sense that they may be used in fragment negative answers (cf. English 'never,' 'nothing,' and 'not at all').

10.9.1 ولا *wala 'no/not'*

The negative determiner ولا wala 'no/not' participates in NC in the sense that it may be licensed by a preceding negative marker (e.g. ما maa 'not'), yet only a single negative meaning is expressed. The indefinite wh-word أي aj 'any' is also used.

ما قلت ولا/أي كلمة

maa gəlt wala/aj kəlma.

not say.perf-I not/any word

'I have not said any word.'

ما حصلوا ولا شي من اللي يبونه هناك

maa ħasˁsˁəl-aw wala ʃaj mən ʔəlli jəb-oon-a hnaak.

not find.perf-they not thing from what want.imperf-they-it there

'They didn't find anything of what they wanted there.'

ما لقت معلومات عن ولا موضوع من اللي كانت تباهم

maa ləg-at maʕluuma-at ʕan wala mawðˁuuʕ mən ʔəlli kaan-at tə-baa-hum.

not find.perf-she information-pl about not topic from that be.perf-she she-want.imperf-them

'She did not find information about any topic she wants.'

If NC occurs with a grammatical subject, Emirati speakers prefer a subject-verb order (Chapter 11), and the negative subject ولا حد wala ħad 'no one' may exist without another negative marker.

ولا حد يا

wala ħad ja.

not one came.perf-he

'No one came.'

The alternative verb-subject word order, such as the following sentence, is considered as degraded by Emirati speakers (Chapter 11). Even if the sentence were accepted by some speakers, the sentence-final negative subject ولا حد wala ħad 'no one' needs to be licensed by a preceding negative marker.

ما يا ولا حد

maa ja wala ħad.

not come.perf-he no one

'No one came.'

As a single negative word, ولا wala can be used to answer the following questions:

أ: في أي طالب في الصف؟

fii ʔaj tˤaaləb fə-sˤ-sˤaf?

there.is any students in-the-classroom

A: 'Is there any student in the classroom?'

ب: ولا حد

wala ħad

not one

B: 'Nobody'

In terms of usage, ولا wala is always used to express new information to the hearer.

ولا حد يا الحفلة أمس

wala ħad ja l-ħafla ʔams.

no one come.perf the-party yesterday

No one came to the party yesterday.

The use of ولا wala in the following examples expresses the speaker's notification of a new situation:

ما في ولا كمبيوتر فالكلاس

maa fii wala kambjuutar f-əl-klaas.
not there.is not computer in-the-classroom
'There is no computer in the classroom!'

ولا شي من اللي كان حسن يباه موجود

wala ʃaj mən ʔəlli kaan ħasan jə-ba-ah mawdʒuud.
not thing from that be.perf-I Hasan he-want.imperf-it available
'Nothing of what Hasan wanted is there.'

10.9.2 أبد *ʔabad 'ever, at all'*

Negative concord may occur with أبد ʔabad (var. أبداً ʔabadan) 'ever, at all,' which must be licensed by the negative marker, resulting in an interpretation of the negative meaning 'never.' If أبد ʔabad is preverbal, it has to precede the negative marker. أبد ʔabad may also be sentence-final.

سمعنا عن الفار بس ما شفناه أبد

səmaʕ-na ʕan əl-faar bas maa tʃəf-naa-h ʔabad.
hear.perf-we about the-mouse but not see.perf-we-it ever
'We have heard about the rat but we have never seen it.'

أبد ما حبيت الكلام اللي انقال

ʔabad maa ħabb-eet əl-kalaam ʔəlli (ə)n-gaal.
at.all not like.perf-I the-talk that pass-say
'I did not like what was said at all.'

The use of أبد ʔabad (var. أبداً ʔbadan) is strongly preferred in generic and individual-level sentences, especially if it means 'never' in a temporal sense.

جون أبد ما سار المكتبة عشان يدرس

dʒoon ʔabad maa saar əl-maktəba ʕaʃaan jə-drəs.
John never not go.perf-he the-library in.order.to he-study.imperf
'John never went to the library to study.'

الأرض ما توقف دوران أبداً

əl-ʔarðˤ	maa	t-waggəf	dawaraan	ʔabadan.
the-earth	not	it.f-caus.stop.imperf	rotation	never

'The Earth never stops rotating.'

الأرانب ما تاكل لحم أبداً

əl-ʔaraanəb	maa	t-aakəl	laħam	ʔabadan.
the-rabbits	not	she-eat.imperf	meat	never

'Rabbits never eat meat.'

As a negative concord, it can be used alone as a fragment answer (Chapter 11), without the negative marker.

أ: جد سرت قصر الإمارات فبوظبي؟

ʧəd	sərt	gasˤr	əl-əmaaraat	f-buðˤabi?
ever	go.perf-you	palace	the-Emirates	in-Abu Dhabi?

A: 'Have you ever been to Emirates Palace in Abu Dhabi?'

ب: أبداً

ʔabadan!

B: 'Never!'

10.9.3 موول *muul 'not at all'*

The negative concord موول muul (var. موولية muulijja) 'not at all' may appear at various positions within the sentence (including the sentence-initial position), as long as it is licensed by another negative marker. It is also used as a fragment answer 'not at all.' موول muul differs from أبد ʔabad 'ever' in that موول muul is preferred in episodic situations, whereas أبد ʔabad 'ever' is used in both episodic and generic statements.

أمريكا ما بتخليهم فحالهم موول

ʔamriikaa	maa	ba-t-xallii-hum	f-ħaal-hum	muul.
America	not	will-it.f-leave.imperf-them	on-own-their	not.at.all

'America will not leave them on their own at all.'

يدوه ما بتتنازل عن حقها موول
jaddooh maa bə-tə-tnaazal ʕan ħag-ha muul.
grandmother not will-she-refl.give.up.imperf about right-her not.at.all
'My grandmother will not give up her right at all.'

شيخة مول ما تحب الحيوانات
ʃeexa muul maa t-ħəb əl-ħajwaan-aat.
Shaikha not.at.all not she-like.imperf the-animal-f.pl
'Shaikha doesn't like animals at all.'

موول ماشفت القطوة وأنا داخله
muul maa ʧəft əl-gatˤwa w ʔana daaxl-a.
not.at.all not see.perf-I the-cat and I part.enter-f
'I did not see the cat at all while I was entering.'

ما جد كتبت حقها رساله موولية
maa ʧəd kətab-t ħag-ha rəsaala muulijja
not not.at.all write.perf-I for-her letter not.at.all
'I have not written her a letter at all.'

أ: طلعتي اليوم من البيت؟
tˤəlaʕt-i əl-joom mən əl-beet
go.out.perf-you.f the-today from the-house
A: 'Have you gone out today?'

ب: موول
muul
B: 'Not at all.'

10.9.4 بالمرة *bəlmarra 'not at all'*

بالمرة bəlmarra 'not at all' (which literally means 'by once') is another common negative concord element used in negative contexts or which exists independently as a fragment answer.

أ: انتي أبداً ما تشربين شاي ، صح؟

ʔənt-i ʔabadan maa tə-ʃrəb-iin ʧaaj sˤaħ?

you-f never not you.f-drink.imperf-you.f tea right?

A: 'You never drink tea, right?'

ب: بالمرة

b-əl-marra

by-the-once

B: 'Not at all.'

أ: سرتي الحديقة قبل؟

sər-ti əl-ħadiiqa gabəl?

go.perf-you the-park before?

A: 'Have you been to the park before?'

ب: بالمرة

b-əl-marra

by-the-once

B: 'Not at all.'

أحمد ما بيروح ويا حد بالمرة

ʔaħmad maa ba-j-rooħ wəjja ħad b-əl-marra.

Ahmad not will-he-go.imperf with one by-the-once

'Ahmad will not go with anyone at all.'

ما سافرت بالمرة

maa saafar-t b-əl-marra.

not travel.perf-I by-the-once

'I have not traveled at all.'

رحت المزرعة بس ما استانست بالمرة

rəħ-t əl-mazraʕa bas maa əstaanas-t b-əl-marra.

go.perf-I the-farm but not caus.refl.enjoy.perf-I by-the-once

'I went to the farm, but I did not enjoy it at all.'

Further reading

For the typological study of negation across various Arabic dialects, see Brustad (2000). For a theoretical discussion of negative polarity items and negative concord, see Benmamoun (1996, 1997, 2000, 2006) for MSA and Moroccan Arabic, and Hoyt (2010) for Levantine Arabic. For negative imperatives, see Benmamoun (2000). For an overview of the historical development of negations in Arabic, see Lucas (2009) and Diem (2014), among many others.

Chapter 11

Word order

In the domain of linguistics, *basic word order* refers to the linear order between major grammatical functions, including the subject (S), object (O) (further distinguished into the direct object (DO) and indirect object (IO) in double-object constructions), and the verb (V). For sentences in which the argument structure does not consist of a verb, basic word order concerns the order between the subject and the predicate. Based on the basic word order, word order permutation (Section 11.4) is possible, with corresponding pragmatic functions, e.g. afterthought and topicalization.

11.1 Subject-verb (SV) and verb-subject (VS)

In many cases, Emirati Arabic allows both subject-verb (SV) and verb-subject (VS) word order. For example:

الولد توه يا

əl-wəlad taww-a jaa

the-boy just-him come.perf-he

'The boy just came.'

يا الولد

jaa-l-wəlad.

come.perf-he-the-boy

'The boy came.'

The preference between SV and VS is influenced by the definiteness of the subject. The VS word order is strongly favored if the subject is indefinite (whereas SV word order is considered as unnatural). However, in existential constructions formed by the existential preposition في fii 'there is,' the indefinite subject may precede the verb.

يا ولد

jaa wəlad.

come.perf-he boy

'A boy came.'

في ولد توه يا

fii wəlad taww-a jaa.

there.is boy just-him come.perf-he

'There is a boy (who) just came.'

As the subject becomes more semantically specific, the SV is more acceptable. The two examples in the following are equally acceptable, given that the subject ولد طويل wəlad tˤwiil 'a tall boy' is more specific (though still indefinite):

ولد طويل يا

wəlad tˤwiil jaa

boy tall come.perf-he

'A tall boy came.'

يا ولد طويل

jaa wəlad tˤwiil.

come.perf-he boy tall

'A tall boy came.'

Emirati Arabic sentences do not always contain a verbal predicate. For the copula sentences (Section 7.1), the subject should always precede the predicate. On the other hand, the reverse predicate-subject order, if acceptable, usually expresses an additional pragmatic function, e.g. an afterthought.

موزة معلمة

mooza mʕalm-a.

Moza teacher-f

'Moza is a teacher.'

معلمة موزة

mʕalm-a mooza.

teacher-f Moza

'(She is) a teacher, Moza.' (afterthought)

هند في المكتبة

hənd f-əl-maktəba.

Hind in-the-library

'Hind is in the library.'

في المكتبة هند

fə-l-maktəba hənd.

in-the-library Hind

'(She is) in the library, Hind.' (afterthought)

هييج الطالبة وايد مجتهدة

hajii-ʧ ətˤ-tˤaalˤb-a waajəd mədʒtahd-a.

that.f the-student-f very hardworking-f

'That student is very hardworking.'

وايد مجتهدة هاييج الطالبة

waajed mədʒtahd-a haajii-ʧ ətˤ-tˤaalˤb-a.

very hardworking-f that-f the-student-f

'(She is) very hardworking, that student.' (afterthought)

The verbless subject-predicate structure may also be expressed by the existential preposition **في** fii which is interpreted as 'there is/are.' The following sentences show that **في** fii may be sentence-initial or intervene between the subject and the predicate. In both cases **في** fii precedes the subject.

في كوبين عالطاولة

fii koob-een ʕa-tˤ-tˤaawla

there.is cup-du on-the-table

'There are two cups on the table.'

على الطاولة في كوبين

ʕa-tˤ-tˤaawla fii koob-een.

on-the-table there.is cup-du

'On the table (there) are two cups.'

في طالبة في الصف

fii tˤaalˤb-a f-əsˤ-sˤaf.

there.is student-f in-the-classroom

'There is a student in the classroom.'

في الصف في طالبة

f-əsˁ-sˁaf	fii	tˁaalb-a.
in-the-classroom	there.is	student-f

'In the classroom (there) is a student.'

11.2 Subject-verb-object (SVO)

For sentences that include a transitive verb and a DO, Emirati Arabic strongly prefers SVO word order.

موزة لاقت مريم أمس فالليل

mooza	laag-at	marjam	ʔams	f-əl-leel.
Moza	meet.perf-she	Mariam	yesterday	in-the-night

'Moza met Mariam last night.'

علي توه صلح الكمبيوتر

ʕəli	taww-a	sˁallaħ	əl-kəmbjutar.
Ali	just-him	caus.fix.perf-he	the-computer

'Ali just repaired the computer.'

أحمد اشترى كتاب لغويات البارحة

ʔaħmad	əʃtəra	ktaab	ləɣawiijat	əl-baarħa.
Ahmad	refl.buy.perf-he	book	linguistics	the-yesterday

'Ahmad bought a linguistics book yesterday.'

The basic SVO word order is not influenced by the animacy of the noun phrases. The following examples are all considered natural by native speakers, even when the subject is less animate than the object:

الكلب خوف شيخة وايد

əʧ-ʧalb	xawwaf	ʃeexa	waajəd.
the-dog	caus.fear.perf-it	Shaikha	a.lot

'The dog frightened Sheikha (i.e. caused Sheikha to fear) very much.'

الموسيقى الكلاسيكية تعيب عهود

əl-musiiq-a	əl-klaasiikij-ja	t-ʕajəb	ʕəhuud.
the-music-f	the-classic-f	it-please.imperf	Uhood

'Classical music pleases Uhood.'

الوضع يضايج أهلي وايد

əl-waðˤʕ j-ðˤaajədʒ ʔahl-i waajəd.

the-situation it-bother.imperf family-my a.lot

'The situation bothers my family a lot.'

نهاية الفلم فاجأت الحضور

nəhaaja-t əl-fəlm faadʒəʔ-at əl-ħəðˤuur.

ending-f the-movie surprise.perf-it the-audience

'The movie ending surprised the audience.'

الحضور تفاجئوا بنهاية الفلم

əl-ħəðˤuur t-faadʒəʔ-aw b-nəhaaj-at əl-fəlm.

the-audience refl-surprise.perf-they by-ending-f the-movie

'The audience were surprised by the movie ending.'

On the other hand, the verb-initial sentence (VSO) is considered unnatural or sounding 'hyper-corrective'—perhaps an influence from MSA.

11.3 Double-object constructions

For ditransitive verbs which select two objects (Section 7.6), the order between the DO and IO may be flexible, depending on the semantic class of the ditransitive verbs and the animacy of the arguments. For the verbs of sending and giving, both S-V-DO-IO and S-V-IO-DO are acceptable. If the objects become pronominal (Section 5.8.1.3), both orders are available. Note that the linking particle ايّا ijja is used to host the DO pronoun.

S-V-DO-IO

علي طرّش كتاب لفاخرة

ʕəli tˤarraʃ ktaab l-faaxra.

Ali send.perf-he book to-Fakhra

'Ali sent a book to Fakhra.'

علي طرَّشه لها

ʕəli tˤarraʃ-a əl-ha.

Ali send.perf-he-it to-her

'Ali sent it to her.'

علي عطى كتاب لفاخرة

ʕəli	ʕatˤa	ktaab	l-faaxra.
Ali	gave.perf-he	book	to-Fakhra

'Ali gave a book to Fakhra.'

علي عطاه حقها

ʕəli	ʕatˤaa-h	ħag-ha.
Ali	gave.perf-he-it	to-her

'Ali gave it to her.'

S-V-IO-DO

علي طرَّش حق فاخرة كتاب

ʕəli	tˤarraʃ	ħag	faaxra	ktaab.
Ali	send.perf-he	for	Fakhra	book

'Ali sent Fakhra a book.'

علي طرشلها اياه

ʕəli	tˤarraʃ-əl-ha	əjja-ah
Ali	send.perf-to-her	Ink-it

'Ali sent it to her.' (lit. Ali sent her it.)

علي عطى حق فاخرة كتاب

ʕəli	ʕatˤa	ħag	faaxra	ktaab.
Ali	gave.perf-he	for	Fakhra	book

'Ali gave Fakhra a book.'

علي عطاها اياه

ʕəli	ʕatˤaa-ha	əjja-ah
Ali	gave.perf-he-her	Ink-it

'Ali gave it to her.' (lit. Ali gave her it.)

If both DO and IO are bare noun phrases (i.e. without any preposition such as لـ l- 'to' or حق ħag 'for'), and the IO is animate (e.g. a person), the S-V-IO-DO order is preferred (Section 7.6). The alternative S-V-DO-IO order is ungrammatical without a dative preposition.

شما عطت حصة كتابها

ʃamma ʕatˁa-t ħəsˁsˁa ktaab-ha.

Shamma give.perf-she Hessa book-her

'Shamma gave Hessa her book.'

سلف أحمد شوية مجلات

salləf ʔaħmad ʃwajja-t madʒall-aat.

lend.imp Ahmad some-f magazine-f.pl

'Lend Ahmad some magazines.'

فر حق أحمد الكورة

fərr ħag ʔaħmad əl-koora.

throw.imp to ahmad the-ball

'Throw Ahmad the ball.'

موزة علمت اختها بعض المهارات

mooza ʕalləm-at ʔəxət-ha baʕðˁ l-mahaar-aat.

Moza teach.perf-she sister-her some the-skill-f.pl

'Moza taught her sisters some skills.'

For non-animate indirect objects, the dative construction S-V-DO-IO is preferred.

رد شوية كتب حق المكتبة

radd ʃwajja-t kətəb ħag l-maktəba

return.perf-he some-f books for the-library

'He returned some books to the library.'

العلماء وفروا بيانات مهمة حق الحكومة

l-ʕəlamaaʔ waffər-aw bajaanaat mhəm-ma ħag əl-ħəkuuma

the-scientist.pl provide.perf-they data important-f for the-government

'The scientists provided the government with some important data.'

Some locative (e.g. حط ħatˁ 'put') and benefactive (e.g. جهز ʤahhaz 'prepared') verbs only allow the dative construction S-V-DO-IO.

حط الكتاب عالرف

ħatˁ lə-ktaab ʕa-r-raf

put.perf-he the-book on-the-shelf

'He put the book on the shelf.'

جهز الاكل حق بنته

ʤahhaz l-ʔakəl ħag bənta-h

prepare.perf-he the-food for daughter-his

'He prepared the food for his daughter.'

11.4 Word order permutation

As mentioned, word order permutation always corresponds to information structure considerations, for instance, the expression of afterthought and topicalization. The following examples have the word order VOS, and they may be described by right-dislocation of the subject toward the end of the sentence.

11.4.1 *Afterthought*

صلح الكمبيوتر علي

sˁallaħ əl-kambjutar ʕəli.

fix.perf-he the-computer Ali

'He repaired the computer, Ali.'

كسر المزهرية أحمد

kəsar əl-mazharijja ʔaħmad.

break.perf-he the-vase Ahmad

'He broke the vase, Ahmad.'

In some cases, the expression of afterthought leads to semantic ambiguity. For instance, in the following example, the right-dislocated noun Latifa may be interpreted as the subject of the sentence (e.g. Latifa went to her friend's house), or as a friend of the sentence subject:

سارت بيت ربيعتها لطيفة

saar-at beet rbiiʕa-t-ha lətˁiifa.

go.perf-she house friend-f-her Latifa

'She went to her friend Latifa's house.' (or 'Latifa went to her friend's house.')

On the other hand, the following example is disambiguated, i.e. Latifa is only interpreted as the sentence subject (i.e. Latifa went with her friends):

طلعت ويا ربيعاتها لطيفة

tˤəlʕ-at	wəjja	rbiiʕa-at-ha	lətˤiifa.
go.out.perf-she	with	friend-f.pl-her	Latifa

'She went with her friends, Latifa.'

Afterthought may be a grammatical constituent (e.g. a noun phrase) or non-constituent. This is shown in the following embedded clause (first example). The second example shows that موزة قالت mooza gaalat 'Moza said' is the afterthought. The third, although viewed somewhat unnatural by native speakers, shows that 'Maryam' is an afterthought of the embedded clause, whereas 'Moza said' is another afterthought of the main clause.

موزة قالت انه مريم كانت تسافر في مصر

mooza gaal-at ʔənn-ah marjam kaan-at t-saafər f-məsˤər.

Moza say.perf-she that-her Maryam be.perf-she she-travel.imperf in-Egypt

'Moza said that Maryam was traveling in Egypt.'

مريم كانت تسافر في مصر، موزة قالت

marjam	kaan-at	t-saafər	f-masˤər	mooza	gaal-at.
Maryam	be.perf-she	she-travel.imperf	in-Egypt	Moza	say.perf-she

'Maryam was traveling in Egypt, Moza said.'

كانت تسافر في مصر مريم، موزة قالت

kaan-at	t-saafər	f-masˤər	marjam,	mooza	gaal-at.
be.perf-she	she-travel.imperf	in-Egypt	Maryam	Moza	say.perf-she

'She was traveling in Egypt, Maryam, Moza said.'

Afterthought is also be used in negative sentences (Chapter 9).

أحمد ما يا حفلتنا

ʔaħmad	maa	jaa	ħafla-t-na.
Ahmad	not	come.perf-he	party-f-our

'Ahmad did not come to our party.'

ما يا حفلتنا أحمد

maa jaa ħafla-t-na ʔaħmad.
not come.perf-he party-f-our Ahmad
'He did not come to our party, Ahmad.'

Word order permutation is overall considered as unnatural or ungrammatical within embedded clauses. For instance, the basic word order of the conditional clauses (Section 14.4) is SVO. Any variant of SVO within the conditional clause is ungrammatical.

لو عطيتني الفلوس بشتريلك اللي تباه

loo ʕatˤ-eet-ni əl-fluus b-aʃtərii-l-ək ʔəlli tə-baa.
if give.perf-you-me the-money will-I.buy.imperf-to-you that you-want.imperf
'If you give me the money, I will buy you what you want.'

مع انه علي شد حيله بس رسب فالأمتحان

maʕ ʔenn-a ʕəli ʃad ħeel-a bas rəsab f-əl-əmtəħaan.
with that-him Ali work.hard.perf but fail.perf-he in-the-exam
'Although Ali worked hard, he failed the exam.'

وقت ما هند كانت تحل واجبها، عليا كانت تلعب

wagt maa hənd kaan-at t-ħəl waadʒəb-ha ʕalja kaan-at tə-lʕab.
while that Hind be.perf-she she-solve.imperf assignment-her Alia be.perf-she she-play.imperf
'While Hind was doing her assignment, Alia was playing.'

11.4.2 Topicalization

Topicalization is a grammatical strategy in which the topic of the sentence (i.e. what the sentence is about) is brought to a prominent (e.g. sentence-initial) position. If the sentential object is topicalized to the sentence-initial position and precedes the subject (OSV), the transitive verb would require an object suffix which co-refers to the object (Section 5.8.1.3).

11.4.2.1 Object-subject-verb (OSV)

مريم ، موزة جافتها أمس فالليل

marjam mooza ʧaaf-at-ha ʔams f-əl-leel.
Mariam Moza met-she-her yesterday at-the-night
'(As for) Mariam, Moza met her last night.'

الكمبيوتر علي صلحه

əl-kəmbjutar ʕəli sˤallaħ-a.
the-computer Ali fix.perf-he-it
'(As for) the computer, Ali repaired it.'

In addition, the anaphoric pronoun of the topic may be used in other structures, e.g. possessives (Section 5.8.2).

أحمد، أمه مب راضية عن درجته في الامتحان

ʔaħmad ʔumm-ah mub raaðˤj-a ʕan daraʤt-ah f-əl-əmtəħaan.
Ahmad mother-his not satisfy.perf-she about mark-his in-the-exam
'(As for) Ahmad, his mother is very unhappy about his exam result.'

Topicalization is also used to establish a contrast. For example:

الكمبيوتر علي صلحه، والدريشة أحمد نظفها

əl-kəmbjutar ʕəli sˤallaħ-a w-əd-dəriiʃa ʔaħmad naðˤðˤaf-ha.
the-computer Ali fix.perf-he-it and-the-window Ahmad clean.perf-he-it
'(As for) the computer, Ali repaired it, and (as for) the window, Ahmad cleaned it.'

It is possible the topic is not coreferential with the argument structure of the whole sentence; instead, the topic expresses the notion of 'aboutness.'

الحريقة ، الحمد لله المطافي يو بسرعة

əl-ħəriiʤa əlħəmdəllaah əl-matˤaafi j-aw b-sərʕa.
the-fire thank.God the-civil.defense come.perf-they with-speed
'(About) the fire, thank God the Civil Defense came quickly.'

Sometimes the topic is resumed in the main sentence. For example:

غدا، ما نتغدا همبرغر

ɣəda	maa	nə-tɣadda	hambərgar.
lunch	not	we-refl.eat.lunch.imperf	burger

'(About) lunch, we don't eat burgers for lunch.'

سباحة، موسى كان يسبح كل يوم

səbaaħ-a	muusa	kaan	jə-sbaħ	kəl	joom.
swimming-f	Musa	be.perf-he	he-swim.imperf	every	day

'(As for) swimming, Musa used to swim every day.'

Emirati Arabic sometimes employs a number of topic markers. For instance:

ذكية، ترى حتى فاطمة ذكية

ðakij-ja	tara	ħatta	faatˤma	ðakij-ja.
smart-f	by.way.of	even	Fatma	smart-f

'(As for being) smart, Fatma is also smart.'

في السيارات، أحمد بس يحب المرسيدس

f-əs-sajjaara-at	ʔaħmad	bass	j-ħəbb	əl-mərsiidəs.
in-the-car-f.pl	Ahmad	only	he-like.imperf	the-Mercedes

'(On the topic of) cars, Ahmad only likes Mercedes.'

اما الصين، سكّانها وايدين

ʔamma	əsˤ-sˤiin	səkkaan-ha	wajd-iin.
As.for	the-China	population-its	a.lot-pl

'As for China, its population is huge.'

11.4.2.2 *Object-verb-subject (OVS)*

Another possible word order which involves object topicalization is object-verb-subject (OVS). In this case, the underlying subject (i.e. the event initiator) is right-dislocated to the sentence-final position, which corresponds to the speaker's intention to demote its pragmatic saliency in the conversation. Sometimes right-dislocation also brings along the effect of an afterthought.

اهلي وايد مضايجنهم الوضع

ʔahl-i waajəd m-ðˤaajʤənn-hum əl-waðˤəʕ

family-my a.lot part-bother-them the-situation

'My family is very much bothered by the situation.' (lit. My family, it is bothering them, the situation.)

نحن وايد منرفزنا الخبر

nəħən waajəd m-narfəzə-na əl-xəbar

we a.lot part-annoy-us the-news

'We were so annoyed by the news.' (lit. We, (it) annoyed us a lot, the news.)

أهلي وايد تعبتهم الرحلة

ʔahl-i waajəd taʕʕəb-at-hum ər-rəħla

family-my a.lot caus.tire.perf-it.f-them the-trip

'My family was so tired by the trip.' (lit. My family, it caused them tired, the trip.)

أحمد وايد أحبطه القرار

ʔaħmad waajəd ʔa-ħbətˤ-a əl-qaraar

Ahmada a.lot it-disappoint.perf-him the-decision

'Ahmad was so disappointed by the decision.' (lit. Ahmad, it disappointed him, the decision.)

فاطمة وايد جرحها الكلام

faatˤma waajəd ʤaraħ-ha əl-kalaam

Fatima a.lot hurt.perf-it-her the-talk

'Fatima was so hurt by the talk.' (lit. Fatima, it hurt her a lot, the talk.)

حصة وايد ظلمها المدير

ħəsˤsˤah waajəd ðˤalam-ha əl-mudiir

Hesah a.lot oppress.perf-he-her the-boss

'Hesah was so oppressed by the boss.' (lit. Hesah, he oppressed her, the boss.)

سالم وايد مزعجتنه السالفة

saaləm waajəd mə-zʕədʒ-tə-nna əs-saalf-a
Salim a.lot part-bother-f-him the-rumor.f
'Salim was so bothered by the rumor.' (lit. Salim, they are bothering him, the rumor.)

11.4.2 *Focus*

In the area of information structure, focus is a grammatical category which introduces new information or some kind of contrast to the relevant discourse. Emirati Arabic speakers prefer the use of relative and cleft structures (Chapters 12 and 13) to express the focused element. The focused element usually attracts phonological prominence, represented here with the use of capitalization in the English translations, following standard conventions:

هو البرتقال اللي شيخة ما تاكله

huu əl-bərtəqaal ʔəlli ʃeexa maa ta-akl-ah.
it th-orange that Sheikha not she-eat.imperf-it
'It is ORANGES that Sheikha does not eat.'

البرتقال هو اللي شيخة ما تاكله

əl-bərtəqaal huu ʔəlli ʃeexa maa ta-akl-ah.
th-orange it that Sheikha not she-eat.imperf-it
'ORANGES are what Sheikha does not eat.'

هو اللي شيخة أبدًا ما تدانيه

huu ʔəlli ʃeexa ʔabadan maa-d-dani-ih.
he that Sheikha completely not-she-like.imperf-him
'HE is who Shekha does not like very much.'

If the focused element is non-argumental, e.g. adverbials (Section 5.4), the cleft structure is not used. In this case, the focused element is left-disclosed and receives phonological prominence.

في المكتبة رقد علي طول اليوم

f-əl-maktaba rəgad ʕəli tˁuul-əl-joom.
in-the-library sleep.perf-he Ali all-the-today
'(It's) IN THE LIBRARY that Ali slept for the whole day.'

Contrastive focus may be expressed by using negation (Chapter 10). Both of the following examples are acceptable, although the second is more felicitous to emphasize the focused element:

هو البروكولي اللي ما أحبه، مب الكوسا

huu	l-brokoli	ʔəlli	maa-ħəbb-ah	məb	əl-kuusa.
it	the-broccoli	that	not-I-like.imperf-it	not	the-zucchini

'It is the BROCCOLI that I do not like, not the ZUCCHINI.'

البروكولي هو اللي ما أحبه، مب الكوسا

əl-brokoli	huu	ʔəlli	maa-ħəbb-ah	məb	əl-kuusa.
the-broccoli	it	that	neg-I-like.imperf-it	not	the-zucchini

'I hate BROCCOLI, not ZUCCHINI.'

11.4.3 *Heavy NP shift*

Heavy NP shift is an operation by which the heavy NP—that is, an NP with a rich internal structure—is shifted toward the end of sentences. While the following two pairs of sentences are grammatical, native speakers strongly prefer the second, in which the heavy noun phrase is shifted toward the end.

سارة عطت الكتاب اللي اشترته الاسبوع اللي طاف لموزة

saara	ʕatˤ-at	lə-ktaab	ʔəlli	əʃtər-at-a	əs-səbuuʕ
ʔəlli	tˤaaf	l-mooza.			
Sara	give.perf-she	the-book	that	refl.buy.perf-she-it	the-week
that	pass.perf-it	to-Moza			

'Sara gave the book that she bought last week to Moza.'

سارة عطت موزة الكتاب اللي اشترته الاسبوع اللي طاف

saara	ʕatˤ-at	mooza	lə-ktaab	ʔəlli	əʃtər-at-a
əs-səbuuʕ	ʔəlli	tˤaaf.			
Sara	give.perf-she	Moza	the-book	that	refl.buy.perf-she-it
the-week	that	pass.perf-it			

'Sara gave to Moza the book that she bought last week.'

خذت لبنت عمي اللي ربت الاسبوع اللي طاف هدية

xaðt	l-bənt	ʕam-mi	ʔəlli	rabb-at	l-əsbuuʕ
ʔəlli	tˤaaf	hadijja.			
buy.perf-I	for-daughter	uncle-my	that	birth.perf-she	the-week
that	pass.perf-it	gift			

'I bought my cousin who gave birth last week a gift.'

خذت هدية لبنت عمي اللي ربت الاسبوع اللي طاف

xað-t	hadij-ja	l-bənt	ʕamm-i	ʔəlli	rabb-at
l-əsbuuʕ	ʔəlli	tˤaaf.			
buy.perf-I	gift-f	for-daughter	uncle-my	that	give.birth.perf-she
the-week	that	pass.perf-it			

'I bought a gift for my cousin who gave birth last week.'

Further reading

For a detailed analysis of the interaction between word order permutation and discourse functions in Gulf Arabic, see Owens et al. (2009, 2013) and Holes (2013). For the syntactic analysis of word order permutation in Arabic, see Fassi Fehri (1993), Mohammad (1999), Brustad (2000), and Aoun et al. (2010). To learn more about word order permutation as a general linguistic observation, consult the relevant chapters in Kiss (1995).

Chapter 12

Relative clauses

Relative clauses are clauses within the NP structure (Chapter 6) which serve to modify the head noun. A relative clause may be restrictive, which limits the reference of the head noun, or non-restrictive, which appends additional meaning to the head noun without further defining the reference of the head noun. In Emirati Arabic, the structure of the relative clause depends upon the definiteness of the head noun (Section 6.1). Relative clauses that modify a definite head noun are always typed by the relative clause marker اللي ʔəlli 'that' (Section 5.7), whereas those that modify an indefinite head noun do not allow the use of اللي ʔəlli. Both types of relative clauses typically require the use of a resumptive pronoun if the head noun is interpreted as the object within the relative clause. The only case in which the objective resumptive pronoun is not required is with headless, free relative clauses (Section 12.3).

12.1 Restrictive relative clauses

Relative clauses always follow the head noun in Emirati Arabic. The verb/predicate inside the relative clause must fully indicate the reference of the head noun in terms of its person (usually the third person), number (singular or plural), and gender (masculine or feminine). If the head noun functions as the object of the relative clause, an objective resumptive pronoun which agrees with the referent of the head noun must be used (Section 5.8.1.9). On the other hand, if the head noun functions as the subject of the relative clause, an overt subject pronoun within the relative clause is disallowed.

12.1.1 Definite head nouns

If the head noun is definite (e.g. الكتاب əlktaab 'the book'), the relative clause must be introduced by the relative clause marker اللي ʔəlli 'that.'

الكتاب اللي اشتريته أمس غالي
lə-ktaab ʔəlli əʃtər-eet-ah ʔams ɣaali.
the-book that refl.buy.perf-I-it yesterday expensive
'The book that I bought yesterday is expensive.'

السيارة اللي اشتريتها أمس غالية
əs-sajjaara ʔəlli ə-ʃtər-eet-ha ʔams ɣaal-jah.
the-car that refl.buy.perf-I-it.f yesterday expensive-f
'The car that I bought yesterday is expensive.'

المكينه اللي تقص الورق ثقيله
əl-məkiina ʔəlli t-gəsˤ əl-warag θədʒiil-ah.
the-machine that it.f-cut.imperf the-papers heavy-f
'The machine that cuts paper is heavy.'

المقص اللي يقص الورق ثقيل
əl-magasˤ ʔəlli j-gəsˤ əl-warag θədʒiil.
the-scissor that it-cut.imperf the-papers heavy
'The scissors that cut the paper are heavy.'

Various types of definite head nouns can be relativized, e.g. thing, person, place, and time. For example:

المدينه اللي أحمد يسكن فيها هي العين
əl-mədiina ʔəlli ʔaħmad jə-skən fii-ha (hii) əlʕeen.
the-city that Ahmad he-live.imperf in-it.f it.f Al Ain
'The city where Ahmad lives is Al Ain.'

الدوله اللي أحمد انولد فيها هي الإمارات
əd-doola ʔəlli ʔaħmad ən-wəlad fii-ha (hii) l-əmaaraat.
the-country that Ahmad pass-born.perf in-it.f it.f the-emirates
'The country where Ahmad was born is UAE.'

اليوم اللي الامتحان يبدأ فيه هو الإثنين
əl-joom ʔəlli l-əmtəħan jə-bda fii-h (huu) l-əθneen.
the-day that the-exam it-start.imperf in-it he the-Monday
'The day on which the exam starts is Monday.'

Other nouns, such as manner and reasons, may not be relativized in Emirati Arabic. Instead of sentences such as 'Hard work is the way through which people get success' and 'Ahmad has a disability because of which he cannot attend classes regularly,' Emirati people prefer to say 'People get success by hard work' and 'Ahmad cannot attend classes regularly because he has a disability.'

Restrictive relative clauses formed by اللي ʔəlli 'that' also modify other quantifiers such as 'some,' 'many,' and 'most.' While these quantifiers are indefinite by nature (Sections 6.1.2 and 6.4.4), they function as the partitives which pick out a specific subset from the set denoted by the head noun. In such cases, the head noun always contains the definite determiner.

حد من الطلاب اللي رسبوا فالامتحان لازم يعيدون المادة

ħad mən ətˤ-tˤəlˤlˤaab ʔəlli rəsba-w f-əl-əmtħaan laazəm jə-ʕiiduun əl-maaddah.

some of the-students that fail.perf-they in-the-exam must they-repeat.pl the-course

'Some (of the) students who fail the exam need to repeat the course.' (i.e. not all failing students need to repeat the course)

أغلب الدول اللي الصين بنتلهم دول نامية

ʔaɣlab əd-duwal ʔəlli əsˤ-sˤiin bana-t-əl-hum duwal namij-a.

most the-countries that the-China build.perf-f-for-them countries developing-f

'Most (of the) countries that China did construction for are developing countries.'

أغلب الطلاب اللي أحمد درسهم أذكياء

ʔaɣlab ətˤ-tˤəlˤlˤaab ʔəlli ʔaħmad darras-hum ʔaðkija.

most the-students that Ahmad caus.teach.perf-he-them smart.pl

'Most (of the) students who Ahmad taught are smart.' (i.e. not all students who Ahmad taught are smart)

It should be noted that definite plural nouns can express a non-specific generic concept—this requires the relative marker اللي ʔəlli 'that' in relativization.

السيايير اللي ياية من اوروبا أحسن

əs-sjajiir ʔəlli jaa-jja mən ʔorobba ʔa-ħsan
the-cars that come.imperf from Europe more-good
'Cars which came from Europe (in general) are better.'

الطلاب اللي تخرجوا من الجامعات التوب غالبا معاشاتهم أعلى

ətˁ-tˁəlˁlˁaab ʔəlli t-xarrədʒ-aw mən
əl-dʒaamʕ-aat ət-tob ɣaaləban maʕaʃaat-hum ʔaʕla
the-students that refl-caus.graduate.perf-they from
the-university-f.pl the-top usually salaries-their higher
'Students who graduate from top universities usually earn higher salaries.'

12.1.2 *Indefinite head nouns*

Indefinite head nouns are less commonly relativized than definite head nouns. Expressions that include a nonspecific indefinite noun such as 'A book everyone bought must be popular' are considered as unnatural to native speakers. An indefinite noun may be relativized if it refers to a specific entity. The relative clause is not typed by the relative clause marker اللي ʔəlli.

تونا اشترينا بيت كلفنا أقل عن مليون درهم

taww-na əʃtəree-na beet kallaf-na ʔaqal ʕan
məljoon dərham.
just-us refl.buy.perf-we house caus.cost.imperf-we less than
million Dirham
'We just bought a house which costs us less than 1 million Dirhams.'

While bare singular nouns (e.g. كتاب ktaab 'book') may be interpreted as indefinite (cf. English 'a/one book'), they are not compatible with the use of relative clauses. Emirati speakers prefer the use of أي ʔaj 'any' and render the head noun a free-choice reading (Section 12.3 and Chapter 10). The relative clause which modifies indefinite head nouns does not have a relative clause marker.

أي كتاب كل حد يقراه لازم يكون زين

ʔaj ktaab kəl ħad jə-graa-h laazəm j-kuun zeen.
any book every person he-read.imperf-it must it-be.imperf good
'Any book everyone reads (it) must be good.'

ماشي كتاب كل حد يقراه يكون رخيص

maaʃaj ktaab kəl ħad jə-graa-h j-kuun rəxiisˤ.
no book every person he-read.imperf-it it-be.imperf cheap
'No book everyone reads (it) is cheap.'

12.2 Nonrestrictive relative clauses

The use of nonrestrictive relative clauses, which serve to present additional information to the head noun, is not very common in Emirati Arabic. In comparison with English, in which nonrestrictive relative clauses are separated from the head noun by a comma in writing or a pause in speech, Emirati Arabic employs the same strategy of marking a nonrestrictive relative clause with the relative clause marker اللي ʔəlli. The way native speakers utter nonrestrictive relative clauses is exactly the same as with restrictive clauses—that is, with no pause between the head noun and the relative clause. Moreover, since the reference of the head noun modified by the nonrestrictive relative clauses must be definite, the use of اللي ʔəlli is obligatory.

توني شفت هاري بوتر اللي كل اليهال شافوه مرتين

taww-ni ʧəf-t haari bootər ʔəlli kəl əl-jahhaal
ʧaafoo-h mart-een.
just-me see.perf-I Harry Potter that all the-children
they-see.imperf-it time-du
'I just watched Harry Potter, which all children have watched twice.'

أمريكا اللي كانت دولة قوية لمدة 50 سنة الحين تواجه مشكلة اقتصادية

ʔamriika ʔəlli kaan-at doola gəwij-ja l-mədda-t xamsiin
səna əl-ħiin t-waaʤəh məʃkəla əqtəsˤaadijj-ah.
America that be.perf-it.f country strong-f the-duration-f fifty
year the-now it.f-face.imperf problem economic-f
'The United States, which has been a superpower for 50 years, is now facing an economic problem.'

12.3 Free relative clauses

A relative clause may sometimes be headless as long as the interpretation of the relative clause is clear enough and exhaustively limits the set of potential referents. In English, the word 'whatever'

Table 12.1 Wh-words for free relatives

شو ما	ʃuu ma	'whatever'
منو ما	mnuu ma	'whoever'
وين ما	ween ma	'wherever'
متى ما	məta ma	'whenever'
كيف ما	keef ma	'however'

as in 'Whatever you bought must be expensive' is self-explanatory and synonymous to 'Anything you bought must be expensive,' which contains the head noun. In Emirati Arabic, the 'headless' free relative clause is formed by the clause-initial wh-word (Section 13.2.1) followed by ما ma '-ever.' The structure of free relative clauses is that of typical wh-questions (Table 12.1). They neither contain the relative clause marker اللي ʔəlli nor the objective resumptive pronoun (Section 5.8.1.9).

شو ما قالت ماله معنى

ʃuu maa gaal-at ma-l-a maʕna.

what ever say.perf-she not-for-it meaning

'Whatever she said was meaningless.'

اطلع منو ما كنت

ətˤlaʕ mnuu maa kənt.

come.out.imp who ever be.perf-you

'Come out, whoever you are.'

بسير وين ما بتسير

ba-siir ween maa bə-t-siir.

will-I-go.imperf where ever will-you-go.imperf

'I will go wherever you go.'

متى ما تي، خبرني

məta maa t-əjj xabbər-ni.

when ever you-come.imperf caus.tell.imp-me

'Whenever you come, let me know.'

كيف ماتسوي الوصفة بتطلع زينة

keef maa t-sawwi əl-wasˤfa ba-t-ətˤlaʕ zeen-ah.

how ever you-do.imperf the-recipe will-it.f-come.out.imperf good-f

'However you follow the recipe it will turn out good.'

شعرج حلو كيف ما تعدلينه

ʃaʕrə-ʧ ħəluu keef maa t-ʕadl-iin-ah.

hair-your beautiful how ever you.modify.imperf-you.f-it

'Your hair looks good however you modify it.'

It is common for native speakers to replace the free relative pronouns with the indefinite determiner أي ʔaj 'any,' e.g. منو ما mnuu ma 'whoever' may be expressed by أي حد ʔaj ħad 'anyone' without losing the interpretation. Since أي ʔaj is not a wh-word, the free relative clause is not structurally interrogative. The relative clause formed by أي ʔaj therefore requires an objective resumptive pronoun if necessary.

أي حد يغش بيرسب

ʔaj ħad j-ɣəʃ b-jə-rsab.

any one he-cheat.imperf will-he-fail.imperf

'Anyone who cheats will fail.'

أي حد اشوفه باجر بعزمه عالعشا

ʔaj ħad a-ʧuuf-ah baaʧər b-a-ʕzəma-h ʕa-l-ʕəʃa.

any one I-see.imperf-him tomorrow will-I-invite.imperf-him over the-dinner

'Whoever I meet (him) tomorrow, I will invite him to dinner.'

It is also possible to use free relatives to express a definite meaning. For instance, in English the sentence 'What you bought yesterday was amazing' suggests a definite reading of the head noun (= 'the thing you bought yesterday was amazing'). In Emirati Arabic, this type of definite free relatives may be expressed by the relative marker اللي ʔəlli, which suggests that the empty head noun is definite. Note that the definite referent may be an entity, a person, or a place.

اللي أحمد شراه أمس غالي

ʔəlli ʔaħmad ʃara-ah ʔams ɣaali.

that Ahmad buy.perf-he-it yesterday expensive

'What Ahmad bought yesterday was expensive.'

باكل اللي اشتريتيه أمس

b-a-a-kəl ʔəlli ʃtaree-tii-h ʔams.

will-I-eat.imperf that refl.buy.perf-you.f-it yesterday

'I will eat what you bought yesterday.'

أنا اللي جون يبا يشوفه

ʔana ʔəlli ʤoon jə-ba j-ʧuuf-ah.

I that John he-want.imperf he-see.imperf-him

'I am who John wants to see.'

باريس هي اللي كل الفنانين يبون يعيشون فيها

baariis hii ʔəlli kəl əl-fannaaniin jə-b-oon jə-ʕiiʃ-uun fii-ha.

Paris she that all the-artists they-want.imperf-they they-live.imperf-they in-it.f

'Paris is where all artists want to live.'

For other nominal expressions such as time, manner, way, and reason, the use of definite free relatives is unavailable. Instead, Emirati Arabic uses expressions such as جي ʧii 'this way' for manner-free relatives and restricted relative clauses for reason-free relatives.

جي أنا أعدل التاير

ʧii ʔana ʔa-ʕaddəl ət-taajər.

this.way I I-caus.fix.imperf the-tire

'This is how I fix the tire.' (lit. This way I fix the tire.)

واترجيت هي السبب انه الرئيس نيكسون استقال

watərgeet hii əs-səbab ʔənna ər-raʔiis nəksən əstaqaal.

Watergate she the-reason that the-president Nixon caus.refl.resign.perf-he

'Watergate is why (=the reason that) President Nixon resigned.'

12.4 Noun complement clauses

Another type of clause, the noun complement clause, functions as a complement to the head noun, yet it is not structurally a relative clause. In English, the noun phrase 'the fact that UAE has seven Emirates is well known to its citizens' contains a full clause which functions as the complement of the head noun 'fact.' In Emirati Arabic, most noun complement clauses are marked by the complementizer انه ʔənn(ah) 'that' followed by a complete clause.

كل حد يعرف عن اشاعة انه أحمد بيتقاعد

kəl ħad jə-ʕarf ʕan əʃaaʕət ʔənna ʔaħmad ba-j-ətqaaʔad.

every one he-know.imperf about rumor that Ahmad will-he-resign.imperf

'Everyone knows the rumor that Ahmad will resign.'

السبب انه أحمد رسب فلمتحان هو عيازته

əs-səbab ʔənnah ʔaħmad rəsab fə-l-əmtəħaan huu ʕəjaaz-t-əh.

the-reason that Ahmad fail.perf-he in-the-exam it laziness-f-his

'The reason that Ahmad failed the exam is his laziness.'

متطلب انه الطلاب لازم ايبون أيي فالرياضيات صعب عالكل

mə-ttˤalˤlˤab ʔənnah ətˤ-tˤəlˤlˤaab laazəm əj-jiib-uun ʔee f-ər-rijaðˤijjaat sˤaʕəb ʕ-al-kəl.

part-refl.requirement that the-students must they-get.imperf-they A in-the-math difficult for-the-all

'The requirement that students need to get an A in math is difficult for everyone.'

If the noun complement clause is not declarative, e.g. interrogatives such as 'the question why Ahmad came late' or conditionals such as 'the fine if you park here,' the complementizer انه ʔənn(ah) 'that' is not used (Section 5.7).

سؤال وين مكان نشأة اللغة العربية وايد صعبة أجابته

suʔaal ween məkaan naʃʔa-t əl-ləɣa əl-ʕarabijja waajəd sˤaʕb-a ʔəʤab-t-ah.

question where place origin-f the-language the-Arabic very hard-f answer-f-it

'The question "Where did Arabic originate?" is very difficult to answer.'

الغرامة إذا بركنت هنيه وايد غالية

əl-ɣaraama ʔəða barkan-t hniih waajəd ɣaal-jah.

the-fine if park.perf-you here very expensive-f

'The fine if you park here is very expensive.'

Further reading

For an overview of the relative strategies in Arabic dialects, see Brustad (2000), Aoun et al. (2001), and Alqurashi and Borsley (2012). For more advanced research on the syntactic properties of resumptive pronouns in relative structures, refer to Sells (1984), McCloskey (1990, 2017), Shlonsky (1992), Sharvit (1999), and Aoun et al. (2001), among others.

Chapter 13

Questions

13.1 Yes-no questions

13.1.1 Intonation patterns

Yes-no questions (sometimes called polar or alternative questions) are questions for which an answer is usually a confirmation or a denial of a statement or fact. In Emirati Arabic, yes-no questions are formed using the same word order as declarative sentences with a change in the intonational pattern—in other words, in the pitch trajectory during its pronunciation. Thus, in a normal declarative sentence, the intonation is globally declining towards the end of the sentence. In contrast, for yes-no questions, the intonation pattern begins with a lower pitch and rises when it reaches the word in question, followed by a continuing increase in pitch in the syllables following this element.

ميرة صكت الباب

miira sˤakk-at əl-baab.

Meera close.perf-she the-door

'Meera closed the door.'

أعتقد مهرة شلت الفلوس

ʔa-ʕtəqəd mahra ʃall-at lə-fluus.

I-think.imperf Mahra take.perf-she the-money

'I think Mahra took the money.'

راشد راح العيادة اليوم

raaʃəd raaħ əl-ʕəjaada əl-joom.

Rashid go.perf-he the-clinic the-today

'Rashid went to the clinic.'

In all these cases, the pitch rises at the beginning of the sentence and returns to a lower flat level for the remainder of the sentence. This is the default intonation pattern for a non-contrastive sentence, i.e. a sentence where no sentence-internal constituent is focused. Figures 13.1 and 13.2 represent the pitch (measured in Hertz) over time for the first two example sentences.

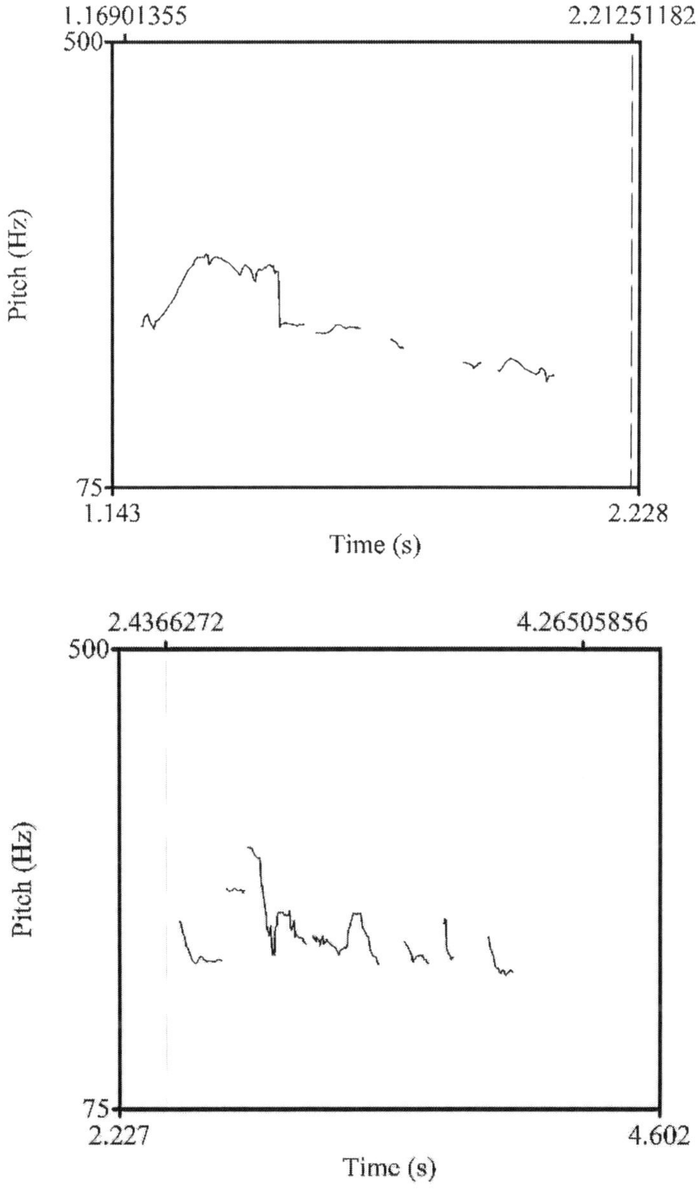

Figure 13.1 The intonation pattern for declarative sentences

In contrast, with the utterance of yes-no questions, the pitch starts at the mid-level and rises at the point of the question focus and remains high for a while before declining. Consider the following sentences as questions:

رحتي الجامعة اليوم؟

rəħ-ti	əl-ʤaamʕa	əl-joom?
go.perf-you.f	the-university	the-today

'Did you go to university today?'

بتروح فاطمة ويانا اليوم؟

ba-t-ruuħ	faatˁma	wəjjaa-nna	əl-joom?
will-she-go.imperf	Fatima	with-us	the-today

'Is Fatima coming with us today?'

حليتي واجب امس؟

ħallee-ti	waaʤəb	ʔams?
solve.perf-you.f	assignment	yesterday

'Did you solve yesterday's assignment?'

ميرة اللي مسويه هالكيكة؟

miira	ʔəlli	m-sawj-a	ha-l-keeka?
Meera	that	part-make-f	this-the-cake

'Did Meera bake this cake?'

The intonation patterns for the first two questions are illustrated in Figure 13.2.

It is clear a sharp increase in pitch occurs as the focus element in the question approaches, and then the pitch remains at a high level until the end of the sentence.

تتحرا عمرك بتروح؟

tə-t-ħarraa	ʕəmr-ək	ba-t-ruuħ?
you-refl-think.imperf	self-your	will-you-go.imperf

'Do you think you are going?'

تتحرين بيعطيج فلوسج؟

tə-t-ħarr-een	ba-ja-ʕtˁii-ʧ	fluus-əʧ?
you.f-refl-think.imperf-you.f	will-he-give.imperf-you.f	money-your.f

'Do you think he will give you your money?'

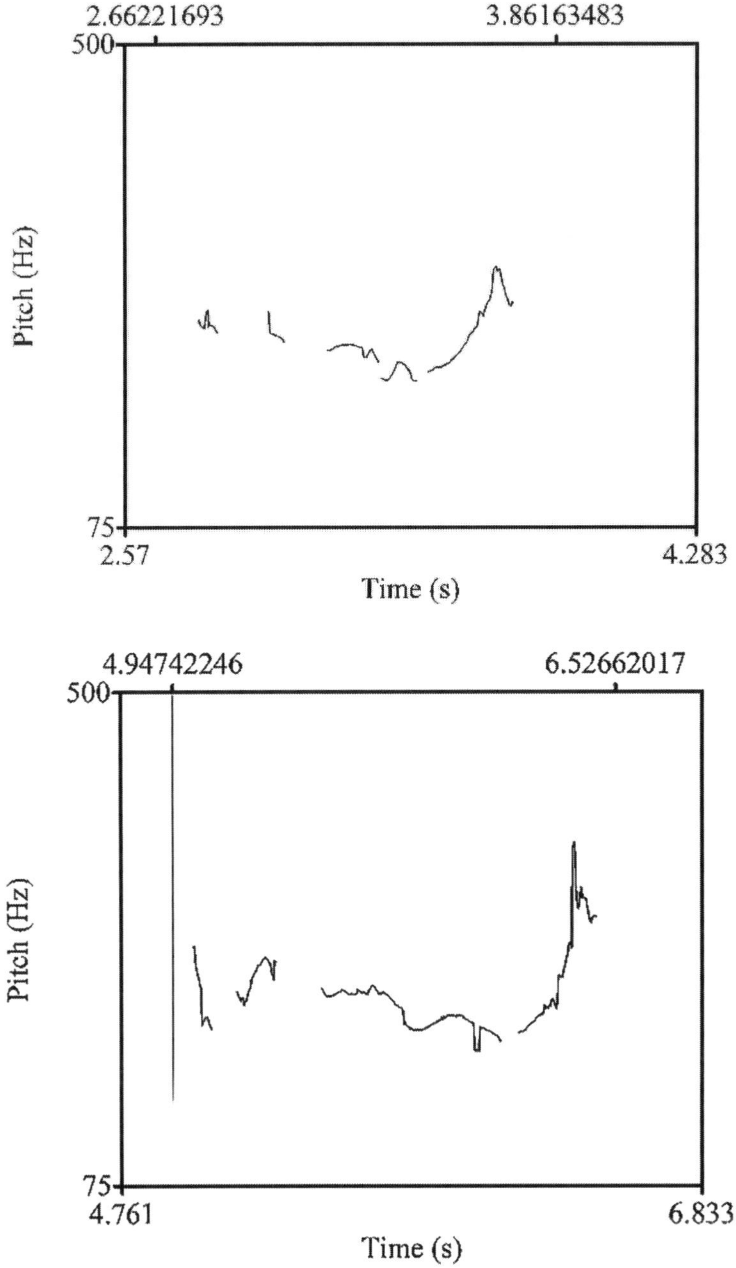

Figure 13.2 The intonation pattern for yes-no questions

أونج بتين ويانا؟

ʔawwann-əʧ	ba-t-tii-n	wəjjaa-nna?
for.real-you.f	will-you.f-come.imperf-you.f	with-us

'Do you think you are coming with us?'

13.1.2 *Tag questions*

In many cases, and especially when a confirmation of the question is expected, the yes-no question is reinforced with a tag. In most instances of a positive question, the tag is the negative particle لا la 'not' (Section 13.5).

أحمد ساق السيارة، لا؟

ʔaħmad	saag	əs-sajjaara,	laa?
Ahmad	drive.perf-he	the-car	not

'Ahmad drove the car, no?'

أحمد رسم وردة، لا؟

ʔaħmad	rəsam	warda,	laa?
Ahmad	draw.perf-he	flower	no

'Ahmad painted a flower, no?

أحمد سار النادي، لا؟

ʔaħmad	saar	ən-naadii,	laa?
Ahmad	go.perf-he	the-gym	no

'Ahmad went to the gym, no?'

ميرة طلعت من البيت، لا؟

miira	tˤəlʕ-at	mən	əl-beet,	laa?
Meera	go.perf-she	from	the-house	no

'Meera has left the house, no?'

علي صلح السيارة، لا؟

ʕəli	sˤallaħ	əs-sajjaara,	laa?
Ali	caus.fix.perf-he	the-car	no

'Ali has fixed the car, hasn't he?'

In contrast, if the speaker wants to confirm a negative statement from the hearer, an alternative question with opposite polarity (i.e. a positive statement) may be uttered. The two sentences are always connected by the coordinator والا wəlla 'or' (Section 15.7).

نورة ما طبخت الغدا؟ ولا طبخته؟

nuura maa tˤəbxa-t əl-ɣədaa, wəlla tˤəbxa-t-ah?
Noora not cook.perf-she the-lunch or cook.perf-she-it
'Has Noora not cooked lunch? Or has she (cooked it)?'

ما بتين وياي المول والا (بتين)؟

maa ba-t-tii-n wijjaa-ja əl-mool, wəlla (ba-t-ii-n)?
not will-you.f-come.imperf-you.f with-me the-mall or will-you.f-come.imperf-you.f
'Will you not come with me to the mall, or will you come?'

Finally, other expressions used as tags include the sequence مب صح mub sˤaħ 'not so?' and, more rarely, مب جي mub ʧii 'not like this?'

أحمد دفع حق البترول ، مب صح؟

ʔaħmad dəfaʕ ħag əl-bətrool, mub sˤaħ?
Ahmad pay.perf-he for the-gas not right?
'Ahmad paid for the gas, is that not so?'

أحمد درس حق الامتحان، مب صح؟

ʔaħmad dəras ħag l-əmtəħaan, mub sˤaħ?
Ahmad study.perf-he for the-exam not right
'Ahmad studied for the exam, is that not so?'

علي صلح السيارة ، مب جي؟

ʕəli sˤallaħ əs-sajjaara, mub ʧii?
Ali caus.fix.perf-he the-car not like.this
'Ali has fixed the car, hasn't he?'

مب جي؟ المفروض علي يصلح السيارة

mub ʧii? əl-ma-frooðˤ ʕəli j-sˤalləħ əs-sajjaara.

not like.this the-part.pass.suppose Ali he-caus.fix.imperf the-car

'Isn't it so? Ali is supposed to fix the car.'

اتبعتي الوصفة، مب جي؟

ettəbaʕ-ti əl-wasˤfaa mub ʧii?

refl.follow.perf-you.f the-recipe not like.this

'You followed the recipe, didn't you?'

13.1.3 Answers to questions

There are many possible answers to a yes-no question, most prominently the interjections هيه heeh or هييه نعم heeh naʔam 'Yes!' and لا laa 'No!' An ingressive apico-alveolar click 'tsk' may be used for a negative answer instead of لا laa (Chapter 17). Other expressions are also used, as in the examples following the yes-no question next:

رحتي الجامعة اليوم؟

riħ-ti əl-ʤaamʕa əl-joom?

go.perf-you.f the-university the-today

'Did you go to university today?'

هيه	heeh	'Yes!'
هيه نعم	heeh naʕam	'Oh, yes!'
أكيد	ʔakiid	'Definitely!'
طبعاً	tˤabʕan	'Of course!'
افا عليج	affa ʕaleetʃ	'You bet!'
تم	tamm	'Done!'
لا	laa	'No!'
يمكن	jəmkən	'Maybe.'

13.1.4 Alternative questions

Alternative questions are a type of yes-no questions in which more than one possible choice is listed in the question. The first part of the alternative question usually states the positive situation and the second part states the negative. The two component questions are coordinated by the disjunction marker والا wəlla 'or' (Section 15.7). For the second conjunct, it is possible that part of the question is elided (Chapter 16).

بتسير مريم المدرسة والا مابتسير ؟

ba-t-siir marjam əl-mədərsa wəlla maa-ba-t-siir?

will-she-go.imperf Maryam the-school or not-will-she-go.imperf

'Will Maryam go to the school or won't she go?'

بتعرض مريم يوم الاثنين والا ما بتعرض؟

ba-tə-ʕrəðʕ marjam joom əl-ʔəθneen wəlla maa-bə-tə-ʕrəð?

will-she-present.imperf Maryam day the-second or not-will-she-present.imperf

'Will Maryam present on Monday or won't she present?'

أحمد بنّد تلفونه والا مابنّده ؟

ʔahmad bannad teləfuun-ah wəlla maa-bannad-ha?

Ahmad caus.switch.off.perf-he phone-his or not-caus.switch.off.perf-he-it

'Did Ahmad switch off his phone or didn't he switch it off?'

The answer to alternative questions cannot be just 'yes' or 'no.' The addressee is required to provide one of the two alternatives as an answer. Thus, for the first question, the possible answers (excluding cases where the information is not available to the addressee) may be one of the following:

هيه مريم بتسير المدرسة

(heeh), marjam ba-t-seer əl-mədrəsa.

yes Maryam will-she-go.imperf the-school

'Yes, Maryam will go to school.'

لا مريم ما بتسير المدرسة

(laa), marjam maa-ba-t-seer əl-mədrəsa.

no Maryam not-will-she-go.imperf the-school

'No, Maryam will not go to school.'

13.2 Wh-questions

The series of interrogative pronouns is used to form information questions; these questions are sometimes called wh-questions because of the English form of the pronouns. Wh-questions ask for an answer about a participant in an event or situation ('who' and 'what'), location ('where'), time ('when'), manner ('how'), reason ('why'), and quantity/degree ('how many/much'). In Emirati Arabic, wh-questions exhibit variable word order with respect to the sentential position of the interrogative pronoun.

شو	ʃuu	'what'
منو	mnuu	'who'
وين	ween	'where'
متى	məta	'when'
كيف	keef	'how'
شقايل	ʃgaajəl	'how'
ليش	leeʃ	'why'
أي	ʔajj	'which'
كم	kam (var. tʃam)	'how many/much'

13.2.1 Wh-fronting

In usual cases, the formation of a wh-questions involves placing the wh-word at the sentence-initial position, regardless of its grammatical function (i.e. subject, object, or adverbials). Grammarians call this construction wh-fronting. Wh-fronting may be productively formed by all types of wh-word. For instance:

شو ʃuu (var. ʃ) 'what'

شو طابخين عالغدا اليوم؟

ʃuu	tˤaabx-iin	ʕalɣəda	əl-joom?
what	cook.perf-you.pl	on-the-lunch	the-today

'What did you cook for lunch today?'

منو mnu 'who'

منو بيحضر المحاضرة باجر؟

mnuu	ba-jə-ħðˤar	əl-muħaaðˤara	baatʃer?
who	will-he-attend.imperf	the-lecture	tomorrow

'Who will attend the lecture tomorrow?'

أي ʔaj 'which'

أي كلاس تبين تسجلين؟

ʔaj	klaas	təb-een	t-sadʒl-iin?
which	class	want.imper-you.f	you-register-you.f

'Which class do you want to register?'

لأي درجة غالي البوك؟

la-ʔaj	daradʒa	ɣaali	əl-buuk?
to-which	degree	expensive	the-wallet

'How (i.e. to which extent) expensive is the wallet?'

متى məta 'when'

متى آخر مرة كلمته؟

məta	ʔaaxər	marra	kallam-t-a?
when	last	time	speak.perf-you-him

'When was the last time you spoke to him?'

وين ween 'where'

وين لقيت كتابي؟

ween	ləgee-t	ktaab-i?
where	find.perf-you	book-my

'Where did you find my book?'

كيف keef 'how'

كيف سرت مطار دبي أمس؟

keef	sər-t	mətˤaar	dbaɪ	ʔams?
how	go.perf-you	airport	Dubai	yesterday?

'How did you go to Dubai airport yesterday?'

شقايل دليت طريج البيت؟
ʃgaajəl daallee-t tˤriidʒ əl-bəət?
how find.perf-you route the-house
'How did you find the way to the house?'

ليش leeʃ 'why'

ليش واعية لين الحين؟
leeʃ waaʕj-a leen əl-ħiin?
why awake-f until the-now
'Why are you still up until now?'

كم kam (var. tʃam) 'how many/much'

كم دبة ماي اشتريت من اللولو؟
kam dabba-t maaj əʃtəree-t mən əl-luulu?
how bottle-f water refl.buy.perf-you from the-lulu
'How many bottles of water did you buy in Lulu Center?'

كم راتبك؟
kam raatb-ək?
how.much salary-your
'How much is your salary?'

For some wh-words, it is possible to attach the pronoun suffix to form a short question. The locative wh-word وين ween 'where' is one such example. For the expression of 'where are we?', native speakers prefer to pronounce the full pronoun نحن nəħən 'we' instead of using the pronoun suffix.

ويني؟
weenn-i?
where-me
'Where am I?'

وينك/وينج؟

ween-ək/ween-əʧ?

where-you/where-you.f

'Where are you?'

وينه؟

ween-a?

where-him

'Where is he?'

وينها؟

ween-ha?

where-her

'Where is she?'

نحن وين؟

nəħən ween?

we where

'Where are we?'

وينهم؟

ween-hum?

where-them

'Where are they?'

With respect to the intonation patterns of information question sentences, the higher pitch contour coincides with the sentence-initial position, where the fronted wh-word is situated. It is followed by a falling contour over the whole utterance. Figures 13.3a and 13.3b illustrate this pitch contour pattern for the wh-question formed by شو ʃuu 'what' and ليش leʃ 'why,' respectively.

Some wh-words, e.g. منو mnuu 'who' and شو ʃuu 'what,' may also be embedded within phrases such as the noun phrases (Chapter 6) and prepositional phrases (Sections 5.4 and 5.5).

شيخة بنت منو؟

ʃeexa bənt mnuu?

Sheikha daughter who?

'Whose daughter is Sheikha?'

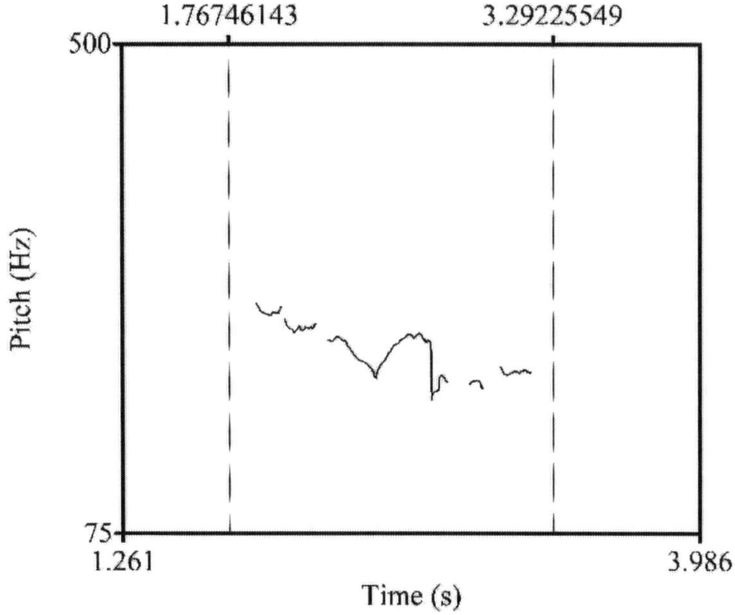

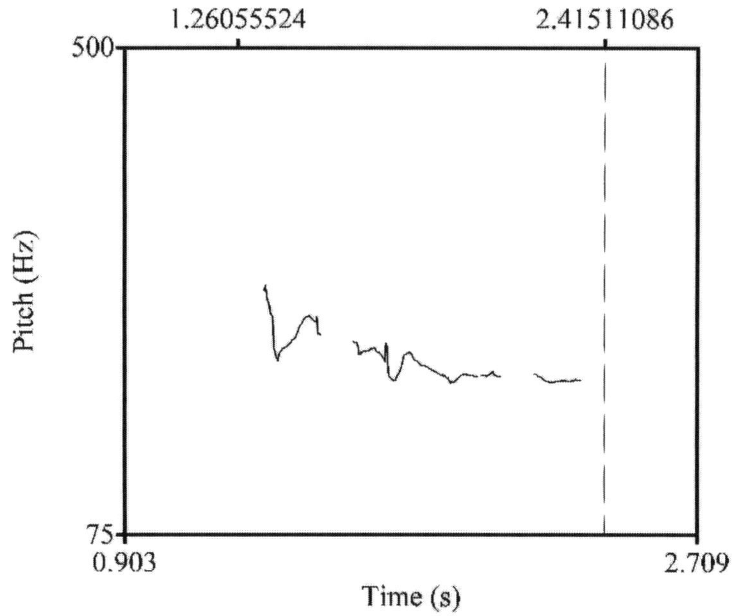

Figure 13.3 The intonation pattern for wh-questions

بشو صلحت الباب؟

b-ʃuu   sˤallaħ-t   əl-baab?

with-what   caus.fix.perf-you   the-door

'With what did you fix the door?'

ويا منو سرت الحفلة؟

wəjja   mnuu   sər-t   əl-ħafla?

with   who   go.perf-you   the-party

'With who did you go to the concert?'

لين اي محطة هالباص بيسير؟

leen   ʔaj   maħatˤtˤ-a   hal   baasˤ   ba-j-siir?

to   which   station-f   this   bus   will-it-go.imperf

'To which station will this bus run?'

The fronted wh-word may be related to its base position, which is further embedded in the structure. For instance, شو ʃuu 'what' is related to the object position of مشتري məʃtəri '(I) have bought' in the following first example sentence, and متى məta 'when' is related to the adverbial position after أوصل ʔawsˤal '(I) arrived' in the second sentence:

شو تحس توني مشتري؟

ʃuu   t-ħəs   taw-ni   mə-ʃtəri?

what   you-feel.imperf   just-me   part-buy

'What do you think I have just bought?'

متى تتوقع لازم أوصل؟

məta   tə-t-waqqaʕ   laazəm   ʔa-wsˤal?

when   you-refl-caus.expect.imperf   should   I-arrive.imperf

'When do you expect I should arrive?'

متى تحسون بتنزل دفعة الكتاب اليديده؟

məta   t-ħəss-uun   bə-tə-nzil   dəfʕ-at
lə-ktaab   əl-jədiid-a?

when   you.pl-feel.imperf-you.pl   will-it-release.imperf   collection-f
the-book   the-new-f

'When do you think the new book collection will be released?'

منو توك قلت رسب فالامتحان؟

mnuu taww-ək gəl-t rəsab f-əl-əmtəħaan?

who just-you say.perf-you fail.perf-he in-the-exam

'Who did you just say failed the examination?'

Further word order perturbation for wh-fronting is possible depending on the speaker's intention. For instance, the sentence subject can be topicalized to the sentence-initial position (Chapter 11).

ميثا وين بتسير؟

meeθa ween ba-t-siir?

Maitha where will-she-go.imperf

'(As for) Maitha, where will she go?'

عهود شو بتاكل؟

ʕəhuod ʃuu b-t-aakəl?

Uhood what will-she-eat.imperf

'(As for) Uhood, what will she eat?'

حلمج متى بيتحقق؟

ħəlm-ətʃ məta ba-jə-t-ħaggag?

dream-your when will-it-refl-caus.realize.imperf

'(As for) your dream, when will it come true?'

If the topicalized item is related to an object position in the main clause, a resumptive pronoun will be used which refers to the topic (Chapter 12 and Section 13.2.3).

عشان الأيلتس، متى بتاخذه فاطمة؟

ʕaʃaan əl-ʔaajəlts məta b-taaxð-a faatˤma?

for the-IELTS when will-she-take.imperf-it Fatima

'(As for) the IELTS, when will Fatima take it?'

عطاري أحمد، وين بيلاقيه علي باجر؟

ʕa-tˤaari ʔaħmad ween ba-j-laagii-h ʕəli baatʃər?

by-mention Ahmad where will-he-meet.imperf-him Ali tomorrow

'(On the topic of) Ahmad, where will Ali meet him tomorrow?'

The subject can also be right-dislocated in wh-fronting. For example:

شو بتاكل عهود؟

ʃuu	b-t-aakəl	ʕuhuud?
what	will-she-eat.imperf	Uhood

'What will Uhood eat?'

وين بتسير ميثا؟

ween	ba-t-siir	meeθa?
where	will-she-go.imperf	Maitha

'Where will Maitha go?'

متى بيتحقق حلمج؟

məta	b-ji-t-ħaggag	ħəlm-əʧ?
when	will-it-refl-caus.realize.imperf	dream-your.f

'When will your dream come true?'

13.2.2 Wh-in-situ

In addition to the sentence-initial position, some wh-words also stay in the 'base' position—that is, the position where the wh-word is interpreted. For instance, the wh-word 'who' as in 'Who did Ahmad meet?' is interpreted as the object of 'meet,' and the object position is usually to the right of the verb, in English and Emirati Arabic. The position where the wh-word is interpreted is also called the in-situ position, and the order in which the wh-word is placed at the in-situ position is called 'wh-in-situ.'

ميثا بتسير وين؟

meeθaa	ba-t-siir	ween?
Maitha	will-she-go.imperf	where

'Where will Maitha go?'

عهود بتاكل شو؟

ʕəhuud	b-t-aakəl	ʃuu?
Uhood	will-she-eat.imperf	what

'What will Uhood eat?'

حلمج بيتحقق متى؟

ħəlm-ətʃ	ba-jə-t-ħaggag	məta?
dream-your.f	will-it-refl-caus.realize.imperf	when

'When will your dream come true?'

13.2.3 *Wh-clefts*

Another major wh-construction involves embedding a cleft and relative clause (Chapter 12). Wh-clefts are similar to wh-fronting in which the wh-word is also sentence-initial. However, they are different in that the wh-cleft structure is marked by the presence of the complementizer اللي ʔəlli 'that,' which is characteristic of a cleft/relative construction (Section 5.7). Another defining property of wh-cleft is the obligatory presence of a resumptive pronoun at the base position (Section 5.8.1.9 and Chapter 12). On the other hand, wh-fronting is strictly incompatible with the presence of resumptive pronouns at the base position. Overall, wh-cleft is more limited than wh-fronting. While the interrogative pronouns 'what' and 'who' may form a wh-cleft question, other wh-words (such as 'where,' 'when,' 'how,' and 'why') may not. The wh-word 'which' also forms a wh-cleft, although most native speakers prefer the wh-fronting construction.

شو اللي اشتريته أمس؟

ʃuu	ʔəlli	əʃtəree-t-ah	ʔams?
what	that	refl.buy.perf-you-it	yesterday

'What did you buy (it) yesterday?'

منو اللي شفته فالمطعم؟

mnuu	ʔəlli	tʃəf-t-ah	f-əl-matˤʕam?
who	that	see.perf-you-him	in-the-restaurant

'Who did you see in the restaurant?'

أي كتاب اللي اشتراه علي؟

ʔaj	ktaab	ʔəlli	əʃtar-aa-h	ʕəli?
which	book	that	buy.perf-he-it	Ali

'Which book did Ali buy?'

Wh-cleft is analogous with cleft structures in general in the sense that both allow the presence of a head noun followed by the complementizer اللي ʔəlli 'that.'

شو الشي اللي اشتريته؟

ʃuu	(əʃ-ʃaj)	ʔəlli	əʃtəree-t-ah?
what	the-thing	that	buy.perf-you-it

'What is the thing that you bought?'

Moreover, the wh-cleft can also be expressed by the copular pronoun or a demonstrative which is anaphoric to the reference of the wh-word. For example:

شو هو اللي اشتريته؟

ʃuu	huu	ʔəlli	əʃtəree-t-ah?
what	he	that	buy.perf-you-it

'What did you buy?' (lit. What is it that you bought?)

منو هاي اللي تمت فالسكن فنهاية الأسبوع؟

mnuu	haaj	ʔəlli	tamm-at	f-əs-sakan	fə-nhaaja-t	l-əsbuuʕ?
who	this.f	that	stay.perf-she	in-the-hostel	in-end-f	the-week

'Who is this who stayed in the hostel at the weekend?'

منو هي اللي تمت فالسكن فنهاية الأسبوع؟

mnu	hii	ʔəlli	tamm-at	f-əs-sakan	fə-nəhaaja-t	l-əsbuuʕ?
who	she	that	stay.perf-she	in-the-hostel	in-end-f	the-week

'Who is she who stayed in the hostel at the weekend?'

13.2.4 *Multiple wh-questions*

It is possible to place more than one instance of wh-words in wh-questions, for example, when the speaker requires a 'pair-list' answer, i.e. who is doing what. For the construction of such multiple wh-questions, the first wh-question appears at the beginning of the sentence (Section 13.2.1) and the second remains in-situ (Section 13.2.2).

منو شاف منو؟

mnuu	ʧaaf	mnuu?
who	see.perf-he	who

'Who saw who?'

منو سمع شو؟

mnuu	səmaʕ	ʃuu?
who	hear.perf-he	what

'Who heard what?'

منو قال شو لمنو؟

mnuu	gaal	ʃuu	lə-mnuu?
who	say.perf-he	what	to-who

'Who said what to whom?'

In other cases, a conjunction is used before the introduction of the second wh-word. These questions always require a single sentence answer (e.g. 'She left last night because she felt unwell').

متى راحت وليش؟

mətaa	raaħa-t	w	leeʃ?
when	go.perf-she	and	why

'When did she leave and why?'

شحقة وليش؟

ʃ-ħagga	w	leeʃ?
what-for	and	why

'What for and why?'

متى ووين شفت شيخة؟

məta	w	ween	ʃəf-t	ʃeexa?
when	and	where	see.perf-you	sheikha

'When and where did you see Sheikha?'

13.3 Echo questions

Echo questions are a subtype of in-situ questions in which the speaker repeats a part of the previous sentence spoken by another person. They are mostly used when the speaker mishears some information and asks for confirmation or clarification, or when the speaker shows disbelief about an aspect of the previous discourse.

أ: جون توه اشترى رواية هاري بوتر

ʤoon tawwa-h əʃtəra rəwaajat haari bootar

John just-him buy.perf-he novel Harry Potter

A: 'John just bought the Harry Potter novel.'

ب: اشترى شو؟؟

əʃtəra ʃuu?

buy.perf-he what?

B: 'He bought what?'

أ: جون يا بيتنا الاسبوع اللي طاف

ʤoon jaa beet-na l-əsbuuʕ ʔəlli tˤaaf.

John come.perf-he house-our the-week that pass.perf-it

A: 'John came to our house last week.'

ب: يا متى؟؟

jaa məta??

come.perf-he when

B: 'He came when??'

أ: العنود يابت ربيعتها البيت

əl-ʕənuud jaab-at rəbiiʕ-at-ha əl-beet.

the-Anood bring-perf-she friend-f-her the-house

A: 'Alanood brought her friend to the house.'

ب: يابت منو؟؟

jaab-at mnuu??

bring.perf-she who

B: 'She brought who??'

أ: أحمد سار الجمعية

ʔaħmad saar əl-ʤamʕijja.

Ahmad go.perf-he the-supermarket

A: 'Ahmad went to the supermarket.'

ب: سار وين؟
saar ween?
go.perf-he where
B: 'He went where?'

أ: مريم بتطرش الهدية عالبريد
marjam ba-tˤtˤarrəʃ əl-hadijja ʕ-al-bariid.
Mariam will-she-caus.send.imperf the-gift through-the-mail
A: 'Mariam will send the gift through the mail.'

ب: بتطرش كيف؟؟
ba-tˤ-tˤarrəʃ keef??
will-she-send.imperf how
B: 'She will send (it) how??'

أ: عطيتها الحلاوة عشان تسكت
ʕatˤee-t-ha əl-ħalaawa ʕaʃaan tə-skət.
give.perf-I-she the-candy in.order.to she-quiet.imperf
A: 'I gave her the candy to keep her quiet.'

ب: عطيتيها ليش؟؟
ʕatˤee-tii-ha leeʃ??
give.perf-you-her why
B: 'You gave (it to) her why??'

عشان تحاول تقنعه يشتري شو؟
ʕaʃaan t-ħaawəl tə-qnəʕ-a jə-ʃtərii ʃuu?
in.order.to you-try.imperf you-persuade.imperf-him he-buy.imperf what
'To try and persuade him to buy what?'

أحمد توه قرا وايد من شو؟
ʔaħmad taww-ah gara waajəd mən ʃuu?
Ahmad just-him read.perf-he a.lot from what
'Ahmad just read a lot of what?'

علي توه سافر لدولتين. علي توه سافر لوين؟

ʕəli taww-ah saafar lə-dawlət-een. ʕəli taw-ah saafar l-ween?

ali just-him travel.perf-he the-country-du Ali just-him traveled to-where

'Ali just traveled to two countries. Where did Ali just travel to?'

أ: في عشرين سؤال صح وخطأ فالامتحان

fii ʕəʃriin suʔaal sˤaħ w xatˤaʔ fə-l-əmtəħaan.

there.is 20 question right and wrong in-the-exam

'There are 20 yes-no questions in the exam.'

ب: عشرين شو؟

ʕəʃriin ʃuu?

20 what

'20 what?'

أ: اسمه محمد الكعبي.

ʔəsm-ah mħammad əl-kaʕbii.

name-his Mohamed the-Kaabi

'His name is Mohamed Al Kaabi.'

ب: محمد شو؟ الكعبي؟

mħammad ʃuu? əl-kaʕbii?

Mohamed what the-Kaabi

B: 'Mohamad what? Al Kaabi?'

13.4 Embedded questions

Both types of questions can be further selected by a main verb (or main predicate) and function as embedded/reported questions (Chapter 16 and Section 5.7).

13.4.1 *Embedded yes-no questions*

Indirect polar questions report on someone's yes-no question, most frequently with the complementizers and conditional marker

إذا ʔiða 'if' and لو law (var. loo) 'if, as long as' (Chapter 16 and Section 5.7).

الدكتور يسأل إذا بتداومون باجر

əd-dəktoor jə-sʔal ʔiða ba-t-daawm-uun baaʧər.
the-doctor he-ask.imperf if will-you-attend.imperf-you.pl tomorrow
'The doctor asked if you're going to attend tomorrow.'

مريم تسألكم تحسون لو لبست احمر بيناسبها

marjam tə-sʔal-kom t-ħəss-uun law ləbs-at ʔaħmar ba-j-naasəb-haa?
Mariam she-ask.imperf-you.pl you-feel.imperf-you.pl if wear.perf-she red will-it-suit.imperf-her
'Mariam asked whether you think wearing red will suit her.'

محمد سأل إذا الدكتور بيحطه غياب لو تأخر

mħammad səʔal ʔiða əd-dəktoor ba-j-ħəttˤa ɣjaab loo t-ʔaxxar.
Mohammed ask.perf-he if the-doctor will-he-mark.imperf-him absence if refl-caus.late.perf-he
'Mohammed asked if the doctor would mark him absent if he was late.'

مهره تخبرت إذا حد عنده فلوس

mahra t-xabbər-at ʔiða ħad ʕənd-aħ fluus.
Mahra refl-caus.ask.perf-she if someone with-him money
'Mahra asked if anyone has money.'

الدكتور يبا يتأكد إذا كلكم شرحتوا

əd-dəktoor jə-ba jə-t-ʔakkad ʔiða kəl-kum ʃaraħ-tu.
the-doctor he-want.imperf he-refl-caus.confirm.imperf if all-you present.perf-you.pl
'The doctor wants to confirm if all of you presented.'

13.4.2 *Embedded wh-questions*

Any wh-question may be further embedded to form embedded wh-questions. For example:

أمي تسأل منو بيحضر العزيمة باجر

ʔumm-i tə-sʔal mnuu ba-jə-ħðˤar əl-ʕəziima baatʃər

mother-my she-ask.imperf who will-he-come.imperf the-gathering tomorrow

'My mom is asking who will come to the gathering tomorrow.'

الدكتور يسأل منو للحين ما شرح

əd-dəktoor jə-sʔal mnuu le-l-ħiin maa ʃaraħ.

the-doctor he-ask.imperf who until-the-now not explain.perf-he

'The doctor is asking who didn't present yet.'

الوالد يتخبر وين حطيتوا الزوليه الجديمه

əl-waaləd jə-t-xabbar ween ħatˤtˤeet-u əz-zuuliijja əl-dʒədiim-a.

the-father he-refl-caus.ask.imperf where put.perf-you.pl the-carpet the-old-f

'My dad is wondering where you put the old carpet.'

منو يعرف متى بينزلن المعاشات؟

mnuu ja-ʕarf mətaa ba-jə-nəzl-ən əl-maʕaaʃ-aat?

who he-know.imperf when will-they.f-come.down.imperf-they.f the-salary-f.pl

'Who knows when the salaries will be deposited?'

أحمد يبا يعرف متى بتبدا المباراة

ʔaħmad j-əba jə-ʕrəf məta ba-tə-bda lə-mbaaraa.

Ahmad he-want.imperf he-know.imperf when will-it-start.imperf the-match

'Ahmad wants to know when the match will start.'

موزة توها سألتني شو اشتريت امس فالليل

mooza taw-ha saʔl-at-ni ʃuu əʃtər-eet ʔams fə-l-ləəl.

moza just-her ask.perf-she-me what buy.perf yesterday at-the-night

'Moza just asked me what I bought last night.'

محد يعرف ليش راشد يبا يستقيل

maħħad jə-ʕarf leeʃ raaʃəd jə-ba jə-stəqiil.

no.one he-know.imperf why Rashid he-want.imperf he-caus.refl.resign.imperf

'No one knows why Rashid wants to resign.'

13.5 Rhetorical questions

Rhetorical questions are structurally formed as questions, yet do not ask for information or confirmation, i.e. they are not usually followed (or expected to be followed) by an answer. They may be used by the speaker to assert a proposition, express an order, or make a request or suggestion (Chapter 9). In some cases, rhetorical questions are merely a pragmatic device for the speaker to express an emotion, exclamation, or interjection (Chapter 17).

For instance, rhetorical yes-no questions are used to assert the speaker's prior understanding or expectation.

ما رحتي بيت يدي امس؟

maa rəħ-ti beet jadd-i ʔams?

not go.perf-you house grandpa-my yesterday

'Didn't you go to my grandpa's house yesterday?' (the speaker thinks the hearer went to grandpa's house).

ما حضرتي اجتماع اليوم؟

maa ħədˤar-ti ədʒtəmaaʕ əl-joom?

not attend.perf-you.f meeting the-today

'Didn't you attend today's meeting?' (the speaker expects the hearer attended today's meeting).

مب توك مكلم شيخة؟

mub tawwə-k m-kalləm ʃeexa?

not just-you part-caus.talk Sheikha

'Haven't you just talked to Sheikha?' (the speaker expects the hearer has just talked to Sheikha).

كم مرة لازم أقولّك لا تصارخ فالبيت؟

kam marra laazəm ʔa-guull-ək laa t-sˤaarəx f-əl-beet?

how.many time must I-tell.imperf-to-you don't you-yell.imperf in-the-house

'How many times do I have to tell you not to yell in the house?' (the speaker has told the hearer many times).

جون يقرا شي أصلًا؟

dʒoon jə-graa ʃaj ʔasˤlan?

john he-read-imperf thing originally

'Does John read anything at all?' (the speaker believes John does not read).

منو شاف هارييت من سنين؟

mnuu tʃaaf haarjet mən sniin?

who see.perf-he Herriet from year.pl

'Who has seen Harriet in years?' (the speaker believes no one has seen Harriet).

في طالب بينكم قرا الحرب والسلم؟

fii tˤaalˤəb been-kum gara əl-ħarb w-əs-səlm?

there.is student among-you.pl read.perf-he the-war and-the-peace

'Has any student among you all read *War and Peace*?' (the speaker expects that no one read *War and Peace*).

كيف لازم أعرف؟

keef laazəm a-ʕarf?

how must I-know.imperf

'How should I know?' (the speaker does not know the answer).

In other cases, the rhetorical question is employed to express the speaker's speech act, e.g. a suggestion or invitation.

ليش نكمّل؟

leeʃ	n-kamməl?
why	we-caus.continue.imperf

'Why do we continue?'

كوب شاي ثاني؟

koob	ʃaaj	θaani?
cup	tea	another

'Another cup of tea?'

أحط أغاني؟

ʔa-ħətˤ	ʔaɣaani?
I-put.imperf	songs

'Shall I put some music on?'

And in some cases, the question merely expresses the speaker's emotion or interjection.

بصراحة، منو يهتم؟

b-sˤaraaħa,	mnuu	j-əhtam?
with-honesty	who	he-care.imperf

'Frankly, who cares?'

ليش تضّايق؟

leeʃ	tə-ðˤ-ðˤaajag?
why	you-refl-bother.imperf

'Why bother?'

ليش أنا؟

leeʃ	ʔana?
why	I

'Why me?'

13.6 Exclamatives

Exclamatives are a particular structure which expresses the speaker's surprise, emotion, appreciation, despair, or disdain. They may be formed by the fronted wh-words such as شو 'what' and كم kam 'how much.' In addition, the MSA word ما maa 'what' may express an exclamation.

شو هالسيارة الطر اللي عندك!

ʃuu	ha-s-sajjaara	ətˤ-tˤar	ʔəlli	ʕənd-ək!
what	this-the-car	the-great	that	have-you

'What a great car you have!'

شو هالتعليق الغبي!

ʃuu	ha-t-taʕliiq	əl-ɣabi!
what	this-the-comment	the-stupid

'What a stupid comment!'

هالخريط شو!

ʃuu	ha-l-xritˤ!
what	this-the-lies

'What lies!'

ما اسخفني!

ma-sxaf-nii!

how-silly-me

'How silly I am!'

ما اسرع يفهم!

ma-sraʕ	jə-fham!
how-quickly	he-understand.imperf

'How quickly he understands!'

عنبو كم يصرف عالسيارات!

ʕənəbuu	kam	jə-sˤrəf	ʕa-s-sajjaara-at!
damn	how.much	he-spend.imperf	on-the-car-pl.f

'Damn! How much he spent on cars!'

Further reading

For the description of questions in Gulf Arabic, see Qafisheh (1977, pp. 172–174), Holes (1990, pp. 2–16), and Feghali (2008, pp. 69–71). For a basic discussion of questions in Emirati Arabic refer to Isleem and Al Hashemi (2018, p. 75). For theoretical discussions of the syntactic properties of wh-questions in Emirati Arabic, see Leung (2014c), Leung and Al Eisaei (2014), and Leung and Shemeili (2014). For an overview of various interrogative strategies in Arabic dialects, see Wahba (1984), Aoun and Choueiri (1999), Shlonsky (2002), and Aoun et al. (2010).

Chapter 14

Subordination

Subordination is a grammatical strategy in which a secondary or subordinate clause is concatenated to the primary or main clause constructing a biclausal configuration. There are two major types of concatenation: embedding and adjunction. For the embedding structure, the subordinate clause functions as an argument of the main predicate (Sections 5.2 and 7.14). The subordinate clause may additionally be adjoined to the beginning or the end of the main clause. In terms of grammatical structure, the subordinate clause may be a complete sentence which contains a subject and a verb, or it may be 'grammatically impoverished,' where some grammatical elements are missing and recoverable only by reference to the main clause. Given its secondary grammatical status, the subordinate clause functions to supplement the main clause by providing secondary information such as time, location, reason, condition, concession, and purpose.

14.1 Temporal clauses

The temporal clause may be marked by various temporal subordinators, including:

Table 14.1 Temporal subordinators

يوم	joom	'when'
قبل	gabəl	'before'
عقب	ʕəgəb	'after'
بعد	baʕad	'after'
لين	leen	'until'
وقت	wagt	'during/while'
من	mən	'since'
دام	daam	'as long as'
أول	ʔawwal	'as soon as'

14.1.1 يوم *joom* 'when'

The temporal clause formed by يوم joom 'when' (lit. 'day') may either precede or follow the main clause. There is no pause between the two clauses in both cases.

يوم علي وصل أنا كنت آكل

joom	ʕəli	wəsˤal	ʔana	kən-t	ʔ-aakəl.
when	Ali	arrive.perf-he	I	be.perf-I	I-eat.imperf

'When Ali arrived, I was eating.'

أنا كنت آكل يوم علي وصل

ʔana	kən-t	ʔ-aakəl	joom	ʕəli	wəsˤal.
I	be.perf-I	I-eat.imperf	when	Ali	arrive.perf-he

'I was eating when Ali arrived.'

يوم توصل باجر، دقلي

joom	t-oosˤal	baatʃer	deg-l-i.
when	you-arrive.imperf	tomorrow	call.imp-to-me

'When you arrive tomorrow, call me.'

يوم تتكلم فخطبة، لازم تتكلم شوي شوي.

joom te-t-kallam f-xetˤbah laazəm te-t-kallam ʃwaj ʃwaj.

when you-refl-caus.talk.imperf in-public.speech must you-refl-caus.talk.imperf little little

'When you make a public speech, you should speak slowly.'

The use of an anaphoric pronoun (if there is any) must be identified by a preceding noun in subordination. For instance, the pronoun in the following sentence refers to Ali, which is in the preceding subordinate clause. In contrast, sentences such as 'When he arrived, Ahmad took a shower,' in which the pronoun 'he' precedes and refers to Ahmad, can never be expressed in Emirati Arabic.

يوم علي وصل البيت متأخر أبوه نازعه

joom ʕəli wəsˤal əl-beet mə-t-ʔaxxər, ʔəbuu-h naazaʕ-ah.

when Ali arrive.perf-he the-home part-refl-late dad-his yell.perf-he-him

'When Ali arrived home late, his dad yelled at him.'

It should be noted that free relatives formed by 'when' (Section 12.3) are expressed by another word كلما kilmaa 'whenever.'

كلما أحمد جاف قطوة لعب وياها

kəl-maa ʔaħmad ʧaaf gatˤwa, ləʕab wəjjaa-ha.
when-ever Ahmad see.perf-he cat play.perf-he with-her
'Whenever Ahmad saw a cat, he started to play with her.'

كلما زدنا ملح فالاكل تحسن الطعم

kil-maa zid-na məlħ fi-l-ʔəkəl t-ħassan
ətˤ-tˤeʕəm.
when-ever add.perf-we salt in-the-food it-caus.improve.imperf
the-taste
'Whenever we add salt to the food, the taste improves.'

14.1.2 قبل *gabəl 'before'*

The subordinator قبل gabəl 'before' may combine with a simple temporal expression. For example:

قبل المباراة

gabəl əl-mubaaraa
before the-match
'before the match'

قبل الغروب

gabəl əl-ɣəruub
before the-sunset
'before sunset'

هند لخصت المادة قبل يوم الامتحان

hənd laxxəsˤa-t əl-maadda gabəl joom
l-əmtəħaan.
Hind caus.summarize.perf-she the-material before day
the-examination
'Hind summarized the material before the examination day.'

الفريق تدرب وايد قبل المباراة

əl-fariiq	t-darrab	waajed	gabəl	əl-mubaaraa.
the-team	refl-caus.practice.perf-it	much	before	the-match

'The team has practiced a lot before the match.'

When قبل gabəl combines with a temporal clause, it can be followed by the negative marker لا laa (Section 10.3) which functions as a relative clause marker 'that/which' (Section 5.7, 7.14.2, Chapter 12). It is possible that such a complementizer-nature of لا laa is the result of grammaticalization (Hopper & Traugott, 2003).

قبل لا تبدا الحصة وصلت المدرسه

gabəl	laa	tə-bda	əl-ħəsˤsˤa	wəsˤal-t	əl-madrəsa.
before	that	it-start.imperf	the-class	arrive.perf-I	the-school

'Before the class starts, I have arrived at school.'

هند قرت الوصفة قبل لا تطبخ

hənd	gara-t	əl-wasˤfa	gabəl	laa	tətˤbax.
Hind	read.perf-she	the-recipe	before	that	cook.imperf-she

'Hind had read the recipe before she cooked.'

أمي اتصلتلي قبل لا أوصل المدرسة

ʔumm-i	əttasˤla-t-li	gabəl	laa	ʔa-wsˤal	əl-madrəsah.
mom-my	call.perf-she-me	before	that	I-arrive.imperf	the-school

'My mom had called me before I arrived school.'

خبريني قبل لا توصلين

xabr-i-ni	gabəl	laa	tuu-sˤəl-iin.
tell.imp-you.f-me	before	that	you.f-arrive.imperf-you.f

'Tell me before you arrive.'

In some cases, it is possible to use the relative marker ما maa 'that' in the formation of subordinate clauses.

قبل ما تبدا الحصة وصلت

gabəl	maa	te-bda	əl-ħəsˤsˤa	wəsˤal-t.
before	that	it-start.imperf	the-class	arrive.perf-I

'Before the class starts, I have arrived.'

ما maa and لا laa cannot co-occur in this situation, i.e. the expression قبل لا ما gabəl laa maa or قبل ما لا gabəl maa laa would be ungrammatical.

14.1.3 عقب ʕəgəb and بعد baʕad 'after'

The subordinator عقب ʕəgəb (var. ʕəgub) and بعد baʕad 'after' may combine with simple nouns.

عقب المباراة الجمهور رد البيت

ʕəgəb lə-mbaaraa əl-dʒəmhuur rad əl-beet.
after the-match the-audience return.perf-he the-home
'After the match, the audience went back home.'

عقب الكلاس كل البنات سطلن

ʕəgəb lə-klaas kəl əl-banaat satˤtˤəl-an.
after the-class all the-girls caus.sleepy.perf-they.f
'After the class, all the girls became sleepy.'

بعد الامتحان بنروح السينما

baʕad l-əmtəħaan ba-n-ruuħ əs-seenəma.
after the-test will-we-go.imperf the-cinema
'After the test, we will go to the cinema.'

When combining with a temporal clause, the relative marker ما maa 'that' is obligatory.

عقب ما دفعت استلمت الطلب

ʕəgəb maa dəfaʕ-t stəlam-t ətˤ-tˤalab.
after that pay.perf-I refl.receive.perf-I the-order
'After I paid, I received the order.'

عقب ما تخرجت مريم اشتغلت فمطعم لمدة سنة

ʕəgəb maa t-xarrədʒ-at marjam əʃtaɣl-at f-matˤʕam le-mədda-t səna.
after that refl-caus.graduate.perf-she Mariam work.perf-she in-restaurant for-period-f year
'After she graduated, Mariam worked in a restaurant for a year.'

عشر سنين بعد ما اشترى اللوحة، علي اكتشف انها مزورة

ʕaʃər sniin baʕad maa əʃtara əl-looħa ʕəli əktəʃaf ʔən-ha mzawwara-a.

ten years after that buy.perf-he the-painting Ali discover.perf-he that-it.f part-caus.fake-f

'Ten years after he bought the painting, Ali discovered that it was fake.'

علي بعد ما اشترى اللوحة بعشر سنين اكتشف انها مزورة

ʕəli baʕad maa əʃtəra əl-looħa b-ʕaʃər sniin əktəʃaf ʔən-ha mzawwara-a.

Ali after that buy.perf-he the-painting by-ten year.pl discover.perf-he that-it.f fake-f

'Ten years after Ali bought the painting, he discovered that it was fake.'

خلنا نسير المول بعد ما نخلص دراسة

xal-na n-siir əl-mool baʕad maa n-xalˤlˤəsˤ dəraasa.

let.imp-us we-go.imperf the-mall after that we-caus.finish.imperf study

'Let's go to the mall after we finish studying.'

14.1.4 وقت *wagt* 'during/while'

The subordinator وقت wagt 'during/while' (it literally means 'time') may combine with a noun or a clause. If a clause is selected, وقت wagt must be followed by the relative marker ما maa 'that.' وقت wagt is used to describe a temporal parallelism between two events which occur at the same time.

وقت ما هند كانت تحل واجبها، عليا كانت تلعب

wagt maa hənd kaan-at t-ħəl waadʒəb-ha ʕalja kaan-at tə-lʕab.

while that Hind be.perf-she she-do.imperf assignment-her Alia be.perf-she she-play.imperf

'While Hind was doing her assignment, Alia was playing.'

وقت ما دقيتيلي، كنت راقدة

wagt maa daggeet-ii-li ken-t raagd-a.

while that call.perf-you.f-to.me be.perf-I asleep-f

'While you called me, I was asleep.'

وقت الصلاة عليا كانت تطبخ

wagt əsˤ-sˤalaa ʕalja kaan-at tə-tˤbax.

during the-prayer Alia be.perf-she she-cook.imperf

'During the prayer time, Alia was cooking.' (lit. At the time of praying, Alia was cooking.)

14.1.5 دام *daam 'as long as'*

دام daam functions as a preposition subordinator which may take an object pronoun suffix (Section 5.8.1.8), followed by a temporal clause.

دامج ما تغديتي ممنوع تحلين

daam-ətʃ maa t-ɣaddee-ti
ma-mnuuʕ t-ħalli-in.

as.long.as-you.f not you.f-caus.have.lunch.imperf-you-f
part-pass.forbid you.f-dessert.imperf-you.f

'As long as you have not had lunch, you are forbidden to have dessert.'

دامج خلصتي شغلج خذيلج كوفي.

daam-ətʃ xalˤlˤasˤ-ti ʃəɣl-ətʃ xeð-ii-l-ətʃ
koofi.

as.long.as-you finish.perf-you.f work-your get.imperf-you.f-for-you.f
coffee

'As long as you finish your work, you can get yourself a coffee.'

14.1.6 من *mən 'since'*

من mən, which literally means 'from,' is interpreted as 'since' if followed by a temporal noun or a temporal clause (without an intervening relative marker). If the subordinate clause linearly precedes the main clause, the coordinator و wa- 'and' is obligatorily required (cf. Chapter 15). On the other hand, و wa- is not required if the main clause precedes the subordinate clause. Note that و wa- does not function as a typical coordinator, but as a linker of two temporally adjacent events (cf. English ' . . . and then . . . ').

من الظهر ونحن نشتغل على المشروع

mən	əðˁ-ðˁəhər	w-nəħən	nə-ʃtəɣəl	ʕa-l-maʃruuʕ.
since	the-noon	and-we	we-work.imperf	on-the-project

'Since noon we were working on the project.'

من رحتي وأنا ما طلعت من البيت

mən	rəħt-i	w-ana	maa	tˁəlaʕ-t	mən	əl-beet.
since	leave.perf-you	and-I	not	leave.perf-I	from	the-house

'Since you left, I have not left the house.'

ريم عدلت رقادها من بدت الجامعة

riim	ʕaddəl-at	rgaad-ha	mən	bəda-t	ədʒ-dʒaamʕa.
Reem	fix.perf-she	sleep-her	since	start.perf-it	the-university

'Reem fixed her sleep pattern since university started.'

14.1.7 أول *ʔawwal* 'as soon as'

The subordinator أول ʔawwal 'as soon as' must be followed by the relative marker ما maa 'that' (Chapter 12). Only a temporal clause may be selected.

أول ما دخلتي الكل سكت

ʔawwal	maa	daxal-ti	l-kəl	sək-at.
as.soon.as	that	walk.in.perf-you.f	the-all	quiet.perf-it

'As soon as you walked in, everyone became quiet.'

بدقلج أول ما أوصل

ba-dəgg-ələ-tʃ	ʔawwal	maa	ʔa-wsˁal.
will-I-call.imperf-to-you.f	as.soon.as	that	I-arrive.imperf

'I'll call you as soon as I arrive.'

14.1.8 لين leen 'until'

The subordinator لين leen 'until' may select a temporal noun or a temporal clause. If a temporal clause is used, the relative marker ما maa 'that' is necessary.

بدرس لين الساعه خمس

b-adrəs leen əs-saaʕa xams.
will-I.study.imperf until the-clock five
'I will study until five o'clock.'

الإجازة لين شهر ثمانيه

l-ədʒaaza leen ʃahar θəmaanja.
the-holiday until month eight
'The holiday is until August.'

ما بتتعلم لين ما اطييح ع ويهك

maa b-tə-tˤʕallam leen maa tˤ-tˤiiħ ʕa-wajh-ək.
not will-you-refl.learn.imperf until that you-fall.imperf on-face-your
'You will not learn until something bad happens to you.' (lit. You fall on your face.)

خلنا نيلس فالبيت لين ما يوقف المطر

xal-na ni-jləs f-əl-beet leen maa j-waggəf əl-mətˤar.
let-us we-sit.imperf in-the-house until that it-stop.imperf the-rain
'Let's stay home until the rain stops.'

شيخة عادي عندها تشتغل فهالشركة لين ما تتقاعد

ʃeexa ʕaadi ʕənd-ha tə-ʃtəɣəl f-ha-ʃ-ʃarəka leen maa tə-t-qaaʕad.
Shikha alright with-her she-work.imperf in-this-the-company until that she-refl-retire.imperf
'Shaikha is fine with working in this company until she retires.'

14.2 Reason clauses

14.2.1 لأن *laʔann* 'because'

The subordinator لأن laʔann (var. لن lann) 'because' may be further suffixed by object pronouns (Section 5.8.1.6).

لأنها متضايجة كانت تصيح

laʔann-ha mðˤðˤaydʒ-a kaan-at ət-sˤiħ
because-her upset-f be.perf-she she-cry.imperf
'Because she is upset, she was crying.'

لأنه عرس خالتي اليوم برد البيت متأخرة.

laʔann-a ʕərs xaalt-i əl-joom b-a-rəd əl-beet mə-t-ʔaxxr-a.
because-it wedding aunt-my the-today will-I-return.imperf the-home part-refl-caus.late-f
'Because it is my aunt's wedding, I will be home late.'

لأن عندها كلاسات نورة لازم كل يوم تنش من وقت.

laʔan ʕənd-ha klaas-aat nuura laazəm kəl-joom t-nəʃʃ mən wagt.
because with-her lecture-f.pl Noura must every-day she-wake.imperf from time
'Because she has classes, Moura must wake up early every day.'

لأنه راشد مش متدرب زين خسر المباراة

laʔann-a raaʃəd məʃ mə-t-darˤrˤəb zeen xəsar lə-mbaaraa.
because-him Rashid not part-refl-caus.train well lose.perf-he the-match
'Because Rashid did not train well, he lost the match.'

أحمد انطرد لأنه سرق معلومات سرية من الشركة.

ʔaħmad ən-tˤərad laʔann-ah sˤarag maʕluumaat sərrijj-a mən əʃ-ʃarəka.
Ahmad pass-fire.perf-he because-he steal.perf-he information confidential-f from the-company
'Ahmad was fired because he stole confidential information from the company.'

14.2.2 دام *daam* 'as long as'

The 'cause' subordinator دام daam 'as long as' may also express the meaning of causal clauses in addition to its temporal meaning (Section 14.1.5). That is, the main clause is the natural consequence based on the truth of the subordinate clause. However, the subordinate clause formed by دام daam may not always underlie the reason for the realization of the main clause.

دامني ما أدل الطريق باخذ تكسي

daam-ni maa ʔa-dall ətˤ-tˤəriig baa-xeð taksi.
as.long.as-me not I-know.imperf the-way will-I.take.imperf taxi
'As long as I don't know the way, I will take a taxi.'

دامني تريقت متأخر ما بتغدى

daam-ni t-rajjag-t mə-t-ʔaxxər maa b-a-tɣadda.
as.long.as-me relf-caus.eat.breakfast.perf-I part-refl-late not will-I-caus.have.lunch.imperf
'As long as I have breakfast late, I will not have lunch.'

14.3 Purpose clauses

14.3.1 عشان *ʕaʃaan* 'in order to'

The subordinator عشان ʕaʃaan 'in order to' is always used to form a control structure (known as adjunct control) (Section 7.9). In such cases, the subject of the control clause (e.g. subject pronoun) is not overtly expressed.

علي شد حيله عشان يدخل الجامعة

ʕəli ʃadd-ħeel-ah ʕaʃaan jə-dxəl əl-dʒaamʕa.
Ali work.hard.perf-he in.order.to he-get.imperf the-university
'Ali worked hard in order to get into university.'

طلعنا عشان ناخذ بيتزا

tˤəlaʕ-na ʕaʃaan naa-xəð biitza.
go.out.perf-we in.order.to we-buy.imperf pizza
'We went out to buy a pizza.'

عشان يدخل جامعة هارفرد، علي درس امتحان الدخول من يوم هو صف عاشر

ʕaʃaan jə-dxal ʤaamʕa-t haarvard ʕəli dəras əmtəħaan əd-dəxuul mən joom huu sˤaff ʕaaʃər.
in.order.to he-enter.imperf university-f Harvard Ali study.perf-he exam the-entrance from when he grade ten
'In order to get into Harvard, Ali studied for the entrance examination since Grade 10.'

أحمد جمع فلوس عشان يشتري قيتار يديد

ʔaħmad ʤammaʕ fluus ʕaʃaan jə-ʃtəri giitaar jədiid.
Ahmad collect.perf-he money in.order.to he-buy.imperf guitar new
'Ahmad collected money in order to buy a new guitar.'

It is possible to use عشان ʕaʃaan to select a clause in which its subject is different from that of the main clause. For example:

أمريكا رفعت ضريبة الموارد المستوردة عشان المواطنين يصرفون فلوس اكثر على المواد المحلية

ʔamriika rəfʕ-at ðˤariib-at əl-mawaarəd əl-məstawrəd-ah ʕaʃaan əl-məwaatˤn-iin jə-sˤrəf-uun fluus ʔakθar ʕa-l-məwaad əl-maħallij-ja.
America increase.perf-it.f tax-f the-imported.items the-imported-f in.order.to the-citizen.pl they-spend.imperf-they money more on-the-items the-domestic-f
'The United States raised the import tax so citizens would spend more money on domestic items.'

14.4 Conditional clauses

14.4.1 لو *law,* اذا *ʔəða and* ان *ʔən 'if'*

لو law (var. loo), إذا ʔəða and إن ʔən 'if' are used to mark a conditional clause. The consequent clause is concatenated to the conditional clause without any coordinator (cf. English 'then').

لو عطيتني الفلوس بشتريلك اللي تباه

law ʕatˤee-t-nii lə-fluus b-aʃtərii-l-ək ʔəlli tə-baah.

if give.perf-you-me the-money will-I-buy.imperf-to-you that you-want.imperf

'If you give me the money, I will buy you what you want.'

لو درستي عدل بتنجحين

law dəras-ti ʕadəl bə-tə-ndʒəħ-iin.

if study.perf-you.f well will-you.f-succeed.imperf-you.f

'If you study well, you will succeed.'

إذا اشتغلتي بتحصلين فلوس

ʔəða ʃtaɣal-ti ba-t-ħasl-iin fluus.

if work.perf-you.f will-you.f-get.imperf-you.f money

'If you work you will get money.'

إن ما عطيتيها الشنطة بتزعل

ʔən maa ʕatˤee-tii-ha əʃ-ʃantˤa ba-tə-zʕal

if not give.perf-you.f-her the-bag will-she-sad.imperf

'If you did not give her the bag, she would be sad.'

14.4.2 لو ما *law maa 'unless'*

لو ما law maa (var. loo maa) 'unless' consists of the typical conditional marker and the negative marker ما maa 'not' (Section 10.1).

لو ما شديت حيلك بترسب فالأمتحان

law maa ʃaddeet ħeelə-k ba-tə-rsab fə-l-əmtəħaan.

if not work.hard.perf-you will-you-fail.imperf in-the-exam

'Unless you work hard, you will fail the examination.'

لو ما درست ما بتتخرج

law maa dəras-t maa ba-tə-ndʒaħ.

if not study.perf-you not will-you-pass.imperf

'If you don't study, you will not pass.'

لو ما انتبهت فالمحاضرة ما بتفهم

law maa əntəbah-t f-əl-muħaaðˤara maa ba-tə-fham.

if not refl.concentrate.perf-you in-the-lecture not will-you-understand.imperf

'If you don't concentrate on the lecture, you will not understand.'

14.4.3 الا اذا əlla ʔəðaa 'unless'

The subordinate clause selected by الا اذا əlla ʔəðaa 'unless' (lit. except if) usually contains a perfective verb. The verb in the main clause is in the imperfective stem affixed by the irrealis modal/ future prefix بـ b- (Section 5.2.16).

ما بسير باجر الحفلة إلا إذا نمت اليوم من وقت

maa ba-siir baaatʃər əl-ħafla əlla ʔəðaa nəm-t əl-joom mən wagt.

not will-I-go.imperf tomorrow the-party except if sleep. perf-I the-today from time

'I will not go to the party tomorrow unless I (go to) sleep early today.'

ما بتعطيج الحلاوة إلا إذا حليتي الواجب

maa bə-ta-ʕtiitʃ əl-ħalaawa əlla ʔəðaa ħallee-ti əl-waadʒəb.

not will-she-give.imperf.you.f the-candy except if solve-you.f the-homework

'She will not give you the candy unless you do your homework.'

14.4.4 Verbs of conditionality

In addition to a conditional marker, the conditional meaning may be expressed by verbs of assumption.

فرضا إني يبت علامة كاملة في الامتحان إحتمال يرتفع المعدل

faraðˤan ʔənn-i jəb-t ʕalaama kaaml-a fə-l-əmtəħaan ʔəħtəmaal jə-rtəfəʕ əl-muʕaddal.

assume that-me get.perf-I mark full-f in-the-exam possibility it-refl.increase.imperf the-average

'Assuming that I got full marks in the examination, my GPA may increase.'

خل نفترض إني وافقت أنا شو بستفيد؟

xal nə-ftərəðˤ ʔənn-i waafag-t ʔana ʃuu b-a-stəfiid?

let.imp we-refl.assume.imperf that-me agree.perf-I I what will-I-refl-benefit.imperf

'Let's assume I agreed, what will benefit me?'

The conditional meaning can also be inferred from the context. For example:

بدون مساعدتج، جان ما عرفت كيف أحل الواجب

bəduun musaaʕadtə-ʧ ʧaan maa ʕa-raf-t keef ʔa-ħəl əl-waaʤəb.

without part.help-your.f would not I-know.perf how I-solve.imperf the-homework

'Without your help, I would not have known how to solve the homework.'

لولا مساعدتج، جان ما عرفت كيف أحل الواجب

loo laa musaaʕadtə-ʧ ʧaan maa ʕa-raf-t keef ʔa-ħəl əl-waaʤeb.

if not part.help-your.f would not know.perf-I how I-solve.imperf the-homework

'If it were not for your help, I would not have known how to solve the homework.'

14.4.5 Comparative correlatives

Across languages, expressions known as comparative correlatives express a conditional meaning (cf. English 'the more . . . the more. . . '). In Emirati Arabic, the structures are realized by كلما kəlmaa 'whenever' (Chapter 12) and اكثر ʔakθar 'more' (Section 5.3.4).

كلما كلتي اكثر، كلما زاد وزنج (أكثر)

kəl-maa kalt-i ʔakθar kəl-maa zaad waznəʧ (ʔakθar).

when-ever eat.perf-you more when-ever gain weight more

'The more you eat, the more weight you gain.'

كلما سويت رياضة كلما تحسنت صحتك (أكثر)

kəl-maa sawwee-t rijaaðˤa kəl-maa t-ħassəna-t sˤaħt-ək (ʔakθar).
when-ever do.perf-you sport when-ever refl-caus.better.perf-it.f health-your more
'The more exercise you do, the healthier you will get.'

14.4.6 *Counterfactual conditionals*

Counterfactual conditionals consist of conditional clauses which are factually unreal. In Emirati Arabic, the meaning of counterfactual conditionals may be expressed by the use of perfective aspect (Section 8.1) in the conditional clause or inferred by the use of past-time adverbs (e.g. 'yesterday'). The main clause may contain the modal auxiliary جان ʧaan 'would' (Chapter 9).

لو سعيد يا الحفلة أمس، جان استانسنا اكثر

law səʕiid jaa əl-ħafla ʔams ʧaan əstaans-na ʔakθar.
if Saeed come.perf-he the-party yesterday would caus.refl.enjoy.perf-we more
'If Saeed had joined the party yesterday, we would have had more fun.'

The 'as if'-clause, which also expresses the counterfactual reading, requires the word جان ʧaan 'would' (with a list of pronoun suffixes). It is possible to place the negative marker ولا wla 'and not' before the modal marker جان ʧaan.

الطلاب دوم يتشكون من البروفسور ولا جنه هو يسمعهم

ətˤ-tˤəlˤlˤaab doom jə-tʃakk-oon mən əl-brofəsoor wa-laa ʧan-nah jə-smaʕ-hum.
the-students always they-refl.complain.imperf-they from the-professor and-not as.if-he he-hear.imperf-them
'The students always complain about the professor as if he can't hear them.'

يوعانة ولا جني ماكله شي

jooʕaan-a w-laa ʧann-i ma-akl-a ʃaj.
hungry-f and-not as.if-me part-eat-f thing
'I am hungry as if I had not eaten anything.'

The counterfactual conditional marker لو بس law bas 'if only' is commonly used to indicate unreal situations. Its subordinate clause always contains a perfective verb, whereas the main clause contains the complex predicate with كان kaan (Section 7.11), indicating that it is a past perfective (or pluperfect) (Section 8.1).

لو بس كان عندي فلوس كنت خذت هالشنطة

law bas kaan ʕənd-i fluus kən-t xað-t ha-ʃ-ʃantˤa.

if only be.perf-I with-me money was.perf-I take.perf-I this-the-bag

'If only I had money, I would have bought this bag.'

لو بس سمعت كلام أمها ما كان بيستويلها جيه

law bas səmʕa-t kalaam ʔum-ha maa kaan ba-jə-stəwii-l-ha ʧii.

If only listen.perf-she talk mother-her not be.perf-I will-it-happen.imperf-to-her like.this

'If only she had listened to her mother, this would not have happened to her.'

14.5 Concessive clauses

14.5.1 معنه *maʕənna 'although'*

معنّه maʕenna 'although,' which literally stems from مع إنّه 'with that,' is always used to express a concessive clause, a type of clause usually contrasting two or more facts or points of view. The main clause may be optionally marked by the conjunction بس bas 'but' (Section 15.6).

مع إنه علي شد حيله بس رسب فالامتحان

maʕə-nna ʕəli ʃad ħeel-a (bas) rəsab f-əl-əmtəħaan.

with-that Ali work.hard.perf-he but fail.perf-he in-the-exam

'Although Ali worked hard, he failed the examination.'

14.5.2 حتى و ħatta wa- 'even though'

The concessive clause expressed by حتى ħatta 'even though' has to be accompanied by the coordinator و wa- 'and' (Section 15.1).

حتى و هي دارسة رسبت فامتحانها

ħatta w-hii daars-a rəsba-t f-əmtəħaan-ha.
even and-she study.perf-she fail.perf-she in-exam-her
'Even though she studied, she failed in her examination.'

حتى و هي شاطرة رسبت

ħatta w-hii ʃaatˁr-a rəsb-at.
even and-she smart-f fail.perf-she
'Even though she is smart, she failed.'

14.5.3 ولو اني walaw ʔən 'even though'

Another subordinate clause marked ولو اني walawu ʔən 'even though' expresses a concessive clause.

ولو إني ما حب هالأماكن بس بسير عشانج

wala-wu ʔən-ni maa ħəb h-al ʔamaakən
bas ba-siir ʕaʃaan-ətʃ.
even.though that-me not I-love.imperf this-the place.pl
but will-I-go.imperf for-you.f
'Even though I don't like these places, I will go for you (for your sake).'

14.5.4 حتى لو ħatta law 'even if'

The clause formed by حتى لو ħatta law (var. ħatta loo) 'even if' simultaneously expresses the conditional (i.e. the concessive clause remains unreal) and concessive meaning.

حتى لو حاولت تقنعه ما بيوافق

ħatta law ħaawal-t t-əqnəʕ-a maa
ba-j-waafəg.
even if try.perf-you you-convince.imperf-him not
will-he-agree.imperf
'Even if you try to convince him, he will not agree.'

حتى لو كلمتها ما بتسمع

ħatta law kallam-t-ha maa ba-tə-smaʕ.

even if talk.perf-you-her not will-she-listen.imperf

'Even if you talked to her, she would not listen.'

14.5.5 لو *law 'no matter'*

Free relatives (Section 12.3) formed by various wh-words may express the concessive meaning. The free relative clause (formed by a wh-word and the relative marker maa) may be optionally preceded by the conditional marker لو law 'if.'

لو شو تسوين ما بسامحج.

law ʃuu t-saww-iin maa b-a-saamħ-əʧ.

if what you.f-do.imperf-you.f not will-I.forgive.imperf-you.f

'No matter what you do, I will not forgive you.'

لو متى ما تقومين بعدج ما بتلحقين عالباص

law mətaa maa t-guum-iin baʕdə-ʧ maa b-te-lħəg-iin ʕ-al-baasˤ.

if when that you.f-get.up.imperf-you.f still-you not will-you.f-reach.imperf-you.f on-the-bus

'No matter when you wake up, you will still not catch the bus.'

لو وين ما تروح بلحقك

law ween maa t-ruuħ b-a-lħag-ək.

if where that you-go.perf will-I-follow.imperf-you

'No matter where you go, I will follow you.'

لو آكل اللي آكله ما بمتن.

law ʔa-akəl əlli ʔaa-kl-ah maa b-a-mtan.

if I-eat.imperf that I-eat.imperf-it not will-I-gain.weight-imperf

'No matter what I eat, I will not gain weight.'

لو آكل كثر ما أبا ما بمتن.

law ʔaa-kəl kəθər maa ʔa-ba maa b-a-mtan.

if I-eat.imperf as.much that I-want.imperf not will-I-gain.weight.imperf

'No matter how much I eat, I will not gain weight.'

14.6 Other subordinators

The abessive subordinator من دون mənduun 'without' marks the lack or missing of some entities/events. For example:

كيف تحكم على كتاب من دون ما تقراه؟
keef tə-ħkəm ʕala ktaab mənduun maa tə-graa-h?
how you-judge.imperf on book without not you-read.imperf-it
'How can you judge a book without reading it?'

Another is the contrastive subordinator بدال bədal 'instead of.'

بدال لا يدرس حق الامتحان، كان يلعب بالكورة طول اليوم
bədaal laa jə-drəs ħag l-əmtəħaan kaan jə-lʕab b-əl-koorah tˁuul əl-joom.
instead.of that he-study.imperf for the-examination be.perf-he he-play.imperf with-the-ball all the-day
'Instead of studying for the examination, he played ball for the whole day.'

14.7 Parentheticals

Parentheticals are expressions which give additional information to the sentence without contributing to the core sentential meaning. They do not belong to the argument structure of the sentence predicate (Chapter 6). The following examples show that parentheticals may occur at various positions within the sentence. Some parentheticals express additional pragmatic meanings such as afterthoughts (Chapter 11).

هو أظني ما عنده وظيفة
huu ʔa-ðˁanni maa ʕənd-ah waðˁiifa.
he I-think.imperf not with-him job
'He, I think, does not have a job.'

مايد مثل ما تعرف مسافر برا للعلاج
maajəd məθəl maa t-əʕarf m-saafər barra l-əl-ʕelaadʒ.
Mayed as what you-know.imperf part-travel abroad for-the-treatment
'Mayed, as you know, is traveling abroad for the treatment.'

الماي بارد، اظني

əl-maaj baarəd ʔa-ðˤanni.

the-water cold I-think.imperf

'The water is cold, I think.'

صحيح، أعترف.

sˤaħiiħ ʔa-ʕtərəf.

true I-admit.imperf

'It is true, I admit.'

Further reading

For a typological survey and grammatical analysis of subordination, see Cristofaro (2003) and Thompson et al. (2007).

Chapter 15

Coordination

Coordination is a grammatical structure which consists of at least two constituents of generally equal grammatical status. The size of the concerned constituents may be lexical (i.e. between nouns), phrasal (i.e. between verb phrases), sentential (i.e. between sentences), or sublexical (i.e. between bound morphemes). Grammatical devices which coordinate constituents—*coordinators*—assume various grammatical, semantic, and discourse functions. From purely grammatical and semantic perspectives, coordinators may constitute a conjunction (e.g. 'and') (Section 15.1) or a disjunction (e.g. 'or') (Section 15.7). Coordination may also express additional pragmatic and discourse functions, e.g. sequential relation between the two conjuncts (e.g. 'go home and take a shower'), conditionals (e.g. 'Work hard and you will pass'), and warnings (e.g. 'Hurry up or you will miss the train') (Section 15.4).

15.1 Conjunction و w-/wa 'and'

The default coordinator in Emirati Arabic is و wa (var. w-) 'and,' which is always shortened to w- in normal speech. While the coordinator functions to combine two constituents of equal status, it is always phonologically attached to the second conjunct. For example:

تفاح وبرتقال
təffaaħ w-bərtəqaal
apples and-oranges
'Apples and oranges'

موز وفراولة
mooz w-farawla
banana and-strawberry
'Banana and strawberry'

The coordinator is always required when more than two conjuncts are coordinated. The following examples show that the coordinator و wa is prefixed to the second and third conjunct. The three conjuncts are uttered without a pause (cf. English).

شفت جون وبيتر وبول وسايمون ليله أمس

ʧəf-t	ʤoon	w-biitar	w-bool	w-saajmən	leela-t	ʔams.
see.perf-I	John	and-Peter	and-Paul	and-Simon	night-f	yesterday

'I met John, Peter, Paul, and Simon last night.'

جون وبيتر وبول وسايمون نجحوا فالامتحان

ʤoon	w-biitar	w-bool	w-saajmən	nəʤħ-aw	f-əl-əmtəħaan.
John	and-Peter	and-Paul	and-Simon	pass.perf-they	in-the-exam

'John, Peter, Paul, and Simon passed the examination.'

The coordinator may combine other grammatical categories, e.g. verbs. If the conjoined verbs are transitive, the object pronoun (Section 5.8.1.2) is obligatory for both conjoined verbs, given that the context is salient so that the pronoun identity does not need to be expressed.

أحمد اشتراه وقراه

ʔaħmad	ʔəʃtaraa-h	w-garaa-h.
Ahmad	buy.perf-he-it	and-read.perf-it

'Ahmad bought it and read it.'

أحمد حضنها وحبها

ʔaħmad	ħəðˤan-ha	w-ħab-ha.
Ahmad	hug.perf-he-her	and-kiss.perf-her

'Ahmad hugged and kissed her.'

On the other hand, if the direct object of the conjoined verb is a referential expression, the conjoined verbs (even if they are transitive) do not require object pronoun suffixes.

أحمد حضن وحب أمه

ʔaħmad	ħəðˤan	w-ħab	ʔumm-ah.
Ahmad	hug.perf-he	and-kiss.perf-he	mom-his

'Ahmad hugged and kissed his mom.'

The coordinator can also combine adjectives (Section 5.3), adverbs (in the form of prepositional phrases), prepositions (Section 5.5), prepositional phrases, numerals (5.6), wh-words and wh-questions (Section 13.2), relative clauses (Chapter 12), and possessives (Section 6.2).

ذكية و عبقرية

ðakijj-ah w-ʕabqarijj-ah

smart-f and-genius-f

'smart and genius'

عالطاوله وفالصندوق

ʕa-tˤ-tˤaawula w-f-əsˤ-sˤannduug

on-the-table and-in-the-box

'on the table and in the box'

مع وضد الرأسمالية

maʕa w-ðˤədd ər-rasmaalijjah

with and-against the-capitalism

'for and against capitalism'

أحمد صلح التاير بسرعة وبطريقة صح

ʔaħmad sˤallaħ ət-taajər b-sərʕa w-b-tˤariiqa sˤaħ.

Ahmad fix.perf-he the-tire with-speed and-with-way correct

'Ahmad fixed the tire quickly (i.e. with speed) and correctly.'

ميثا ويمكن ريم ما عيبهم الأكل

meeθa w-jəmken riim maa ʕijab-hum əl-ʔakəl.

maitha and-maybe reem not like.perf-they the-food

'Maitha and probably Reem did not like the food.'

بيوصلون بعد أو قبل لا يبدا العرض

b-j-oosˤl-uun baʕd ʔaw gabəl laa jə-bda əl-ʕarðˤ.

will-they-arrive.imperf-they after or before that it-begin.imperf the-show

'They will arrive before or after the show begins.'

فهالمحاضرة برمس عن تركيب الجملة وعن المعاني

f-h-al-muħaaðˤara b-a-rməs ʕan tarkiib əl-ʤəmla w-ʕan əl-maʕaani.

in-this-the-lecture will-I.talk.imperf about composition the-sentence and-about the-meanings

'In this lecture I will talk about syntax and about semantics.'

زين مني ومنك انه نساعد الثانيين

zeen mənn-i w-mənn-ək ʔən-nah n-saaʕəd əθ-θaaniin.

good from-me and-from-you that-it we-help.imperf the-others

'It is good of me and of you that we help others.'

ألف وثلاثميه وخمس وأربعين

ʔalf w-θalaaθ-əmja w-xamsa w-ʔarbəʕiin.

thousand and-three-hundred and-five and-forty

'One thousand three hundred and forty-five'

أحمد قابل من ومن؟

ʔaħmad gaabal mən w-mən?

Ahmad meet.perf-he who and-who

'Whom and whom did Ahmad meet?'

شو اشترى أحمد ومن وين شراه؟

ʃuu ʃtara ʔaħmad w-mən ween ʃaraa-h?

what buy.perf-he Ahmad and-from where buy.perf-he-it

'What did Ahmad buy and from where did he buy it?'

البنت اللي يت الكلاس امس و(اللي) درست زين هي اختي

əl-bənt ʔəlli jat əl-klaas ʔams w-(əlli) dərs-at zeen hii ʔəxt-i.

the-girl that come.perf-she the-class yesterday and-that study.perf-she well she sister-my

'The girl who came to class yesterday and (who) studied well is my sister.'

علي هو أخو أحمد وموزه

ʕəli huu ʔuxu ʔaħmad w-mooza.

Ali he brother Ahmad and-Moza

'Ali is Ahmad and Moza's brother.'

Some cases of coordination involve other grammatical operations, e.g. ellipsis (Chapter 16).

أحمد شاف من ووين؟

ʔaħmad	ʃaaf	mən	w-ween?
Ahmad	see.perf-he	who	and-where

'Whom did Ahmad see and where?'

أحمد قتل من ووليش؟

ʔaħmad	ʤətal	mən	w-leeʃ?
Ahmad	kill.perf-he	who	and-why

'Whom did Ahmad kill and why?'

شو أشترى أحمد ، ومن وين، وليش؟

ʃuu	ʃtara	ʔaħmad	w-mən	ween	w-leeʃ?
what	buy.perf-he	Ahmad	and-from	where	and-why

'What did Ahmad buy, from where (did he buy it) and why?'

In contrast, it is generally considered as ungrammatical to conjoin distinct categories, and sentences such as 'The car sales explained the mechanics and where it was made' and 'The group will leave Rome and next week' are illegitimate in Emirati Arabic.

The use of a coordinator may combine expressions generally not considered as grammatical constituents. There is a grammatical construction called 'gapping' which is attested across languages (Section 16.1). This is also observed in Emirati Arabic.

أحمد درس لغويات وعلي رياضيات

ʔaħmad	dəras	ləɣawijjaat	w-ʕəlii,	rjaaðˤijj-aat.
Ahmad	study.perf-he	linguistics	and-Ali	math-f

'Ahmad studied linguistics, and Ali, (studied) mathematics.'

عطيت 10 حق كيم و5 حق بات

ʕatˤee-t	ʕaʃər	ħagg	kəm	w-xams	ħagg	baat.
give.perf-I	ten	for	Kim	and-five	for	Pat

'I gave $10 to Kim and $5 to Pat.'

جل اشترت حق كيم قميص وحق بات بنطلون

dʒəl	əʃtər-at	ħagg	kəm	qamiisˤ	w-ħagg	baat	bantˤəloon.
Jill	buy.perf-she	for	Kim	shirt	and-for	Pat	pants

'Jill bought Kim a T-shirt and Pat some pants.'

Conjunctions may also license elliptical structures (Chapter 16). In addition to the previous examples which involve coordination of wh-words (Section 13.2), it is common for a conjunction to license other constituents. For instance, the verb/verb phrase of the second clause in the following examples may be elided (VP-ellipsis):

أحمد سار الحفلة وعلي بعد

ʔaħmad	saar	əl-ħaflah	w-ʕəli	baʕad.
Ahmad	go.perf-he	the-party	and-Ali	also

'Ahmad went to the party, and Ali also (went).'

الصين يمكن تكون فحرب تجارية ويا امريكا وروسيا بعد

əsˤ-sˤiin	jəmkən	t-kuun	f-ħarb	tədʒaarijj-ah	wəjja
ʔamriika	w-ruusjaa	baʕad.			
the-China	may	she-be.imperf	in-war	trade.adj-f	with
America	and-Russia	also			

'China may have a trade war with America, and Russia (too).' (= China may have a trade war with both America and Russia.)

Conjunction between verbs with different subjects, but with the same direct object (cf. English 'John likes but Mary hates Peter'), may only be expressed by spelling out the two clauses completely. In such cases, the object pronoun is usually used for the second conjoined verb.

أحمد يحب موزة بس علي يكرهها

ʔaħmad	j-ħəb	mooza	bas	ʕəli	jə-krah-haa.
Ahmad	he-like.imperf	Moza	but	Ali	he-hate.imperf-her

'Ahmad likes Moza but Ali hates her.'

If the two conjuncts formed by و wa- are scoped over by the negation (Chapter 10), one of De Morgan's laws (i.e. the negation of a conjunction is the disjunction of the negations) applies. In the following example, the only scenario which is ruled out is that a single person stood up and complained:

محد نش وتشكّى

mahħad naʃʃ w-ətʃakka.

no.one stand.up.perf-he and-refl.complain.perf-he

'No one stood up and complained.' (i.e. It is still possible that someone stood up or complained, but not both.)

15.2 Agreement in coordination

A single noun may be modified by conjoined adjectives (Section 5.3). Both conjoined adjectives must agree with the head noun with respect to gender and number.

المكتبة تبيع كتب يداد وجدام

əl-maktəba t-biiʕ kətəb jədaad w-ʤdaam.

the-bookstore she-sell.imperf books new.pl and-old.pl

'The bookstore sells new and old books.'

On the other hand, conjoined nouns may be modified by a single adjective. Note that ambiguity may arise depending on whether the adjective modifies both conjoined nouns or its adjacent noun only. The following examples are ambiguous, especially because the adjectives agree with the two nouns in number and gender:

مريم تحب تكتب قصايد وتقارير طوال

marjam t-ħəb t-əktəb gəsˤaajəd w-taqaariir ətˤwaal.

Mariam she-like.imperf she-write.imperf poems and-essays long.pl

'Mariam loves to write long poems and essays.'

The following example, however, allows only a single reading—that the poem is long:

مريم قرت كتاب وقصيدة طويلة

marjam gar-at ktaab w-gəsˤiid-a tˤəwiil-a.

Mariam read.perf-she book and-poem-f long-f

'Mariam read a book and a long poem.'

A gender asymmetry affects the agreement between the adjective and conjoined nouns. The plural masculine agreement on the adjective is always preferred for conjoined nouns formed by both genders. If the agreement on the adjective is singular, it always agrees with the gender of its adjacent noun.

اشتريت كتاب ولوحة غاليين

əʃtəree-t	ktaab	w	looħ-a	ɣaalj-iin
buy.perf-I	book.m	and	board-f	expensive-m.pl

'I bought an expensive book and an expensive board.'

اشتريت كتاب ولوحة غالية

ʔəʃtər-eet	ktaab	w	looħ-a	ɣaalj-a
buy.perf-I	book.m	and	board-f	expensive-f

'I bought a book and an expensive board.'

15.3 Fixed expressions formed by و w-/wa

A number of coordinative structures are considered as fixed expressions by Emirati speakers. In English, we encounter expressions such as 'bread and butter' and 'hide and seek'; these are fixed expressions in the sense that the linear order between the conjoined elements cannot be altered. See Table 15.1.

Among these conjunctions, some receive a unitary interpretation, i.e. they are interpreted as a single entity. This is verified by the use of the third-person singular as the copular subject (Section 5.8.1).

القانون والنظام هو اهتمام الإدارة اليديدة الأساسي

əl-qaanuun w-ən-nəðˤaam huu əhtəmaam əl-ʔədaara əl-jədiid-ah əl-ʔasaasi.

the-law and-the-order it concern the-administration the-new-f the-primary

'Law and order is a primary concern of the new administration.'

The following example shows that the activity of eating and drinking is perceived as a singular event, which is further verified by the use of the passive participle ممنوع mammnuuʕ 'prohibited' (Section 5.2 and Chapter 7), which is singular:

الأكل والشرب فالقطار ممنوع

əl-ʔakəl	w-eʃ-ʃərb	f-əl-qətˤaar	ma-mnuuʕ.
the-eating	and-the-drinking	in-the-train	part-pass.prohibit.perf

'Eating and drinking on the train is prohibited.'

Table 15.1 Fixed expressions formed by و w-/wa

عيش وروب ʕeeʃ w-roob rice and-yogurt 'rice and yogurt'	العروس والمعرس əl-ʕaruus w-əl-məʕrəs the-bride and-the-groom 'bride and groom'
سيداتي سادتي sajjədaat-ii saadat-ii ladies-my gentlemen-my 'ladies and gentlemen'	ابتدائي وثانوي əbtedaaʔi w-θaanawi primary and-the-secondary 'primary and secondary'
أب وولد ʔabb w-walad father and-son 'father and son'	أول واخير ʔawwal w-axiir first and-last 'first and last'
القانون والنظام əl-qaanuun w-ən-nəðˤaam the-law and-the-order 'law and order'	إيدين وريول ʔiid-een w-rjuul hand-du and-feet '(two) hands and feet'
نقاط قوة ونقاط ضعف ngaatˤ quwwah w-ngaatˤ ðˤaʕf point.pl strength and-points weakness 'strengths and weaknesses'	حاضر ومستقبل ħaaðˤər w-mustaqbal present and-future 'present and future'
أخوان وخوات əxwaan w-xawaat brothers and-sisters 'brothers and sisters'	القلب والكبد əl-galb w-ətʃ-tʃabd the-heart and-the-liver 'heart and liver'
علاقة زوج وزوجة ʕəlaaqat zoodʒ w-zoodʒah relationship husband and-wife 'husband-and-wife relationship'	يمين ويسار jəmiin w-jəsaar right and-left 'left and right'
تفاعل الطالب والمعلم tafaaʕəl ətˤ-tˤaalˤəb w-əl-mʕalləm interaction the-student and-the-teacher 'student-and-teacher interaction'	ذكر وانثى ðakar w-ʔunθa male and-female 'male and female'

ذهب وفضه
ðahab w-fəðˤðˤah
gold and-sliver
'gold and silver'

هذا وهاذاك
haaða w-haaðaak
this and-that
'this and that'

الشرق والغرب
əʃ-ʃarg w-əl-ɣarb
the-east and-the-west
'East and West'

أمير وأميرة
ʔamiir w-ʔamiirah
prince and-princess
'prince and princess'

ريابيل وحريم
rəjaajiil w-ħəriim
men and-women
'men and women'

قبل وبعد
gabəl w-baʕad
before and-after
'before and after'

نظري وعملي
naðˤari w-ʕamali
theoretical and-practical
'theory and practice'

فنون وعلوم
funuun w-ʕluum
Arts and-Science
'Arts and Science'

جاهي وقهوة
ʧaahi w-gahwa
tea and-coffee
'tea and coffee'

اولاد وبنات
ʔawlaad w-banaat
boys and-girls
'boys and girls'

ايجابي وسلبي
ʔiiʤaabi w-salbi
positive and-negative
'positive and negative (e.g. in debate)'

الإيجابيات والسلبيات
l-iʤaabiijjaat w-əs-salbiijjaat
the-pros and-the-cons
'the pros and cons'

الصادرات والواردات
əsˤ-sˤaadəraat w-əl-waarədaat
the-imports and-the-exports
'the exports and the imports'

سبب وتأثير
səbab w-taʔθiir
cause and-effect
'cause and effect'

آباء وعيال
ʔaabaaʔ w-ʕjaal
parents and-children
'parents and children'

جنه ونار
ʤanna w-naar
heaven and-hell
'heaven and hell'

صح وغلط
sˤaħ w-ɣalatˤ
right and-wrong
'right and wrong'

أسود وأبيض
ʔaswad w-abjaðˤ
black and-white
'black and white'

Many function as a single adjective modifying the singular head noun.

العيش والروب لذيذ

əl-ʕeeʃ w-əl-roob laðiið
the-rice and the-yogurt delicious
'delicious rice and yogurt'

تفاعل الطالب والمعلم

tafaaʕul ətˤ-tˤaaləb w-əl-mʕalləm
interaction the-student and-the-teacher
'the teacher-student interaction'

علاقة الأبو والولد يالسه تستوي أسوء

ʕəlaaqat əl-ʔəbuu w-əl-walad jaals-a tə-stəwi ʔa-swaʔ.
rəlation the-father and-the-son part.sit-f it.f-refl.get.imperf more-bad
'The father-and-son relation is getting worse.'

In many other cases, the coordinative expressions are semantically plural, as shown by the use of a plural verb agreement.

أحمد وموزة عرسوا السنة اللي طافت

ʔaħmad w-mooza ʕarrəs-aw əs-səna ʔəlli tˤaaf-at.
Ahmad and-Moza marry.perf-they the-year that pass.perf-f
'Ahmad and Moza married last year.'

Emirati Arabic expresses the function of quantifiers such as English 'both' and 'each' by means of a partitive expression (Section 6.1.1). The use of كل واحد kəl waaħəd 'everyone' and اثنيناتهم əθneenaathum 'the two of them' in the following pair differs in terms of verbal agreement, namely, كل واحد kəl waaħəd is masculine singular, whereas اثنيناتهم əθneenaathum is masculine plural.

جون وماري كل واحد منهم فاز بجوائز

ʤoon w-maari kəl waaħəd mən-hum faaz b-ʤawaaʔəz.
John and-Mary every one from-them win.perf-he with-prize.pl
'John and Mary have each won prizes.'

جون وماري اثنيناتهم فازوا بجوائز

ʤoon	w-maari	əθneen-aat-hum	faaz-aw	b-ʤawaaʔəz.
John	and-Mary	two-f-them	win.perf-they	with-prizes

'John and Mary (both) won prizes.'

15.4 Pragmatic uses of و w-/wa

In addition to merely concatenating two grammatical expressions, the use of coordination may express pragmatic meanings. Cross-linguistically, coordination of sentences implies a temporal sequence between the conjoined events, which is unsurprisingly observed in Emirati Arabic.

غسلت الصحون ونشفتهن

ɣassal-t	əsˤ-sˤəħ-uun	w-naʃʃaft-hən.
wash.perf-I	the-dish-pl	and-caus.dry.perf-I-them

'I washed the dishes and (then) I dried them.'

Coordination of sentences gives rise to further pragmatic meanings such as conditionals, explanations, concessions, and warnings.

ادرس زين و بتييب إيي

ədrəs	zeen	w-ba-t-jiib	ʔee.
study.imp	good	and-will-you-get.imperf	A

'Study well and you will get an A.' (conditional)

عطني فلوس وبساعدك تشرد

ʕatˤ-nii	fluus	w-ba-saaʕd-ək	tə-ʃrəd.
give.imp-me	money	and-will-I.help.imperf-you	you-escape.imperf

'Give me some money and I'll help you escape.' (conditional)

حاولت وبعدها رسبت

ħaawəl-at	w-baʕad-ha	rəsb-at.
try.perf-she	and-still-she	fail.perf-she

'She tried and (with that) she failed.' (concession)

كلمه ثانيه منك وبدق للشرطة

kəlm-a	θaanj-a	mən-k	w-b-a-dəgg	l-əʃ-ʃərtˤa.
word-f	another-f	from-you	and-will-I-call.imperf	to-the-police

'Another (i.e. one more) word from you and I will call the police.' (warning)

باقي شيء واحد تسويه وهو إنك تعتذر

baagi ʃaj waaħəd t-sawwii-h w-huu ʔənn-ək t-əʕtəðər.

still thing one you-do.imperf-it and-it that-you you-refl.apologize.imperf

'There's only one thing left for you to do, and (it is that) to apologize.' (explanation)

Sometimes, و wa can start a sentence without a preceding conjunct in the same sentence, as long as the context is salient. For instance, the following conversation:

هي معلمة زينه

hii mʕalm-ah zeen-ah.

she teacher-f good-f

'She is a good teacher.'

هيه وبعد طالباتها يحبنها

heeh w-baʕad tˤaalˤəbaat-haa j-ħəbb-ən-ha.

yes and-also students.f-her they-like.imperf-they.f-her

'Yes, and also her students like her.'

15.5 Informal use of و w-/wa

In spoken contexts, the coordinator و wa/w- may be used to coordinate an unnamed (mostly indefinite) entity. In English, people say ' . . . and stuff/things (like that),' meaning there is an entity additional to the previously mentioned entities. In Emirati Arabic, the corresponding expression is وجي wʧii 'and so.'

سألوني عن مخططاتي للمستقبل وجي

səʔl-oo-ni ʕan mu-xatˤtˤətˤaa-ti l-əl-mustaqbal w-ʧii.

ask.perf-they-me about part-caus.plans-my for-the-future and-like.this

'They asked me about my plans for the future and stuff.'

المحل يبيع تلفزونات ومسجلات وجي

əl-maħal j-biiʕ tәlfәzjuun-aat w-msadʒdʒәl-aat w-ʧii.

the-store it-sell.imperf television-f.pl and-part.stereo-f.pl and-like.this

'The store sells TVs and stereos and stuff.'

عنده وايد معارف وجي

ʕәnd-ah waajәd ma-ʕaarәf w-ʧii.

with-him lot part-acquaintance and-like

'He has a lot of acquaintances and stuff.'

أحمد سار السينما وجي

ʔaħmad saar әs-seenәma w-ʧii.

Ahmad go.perf-he the-cinema and-like.this

'Ahmad went to the movie theater and so on.'

15.6 بس bas 'but'

بس bas (var. bs) 'but' is a coordinator which establishes a contrast between the two conjuncts. It is logically equivalent to 'and,' which entails that the two conjoined items are simultaneously true, yet differs in that 'but' expresses a *concessive* meaning—that is, the second conjunct expresses a predicate/situation not normally predicted by the interpretation of the first conjunct. In Emirati Arabic, this concessive conjunction is expressed by بس bas 'but.' It may conjoin two categorically equivalent constituents such as adjectives and nouns.

ذكيه بس عيازه

ðakiijj-a bas ʕajjaaz-a.

smart-f but lazy-f

'smart but lazy'

معارف وايدين بس اصدقاء شوي

ma-ʕaarәf wajd-iin bas ʔasˁdәqaaʔ ʃwaj.

part-know many-pl but friends little

'many acquaintances but few friends'

In most cases, بس bas conjoins two full sentences.

أحمد يحب موزة بس علي يكرهها

ʔaħmad	j-ħəb	mooza	bas	ʕəli	jə-krah-ha.
Ahmad	he-like.imperf	Moza	but	Ali	he-hate.imperf-her

'Ahmad likes Moza, but Ali hates her.'

آسفه بس لازم أروح الحين

ʔaasf-ah	bas	laazəm	ʔa-ruuħ	əl-ħiin.
sorry-f	but	must	I-leave.imperf	the-now

'I am sorry, but I have to leave now!'

Given the concessive meaning, بس bas can start a sentence without a preceding conjunct, or conjoin fragments, if the context is clear.

بس ها مب معقول!

bas	haa	mub	maʕquul!
but	this	not	possible

'But this is not possible!'

The following conversation is another example:

أ: بيكون شي امتحان باجر

ba-j-kuun	ʃaj	ʔemtəħaan	baatʃər.
will-it-be.imperf	there.is	test	tomorrow

A: 'There will be a test tomorrow.'

ب: أدري بس

ʔa-dri	bas
I-know.imperf	but

B: 'I know, but.'

أ: لا بس ولا غيره

laa	bas	wa-laa	ɣeer-ah.
no	but	and-no	other-it

A: 'No buts.' (i.e. the speaker will not change their mind in giving out a test tomorrow)

Similar to و wa 'and,' بس bas can license grammatical structures such as gapping:

كنت أبا الهند يفوزون، بس حرمتيه إيطاليّة

kən-t ʔa-ba l-hənd j-fuuz-uun bas ħərmat-jah ʔiitˤaalijj-a.

be-perf-I I-want.imperf the-India they-win.imperf-they but wife-my Italian-f

'I wanted India to win, but my wife is Italian.'

Similar to و wa, if a single entity appears in both conjuncts, the second one can be expressed by an object pronoun suffix. Alternatively, the object pronoun suffix is used in both conjuncts, followed by the postposed referential expression (Chapter 11).

ماكس ضيع المفتاح لكن سو حصلته

maaks ðˤajjaʕ əl-məftaaħ bas suu ħasˤsˤəl-at-ah.

Max caus.lose.perf-he the-key but Sue caus.find.perf-she-it

'Max lost the key but Sue found it.'

ماكس ضيعه بس سو حصلته، المفتاح

maaks ðˤajjaʕ-ah bas suu ħasˤsˤəl-ət-a əl-məftaaħ.

Max caus.lose.perf-it but Sue caus.find.perf-she-it the-key

'Max lost it but Sue found it, the key.'

بس bas may combine with the negative marker مب mub 'not' (Section 10.2) and إلا ʔəlla 'only' in the first conjunct to form the parallel (or correlative) structure 'not only . . . but also' (Section 14.4.5).

المشروع مب بس إلا بيدمر البيئة بعد بيعرض الناس للخطر

əl-maʃruuʕ mub bas ʔəlla ba-j-dammər əl-biiʔa baʕad bi-j-ʕarrəðˤ ən-naas l-əl-xatˤar.

the-project not but only will-it-caus.destroy.imperf the-environment also will-it-caus.expose.imperf the-people to-the-danger

'This project will not only destroy the environment but will also put people in danger.'

مب بس إلا دخلوا مكتبه وسرقوا كتبه بعد طرطرو مخططاته
mub bas ʔəlla dəxl-aw maktəb-ah w-sərg-aw
kətb-a baʕad tˁartˁər-aw mə-xatˁtˁatˁ-aat-ah.
not but only enter.perf-they office-his and-steal.perf-they
books-his also tear.perf-they part-manuscripts-his
'They not only broke into his office and stole his books, but (they) (also) tore up his manuscripts.'

توم كروز مب بس إلا ممثل، بعد منتج
toom kruuz mub bas ʔəlla mumaθθəl baʕad muntəʤ.
Tom Cruise not but only actor also producer
'Tom Cruise is not only an actor but also a producer.'

هالسياره مب بس إلا سريعه بعد إقتصاديه
h-as-sajjaara mub bas ʔəlla sariiʕ-a baʕad əqtəsˁaadijj-a.
this-the-car not but only fast-f also economical-f
'This car is not only fast but also economical.'

Alternatively, another (although less common in colloquial speech) conjunction لكن laakən 'but' can be used without any meaning change.

ماكس ضيع المفتاح لكن سو حصلته
maaks ðˁajjaʕ əl-məftaaħ laakən suu ħasˁsˁəl-ət-ah.
Max caus.lose.perf-he the-key but Sue caus.find.perf-she-it
'Max lost the key, but Sue found it.'

عنا امتحان اليوم لكن محد درس
ʕən-na əmtəħaan əl-joom laakən ma-ħħad daras.
with-us test the-today but no-one study.perf-he
'We have a test today, but no one (has) studied.'

15.7 Disjunction والا wəlla 'or'

والا wəlla 'or' is commonly used to connect words and phrases of the same grammatical category to express the meaning of a typical disjunction.

أحمد بيي يساعدني والا علي بيي

ʔaħmad b-ijji j-saaʕəd-nii wəlla ʕəli b-ijji.

Ahmad will-he.come.imperf he-help.imperf-me or Ali will-he.come.imperf

'Ahmad will come to help me, or Ali will come (to help me).'

سواء كانت النتيجة زينة والا لا لازم تشد حيلك

sawaaʔ kaan-at ən-nətiidʒ-ah zeen-ah wəlla laa laazəm tʃəd ħeel-ək.

whether be.perf-it.f the-result-f good-f or not must pull will-your

'Whether the result is good or bad, you have to work harder.' (lit. Pull your will!)

والا wəlla is used to combine various categories. In some cases, the order of the disjunction is linearly fixed (Table 15.2).

The second conjunct is not always categorically identical to the first one. For instance, والا wəlla 'or' may combine with the negative marker لا laa 'not' to express alternatives. In this case, the second conjunct linked by لا laa may be left empty. It can be analyzed as a result of ellipsis (Chapter 16).

زين والا لا

zeen wəlla laa

good or not

'good or not'

جان بتي الحفلة والا لا، خبرني

tʃaan bə-t-ti əl-ħafla wəlla laa xabbər-nii.

whether will-you-come.imperf the-party or no caus.tell.imperf-me

'Whether you will join the party or not, please let me know.'

المطعم رخيص والا؟

əl-matˤʕam rəxiisˤ wəlla (laa)?

the-restaurant cheap or not

'The restaurant is cheap or not?'

Table 15.2 Fixed expressions formed by والا wəlla 'or'

زين والا مب زين zeen wəlla mub zeen good or not good 'good or bad'	يمين والا يسار jəmiin wəlla jəsaar right or left 'right or left'
بنت والا ولد bənt wəlla walad girl or boy 'Girl or boy' (the alternative order ولد والا بنت walad wəla bənt is occasionally heard and not completely ruled out)	الأول والا الأخير əl-ʔawwal wəlla əl-ʔaxiir the-first or the-last 'the first or the last'
الأول والا الثاني əl-ʔawwal wəlla əθ-θaani the-first or the-second 'the first or the second'	صح والا غلط sˤaħ wəlla ɣalatˤ right or wrong 'right or wrong'
أيي والا بي ee wəlla bii A or B 'A or B'	ملح والا فلفل məlħ wəlla fəlfəl salt or pepper 'salt or pepper'

والا wəlla can also coordinate different categories. For example:

بيرد الأسبوع الياي والا عآخر الشهر
ba-rəd lə-esbuuʕ əl-jaaj wəlla ʕa-ʔaaxər əʃ-ʃahar.
will-I-return.imperf the-week the-coming or at-end the-month
'I will return next week or at the end of the month.'

Similar to the use of conjunctions, والا wəlla 'or' may also combine with an unnamed indefinite entity (cf. English ' . . . or something like that').

تستخدم محضر الطعام والا شي جي
t-əstaxdəm mə-ħaðˁðˁər ətˁ-tˁaʕaam wəlla ʃaj ʧii.
she-caus.refl.use.imperf part-caus.processor the-food or thing like.this
'She uses a food processor or something (like that).'

In addition to the semantics of disjunctions, والا wəlla expresses the pragmatic function of 'otherwise,' which may further express warnings, advice, and reasons.

عطني فلوس والا تراني بستقيل
ʕatˁ-ni fluus wəlla taraa-ni b-a-stəqiil.
give.imp-me money or well-me will-I-resign.imperf
'Give me money or, (well), I will resign.' (warning)

لا اتم وايد والا بتتأخر عالكلاس
laa t-tamm waajəd wəlla bə-t-əttaxxar ʕa-lə-klaas.
not you-stay.imperf lot or will-you.refl.late.imperf on-the-class
'Don't stay too long, or you will be late for class.' (advice)

أكيد عيبتهم الشقة والا ما كانوا بيتمون هالكثر
ʔakiid ʕiiba-t-hum əʃ-ʃaqqah wəlla maa kaan-aw ba-j-tamm-oon ha-l-keθər.
surely appeal.perf-it.f-them the-apartment or not be.perf-they will-they-stay.imperf-they this-the-much
'They liked the apartment for sure, or (otherwise) they would not have stayed for that long.' (reason)

In Emirati Arabic, the exclusive disjunction (cf. English 'either . . . or') is expressed by the correlative structure يا . . . يا ja . . . ja. . ., which is covered in Section 15.13.1.

15.8 أو ʔaw 'or'

Emirati Arabic speakers occasionally use the disjunctor أو ʔaw 'or.'

حياة أو موت
ħayaah ʔaw moot
life or death
'life or death'

مع أو بدون مساعدتك
maʕ ʔaw bəduun m-saaʕəd-tək
with or without part-help-your
'with or without your help'

قبل أو بعد العشا
gabəl ʔaw baʕad əl-ʕəʃa
before or after the-dinner
'before or after dinner'

فوق أو تحت
foog ʔaw taħat
above or below
'above or below'

15.9 فـ- fa- 'and then/so'

Another coordinator - فـ fa- 'and then/so' may be used to conjoin the antecedent clause and the consequent clause.

سمع الانفجار فدق للشرطة
səmaʕ l-ənfədʒaar fa-dag l-əʃ-ʃərtˤah.
hear.perf-he the-explosion so-call.perf-he to-the-police
'He heard an explosion, so he called the police.'

شفت جلب يربع صوبي، فشردت.
ʧef-t ʧalb jə-rbaʕ sˤoob-i fa-ʃərad-t.
see.perf-I dog he-run.imperf toward-me so-run.away.perf-I
'I saw a dog running towards me, so I ran away.'

15.10 Contrastive coordinator أما ʔamma 'as for'

The coordinator أما ʔamma 'as for' is used to conjoin two contrastive clauses.

روبرت كتوم أما ديفد صريح
robərt katuum ʔamma deevəd sˤariiħ.
Robert secretive as.for David candid
'Robert is secretive and (in contrast) David is candid.'

مريم تدرس دكتوراه فاللغويات، أما اختها تدرس هندسة.

marjam tə-drəs dəktooraah f-əl-ləɣawijjaat ʔamma ʔəxət-haa tə-drəs handəsa.

Mariam she-study.imperf doctorate in-the-linguistics as.for sister-her she-study.imperf engineering

'Mariam studies for a doctorate in linguistics, (in contrast) her sister studies engineering.'

بوظبي فيها رطوبة أما العين لا

buu-ðˤabi fii-haa rtˤuuba ʔamma l-ʕeen laa.

Abu-Dhabi in-her humidity as.for Al Ain not

'Abu Dhabi has humidity, (in contrast) Al Ain does not.'

15.11 Comparative coordinator عن ʕan 'than'

The preposition عن ʕan 'than' (Section 5.5) functions as a coordinator in the expression of comparison (Section 5.3).

البيوت أرخص فبيرث عن فسيدني والا ميلبورن

lə-bjuut ʔa-rxasˤ f-bərθ ʕan f-sidni wəlla məlboorn.

the-house.pl more-cheap in-Perth than in-Sydney or Melbourne

'Houses are cheaper in Perth than in Sydney or Melbourne.'

موزة سريعة أكثر عن انها ذكية

mooza sariiʕ-a ʔakθthar ʕan ʔən-ha ðaki-jja.

Moza fast-f more than that-her smart-f

'Moza is faster than (she is) smart.'

علي قرر إنه يتم فالبيت عن إنه يسافر هالإجازة

ʕəli qarrarr ʔənn-ah j-tamm f-əl-beet ʕan ʔənn-ah j-saafər ha-l-əʤaaza.

Ali caus.decide.perf-he that-him he-stay.imperf in-the-house than that-him he-travel.imperf this-the-break

'Ali decided to stay home rather than to travel for this break.'

الرياضيين غالباً يشربون ماي عن انهم يشربون مشروبات طاقه عقب أي مباراة

ər-rəjaað^ʕijj-iin ɣaaləban jə-ʃrəb-uun maaj ʕan ʔən-hum jə-ʃrəb-uun ma-ʃruub-aat t^ʕaaq-a ʕəgəb ʔajj mbaaraa.

the-athlete-pl usually they-drink.imperf-they water than that-them they-drink.imperf-they part-drink-f.pl energy-f after any match

'Athletes usually drink water rather than energy drinks after a match.'

المشكلة اقتصاديه عن إنها سياسيه

əl-məʃkəlah əqtəs^ʕaadijj-a ʕan ʔən-haa sijaasijj-a.

the-problem economical-f than that-her political-f

'The problem is economical (rather) than political.'

15.12 Negative coordinator مب mub 'not'

The negative marker مب mub 'not' (Section 10.2) also functions as a coordinator. The following examples show that مب mub may coordinate two nouns. Note there is no pause between the first conjunct and مب mub.

يابت أعلى درجة فالامتحان عليا مب موزه الي

ʕalja mub mooza ʔəlli jaab-at ʔa-ʕla daradʒah f-əl-əmtəħaan.

Alia not Moza that get.perf-she most-high grade in-the-exam

'(It's) Alia not Moza who scored the highest in the examination.'

شريت دياي مب سمج حق العشا

ʃaree-t dəjaaj mub səmatʃ ħag əl-ʕəʃa.

buy.perf-I chicken not fish for the-dinner

'I bought chicken not fish for dinner.'

مات ف 1984، مب 1983

maat f-ʔalf w-təsʕəmja w-ʔarbaʕ w-θəmaaniin mub ʔalf w-təsʕəmja w-θalaaθ w-θəmaaniin.

die.perf-he in-thousand and-nine-hundred and-four and-eighty not thousand and-nine-hundred and-three and-eighty

'He died in 1984, not 1983.'

If a pause is added between the two conjuncts, the second conjunct should be combined with the coordinator بس bas 'but.' In this case the negation may not have the conjunction function.

عزموا جيل بس مب ريلها

ʕəzm-aw	ʤəl	bas	mub	rajəl-ha.
invite.perf-they	Jill	but	not	husband-her

'They had invited Jill, not her husband.'

15.13 Correlatives in coordination

Correlative constructions (*correlatives* for short) are a type of coordinate structure in which the two conjoined clauses are grammatically marked simultaneously. That is, the two markers of correlatives are 'paired' so that the intended meaning is properly expressed. In English, correlative conjunctions such as 'either . . . or,' 'neither . . . nor,' and 'whether . . . or' are well-known examples. In Emirati Arabic, the constructions for comparative correlatives and exclusive disjunctions are considered as correlatives.

15.13.1 Comparative correlatives . . . كلما . . . كلما kəlma . . . kəlma. . . 'the more . . . the more'

Emirati Arabic expresses the comparative correlative structures (cf. English 'the more/-er . . . the more/-er . . .) by placing the universal quantifier كلما kəlma (Section 5.6.5) at the beginning of the conjoined clauses (Section 5.3.4).

كلما تشتغل زين كلما كان راتبك أحسن

kəl-ma	tə-ʃtəɣəl	zeen	kəl-ma	kaan	raatb-ək	ʔa-ħsan.
all-ever	you-work.imperf	good	all-ever	be.perf-you	salary-your	more-good

'The better you work, the better salary you will get.'

كلما تاكل أكثر كلما تمتن أكثر

kəlma	taa-kəl	ʔakθar	kəl-ma	tə-mtan	ʔakθar.
all-ever	you-eat.imperf	more	all-ever	you.get.fat.imperf	more

'The more you eat, the fatter you will get.'

كلما كان أكثر كلما كان أحسن

kəl-ma kaan ʔakθar kəlma kaan ʔa-ħsan.
all-ever be.perf-it more all-ever be.perf more-good
'The more (it was), the better (it was).'

كلما كان الكمبيوتر أسرع كل ما كان أغلى

kəlma kaan əl-kambjuutar ʔa-sraʕ kəlma kaan ʔa-ɣla.
all-ever be.perf-it the-computer more-fast all-ever be.perf more-expensive
'The faster the computer, the more expensive it is.'

15.13.2 *Exclusive disjunction . . . يا . . . يا ja . . . ja 'either . . . or . . . '*

The exclusive disjunction (cf. English 'either . . . or') is expressed by the correlative structure . . . يا . . . يا ja . . . ja. . . .

يا فاطمة يا أحمد بييون الكلاس باجر

ja fatˤmah ja ʔaħmad ba-jj-uun lə-kəlaas baatʃər.
either Fatima or Ahmad will-they-come.imperf-they the-class tomorrow
'Either Fatima or Ahmad will come to class tomorrow.'

The number of conjuncts can be more than two. For example:

لو سمحتي اختاري يا دياي يا سمج يا لحم من مينيو الغدا

loo səmaħ-ti xtaar-aj ja dəjaaj jaa səmatʃ ja laħam mən manju l-ɣəda.
if allow.perf-you choose.imp-you either chicken or fish or meat from menu the-lunch
'Please choose either chicken or fish or beef in the lunch menu.'

Moreover, the two conjuncts may belong to distinct categories.

أحمد يا شيف يا يعرف شيف

ʔaħmad ja ʃeef ja jə-ʕarf ʃeef.
Ahmad either chef or he-know.imperf chef
'Ahmad is either a chef or knows someone who is a chef.'

Because of the exclusive nature, . . . يا . . . يا ja . . . ja . . . can be further used to express warnings.

يا تشتغل يا تروح! لا تزعجني أنا والثانين

ja tə-ʃtəɣəl ja t-ruuħ laa tə-zʕədʒ-ni ʔana w-əθ-θaaniin.

either you-work.imperf or you-leave.imperf don't you-disturb.imperf-me I and-the-others

'Either you work or leave! Don't disturb me and others!'

The use of verbal agreement to the disjoined subjects (e.g. 'Either Fatima or Ahmad') is subject to some variation depending on the speakers. The previous example shows that plural verbal agreement (e.g. بييون bijuun 'they will come') may be used for disjoined subjects. It is also possible to use a singular verbal agreement. For instance, the following example shows the use of two singular verbs which agree with the two subjects respectively:

يا فاطمه يا أحمد بتي أو بيي الكلاس باجر

ja fatˤmah ja ʔaħmad bə-t-tii ʔaw bə-j-ji lə-klaas baatʃər.

either Fatima or Ahmad will-she-come.imperf or will-he-come.imperf the-class tomorrow

'Either Fatima or Ahmad (he or she) will come to class tomorrow.'

15.13.3 *Negative correlatives . . . لا و . . . لا laa . . . w-laa . . . 'neither . . . nor . . . '*

The coordination of negative predicates may be expressed by و wa (cf. English 'neither . . . nor'). The two predicates are preceded by the negative marker لا la 'not' (Section 10.3). Note that ولا wlaa 'and not/nor' is pronounced differently from the disjunctor wəla 'or' (Section 15.7).

سام لا يلبس بدلات و لا يلبس قمصان بولو

saam laa jə-lbas badl-aat w-laa jə-lbas gəmsˤaan booloo.

Sam not he-wear-imperf suit-f.pl and-not he-wear.imperf shirts polo

'Sam neither wears suits nor polo shirts.'

ماري ما كانت مستانسه ولا حزينه

maari maa kaana-t məstaans-a w-laa ħaziin-a.
Mary not be.perf-she happy-f and-not sad-f
'Mary was neither happy nor sad.'

لا بيتر ولا حرمته بغوا المسؤوليه

laa biitar w-laa ħərmət-ah bəɣ-aw əl-masʔuulijja.
not Peter and-not wife-his want.perf-they the-responsibility
'Neither Peter nor his wife wanted the responsibility.'

ولا طالب يعرف متى الامتحان ولا وين مكانه

wala tˤaaləb jə-ʕrəf məta l-əmtəħaan w-laa ween məkaan-ah.
no student he-know.imperf when the-exam and-not where place-its
'No student knows when the exam is or where it is.'

مب طايع يقول السبب ولا منو خبره

mub tˤaajəʕ j-guul əs-səbab w-laa mnuu xabbar-ah.
not part.want he-say.imperf the-reason and-not who caus.tell.perf-he-him
'He neither wants to say the reason nor who told him.'

محد سمع عن المتحف ولا وين مكانه.

maħħad səmaʕ ʕan əl-mətħaf w-laa ween məkaan-ah.
noone hear.perf-he about the-museum and-not where place-its
'Nobody heard about the museum nor where it is.'

15.14 Paratactic coordination

In rare situations it is possible to conjoin two clauses without the use of a coordinator. This type of paratactic coordination is always used to express some idiomatic or fixed expression (Chapter 18). For instance:

ماشي شغل، ماشي فلوس

maa-ʃajj ʃəɣəl maa-ʃajj fluus!
not-thing work not-thing money
'No work, no money!'

فلوس أكثر مشاكل أكثر

fluus ʔakθar məʃaakəl ʔakθar!
money more problems more
'More money, more problems!'

Further reading

For a theoretical analysis of agreement in conjunction in Arabic dialects, refer to Aoun et al. (1994, 1999) and Bahloul and Harbert (1993). For negative correlatives/coordination in Arabic, see Alqassas (2019). For a cross-linguistic introduction to coordination, see Haspelmath (2007).

Chapter 16

Ellipsis

Ellipsis and elliptical structures are a major universal language property. Ellipsis allows lexical items or grammatical constituents to be left unsaid by the speaker, yet the listener has no difficulty restoring the intended meaning. In most cases, ellipsis is possible if the 'elliptical site' is discourse-salient. Most linguists agree that the elliptical site is a grammatical constituent, or at least consists of lexical items which are unpronounced. In Emirati Arabic, ellipsis may be observed at various grammatical levels.

16.1 Gapping

Gapping is a type of elliptical structure found in coordination (Chapter 15), in which the verb of the second conjunct is left unsaid.

محمد يركض برا و حامد داخل

mħammad jə-rkəðˤ bara w ħaaməd daaxəl.

Mohammad he-run.imperf outside and Hamed inside

'Mohammad is running outside and Hamed (is running) inside.'

بيي بسيارتي وهي بسيارتها

b-a-jji b-sajjaart-i w hii b-sajjaart-ha.

will-I-come.imperf by-car-my and she by-car-her

'I will come in my car and she (will come) in her car.'

سمعت فونج يدق وفون حمده

səmaʕt foon-ətʃ jə-dəgg w foon ħamda.

hear.perf-I phone-your.f it-ring.imperf and phone Hamda

'I heard your phone ringing and Hamda's phone (ringing).'

Sometimes, the gap contains more than one verb, e.g. the modal verb (Chapter 9). For example:

إيمان تقدر تعزف بيانو وحسين غيتار

ʔiimaan tə-gdar tə-ʕzəf bijaano w ħseen giitaar.

Eiman she-can.imperf she-play.imperf piano and Husain guitar

'Eiman can play piano and Husain (can play) guitar.'

It is not uncommon to see more than one instance of ellipsis in a sentence, e.g. gapping and NP ellipsis (Section 16.3).

هلالة تكتب بالإيد اليمين ومريم باليسار

hlaala tə-ktəb b-əl ʔiid əl-jəmiin w marjam b-əl-jəsaar.

Helala she-write.imperf with-the hand the-right and Mariam with-the-left

'Helala writes with her right hand and Mariam (writes) with the left (hand).'

16.2 Stripping

Stripping is another elliptical structure in which the 'remnant' after ellipsis has only one lexical item (usually a noun or a noun phrase). Usually, the 'stripped' remnant appears after negation (Chapter 10) and coordination (Chapter 15). Sometimes the stripped item is followed by the adverb بعد baʕad 'too' or the negative marker لاء laaʔ 'no' (Section 10.3).

سلطان اللي لعب مب خالد

səltˤaan ʔəlli laʕab mub xaaləd.

Sultan that play.perf-he not Khaled

'Sultan (was the one who) played, not Khaled (was the one who played).'

حمدان يلعب سوني و مريم بعد

ħamdan jə-lʕab soonii w marjam baʕad.

Hamdan he-play.imperf PlayStation and Mariam too

'Hamdan plays PlayStation and Mariam (plays PlayStation) too.'

جو كانت شوية مظايقة وأنا بعد

dʒoo kaan-at ʃwajja mə-ðˤðˤaajga w ʔana baʕad.
Joe be.perf-she little part-upset and I too
'Joe was a little upset, and me too.'

مريم شكلها مستانسة على درجة الامتحان وفاطمة بعد

marjam ʃakəl-ha mə-stans-a ʕala daradʒ-at l-əmtəħan w faatˤma baʕad.
Mariam apparently-her part-happy-f on score-f the-exam and Fatima also
'Mariam seemed happy with the exam score, and Fatima also.'

وايد طلاب يو من الصين و(من) الهند بعد

waajəd tˤəlˤlˤaab ja-w mən ə-sˤsˤiin w (mən) əl-hənd baʕad
Many students come.perf-they from the-china and from the-India too
'Many students came from China, and India too.'

فاطمة بتييب بنتها الحفلة وموزة بعد

faatˤma ba-t-jiib bənt-ha l-ħafla w mooza baʕad.
Fatima will-she-bring.imperf daughter-her the-party and Moza too
'Fatima will bring her daughter to the party, and Moza too.'

كل حد يحب هالفلم بس أنا لا

kəl ħad j-ħəb h-al-fəlm bas ʔana laaʔ.
every one he-love.imperf this-the-movie but I no
'Everyone loves this movie, but not me.'

16.3 NP ellipsis

Noun phrase (NP) ellipsis may be licensed by various grammatical categories, including lexical categories such as verbs (Chapter 7) and possessive prepositions (Section 6.2.3), and functional categories such as numerals (Sections 5.6.1–5.6.2) and demonstratives (Section 5.8.4).

منى حصلت كتاب، و هدى بعد حصلت

muna ħasˤsˤəl-at ktaab, w huda baʕad ħasˤsˤəl-at.
Mona caus.find.perf-she book and Huda also caus.find-perf-she
'Mona found a book, and Huda also found (a book).'

أتمنى اشتري سيارة حمرة و ثلاث زرق

ʔa-tmanna ʔa-ʃtəri sajjaara ħamra w θalaθ zərg
I-wish.imperf I-buy.imperf car red and three blue
'I wish to buy a red car and three blue (cars).'

إذا دانة جربت الچامي مالي، بجرب مالها

ʔəða daana ʤarrəb-at əl-ʧaami maal-i, b-a-ʤarrəb maal-ha.
if Dana try.perf-she the-chami poss-me will-I-try.imperf poss-her
'If Dana tried my Chami (an Emirati dish), I will try hers.'

أنا مب مدرّس، بس كنت

ʔana mub m-darrəs bas kənt.
I not part-teacher but be.perf-I
'I am not a teacher, but I was (a teacher).'

عيسى حل خمس أسئله لان ه فاطمه حلت أربعه

ʕiisa ħall xams ʔasʔil-ah lanna fatˤma ħall-at ʔarbaʕa.
Eisa answer.perf-he five questions-f because Fatima answer.perf-she four
'Eisa answered five questions because Fatima answered four (questions).'

القطار الأول توه تحرك، والثاني ياي

əl-qətˤaar əl-ʔawwal taww-ah ət-ħarrak w-əθ-θaani jaaj.
the-train the-first just-it refl-move.perf-it and-the-second part.come
'The first train just left, and the second (train) is coming.'

هالدفتر مالي وها مالك

ha-d-daftar maal-i w haa maal-ək.
this-the-notebook poss-me and this poss-you
'This notebook is mine, and this (notebook) is yours.'

It is common to use the numeral واحد waaħəd 'one' (Section 5.6.1–5.6.2) and the partitive structure (Section 6.1) to replace the elided noun phrase. For example:

الطلاب ساروا المكتبة وكل واحد اشترى كتاب

ətˤ-tˤəllaab saar-aw əl-maktəba w kəl waaħəd əʃtəra ktaab.
the-student.pl go.perf-they the-bookstore and each one buy.perf-he book
'The students went to the bookstore and each one bought a book.'

سلطان عنده قناعين حمر وواحد أخضر بعد

səltˤaan ʕənd-ah qənaaʕ-een ħəmər w waaħəd ʔaxðˤar baʕad.
Sultan with-him mask-du red.pl and one green too
'Sultan has two red masks, and a green one too.'

الصيف اللي طاف راشد زار قرية فرأس الخيمة ووحدة ثانية فالفجيرة

əsˤ-sˤeef ʔəlli tˤaaf raaʃəd zaar qarja f-raas-əl-xeema w wəħda θaanja f-əl-fədʒeera.
the-summer that pass.perf-he Rashid visit.perf-he village in-Ras-Al-Khaimah and one another in-the-Fujairah
'Last summer Rashid visited a village in Ras Al Khaima, and another one in Fujairah.'

وايد طلاب نجحوا فالامتحان بس في منهم لا

waajəd tˤəlˤlˤaab nədʒħ-aw f-əl-əmtəħaan bas fii mən-hum laaʔ.
many students succeed.perf-they in-the-exam but there from-them not
'Many students passed the exam, but not some of them.'

البنات حظروا الحفلة و كل وحدة فيهم يابت هدية

əl-banaat ħəðˤr-aw əl-ħafla w kəl-wəħd-a fii-hum jaab-at hədijja.

the-girl.pl attend.perf-they the-party and each-one-f in-them bring.perf-she gift

'The girls attended the ceremony and each one of them brought a gift.'

16.4 VP ellipsis

Verb phrase (VP) ellipsis is one of the most productive elliptical structures in Emirati Arabic. The following example shows that the entire verb phrase (Chapter 7) to the exclusion of the temporal adverb is elided in the second clause:

بيلس مع اليهال اليوم بس إنت باجر

b-a-jləs maʕa əl-jahhal əl-joom bas ʔənt baatʃər.

will-I-sit.imperf with the-kids the-today but you tomorrow.

'I will stay with the kids today but you (will stay with the kids) tomorrow.'

خليفة راح المول عالساعة خمس و مريم عالست

xəliifa raaħ əl-muul ʕa-əs-saaʕa xams w marjam ʕa əs-sət.

Khalifa go.perf-he the-mall at-the-hour five and Mariam at the-six

'Khalifa went to the mall at five and Mariam (went to the mall) at six.'

امتحنت بس هي بعدها

ʔə-mtaħan-t ʔa-mtəħən bas hii baʕad-ha.

finish.perf-I I-refl.examine.imperf but she still-her

'I finished being examined but she is still (being tested).'

For complex predicate constructions (Section 7.11), it is possible to elide the main (e.g. the second) predicate and leave the first predicate intact in the second clause.

ريم بدت تدرس حق الفاينل وأنا بعد (بديت)

riim bəd-at tə-drəs ħagg əl-faajnal w-ana baʕad bəd-eet.

Reem start.perf-she she-study.imperf for the-final and-I also start.perf-I

'Reem started studying for the final, and I also started (studying for the final).'

خل نكمل ندرس عشان هم بعد يكملون

xal n-kamməl nə-drəs ʕaʃaan hum baʕad əj-kaml-uun.

let we-caus.continue.imperf we-study.imperf in.order.to they also they-continue.imperf-they

'Let's continue studying so that they also continue (studying).'

خلصت امتحن بس هي بعدها ما خلصت

xalˤlˤasˤ-t ʔa-mtəħn bas hii baʕad-ha maa xalˤlˤəsˤ-at.

finish.perf-I I-refl.examine.imperf but she still-her not finish.perf-she

'I finished taking the examination, but she has not yet finished (taking the exam).'

علي يقدر يتكلم ايطالي، و سعيد بعد يقدر

ʕəli jə-gdar jə-t-kallam ʔiitˤaali w sʕiid baʕad jə-gdar.

Ali he-can.imperf he-refl-speak.imperf Italian and Saeed also he-can.imperf

'Ali can speak Italian, and Saeed can (speak Italian) too.'

أغلب الناس يبون يشتغلون في المدن الكبيرة بس احمد ما يبا

ʔaɣlab ən-naas jə-b-oon jə-ʃtaɣl-uun fi əl-məden əl-kəbeer-a bas ʔaħmad maa jə-ba.

most the-people they-want.imperf-they they-work.imperf-they in the-cities the-big-f but Ahmad not he-want.imperf

'Most people want to work in big cities, but Ahmad does not want to (work in big cities).'

الكبار كانوا يقدرون يشترون سيارات بس اليهال ما كانوا يقدرون

lə-kbaar kan-aw jə-gdər-uun jə-ʃtər-uun sajjaar-aat bas əl-jahhaal maa kan-aw jə-gdər-uun.

the-adult.pl be.perf-they they-can.imperf-they they-buy.imperf-they car-f.pl but the-kid.pl not be.perf-they they-can.imperf-they

'Adults were able to buy cars, but kids were not able to (buy cars).'

لأن راشد ما رام، سرت أنا السوق

ləʔan raaʃəd maa raam sər-t ʔana əs-suug.

because Rashid not can.perf-he go.perf-I I the-market

'Because Rashid could not (go to the market), I went to the market.'

16.5 PP ellipsis

It is also possible to elide a prepositional phrase (PP) (Section 5.5 and Chapter 14) in the elliptical clause.

ايمان طرشت بيزات حق اهلها، وهدى طرشت هدايا

ʔiimaan tˤarrəʃ-at beez-aat ħagg ʔahəl-ha w huda tˤarrəʃ-at hadaaja.

Eman caus.send.perf-she money-f.pl for family-her and Huda caus.send.perf-she gifts

'Eman sent money to her family, and Huda sent gifts (to her family).'

ميرة سوت كيكة عشان الحفلة و حسن سوا عصير

miira saww-at keeka ʕaʃaan əl-ħafla w ħəsan sawwa ʕəsiir.

Meera make.perf-she cake for the-party and Hasan make.perf-he juice

'Meera made a cake for the party, and Hasan made juice (for the party).'

16.6 Clausal ellipsis

An entire embedded clause (Chapter 14) may be elided. The following is an example of clausal ellipsis, in which the embedded question (Chapter 13) is left unsaid in the elliptical clause:

موزة فهمت كيف تحسب بس مريم بعدها ما فهمت

mooza fəhm-at keef tə-ħsəb bas marjam baʕad-ha maa fəhm-at.

Moza understand.perf-she how she-calculate.imperf but Mariam still-her not understand.perf-she

'Moza understood how to calculate, but Mariam still did not understand (how to calculate).'

On the other hand, if the embedded clause is declarative (e.g. a statement), the elliptical clause usually contains the adverb **جي** ʧii 'so/like that,' which follows the verb.

أحمد عباله إنه مريم ذكية وايد وعلي بعد عباله جي

ʔaħmad ʕa-baal-a ʔənna marjam θakijja waajəd w ʕəli baʕad ʕa-baal-a ʧii.

Ahmad on-mind-his that Mariam smart very and Ali also on-mind-his so

'Ahmad thought that Mariam was very smart, and Ali also thought so.'

شكله أحمد المشتبه فيه الرئيسي بس ما أتوقع جي

ʃakl-a ʔaħmad əl-mu-ʃtabah fii-h ər-raʔiisi bas maa ʔa-t-waqqaʕ ʧii.

apparently-him Ahmad the-part-suspect in-him the-prime but not I-refl-think.imperf so

'Ahmad seems to be the prime suspect, but I don't think so.'

إذا تبا تسير البيت بس قول جي

ʔəθa tə-ba t-siir əl-beet bas guul ʧii.

if you-want.imperf you-go.imperf the-home just say so

'If you want to go home, just say so.'

16.7 Comparative deletion

Comparative deletion is another elliptical construction in which part of the 'than'-clause is elided (Section 5.3.4). The following examples show that what is elided is the degree to which the adjective/verb applies, when the comparison is made between two degrees:

الأفلام ممتعة أكثر من اللي كنت متوقعتنه

əl-ʔaflaam mumtəʕ-a ʔakθar mən ʔəlli kən-t mə-t-waqqəʕ-tənn-ah.

the-movies part.entertaining-f more than that be.perf-I part-refl-caus.expect-f-it

'The movies were more entertaining than I was expecting.'

الفريق يسجل أهداف أكثر من اللي كنت متوقعتنه

ʔəl-fariiq j-sadʒdʒəl ʔahdaaf ʔakθar mən ʔəlli kən-t mə-t-waqqəʕ-tənn-ah.

the-team it-caus.score.imperf goals more than that be.perf-I part-refl-caus.expect-f-it

'The team scores more goals than I expected.'

If the verb in the 'than'-clause is transitive (Section 5.2 and Chapter 7), a resumptive pronoun which refers to the antecedent noun should be affixed to the verb.

أحمد مدّين فلوس أكثر من اللي جمّعته

ʔaħmad mə-d-dajjən fluus ʔakθar mən ʔəlli dʒammaʕ-t-ah.

Ahmad part-refl-owe money more than that caus.collect.perf-I.f-it

'Ahmad has owed more money than I collected.'

طلبت وايد كرك أكثر عن اللي نقدر نشربه

tˤəlˤb-at wajəd karak ʔakθar ʕan ʔəlli nə-gdar nə-ʃrab-ah.

order.perf-she a.lot Karak more than that we-can.imperf we-drink.imperf-it

'She ordered more Karak than we could drink.'

A subject resumptive pronoun is generally not needed in the 'than'-clause as long as verb agreement is evident.

عزمنا ناس أكثر من اللي كانوا يبون ايّون

ʕəzam-na naas ʔakθar mən ʔəlli kan-aw jə-b-oon ʔəjj-uun.

invite.perf-we people more than that be.perf-they they-want.imperf-they come-pl

'We invited more people than wanted to come.'

16.8 Sluicing

In the literature of syntax, sluicing refers to the use of a bare wh-word (Section 13.2) in the elliptical clause. In these cases, the interpretation of the bare wh-word (called 'wh-sluice') may be referred back to an indefinite expression (Section 6.1) at the antecedent clause or the current discourse. Sluicing in Emirati Arabic is productive, and all wh-words can function as the wh-sluice. The following example shows that what is elided in the second clause (after منو mnuu 'who') is a verb phrase in the first clause (called the 'antecedent clause'):

أحمد توه التقى بربيعه، بس ماعرف منو

ʔaħmad taww-ah əltəga bə-rbiiʕ-ah bas ma-a-ʕarf mnuu.

Ahmad just-him refl.meet.perf-he with-friend-his but not-I-know.imperf who

'Ahmad just met his friend, but I don't know who (Ahmad just met).'

Some wh-sluices, for instance شو ʃuu 'what' and منو mnu 'who,' may be followed by the copular pronoun (Section 5.8 and Chapter 7) without any change of meaning. The wh-sluice may also refer to an indefinite expression within a prepositional phrase (Section 5.5) at the antecedent clause.

عبدالله شرب قهوة ويا ربيعه، بس ماعرف أي ربيع

ʕabdallah ʃərab gahwa wijja rbiiʕ-ah bas ma-a-ʕarf ʔaj rbiiʕ.

Abdulla drink.perf-he coffee with friend-his but not-I-know.imperf which friend

'Abdulla drank coffee with his friend, but I don't know which friend.'

إبراهيم كتب بحثه فكمبيوتر، بس ماعرف أي كمبيوتر

ʔəbrahiim kətab baħθ-ah f-kəmbjuutar, bas maa ʕarf ʔajj kəmbjuutar.

Ibrahim write.perf-he research-his in-computer but not I-know.imperf which computer

'Ibrahim wrote his research on a computer, but I don't know which computer.'

It is possible to combine various wh-sluices in the same elliptical clause. For example:

أحمد كسر ايده، بس محد يعرف متى وكيف، وليش

ʔaħmad kəsar ʔiid-ah, bas maħħad jə-ʕarf məta w-keef, w-leeʃ.

Ahmad break.perf arm-his but no.one he-know.imperf when and-how and-why

'Ahmad broke his arm, but no one knows when, how, and why.'

There are also cases in which the wh-sluice refers to a person or entity not explicitly mentioned in the antecedent clause.

صب الشاي بس ماعرف لمنو

sˤabb əʧ-ʧaaj bas ma-ʕarf lə-mnuu.

pour.perf-he the-tea but not-I-know.imperf to-whom

'He served the tea, but I don't know to whom (he served the tea).'

قاعدة تقرا الحين بس ماعرف شو

gaaʕd-a tə-gra l-ħiin bas ma-ʕarf ʃuu.

part.sit-f she-read.imperf the-now but not-I-know.imperf what

'She's reading now, but I don't know what (she is reading now).'

As the wh-sluice is anaphoric, it may be used to refer to an argument or an adverbial expression in the preceding discourse. For instance, it is used as a fragment answer to a question (Chapter 14).

أ: هو يعرف شو المشكله

huu jə-ʕarf ʃuu əl-məʃkəla.

he he-know.imperf what the-problem

A: 'He knows what the problem is.'

ب: من متى؟

mən məta?

since when

B: 'Since when (did he know what the problem is)?'

أ: شي مب طبيعي استوا.

ʃajj mub tˤabiʕii əstəw-a.

thing not normal refl.happen.perf-it

A: 'Something abnormal has happened.'

ب: شو؟

ʃuu?

what

B: 'What (abnormal thing has happened)?'

While the majority of sluicing requires an antecedent clause, which is usually the first clause of the sentence, it is possible for the wh-sluice to receive its interpretation by referring to a following clause.

ماعرف متى بس أبوي أكيد بيدق

maa-ʕarf	məta	bas	ʔəbuu-j	ʔakiid	ba-j-dəgg.
not-I-know.imperf	when	but	father-my	definitely	will-he-call.imperf

'I don't know when (my father will call), but my father will definitely call.'

نسيت منو بس أحمد ياب سيرة حد أمس فالليل

nəsee-t	mnuu	bas	ʔaħmad	jaab	siira-t
ħad	ʔams		f-əl-leel.		
forget.perf-I	who	but	Ahmad	bring.perf-he	topic-f
someone	yesterday		in-the-night		

'I forgot who, but Ahmad mentioned someone last night.'

Further reading

There is a vast literature on the study of ellipsis (particularly sluicing). For a linguistic discussion of ellipsis, see Ross (1969), Merchant (2001), van Craenenbroeck (2010a, 2010b), and Merchant and Simpson (2012), among others. For a discussion of particular types of ellipsis in Arabic dialects, see Algryani (2007, 2012a, 2012b), Leung (2014a, 2014b, 2014c), Al-Bukhari (2016), Albuarabi (2019), and Alshaalan and Abels (2020).

Chapter 17

Interjections

Interjections are linguistic elements that are mainly vocal gestures or unformed words used by speakers to express a mental state, action, attitude, or reaction to a situation. Linguistically speaking, interjections fall into two major classes, depending on their lexical sources. *Primary* interjections are language elements exclusively used in the formation of interjective and exclamative expressions. They are said to be utterance-independent in the sense that they need to form no grammatical constituent nor interact with the core constituents of the sentence to be meaningful. They may have a phonological structure distinct from the native language system, and morphologically, they may not be affixed by inflectional or derivational morphemes. Typical examples of interjections in English include 'ouch,' 'oh,' 'sh,' and 'gosh.' Secondary interjections are similar to primary interjections in that they are conventionally used to express a particular mental state or attitude of the speaker. The two classes differ in that secondary interjections usually stem from lexical sources and therefore possess semantic values on their own. The lexical meaning of the secondary interjection is still valid in some cases, although it is sometimes overwritten by the function of the interjection. Morphologically speaking, secondary interjections stem from native-language words and may have an internal morphological structure, e.g. English 'dear me,' 'goodness me,' 'thank you,' and 'please.'

17.1 Primary interjections

The most common primary interjections in Emirati Arabic are listed in Table 17.1.

Table 17.1 Primary interjections

أهاا	ʔahaa	‘Aha’	ها/هاااا	haa	‘Huh’
آااه	ʔaaa	‘Oh’	اشش	ʔəʃʃ	(request silence)
هيه	heeh	‘Yes’	اصص	ʔesˤsˤ	(request silence)
تت	tu (click)	‘No’	آيي	ʔaaj	‘Ouch’
هاااا	haa	(surprise)	آخ	ʔaax	‘Ouch’
أوووفف	ʔoff	(annoyance)	اخييه	ʔaxxiih/	‘Eww’
أووف	ʔuff	(annoyance)		ʔaxxeeh	
أوووففف	ʔoooff	(annoyance)	يع	jaʕ	(disgusting)
أوهوو/	ʔoohoo	(annoyance)	يخ	jax	(disgusting)
ايه	ʔeeh	‘Hey’	أخييه	ʔaxxii	‘Eww’
حووه	ħooh	‘Hey’ (disrespectful)	هش هش	həʃʃ həʃʃ	(warding off animals)
هيييه	heeeeh	‘Hooray’	كخ	kəx	‘disgusting’ (to babies)
ها ها ها	ha ha ha	(ironic laughter)	وييه	weeh	‘Oh’ (remind of s.th)
واا	waa	(irony)	أفاااا	ʔaffaa	(sorrow)
واالك	waak	(irony)	واو	waaw	‘Wow’
وييه	wiih	(irony)	يسس	jəss	‘Yes’
برافوو	bravoo	‘Bravo’	ماشاءالله	maaʃaalˤlˤah	‘Wow’
أوبس	ʔobs	‘Oops’			

17.1.1 أهاا ʔahaa 'aha' and آاااه ʔaaa 'oh'

In Emirati Arabic, the interjections أهاا ʔahaa 'aha' and آاااه ʔaaa 'oh' with a long vowel and intonation are used to express understanding and realization. This may be demonstrated by the following short conversation:

أقولك كلّمته و ما طاع

ʔa-guul-l-ək! kallam-t-a w maa tˤaaʕ.

I-say.imperf-to-you talk.perf-I-him and not accept.perf-he

A: 'Listen! I have talked to him and he didn't accept.'

آااه, الحين فهمت، عبالي ما كلمتيه أصلًا

ʔaaa, əlħiin fəham-t, ʕa-baal-i maa kallam-tii-h ʔasˤlan.

Oh, now understand.perf-I on-mind-my not talk.perf-you.f-him yet

B: 'Oh, now I understand, I thought you haven't talked to him yet.'

أ: شو يالسة تسوين؟ شكلج مشغولة

ʃuu jaals-a t-saww-iin? ʃaklə-ʧ ma-ʃɣool-a.

what part.sit-f you.f-do.imperf-you.f apparently-you.f part-busy-f

A: 'What are you doing? You seem to be busy.'

ب: يالسة أقرا كتاب

jaals-a ʔa-gra ktaab.

part.sit-f I-read.imperf book

B: 'I am reading a book.'

أ: أهاااا

ʔahaaa!

A: 'Aha!'

أ: ليش ماسرتي الجامعة اليوم؟

leeʃ maa sərt-i əl-dʒaamʕa əl-joom?

why not go.perf-you the-university the-today

A: 'Why didn't you go to the university today?'

ب: كلاساتي تكنسلت

klaas-aat-i	t-kansəl-at.
class-f.pl-my	pass-cancel-f

B: 'My classes were canceled.'

أ: أهااا

ʔahaaa!

A: 'Aha!'

17.1.2 هيه *heeh*

هيه heeh is used to reply to yes/no questions (Chapter 13) to mean 'yes,' as in the following conversations:

أ: سلمتي على يدّتج اليوم؟

sallamt-i	ʕala	jadda-ʧ	əl-joom?
caus.greet.perf-you	to	grandmother-your	the-today

A: 'Did you greet your grandmother today?'

ب: هيه

heeh

B: 'Yes.'

أ: كلتي عدل؟

kalt-i	ʕadəl?
eat-perf-you.f	well

A: 'Did you eat well?'

ب:هيه

heeh

B: 'Yes.'

أ: خبرتيها إنّا بنطلع من وقت؟

xabbar-tii-ha	ʔən-na	ba-nə-tˤlaʕ	mən	wagt?
caus.tell.perf-you-her	that-us	will-we-leave.imperf	from	time

A: 'Have you told her that we will leave early?'

ب: هيه

heeh

B: 'Yes.'

17.1.3 تت *tu*

Using an ingressive apico-alveolar click تت tu (cf. English 'tut tut') along with a simultaneous head-raising gesture is used to express disapproval or to mean 'no.' If these clicks are repeated many times, they may imply a sense of disappointment or sadness. This interjection is used when the speaker is sad, tired, or angry, in addition to saying a simple 'no.' For example:

أ: تغديتي اليوم؟

təɣadee-t-i	əl-joom?
eat.lunch.perf-you-f	today

A: 'Did you have your lunch today?'

ب: تت

tu

B: 'No.' (with the head raising slightly)

ب: طلعتي البارحة؟

tˤəlaʕ-t-i	əl-baarħa?
hang.out.perf-you-f	the-yesterday

A: 'Did you hang out yesterday?

ب: تت

tu

B: 'No.' (with the head raising slightly)

أ: تعرفين سمعت إنَّ علي سوا حادث

tə-ʕarfiin	səmaʕt	ʔənna	ʕəli	sawwa	ħaadəth.
you.f-know.imperf-you.f	hear.perf-I	that	Ali	have.perf-he	accident

A: 'Do you know, I heard that Ali had a car accident.'

ب: تتتتتتت لاحول ولا قوة إلا بالله

tututu	laa	ħawla	wa-laa	quwwata	ʔəllaa	b-əllah.
no	no	power	and-no	strength	except	by-Allah

B: 'No, no, no! There is not might or strength except by Allah.'

17.1.4 لا *laa,* هاا *haa, and* شو *ʃoo*

Feelings of surprise, astonishment, and shock are expressed in Emirati Arabic by a variety of interjections. One is the repetition of the word لا laa 'no'; another is هاا haa. The question word شو ʃuu 'what' (with a lengthened vowel) (Section 13.2) is also used to express feelings of surprise or shock.

أ: سمعتي الخبر؟

səmaʕ-t-i	əl-xəbar?
hear.imperf-you-f	the-news

A: 'Have you heard the news?'

ب: شو؟

ʃuu?

B: 'What?'

أ: بيحطون مديرة يديدة

ba-j-ħəttˁ-uun	mudiir-a	jdiid-a.
will-they-appoint.imperf-they	manager-f	new-f

A: 'They will appoint a new (female) manager.'

ب: لا لا لا. هاااا. شووو!

laa	laa	laa	haaa	ʃuu!
no	no	no	haaa	what

B: 'No, no, no. . . . What!'

The interjection هاا haa is also inferred as 'here you go' when uttered by a different intonation/tone with the surprise هاا haa.

أ: وين تيلفوني؟

ween	teelfoon-i?
where	phone-my

A: 'Where is my phone?'

ب: هاا!

Haa

B: 'Here you go.' (and then handing the phone over)

Another use of هاا! haa is along with interrogatives (Section 13.2) in the sense that the speaker signals to the hearer that a question has been asked and is requesting a direct answer. This is somewhat compatible with English 'eh' or 'həh.' This class of interjection, which requires an action from the hearer, is known as conative interjections.

شو بتسوين اليوم؟ ها؟

ʃuu	bə-t-saww-iin	əl-joom?	haa?
what	will-you.f-do.imperf-you.f	the-today	haa

'What are you going to do today? Huh?'

17.1.5 آاه əaah, آخ əaax, and آي əaaj

The interjections آاه əaah, آخ əaax, and آي əaaj express the speaker's sadness and physical/emotional pain.

آيي ! دستي على ريلي

ʔaaj	dəst-i	ʕalaa	riil-i!
ouch	step.perf-you.f	on	foot-my

'Ouch! You stepped on my foot!'

آخ ! القطوة شمختني

ʔaax	əl-gatˁw-a	ʃamməx-at-ni!
ouch	the-cat-f	caus.scratch.perf-it.f-me

'Ouch! The cat scratched me!'

17.1.6 الله ʔalˁlˁa 'God'

The interjection الله ʔalˁlˁa 'God' (usually uttered with vowel lengthening) expresses amazement, surprise, or admiration by the speaker.

الله وايد حلو فستانج!

ʔalˁlˁaa	waajəd	ħəlu	fəstaanə-ʧ!
God	so	nice	dress-your.f

'Wow, your dress is very nice!'

الله من وين اشتريتي ها الكفر؟

ʔaalˤlˤaa	mən	ween	əʃtəree-ti	ha-l-kavar?
God	from	where	refl.buy.perf-you-f	this-the-cover

'Wow, from where did you buy this cover?'

الله أنا بعد أبا اسكريم !

ʔalˤlˤaa	ʔana	baʕad	ʔa-ba	ʔaskəriim!
God	I	also	I-want.imperf	ice-cream

'Wow, I also want ice-cream!'

17.1.7 أووف *əoff,* افففف *uffff, and* أوهوو *əohooo*

أووف ʔoff, افففف ʔuffff, and أوهوو ʔoohooo indicate the speaker's feeling of annoyance, irritation, or vexation. The vowels and coda consonants may be lengthened for exaggeration.

أووففف/افففف ما أبا أطلع الحين!

ʔoofff/ʔuff	maa	ʔa-baa	ʔa-tˤlaʕ	əl-ħiin!
Oofff	not	I-want.imperf	I-hang.out.imperf	the-now

'I don't want to hang out now!'

أووفف ليش ما خبرتيني من زمان!

ʔoff	leeʃ	maa	xabbar-tii-ni	mən	zəmaan!
Ooff	why	not	caus.tell.perf-you.f-me	from	before

'Why didn't you tell me before!'

17.1.8 يع *jaʕ,* يخ *jax,* أفف *əof,* أوهوو *uhoo, and* أخييه *ʔaxxii*

These interjections signify feelings of disgust, revulsion, sickness, or nausea. أخييه ʔaxxii may also express a sense of disappointment and discontent.

يع صوته خايس!

jaʕ	sˤoot-ah xaajis!
eww	voice-hisbad

'He has a terrible voice!'

أخييه حطولنا مسؤول يديد!

ʔaxxiitʃ	ħatˤtˤ-oo-l-naa	masʔuul	jdiid!
eww	put.perf-they-for-us	manager	new

'They employed (for us) a new manager!'

أخييج شو بيسكته هذا الحين!

ʔaxxiitʃ	ʃuu	ba-j-sakt-a	haaða	əl-ħiin!
ouff	what	will-it-silence.imperf-him	this	the-now

'What will shut him up now!'

أوهوو الحين بتبدا تصارخ!

ʔoohoo	əl-ħiin	ba-tə-bda	t-sˤaarəx!
Ohoo	the-now	will-she-start.imperf	she-yell.imperf

'Oh no, now she will start yelling!'

17.1.9 ايه əajh and حووه ħooh

The interjection ايه əajh has two different uses—it calls for someone's attention or it expresses an encouraging remark to the hearer (cf. English 'c'mon'). For example:

اييه أحمد! تعال هني!

ʔeeh	ʔaħmad	ta-ʕal	hnii!
hey	Ahmad	you-come.imperf	here

'Hey Ahmad, come here!'

اييه يالله عاد، خلينا نطلع!

ʔeeh	jalˤlˤa-ʕaad	xallii-na	nə-tˤlaʕ!
hey	come-on	let.imp-us	we-go.out.imperf

'C'mon, let's go out!'

اييه ، أنا من متى أبا أسير المول !

ʔeeh,	ʔana	mən	məta	ʔa-baa	a-siir	əl-mool!
hey	I	from	time	I-want.imperf	I-go.imperf	the-mall

'Hey, since when have I been wanting to go to the mall?'

Another interjection with a similar function but uttered in a disrespectful manner is حووه ħooh.

حووه! وين تتحرا عمرك ساير؟

ħooh! ween tə-tħarra ʕəmr-ək saajər?

hooh where you-refl.think.imperf self-your part.go

'Hey! Where do you think you're going to?'

حووه! ليش ماتردين علي؟

ħooh leeʃ maa trədd-iin ʕalaj?

hooh why not answer.imperf-you.f me

'Hey! Why aren't you answering me back?'

حووه! اسمعني !

ħooh ʔəsmaʕ-ni!

hooh listen.imp-me

'Hey! Listen to me!'

17.1.10 هيييه *heeeeh*

هيييه heeeeh is often used by children to express happiness (by shouting) (cf. English 'hooray').

هيييه بنسير عند عمي اليوم !

heeeeh bə-n-siir ʕənd ʕamm-i əl-joom!

hooray will-we-go.imperf to uncle-my the-today

'Hooray! We are going to my uncle's house today!'

هيييه يبت درجة كامله!

heeeeh jəb-t daradʒa kaaml-a!

hooray get.perf-I mark full-f

'Hooray! I have got full marks!'

17.1.11 اشش *əʃʃ*, اص *esˤ*, and هش هش *hiʃʃ hiʃʃ*

اشش əʃʃ and اص esˤ are hissing sounds to ask the hearer to stop talking. They are therefore conative interjections.

اصص ولا كلمة !

ʔəsˤsˤ wa-la kəlma!
sh and-no word
'Sh, not a word!'

اشش لا تسوون حشره

ʔəʃʃ laa t-saww-uun ħaʃra.
sh don't you-make.imperf-you noise
'Sh, don't make any noise.'

The interjection هش هش hiʃʃ hiʃʃ is used to drive away birds or flies. For example:

هش هش قوم عني !

həʃʃ həʃʃ guum ʕann-i!
hsh hsh go.away from-me
'(To birds) Get away from me!'

17.1.12 ها ها ها *ha ha ha,* واا *waa,* وااك *waak, and* وييه *wiih*

ها ها ها ha ha ha is used to imitate the sound of laughter and express irony, sarcasm, or bitterness. Alternatively, واا waa, وااك waak, and وييه wiih express the same pragmatic function as ها ها ها ha ha ha.

ها ها ها محد قالج تاكلين حلاوتي!

ha ha ha ma-ħħad gaal-l-ətʃ t-aakl-iin ħalaaw-ti!
ha ha ha no-one say.perf-to-you.f you.f-eat.imperf-you.f candy-my
'No one told you to eat my candy!'

واا ماسولها سالفه!

waa maa saww-oo-l-ha saalfa!
waa not make.perf-they-for-her attention
'No one gave her attention!'

وا ما بتطلعين اليوم!

waa	maa	bə-tə-tˁləʕ-iin	əl-joom!
waa	not	will-you.f-go.out.imperf-you.f	the-today

'You won't go out today!'

واااك خسرتي الجيم!

waak	xəsar-tii	əl-geem!
waak	lose.perf-you-f	the-game

'You have lost the game!'

وييه سكّتوها!

wiih	sakkət-oo-haa!
wiih	caus.shut.up.perf-they-her

'They shut her up!'

17.1.13 كخ *kəx 'ugh'*

كخ kəx 'ugh' is an interjection used to signify disgust or horror, mainly about the behavior of babies.

كخ ما ياكلون جي!

kəx	maa	j-aakl-uun	ʧii!
ugh	not	they-eat.imperf-they	like.this

'Ugh, people don't eat like this!'

كخ لا تصك الحشرة!

kəx	laa	t-sˁək	əl-ħaʃara!
ugh	don't	you-touch.imperf	the-bug

'Ugh, don't touch the bug!'

17.1.14 وييه *weeh*

وييه weeh is used when the speaker is recalling something.

ويه ! وين حطيت البوك؟

weeh! ween ħatˤtˤ-eet əl-buuk?

oh where put.perf-I the-wallet

'Oh, where did I put the wallet?'

وييه! وين ولدي؟

weeeeeh! ween wəld-i?

oh where boy-my

'Oh, where is my son?'

وييييه ، نسيت أخبرك السالفه!

weeh, nəsee-t ʔa-xabbər-k əs-saalfa

oh forget.perf-I I-caus.tell.imperf-you the-story

'Oh, I forgot to tell you the story!'

وييييه ، منو بيّنا الحين؟

weeh, mnuu bə-j-jii-na əl-ħiin

oh who will-he-come.imperf-us the-now

'Oh, who will come to us now?'

17.1.15 أفاا ʔafaa

أفاا ʔafaa expresses either sorrow or regret for the hearer, or disappointment or frustration with the hearer.

أفاا ما توقعت تقول جي!

ʔaffaa maa t-waqqaʕ-t ət-guul ʧii!

oh not refl-caus.expect.perf-I you-say.imperf like.this

'Oh, I didn't expect you to say this!'

أفاا كيف ما خبرتوني!

ʔaffaa keef maa xabbar-tuu-ni!

oh how not caus.tell.perf-you.pl-me

'Oh, how come you didn't tell me!'

أفاا ليش ما صمت اليوم؟

ʔaffaa	leeʃ	maa	sˤəm-t	əl-joom?
oh	why	not	fast.perf-you	the-today

'Oh, why didn't you fast today?'

17.2 Borrowed interjections

There are a few English-origin interjections used by younger people. They include:

برافوو! حصلتي الميدالية الذهبية !

bravoo!	ħasˤsˤal-ti	əl-miidaalijja	əð-ðahabijj-a!
bravo	caus.get.perf-you.f	the-medal	the-golden-f

'Bravo! you have got the gold medal!'

اوبس! كبيت العصير!

ʔobs!	ʧabb-eet	əl-ʕasˤiir!
oops	spill.perf-I	the-juice

'Oops! I spilled the juice!'

واو! كان الفلم رهيب!

waaw!	kaan	əl-fələm	rahiib!
wow	be.perf-it	the-movie	awesome

'Wow! The movie was awesome!'

واو! ها اللون حلو!

waaw!	ha-l-loon	ħəlu!
wow	this-the-color	nice

'Wow! This color is nice!'

يسس فزت !

jass	fəz-t!
yes	win.perf-I

'Yes! I won!'

17.3 Secondary interjections

Secondary interjections always stem from lexical sources, and they may express the literal (i.e. lexical) meaning and pragmatic meaning simultaneously. The grammatical category of the lexical source of secondary interjection varies, including verbs (e.g. 'help!'), nouns (e.g. 'fire!'), and adjectives (e.g. 'well'). Some secondary interjections contain an internal grammatical structure (e.g. 'my goodness' and 'excuse me') (Table 17.2). In Emirati Arabic, some secondary interjections stem from sacred expressions, e.g. الله ʔalˤlˤaaaa 'God!' and يالله jaʔalˤah 'my God!' Some consist of more than one word, e.g. عيب عليك ʕeeb ʕalək 'shame on you!' and لو سمحت loo səmaħt 'excuse me.' Based on the influence of Western culture, it is common to use English interjections such as سوري soori 'sorry' and شيت ʃət 'shit!'

الحمدالله يبت فل مارك في الامتحان

əl-ħamd-l-əlah	jəb-t	ful	maark	f	əl-əmtəħaan.
the-praise.to.God	bring.perf-I	full	mark	in	the-test

'Thank God! I got full marks in the test.'

انزين شو بعد قالك الريال

ənzeen	ʃuu	baʕad	gall-l-ək	ər-rajjaal?
okay	what	else	tell.perf-he-to-you	the-man

'Okay, what else (has) the man told you?'

عيب عليك لا تتكلم عن الريال جيه

ʕeeb	ʕal-eek	la	tə-t-kallam	ʕan	ər-rajjaal	ʧiih.
shame	on-you	don't	you-refl-caus.talk.imperf	about	the-man	like.that

'Shame on you! Don't you talk about the man like that.'

خيبه دعمت سيارة أبويه

xeebah	dəʕam-t	sajjara-t	ʔubuu-jah.
omg	bang.perf-I	car-f	father-my

'OMG! I crashed in my father's car.'

Table 17.2 Secondary interjections

الله	ʔalˤlˤaaaa/	'God!'	انزين	ənzeen	'Okay'
	ʔaalˤlˤa		يالله	jaʔalˤlˤaah	'My God!'
والله	walˤlˤah	'Really!'	عيب عليك	ʕeeb ʕaleek	'Shame on you!'
دخيلك	daxiilək	'Please!'	الحمدلله	əl-ħamdəlllaah	'Thank God!'
شكرا	ʃəkran	'Thank you'	لو سمحت	loo səmaħt	'Excuse me' (if you allow)
باي	bai	'Bye'	سوري	soori	'Sorry'
جب	ʧabb	'Shut up!'	خيبه	xeebah	'Oh my God!'
فك	fak	'Fuck!'	حريج	ħriiʤ	'Fire!'
تعال	taʕaal	'Hey!' (come)	شيت	ʃeet	'Shit!'

أ: ماحصلت أبوي في الصاله

maa	ħasˤsˤalˤ-t	ʔubuu-j	f-əsˤ-sˤaalˤa.
not	caus.find.perf-I	father-my	in-the-living.room

A: 'I didn't find my father in the living room.'

ب: و الله؟

walˤlˤah?

B: 'Really?'

أ: هيه

heeh

A: 'Yes!'

دخيلك لا تروح الحين!

daxiilək	laa	truuħ	əl-ħiin!
please	don't	leave	the-now

'Please don't leave now!'

تعال شفيك كنت معصب الصبح؟

taʕaal	ʃ-fii-k	kənt	mʕasˤsˤəb	əsˤ-sˤəbħ?
come	what-in-you	be.perf-you	part.angry	the-morning

'Hey, why were you angry this morning?'

Further reading

See Ameka (1992a, 1992b) and Wierzbicka (1992) for a semantic study of interjection as a class of linguistic items.

Chapter 18

Speech conventions

Emirati Arabic has a plethora of expressions which express various pragmatic functions such as politeness, felicitation, and apology, or express honorific forms of address for the speaker and the hearer. While some of these expressions are common to other Arabic dialects, Emirati Arabic possesses some unique terms of address and examples of 'trendy' language.

18.1 Politeness

Emirati Arabic has several politeness conventions to express gratitude, guilt, sociability, hospitality, felicitation, respect, and benevolence, to ask for permission, make a request, or even initiate a conversation. A common politeness expression is لو سمحت law səmaħt 'excuse me' (Chapter 17), which is used to initiate a question (Chapter 13) by the speaker to a stranger.

لو سمحت، ممكن/عادي . . . .

law	səmaħ-t	mumkən	/ʕaadi. . .
if	allow.perf-you	may	can

'Excuse me, may/can I. . . ?'

To ask for directions to the mall, the conversation may start as follows:

لو سمحت ، ممكن تقول لي كيف أروح ياس مول ؟

law	səmaħ-t,	mumkən	t-guul-l-i	keef
ʔa-ruuħ		jaas	mool?	
if	allow.perf-you	can	you-tell.imperf-to-me	how
I-go.imperf		Yas	mall	

'Excuse me, can you tell me how to go to Yas Mall?'

The question can be further inferred as a speech act of request.

لو سمحتوا، ممكن تخفون صوتكم شوي؟

law səmaħ-tuu mumkən t-xəff-uun
sˤoot-kum ʃwaj?
if allow.perf-you.pl can you-lower.imperf-you
voice-your.pl little
'Excuse me, can you lower your voice please?'

لو سمحتي، ممكن تناوليني القلم؟

law səmaħ-ti mumkən t-naawl-ii-ni əl-galam?
if allow.perf-you.f can you.f-give.imperf-you.f-me the-pen
'Excuse me, can you pass me the pen?'

لو سمحت، عادي تبند الدريشة؟

law səmaħ-t ʕaadi t-bannəd əd-dəriiʃa?
if allow.perf-you can you-caus.close.imperf the-window
'Excuse me, can you close the window?'

18.1.1 Requests

In addition to لو سمحت law səmaħt 'excuse me,' ما عليك أمر maa ʕaleek ʔamər 'not an order on you' may also express a request to the hearer.

ما عليك أمر ممكن تعطيني الورقة؟

maa ʕal-eek ʔamər mumkən ta-ʕtˤiin-ni əl-wərga.
not on-you order can you-give.imperf-me the-paper
'Please can you give me the paper?'

ما عليك أمر ممكن تصك الباب وراك؟

maa ʕalee-k ʔamər mumkən t-sˤəkk əl-baab waraa-k?
not on-you order can you-close.imperf the-door behind-you
'Please can you close the door behind you?'

It is a semi-fixed expression in that it may be suffixed by different personal pronouns, e.g. the second-person singular feminine ج- -ʧ.

ما عليج أمر ممكن تعطينها الملف؟

maa ʕalee-ʧ ʔamər mumkən ta-ʕtˁ-iin-ha əl-malaf?
not on-you.f order can you.f-give.imperf-you.f-her the-file
'Please can you give her the file?'

ما عليج أمر ممكن توصفيلي المكان؟

maa ʕalee-tʃ ʔamər mumkən tə-wsˁəf-ii-l-i əl-məkaan?
not on-you.f order can you.f-describe.imperf-you.f-for-me the-place
'Please can you describe the place for me?'

Another way to express a request is the sacred expression الله يخلي ʔalˁlˁah jxalli (with different personal pronoun suffixes) 'May God preserve you.'

الله يخليك ودنا المول

ʔalˁlˁah j-xallii-k wad-na əl-mool.
God he-preserve.imperf-you drive.imp-us the-mall
'May God preserve you, drive us to the mall.'

الله يخليكم ذاكروا عدل

ʔalˁlˁah j-xallii-kum ðaakr-u ʕadəl.
God he-preserve.imperf-you.pl study.imp-you.pl well
'May God preserve you, study well.'

الله يخليج سوييلي كوفي وياج

ʔalˁlˁah j-xallii-ʧ saww-ii-l-i koofi wəjjaa-ʧ.
God he-preserve.imperf-you.f make.imp-you.f-for-me coffee with-you.f
'May God preserve you, make a coffee for me as well.'

Another sacred expression which bears the same pragmatic function is the following:

الله لا يهينك

ʔalˁlˁah laa j-hiin-ək.
God not he-humiliate.imperf-you
'May God preserve you from any humiliation.' (= if you don't mind)

18.1.2 *Responsiveness*

Answering requests politely is achieved through expressions such as:

ان شاء الله	حاضر
ʔənʃaalˤlˤah	ħaaðˤər
if-willed-God	present
'God willing, it will be done.'	'I am here (for you).'

فالشوفة	لبيه
fəʃ-ʃoofah	labbeeh
in-the-support	'Here I am at your service.'
'Here to help or support.'	

While these expressions give an impression of seniority, they are mainly used in familial situations to express respect and intimacy in responses. They may additionally express obedience in cases of seniority.

To respond in informal contexts, which involve an intimate relationship, the following can be used:

من عيوني	على هالخشم	على راسي
mən ʕəj-uun-ii	ʕalaa ha-l-xaʃəm	ʕalaa raas-i
from eye-pl-my	on this-the-nose	on head-my
'from my eyes'	'On this nose (mainly used by men)'	'On my head'

The following short conversation between an Emirati woman and her neighbor is an example:

اذا ما بنعبل عليكم، علمونا وصفة الهريس؟

ʔiða maa bə-n-ʕabbəl ʕalee-kum, ʕalm-uun-na wasfat əl-həriis.

if not will-we-burden.imperf-you on-you.pl teach.imp-you-us recipe the-hariis

'If it is not a burden on you, teach us the recipe for haris.'

إن شا الله، من العين

ən-ʃaa-lˤlˤah, mən-əl-ʕeen.

if-willed-God from-the-eye

'God willing, we will be glad to.'

Another polite expression, mainly used as a response, is حاضرين للطيبين ħaað^{ʕ}riin ləlt^{ʕ}t^{ʕ}ajbiin (cf. English 'you are welcome').

حاضرين للطيبين

ħaað^{ʕ}r-iin	lə-t^{ʕ}-t^{ʕ}ajb-iin.
part.present-pl	for-the-kind.people-pl

A: 'I/We will be glad to do this.' (lit. 'We are here for the kind people.')

For example it can be used in the following conversation:

أ: ما بتعزمنا على بيتك؟

maa	ba-t-əʕzəm-na	ʕala	beet-kum?
not	will-you-invite.imperf-us	to	house-your.pl

A: 'Won't you invite us to your house?'

ب: البيت بيتكم

əl-beet	beet-kum.
the-house	house-your.pl

B: 'The house is your house.'

أ: مشكور

ma-ʃkuur.
part-pass.thank
A: 'Thank you.' (lit. You are thanked.)

ب: حاضرين للطيبين

ħaað^{ʕ}r-iin	lə-t^{ʕ}-t^{ʕ}ajb-iin.
part.present-pl	for-the-kind.people-pl

B: 'I/We will be glad to do this.'

18.1.3 Appreciation

Appreciation (Table 18.1) is usually expressed by sacred expressions. They include:

ما قصّرت

maa	gas^{ʕ}s^{ʕ}ar-t.
not	underdo.perf-you

'You have done a lot for me.'

Table 18.1 Conventional expressions of appreciation

ما قصّرت	maa gasˤsˤart	'You have done a lot for me'
يزاك الله خير	jzaak ʔalˤlˤah xeer	'May God reward you well'
بارك الله فيك	baarak ʔalˤlˤah fii-k	'May God bless you'
بيض الله ويهك	bajjaðˤ ʔalˤlˤah wajhək	'May God whiten/ lighten your face'
كثر الله خيرك	kaθθar ʔalˤlˤah xeerək	'May God increase your blessings'
الحمدلله	əlħamdləllah	'Praise to God'

يزاك الله خير

jzaa-k ʔalˤlˤah xeer.

reward.perf-he-you God goodness

lit. 'May God reward you good.'

بارك الله فيك

baar-ak ʔalˤlˤah fii-k.

bless.perf-he-you God in-you

'May God bless you.'

بيض الله ويهك

bajjaðˤ ʔalˤlˤah wajh-ək.

whiten.perf-he God face-your

lit. 'May God whiten/lighten your face.'

كثر الله خيرك

kaθθar ʔalˤlˤah xeerə-k.

caus.increase.perf-he God blessing-your

lit. 'May God increase your blessings.'

The most common expression is to express gratitude and thankfulness to God.

الحمدلله

əl-ħamd-li-llah.

the-praise-to-God

lit. 'Praise to God.'

This expression of appreciation is further interpreted as an indirect answer to the hearer's queries.

أ :شو الأخبار؟

ʃuu əl-ʔaxbaar?

what the-news

A: 'What's the news?'

ب: الحمدلله كل شي بخير

əl-ħəmd-əl-llaah kəl ʃaj b-xeer.

the-praise-to-God every thing with-goodness

B: 'Praise to God, everything is good.'

أ :شو صحتك اليوم؟

ʃuu sˤaħt-ək əl-joom?

what health-your the-today

A: 'How is your health today?'

ب: الحمدلله أحسن

əl-ħəmd-əl-llaah ʔaħsan.

the-praise-to-God better

B: 'Praise to God, (it's getting) better.'

أ :خلصت أكل؟

xalˤlˤasˤ-t ʔakəl?

finish.perf-you eating

A: 'Have you finished eating?'

ب: الحمدلله هيه خلصت

əl-ħəmd-əl-llaah heeh xalˤlˤasˤ-t.

the-praise-to-God yes finish.perf-I

B: 'Praise to God, yes, I finished.'

18.1.4 *Condolences*

Expressions of condolence always make reference to God.

البقاء لله

əl-baqaaʔ	lə-llaah.
the-immortality	to-God

lit. 'Immortality belongs to God.'

عظّم الله أجركم

ʕaðˤðˤam	ʔalˤlˤaah	ʔadʒər-kum.
glorify.perf-he	God	reward-your.pl

lit. 'May God glorify your reward.'

جبر الله خاطرك

dʒəbar	ʔalˤlˤaah	xaatˤr-ək.
heal.perf-he	God	heart-your

'May God heal your heart.'

الله يصبركم

ʔalˤlˤah	j-sˤabbər-kum.
God	he-caus.patience-you.pl

'May God grant you patience.'

The person can respond by saying:

خلّاف الله

xallaaf	ʔalˤlˤah.
compensator	Allah

'God will compensate.'

إنا لله و إنا إليه راجعون

ʔinna	lə-llaah	wa	ʔinna	ʔilaj-hi	raadʒiʕ-uun.
we	to-God	and	we	to-him	returning-pl

'We all belong to God, and to him we shall return.' (from Quran)

البركة فيكم
əl-əbrəka fii-kum.
the-blessing in-your.pl
'The blessing is with you.' (mainly used for family members)

18.1.5 *Sympathy*

To express sympathy and compassion to the hearer (cf. English 'good luck'), speakers use the following:

الله يعين
ʔalˤlˤah j-ʕiin.
God he-aid.imperf
'God is the aider.'

الله يكون في العون
ʔalˤlˤah j-kuun f-əl-ʕoon.
God he-be.imperf in-the-aid
'May God be the aider.'

الله معاكم
ʔalˤlˤah maʕaa-kum.
God with-you.pl
'God be with you.'

الله يحفظك
ʔalˤlˤah jə-ħfaðˤ-k.
God he-protect.imperf-you
'May God protect you.'

الله فوق
ʔalˤlˤah foog.
God up
lit. God is up there. (i.e. watching over everyone)

To express sympathy to people suffering from disgrace, humiliation, or hard times such as accidents or medical conditions, the following may be used:

ما تشوف شر
maa ətʃuuf ʃar.
neg you-see.imperf harm
'May you never experience any harm.'

سلامات
salaam-aat.
peace-f.pl
'Get well soon.'

تستاهلين السلامة
tə-staahl-een əs-salaama.
you.f-deserve.imperf-you.f the-safety
'You deserve being well.'

أجر وعافية
ʔadʒər w ʕaafja.
reward and well.being
'May you get well soon.' (lit. May you get reward and well-being.)

لا باس عليك
laa baas ʕalee-k.
no harm on-you
'No harm on you.'

18.1.6 *Apology*

The following is a list of common expressions of apology (see also Chapter 17):

السموحة
əs-səmuuħa
the-forgiveness
'Forgive me.'

أنا آسف
ʔanaa ʔaasəf
I sorry
'I am sorry.'

حقك علي
ħagg-ək ʕala-j
right-your on-me
'Your right is on me.'

سامحيني
samħ-ii-ni
forgive.imp-you.f-me
'Forgive me.'

Acceptance of apologies can be expressed with the following:

مسموح
ma-smuuħ
pass-forgive.perf
'You are forgiven.'

الله يسامحك
ʔalˤlˤah jə-saaməħ-k
God he-forgive.imperf-you
'May God forgive you.'

حصل خير
ħasˤal xeer
happen.perf-it good
'It's ok.'

ولا يهمّك
wala j-həmmə-k
never it-matter.imperf-you
'It doesn't matter.'

الأمور طيبة
əl-ʔəmuur tˤajb-a
the-things good-f
'Things are ok.'

18.1.7 *Hospitality*

Emirati hosts may express hospitality to their guests by uttering the following expressions (cf. English 'welcome'):

يا مرحبا الساع

jaa	marħəba	əs-saaʕ.
calling-expression	welcome	the-part.seek

lit. This is a happy moment. (You are welcome in this hour or this is a good hour.)

حياكم الله

ħajjaa-kum	ʔalˤlˤah.
greet.imperf-you.pl	God

'May God bless you.' (for greeting)

أسفرت وأنورت

ʔasfar-at	w	ʔanwar-at.
lighten.perf-it.f	and	brighten.perf-it.f

lit. 'Your presence is illuminating.'

نوّرتونا

nawwar-tuu-na.

brighten.perf-you.pl-us

'You blessed us with your presence.'

البيت بيتكم

əl-beet	beet-kum.
the-house	house-your

'Make yourself at home.' (lit. This house is yours.)

In reciprocity, the guest can reply with the following:

أكرمكم الله

ʔakram-kum	ʔalˤlˤah.
bless.imperf-he-you	God

'May God bless you.'

بيتٍ عامر

beetən ʕaamər.

house full.of.blessings

'(May God keep) your house always full of blessings.'

The following short conversation is always heard after a home visit:

وبيتكم عامر

w beet-kum ʕaamər.

and house-your blessed

'And your house is blessed.'

عامر بوجودكم

ʕaamər bə-wdʒuud-kum.

blessed by-presence-your

'I am blessed by your presence.'

18.1.8 Felicitations and wishes

A number of conventional expressions are used for occasions such as birthdays, graduations, weddings, travels, and religious occasions such as Ramadan, Umrah, Eid, and Hajj or 'pilgrimage.'

The most common expression of general felicitations is مبروك mabruuk 'congratulations/blesses.' In addition, for congratulatory remarks to new parents, the following may be used:

الحمدلله ع/على السلامة

əl-ħəmd-əl-llah ʕa(la) s-salaama.

the-thanks-to-God on the-safety

'Thanks to God for your health.'

مبروك ما ياكم

mabruuk maa jaa-kum.

congratulations what come.perf-you.pl

'Congratulations on the newborn.' (lit. 'what just came to you')

يتربا في عزكم

jə-t-rabba f ʕəz-kum.
he-refl-raise.imperf on blessing-your.pl
'May he/she grow up under your blessings.'

Emirati Arabic has two words for newborns based on their gender.

مبروك الطارش/الحاسر

mabruuk ətˤ-tˤaarəʃ /əl-ħaasər.
congratulations the-baby.boy /the-baby.girl
'Congratulations on the baby boy/girl.'

The person then replies:

إن شاء الله الفال لك

ʔənʃaalˤlˤah əl-faal l-ək.
if.willed.God the-good.omen to-your
'God willing, the good omen is yours.'

بالبركة عليكم الصّغيرون

bə-lə-brəka ʕalee-kum əsˤ-sˤəɣajruun.
with-the-blessing on-you.pl the-little.one
'Congratulations on the little one.'

There are also felicitations for travelers. The following two conversations are typical examples:

الحمدلله على السلامة

əl-ħəmd-əl-llah ʕa s-salaama.
the-thanks-to-God for the-safety
'Thank God for your safety.'

الله يسلمك

ʔalˤlˤah j-salləm-k.
God he-caus.safeguard.imperf-you
'May God keep you safe.'

نوّرت البلاد

nawwar-t lə-blaad.
caus.lighten.perf-f the-country
'You illuminated the country (by your presence).'

بوجودك/النور نورك

bə-wdʒuud-ək /ən-nuur nuur-ək.
by-presence-your/the-light light-your
'By your presence/the light is yours.'

During the first day of Ramadan, the fasting month for Muslims, people use the following expressions:

مبروك عليكم الشهر

mabruuk ʕalee-kum əʃ-ʃahar.
congratulations for-you the-month
'Congratulations for this month.'

On Ramadan nights, and specifically after breaking their fasts, these expressions are used:

تقبل الله طاعتكم

ta-qabbal ʔalˁlˁaa tˁaaʕa-at-kum.
refl-accept.perf-he God obedience-pl-your.pl
'May God reward you for your obedience.'

تقبل الله صيامكم

ta-qabbal ʔalˁlˁaa sˁjaam-kum.
refl-accept.perf-he God fasting-your.pl
'May God accept your fasting.'

Several expressions of felicitation are used on the occasion of Eid, including:

هنيتوا ببركة العيد

hənee-tu bə-brəka-t əl-ʕiid.
congratulation-pl the-blessing-f the-Eid
'Congratulations on the blessing of Eid.'

كل عام وإنتوا بخير

kəl-ʕaam w-əntu b-xeer.
every-year and-you with-goodness
'May you be well every year.'

The addressee will always answer with one of the following:

و إنتوا بخير وصحة و سلامة

w-əntu b-xeer w sʕəħħ-a w salaam-a.
and-you with-goodness and health-f and good.health-f
'And may you be well, in good health and safe every year.'

عيدكم مبارك

ʕiid-kum mbaarak.
Eid-you.pl blessed
'Wish you a blessed Eid.'

عساكم من العايدين والسالمين

ʕasaa-kum mən əl-ʕajd-iin w ə-ssaalm-iin.
wish.imp-you.pl from the-returner-pl and the-healthy.people-pl
'Wish you all celebrate it again and in good health.'

عساكم من عواده

ʕasaa-kum mən ʕawwaad-a.
wish.imp-you from returner.pl-it
'I wish you many returns on this occasion.'

ينعاد علينا وعليكم بالخير

jə-nʕaad ʕalee-na w ʕalee-kum b-əl-xeer.
it-pass.return.imperf on-us and on-you.pl with-the-goodness
'May we and you celebrate it again with goodness.'

من العايدين و السالمين

mən əl-ʕaajd-iin w ə-ssaalm-iin.
from the-part.return-pl and the-healthy.people-pl
'May you celebrate it again and in good health.'

من الفايزين و الغانمين

mən	əl-faajz-iin	w	əl-ɣaanm-iin.
from	the-part.win-pl	and	the-part.rich-pl

'May you be from the winners and wealthy people (in the afterlife/in rewards).'

Some expressions are used to welcome pilgrims back home. For example:

حج مبرور

ħadʒ	ma-bruur.
pilgrimage	pass-righteous

'Congratulations on the pilgrimage.'

تقبل الله طاعتكم

ta-qabbal	ʔalˤlˤaah	tˤaaʕa-t-kum.
refl-accept.perf-he	God	obedience-f-your.pl

'May God accept your obedience.'

مبروك بيتٍ زرتوه

mabruuk	beetən	zərt-uuh.
congratulations	house	visit.perf-you.pl

'Congratulations on visiting the holy city of Mecca.'

On the occasion of marriage, in addition to مبروك mabruuk 'congratulations,' one can always say:

الله يتمم على خير

ʔalˤlˤah	j-tammən	ʕala	xeer.
God	he-make.complete.imperf	on	goodness

'May it be brought to a happy end.'

منك المال و منها العيال

mənn-ək	əl-maal	w	mən-ha	lə-ʕjaal.
from-you	the-expenses	and	from-her	the-children

'Hopefully this marriage brings you wealth and children.'

مبروك ما دبرتوا

mabruuk maa dabbar-tu.
congratulations what caus.plan.perf-you.pl
'Congratulations on your marriage.'

18.2 Terms of address

Emirati Arabic has an intricate system of terms of address. The terms vary according to the relationship between the speaker and the addressee, as well as the status and age of the addressee.

شيخ əʃʃeex 'Sheikh'

الشيخ əʃʃeex 'Sheikh' is the head of the tribe or the ruler of any of the Emirates.

الشيخ سلطان القاسمي تكلم اليوم في الإذاعة

əʃ-ʃeex səltˤaan əl-qaasəmi t-kallam əl-joom fi-l-ʔiðaaʕa.
the-Sheikh sultan Al-Qassemi he-talk.imperf the-today on-the-radio
'Sheikh Sultan Al-Qassemi spoke on the radio today.'

الشيخ əʃʃeex 'Sheikh' (or الشيخة əʃʃeexa 'Sheikha) is also used to address an unknown adult.

الشيخة عندنا عرض اليوم على العطور

əʃ-ʃeexa ʕəndə-na ʕarðˤ əl-joom ʕala əl-ʕətˤuur.
the-sheikha with-us promotion the-today on the-perfume.pl
'Sheikha, we have a promotion on perfumes today.'

الشيخ əʃʃeex is used in forming honorific terms such as:

فضيلة الشيخ

faðˤiil-at əʃ-ʃeex
honor-f the-Sheikh
'His Honor'

سماحة الشيخ

samaaħ-at əʃ-ʃeex
eminence-f the-sheikh
'His Eminence' (for religious men)

There are also honorific terms to address statesmen, such as:

			Addressees
سموّ	səmuw	'His/Her Highness'	country leaders, royal family members
معالي	maʕaali	'His/Her Highness'	non-royal ministers
سعادة	saʕaadat	'His/Her Excellency'	top officials

سعادة مدير الجامعة زار المكتبة اليوم

saʕaada-t mudiir əl-dʒaamʕa zaar əl-maktəba əl-joom.
excellency-f headmaster the-university visit.perf-he the-library today
'His Excellency the University Chancellor visited the library today.'

The following expression is commonly used to address the aforementioned people and show utmost respect to anyone. It is not uncommon for this expression to be heard between sons and parents, employees and supervisors, or even friends.

طال عمرك

tˁaal ʕəmr-ək.
lengthen.perf-it age-your
'May you live long.'

18.3 General honorific terms

18.3.1 *Honorifics*

Emirati Arabic uses general honorific and kinship terms (Section 18.3.2) to address non-family members for honorific purposes.

الحاي/الوالد/عمي تحتاي مساعدة؟

əl-ħaaj/əl-waaləd/ʕam-mi tə-ħtaaj musaaʕad-a.
pilgrim/father/uncle-my you-need.imperf help-f
lit. 'Pilgrim/Father/Uncle, do you need any help?'

If the addressee is an adult female who is unfamiliar to and older than the speaker, then she will be addressed by these terms:

في شو أقدر أساعدج، الوالده/الحايّة/خالوه ؟

f ʃuu ʔa-gdar ʔa-saaʕdə-ʧ əl-waalda /əl-ħaajj-a /xaalˤoo-h?

on what I-able.imperf I-help.imperf-you the-mother /the-pilgrim-f /aunt-f

'How can I help you, mother/pilgrim/aunt?'

However, if the addressee is almost the same age as the speaker he will be addressed by one of the terms in Table 18.2.

Table 18.2 Terms of honorifics

أخوي	ʔəxuuj	'my brother'	(same status)
ولدي	wəldi	'my son'	(senior addressing young people)
بابا	baabaa	'dad'	(senior addressing young people)
حبيبي	ħabiibi	'my love'	(senior addressing young people, between people with an intimate relation)
حبي	ħubbi	'my love'	(between people with an intimate relation)
حياتي	ħajaati	'my life'	(between people with an intimate relation)
عمري	ʕəmri	'my life'	(between people with an intimate relation)
عيوني	ʕjuuni	'my eyes'	(between people with an intimate relation)
قلبي	galˤbi	'my heart'	(between people with an intimate relation)
غناتي	ɣanaati	'my everything'	(between people with an intimate relation)
ولد العم	wəld əl-ʕam	'male cousin' (uncle's son)	(between tribal members)
بنت العم	bənt əl-ʕam	'female cousin' (uncle's daughter)	(between tribal members)

18.3.2 *Kinship terms*

Kinship terms are categorized in terms of consanguinity (i.e. blood relationship) (Table 18.3). This is necessary because polygamy is not uncommon in the Arab world. There are also systems of kinship terms through marriage (Table 18.4), for step-siblings and step-parents (Table 18.5), and for foster siblings and parents (Table 18.6).

Table 18.3 Kinship terms for consanguineous family members

أبويا/بابا	ʔəbuuja/baabaa	'(my) father'
أمي/أُمايا/ماما/ أماه	ʔummi/ʔəmmaaja/ maamaa/ʔəmmaah	'(my) mother'
ولد	wəld	'son'
بنت	bənt	'daughter'
أخوي	ʔuxuui	'brother'
الرضيعة	ərrəðˤiiʕa	'sister' (used by brothers with non-family members)
أختي	ʔəxti	'sister'
يدي/أبوي العود	jaddi/ʔubuujə əlʕood	'my grandfather'
أمي العودة/العودة	ʔummi əlʕoodəh/ əlʕoodəh	'my grandmother'
عمه/عموه/عموتي	ʕammah/ʕammooh/ ʕammooti	'aunt' (father's sister)
خال	xaal	'uncle' (mother's brother)
خالة	xaalah/xaalti	'aunt' (mother's sister)
حفيد/ولد الولد/ ولد البنت	ħəfiid/wəld əlwəlad/ wəld əlbənt	'grandson/son's son/ daughter's son'
حفيدة/بنت الولد/بنت البنت	ħəfiida/bənt əlwəlad/ bent əlbənt	'granddaughter/son's daughter/daughter's daughter'
ولد العم	wəld əlʕamm	'cousin' (paternal uncle's son)
بنت العم	bənt əlʕamm	'cousin' (paternal uncle's daughter)

(*Continued*)

Table 18.3 (Continued)

ولد الخال	wəld əlxaal	'cousin' (maternal uncle's son)
بنت الخال	bənt əlxaal	'cousin' (maternal uncle's daughter)
ولد الأخ	wəld əlʔaxx	'nephew' (brother's son)
ولد الإخت	wəld əlʔəxt	'nephew' (sister's son)
بنت الأخ	bənt əlʔaxx	'niece' (brother's daughter)
بنت الأخت	bənt əlʔəxt	'niece' (sister's daughter)

Table 18.4 Kinship terms through marriage

زوي/زوج/رّيال/ريل	zooj/zoodʒ/rajjaal/ rajəl	'husband'
زويه/زوجة/حرمه	zoojah/zoodʒa/ħərma	'wife'
الطارش	ətˤtˤaarəʃ	'newborn boy'
الحاسر	əlħaasər	'newborn girl'
عمة	ʕamma	'mother-in-law'
عم	ʕamm	'father-in-law'
زوج/ ريل/ زوي نسيب /الأخت	zooj/rajəl/zoodʒ əlʔəxt/nəsiib	'brother-in-law' (sister's husband)
الأخ زوجة/زوية	zoojat/zoodʒat əlʔax	'sister-in-law' (brother's wife)
الزوجة //الزوي أخ الرّيال/نسيب	ʔax əzzooj/əzzoodʒ/ ərrajəl/nsiib	'brother-in-law' (husband's brother)
الزوي/أخت الرّيال	ʔəxt əzzooj/ərrajjaal	'sister-in-law' (husband's sister)
أخ الزوجة-الحرمة-الزوج نسيب	ʔəx əzzoojah/ əlħərma/əzzoodʒ nəsiib	'brother-in-law' (wife's brother)
الحرمه/أخت الزوج	əxt əzzoojah/ əlħermah	'sister-in-law' (wife's sister)
النسيب/العضيد	əlʕəðˤiid/ənnəsiib	'brother-in-law' (wife's sister's husband)

ريل البنت/النسيب	rajəl əlbənt/ənnəsiib	'son-in-law' (daughter's husband)
حرمة الولد	ħərmat əlwəlad	'daughter-in-law' (son's wife)
حرمة العم	ħərmat əlʕamm	'paternal uncle's wife'
حرمة الخال	ħərmat əlxaalˁ	'maternal uncle's wife'
ريل العمة	rajəl əlʕamma	'paternal aunt's husband'
ريل الخالة	rajəl əlxaalah	'maternal aunt's husband'

Table 18.5 Kinship terms for step-siblings and step-parents

ريل الأم/عم	rajəl əlʔum/ʕamm	'stepfather'
حرمة الأب	ħərmat əlʔab	'stepmother'
أخ من الأب	ʔax mən əlʔab	'half-brother' (shared father)
أخ من الأم	ʔax mən əlʔuom	'half-brother' (shared mother)
أخت من الأب	ʔəxt mən əlʔab	'half-sister' (shared father)
أخت من الأم	ʔəxt mən əlʔum	'half-sister' (shared mother)

Table 18.6 Kinship terms for foster siblings and parents (with breast-feeding)

أخ من الرضاعة	ʔax mən ərrəðˁaaʕa	'foster brother'
أخت من الرضاعة	ʔəxt mən ərrəðˁaaʕa	'foster sister'
أم من الرضاعة	ʔum mən ərrəðˁaaʕa	'foster mother'

18.4 Trendy language

There are many new, widely used expressions in Emirati society that are considered as trendy and colloquial (Table 18.7). Some expressions function as interjections (Chapter 17), while others are code-switching expressions adopted from English.

Table 18.7 Trendy expressions

كشخة	kaʃxa	'fancy/elegant'
أونه	ʔawanna	'Really!'
أويه	ʔawweeh	'Oh no!'
خيبة	xeebah	'Damn!'
يا ريال	jaa rajjaal	'Unbelievable!' (lit. 'Oh man!')
يالله	jaa ʔalˤlˤaah	'Oh God!'
أوكيه	ʔookeeh	'Okay!'
تمام	tamaam	'Okay!'
بيبي	beebi	'baby'
وايبي	waaji	'Oh!' (describing s.th cute)
ياليل	jaa leel	'Oh Lord!'
يا سلاام	jaa salaam	'Oh really?'
لا والله	la walˤlˤah	'Seriously?'
واو	waaw	'Wow!'
أوو أمم جيي	ʔoo əmm dʒii	'Omg!'
فون	foon	'phone'
سناب	snaab	'snap' (as in Snapchat)
منشن	mənʃən	'mention'
نود	nuud	'nude'
مات	maat	'matte' (lipstick)
تويته	twiitah	'tweet'
طر/طرطريشن	tˤar/tˤartˤəreeʃən	'cool/nice'
بلّك	ballək	'block' (as a verb)
سيريس	siirjəs	'serious' (as an adjective)
كلاس	klaas	'class' (in schools)
باي ذا وي	baj ðaa weej	'by the way'
كويز	kwiz	'quiz'
بيرفيكت	beerfekt	'Perfect!'
عسول	ʕassuul	'cute and nice' (lit. 'like honey')
كياته-كتاته/كيوت	kataatah/kəjaatah	'cute'
المهم	əlmuhəm	'Anyway.'
اني وييز	ʔənii weejz	'Anyway.'

These trendy words and expressions have become nativized in Emirati Arabic. For instance, some nouns (Section 5.1) may be affixed by other Emirati Arabic suffixes and need to observe the word order of Emirati Arabic. Trendy verbs (Section 5.2) may exhibit a full list of declensions, whereas adjectives may sub-categorize particular prepositions (Section 5.5).

اليوم قريت تويته اتضحك

əl-joom	garee-t	twiita	eðˁ-ðˁaħħək.
the-today	read.perf-I	tweet	refl-caus.laugh.imperf

'Today I read a funny tweet.'

سايره الكلاس

saajr-a	lə-klaas.
part.go-f	the-class

'I am going to class.'

ببلّك هالأكاونت

b-a-ballək	ha-l-ʔakkaawnt.
will-I-block.imperf	this-the-account

'I will block this account.'

خذت روج مات

xaðt	roodʒ	maat.
buy.perf-I	lipstick	matte

'I bought a matte lipstick.'

خلج سيريس شوي

xallə-ʧ	siirijəs	ʃwaj.
be.imp-you	serious	little

'Be a bit serious.'

الدريس بيرفيكت عليج!

əd-dres	beerfekt	ʕalee-ʧ!
the-dress	perfect	on-you.f

'The dress looks perfect on you!'

Further reading

Mazid (2006) describes how various politeness strategies are expressed by Emirati Arabic. For a general discussion of the pragmatic aspect of politeness, see Brown and Levinson (1987). For the expression of politeness in other Arabic dialects, see El-Shafey (1990), Atawneh (1991), and Farghal (1995). Isleem and Al Hashemi (2018) discusses how speech conventions are expressed in cultural contexts.

Glossary of terms

Abessives are the grammatical **case** which marks the lack or absence of some entities or events.

Adjectives are a word class which functions to modify or specify the reference of a noun. They may be **predicative** (e.g. The boy is tall) or **attributive** (e.g. the tall boy).

Adjuncts are optional or secondary grammatical units which provide additional information on an event (or property) (e.g. place, time, manner, degree, reason) but may usually be removed without affecting the identity of the remaining structure.

Adjunct control is a type of **control** structure in which the control clause is an adjunct (i.e. grammatically optional unit) in the **argument structure**.

Adverbs are a word class which indicates the time, place, manner, modality, reason, etc. of an event or situation.

Adverbials are grammatical constructions which serve the same function as **adverbs**. They may be phrases or clauses.

Affixes are **bound morphemes** added to a stem or root.

Afro-Asiatic is a primary language family that includes subdivisions such as Berber, Cushitic, Chadic, and Semitic languages.

Agentive nominals/nouns are nominalizations that refer to the agent participant/initiator of the event denoted by the source verb. They are frequently used to name professions.

Agreement is a relation established between two grammatical elements in a sentence, whereby some grammatical features of an element match with the corresponding features of a second element. Agreement usually affects features of person, gender, number, definiteness, and case.

Aktionsart is the **lexical** (or inner) **aspect** of the **predicate** of the sentence.

Allophone is a variant form of a **phoneme**.

Anaphora is the provision of reference to an element (termed an **anaphor**) by a discourse-salient **antecedent**.

Antecedent is an umbrella term for nouns (or noun phrases) to which a subsequent **pronoun** or **reflexive** is **anaphoric** and **coreferential**.

Antecedent clause is a clause that contains an **antecedent**.

Antepenultimate stress is a **stress** on the third to last syllable.

Appositive is a noun or noun phrase that provides further information about another noun/noun phrase.

Argument of a proposition describes the semantic role played by the **noun phrase**. In other words, arguments are event participants.

Argument structure consists of the lexical information of **arguments** as determined by the sentence **predicate**.

Aspect is a grammatical category that indicates the internal structure of a verbal event or situation. The aspectual property may be expressed by the semantics of verbs (**lexical aspect**), verbal morphology, or grammatical constructions (**grammatical aspect**).

Assimilation is a sound change in which a sound becomes similar to another, usually adjacent, sound in terms of phonological properties.

Attributive adjectives describe the attributes or properties of the noun and which form part of the noun phrase.

Auxiliary verbs accompany the main verb and express grammatical functions such as **tense**, **aspect**, and **modality**.

Bound morpheme is a **morpheme** that cannot exist independently and needs to attach to a stem.

Boundedness in event semantics is the aspectual property which applies to events and objects involved in the events. An event is bounded (or delimited) if it encodes an endpoint in time, whereas an object is bounded if it is specific in the spatiotemporal dimension. In some cases, the object can also delimit the event, e.g. the verb 'draw' constitutes an unbounded event as there is no internal endpoint, whereas the verb phrase 'draw a circle' is bounded.

Broken plural is a **plural** form that derives from changing the vocalic pattern of the **singular**.

Cardinal numeral is a **numeral** used for counting, e.g. one, two.

Case is the syntactic and/or semantic function of a noun phrase which can be determined by its position or grammatical function in the sentence.

Causative is a grammatical structure in which the predicate selects for an argument which acts as a causer, i.e. causes an event to happen or causes someone else to perform an action, e.g. 'have John clean my room,' 'let him finish the task.'

Circumfix is an **affix** which consists of a **prefix** part and a **suffix** part, simultaneously attaching to the stem or root but providing a single meaning.

Clause is a grammatical unit which consists of a subject and a predicate.

Clefts are constructions in which some words/phrases are displaced from their original position to produce great emphasis.

Clitic is a **bound morpheme** which is phonologically weak/unstressed and thus cannot exist independently of a stem or root, yet differs from an **affix** in that it attaches to whatever word is adjacent to it, i.e. its attachment is not category-specific.

Coda is the consonant(s) which ends a syllable.

Comparatives are grammatical structures which convey the meaning of comparison between the properties of two entities (e.g. 'John is taller than Mary') or the degrees to which the verb applies (e.g. John ate more than Mary did).

Comparative deletion is a type of **ellipsis** in which part of the comparative clause is elided, e.g. 'Ahmad ate more burgers than I did [ate burgers].'

Complement is a **noun phrase** or a **clause** which functions as an **argument** of a **verb**.

Complementizer is a grammatical category of functional elements which introduce a complement clause.

Complex predicates consist of a series of concatenated verbs in the expression of a single event.

Concessive clauses are adverbial clauses which mark a concession that contrasts two or more facts or points of view. They are always expressed by conjunctions or subordinators such as 'though' and 'in spite of.'

Conditionals are grammatical structures in which an event (described by the main clause) will be realized if certain conditions (described by the conditional clause) are fulfilled.

Conjunctions are a grammatical category of words which connect phrases or clauses and moreover assign a semantic relation between them. Conjunctions can derive structures of **coordination** and **subordination**.

Construct state is a **genitive/possessive** relation expressed by concatenating two noun phrases, whose **definiteness** is expressed by the definite **determiner** on the possessor noun phrase.

Control is a grammatical structure which consists of a verb whose subject or object is coreferential with the (usually covert) subject of an **embedded clause**.

Control verbs are verbs, the subject/object of which controls the referent of the understood subject of the **embedded clause**, e.g. the subject 'John' in 'John tried to come' controls the embedded subject of 'to come.'

Conversion is a word-formation process in which an existing word is assigned another grammatical category.

Co-occurrence restriction applies to two lexical items which cannot co-occur in the same sentence. Co-occurrence restriction is always considered as a piece of evidence for the two items to be considered as categorically identical.

Coordination is a structure in which the **coordinator** combines two or more linguistic units of equal grammatical status and categories.

Copula (or **copular verb**) is a linking element between a **predicate** and its **subject**.

Correlative constructions are a type of coordination in which the two coordinated units are marked by a particular word, e.g. 'either . . . or,' 'neither . . . nor,' and 'if . . . then.'

Counterfactuals are grammatical constructions which express a contrary-to-fact (or irrealis) event or situation.

Defective verbs contain a **weak root** in which the initial or the last root consonant is [ʔ], [w] or [j], or the long vowel [aa].

Deictic pronouns are pronouns whose reference must be fixed through the context of the discourse (or by pointing to the referent).

Demonstrative determiner or **pronoun** refers to a specific entity in the context, in many cases with respect to the entity's real or metaphorical proximity to the speaker or the addressee.

Deontic modality is a **modality** which expresses the speaker's degree of obligation, ability, or commitment to the realization of the proposition.

Derivational morphemes are bound morphemes which are attached to the stem and derive another lexical item. The original and the derived words may belong to distinct grammatical categories.

Diminutive is a derived noun which expresses a smaller degree of the property denoted by its source noun.

Diphthong refers to a vowel consisting of two vocalic places of articulation (or a vowel and a glide).

Direct object is the object which is directly involved and affected by the verbal action.

Disjunction is a type of **coordination** formed by the **coordinator** '(either) or.'

Distal demonstrative determiner or **pronoun** is used for entities which are far from the speaker in a physical or mental sense.

Distributive quantifiers are a type of **universal quantifiers** which, when applying to a noun, express that all individual things/people of which the proposition can be said to be true. Typical distributive quantifiers include 'each' and 'every.'

Ditransitive verb is a verb which takes two objects as **arguments**.

Dual is a morphological number feature which denotes two (or a pair of) items.

Echo question is a type of question which repeats a word or a phrase mentioned in the immediately preceding discourse, because it is misheard or is considered surprising.

Ellipsis is a linguistic process in which some part of a sentence is elided, yet can still be interpreted by the context.

Elliptical clause is a clause part of which is elided.

Embedded clause is a clause which is inserted into another.

Embedding is an operation which inserts one grammatical unit into another.

Emphatic spread is a phonological process through which the pharyngeal feature of an emphatic consonant is spread toward other consonants, making them emphatic.

Epenthesis is the insertion of an extra phonological segment.

Episodic sentence/situation expresses a specific episode of an event.

Epistemic modality expresses the speaker's evaluation of the likelihood or possibility of a state of affairs.

Equatives are used to describe things that are equal or identical, e.g. 'as tall as' and 'as good as.'

Evidential modality is a type of **modality** which indicates the source of evidence the speaker has regarding a state of affairs.

Exclamatives are grammatical expressions which encode the speaker's surprise and emotion.

Existential (construction) is a grammatical structure which expresses the existence or appearance of someone/something in the proposition.

Existential quantifiers are **quantifiers** which, when applying to a noun, express that something/someone exists of which the proposition can be said to be true. Typical existential quantifiers include 'some,' 'a,' and 'a few.'

Feminine is a grammatical feature of **gender**.

Fragment answer is a non-sentential word or phrase which acts as a short answer to a question.

Fragment question is a short question, which is similar to a **wh-sluice**.

Free relatives are a type of **relative clause** headed by a **wh-word** instead of a **head** noun, e.g. 'John likes [what I bought].'

Functional category/word serves a particular grammatical function in the sentence, and does not usually have a clear lexical content. Compare **Lexical category/word**.

Gapping is an **elliptical structure** in which the verb head of a verb phrase (or sometimes the head noun of a noun phrase) is elided.

Geminates are consonants with approximately double the duration of the articulation of a single consonant.

Gemination is a phonological process in which a consonant becomes a **geminate**.

Gender is a grammatical feature of nouns and adjectives established by **convention**. In Arabic, gender can be masculine or feminine.

Generic statement is a statement regarded as true regardless of time and situation, e.g. 'Chickens hatch eggs' or 'The Earth revolves around the sun.'

Genitive is a morphological or abstract **Case** which marks usually grammatical constructions for possession.

Grammatical aspect expresses the aspectual property of the sentence by means of verbal morphology (e.g. **perfective** vs. **imperfective** aspect), or grammatical constructions (e.g. **complex predicates**).

Grammatical functions are the grammatical roles played by the participants in the sentence (e.g. subject and direct object).

Grammaticalization is a process of language change through which a lexical item becomes a grammatical or functional item.

Head is the element in a syntactic phrase (or complex morphological word) which determines the grammatical property (and label) of the phrase (or word).

Hollow verbs contain a **weak root** in which the medial root consonant is [ʔ], [w], [j], or the long vowel [aa].

Honorifics are grammatical words or constructions which express the speaker's respect and politeness towards the addressee. They may also express differences in social class or age between the speaker and the addressee.

Imperatives are a type of verbal clauses whose **modality** expresses the speaker's command and request towards the hearer.

Imperfect/imperfective verb denotes the aspectual property of an incomplete or ongoing action.

Indefiniteness marks a referent not known/salient to the addressee and not capable of specific identification (see also **definiteness**).

Indirect object is the entity which is affected by the action, yet is not the primary object of action but usually denotes the 'end point' of an event. Indirect objects are usually (but not always) prepositional phrases and appear in ditransitive constructions (see also **direct object**).

Infix is a **bound morpheme** which is inserted within the stem or root of a word.

Inflection is the set of morphological markers of a language which express various grammatical functions such as **tense, aspect, modality, number, person, gender, case**, and **degree**.

In-situ wh-questions are questions in which the **wh-words** are at their base position, i.e. the position where the wh-word is interpreted. See also **wh-in-situ**.

Instrumental nominals/nouns are nouns derived from verbs which refer to **instruments** used to bring about the event denoted by the verb.

Instruments are arguments of the verb which refer to the tool used to bring about the event denoted by the verb and are usually headed by prepositions such as 'with' and 'by.'

Interjections are linguistic expressions, which are formed by one syllable or word, and are used as an exclamation. They are usually sentence-initial.

Interrogative is the structure used to ask a question.

Interrogative pronouns are a type of pronouns used in asking information questions (e.g. 'who' or 'what').

Intonation is the melodic pattern (i.e. pitch distribution) of a sentence.

Intransitive verbs do not take a direct object. See also **unaccusative verbs** and **unergative verbs**.

Irrealis modality is a type of **modality** which expresses that the particular state of affairs has not been realized at the utterance time.

Koine is a widespread language variety which evolves from dialectal contact and/or mixing of various related dialects.

Lenition is a phonological process which makes a consonant more sonorous.

Lexical aspect of a verb is its inherent semantic property of eventuality. See also **Aktionsart**.

Lexical category/word serves to provide the substantive content to the sentence. Compare **functional category/word**.

Locative noun refers to the location where the event denoted by the verb takes place.

Main clause is a clause which can exist independently and expresses a complete proposition.

Masculine is a grammatical feature of **gender**.

Mediopassive is a single grammatical **voice** morphology which combines the meanings of the **middle** voice and the **passive** voice.

Middle verb is an intransitive verb in which its grammatical subject is not the event initiator, but corresponds to the object of the verb. It differs from a **passive** verb in that the initiator cannot be expressed (e.g. as a by-phrase).

Modality is a system of concepts which encode the speaker's intention, belief, wish, and request toward the proposition.

Modal verbs express speaker's intentions in terms of **mood**, e.g., possibility, probability, and necessity.

Mood is the grammatical marker of **modality** which is encoded on verbs.

Moon letters are letters in Arabic which correspond to non-coronal (e.g. bilabial, dorsal) consonants. They do not license the assimilation of their preceding definite determiner [al-] in Arabic. See also **sun letters**.

Morpheme is the smallest meaningful unit of language.

Morphology is the study of word-internal structure and word formation.

Negation is a grammatical operation which transforms a positive sentence to a negative one. It can refer to particular negative items.

Negative concord is the existence of more than one negative item within a sentence, yet only a single negative interpretation is possible. It can also be understood as a negative item which can exist independently as a fragment answer, but must be licensed by negative contexts.

Negative polarity item is an item which must be licensed in negative contexts.

Nominalization is a grammatical/morphological process through which a non-nominal category derives a nominal category.

Nonrestrictive relative clause is a **relative clause** which provides additional information to the noun which it modifies. See also **restrictive relative clause**.

Noun is a grammatical category which denotes an entity, a place, a person, or an abstract concept.

Noun phrase is a phrase formed by a noun as its head.

Number is a grammatical and semantic feature distinguishing between singular, **dual** and plural.

Numerals are a word class which consists of **cardinal numerals** and **ordinal numerals**.

Object is a noun or noun phrase which is affected by the action/effect of the verb.

Object control is a type of **control structure** in which the object of the main clause controls/determines the subject of the **embedded clause**, e.g. 'John asked Mary to come,' in which the object 'Mary' in the main clause is also the subject of 'come.'

Onomatopoeia, or sound symbolism, refers to the creation of words by imitating directly how their referents sound in the natural world (e.g. English word 'splash').

Onset is the initial consonant(s) of a syllable.

Ordinal numerals are the numerals which indicate the rank, order, or position within a sequence, e.g. first, second, last.

Parentheticals are expressions inserted within or next to a well-formed sentence, which function to provide additional clarification to the statement. See also **nonrestrictive relative clause**.

Participle is a category of words morphologically derived from verbs. A participle can be active (**active participle**), i.e. it modifies the subject of the sentence as an agent (e.g. the singing man = a man who sings), or passive (**passive participle**), i.e. it modifies the object of the sentence as the undergoer of the event (e.g. 'the closed door' = 'the door has been closed').

Partitives are expressions which refer to a partial subset of a larger set of things.

Passive voice refers to a morphologically marked **voice** property of a verb. The sentence subject of a passive verb is always the understood object of the verb (e.g. 'John was beaten' implies that someone beat John).

Patterns (or templates) in Arabic words are ordered sequences of **root** consonants and vowels, which derive different forms of the verb or other grammatical categories.

Penultimate stress is a **stress** on the second to last syllable.

Perfect/perfective verb is a verb whose aspectual properties refer to a completed action or event.

Person is a grammatical feature which includes the first person (i.e. 'I,' 'we') referring to the speaker, the second person (i.e. 'you') referring to the addressee and the third person (i.e. 'he,' 'she,' 'it,' 'they') referring to everyone else.

Phoneme is the minimal contrastive unit of the sound system of a language.

Phonetics studies the sound system of a language.

Phonology studies the processes and changes that sounds undergo in a language in specific environments.

Phonotactics is the study of possible combinations of sounds and syllables in a language.

Phrase is a grammatical unit which consists of a **lexical** or **functional category** acting as the **head** and possibly other modifying elements.

Pitch is a perceptual property of sounds, which corresponds to the highness or lowness of a sound's tone.

Pluperfect is the aspectual form of the verb which corresponds to the completion of an event or action before the time of some other event.

Plural is a grammatical and semantic value of the nominal feature **number**, which indicates more than one entity.

Polar questions are **yes-no questions**.

Postposing is a grammatical operation which shifts some grammatical unit to the right of their original position for pragmatic or processing reasons.

Predicate is the part of a **proposition** which expresses what is true of the subject.

Predicative adjective usually appears after a linker or a **copula** of the sentence and ascribes a property to the subject, simultaneously acting as the sentence **predicate**.

Prefix is an **affix** added to the left of a stem.

Preposing places a noun, phrase, or clause to a position on the left edge of the sentence or clause.

Prepositions are a grammatical category of words which indicate a spatiotemporal or circumstantial relationship between two nouns or noun phrases in the sentence.

Progressive is an **aspect** which denotes an ongoing event.

Pronoun is a category of words which substitute for (and take their reference from) a **noun** or **noun phrase**.

Propositions are the states of affairs or events denoted by sentences, whose truth conditions (i.e. whether they are true or false) can be determined.

Proximal demonstrative determiner or **pronoun** refers to an entity which is close to the speaker in the physical or mental sense.

Quadriliteral root is a **root** which consists of four consonants.

Quantifiers are words which express quantity.

Radical is a consonant forming part of the **root**.

Raising structures are grammatical structures formed by a **raising verb** and an **embedded clause**.

Raising verbs (and predicates in general) include verbs such as 'seem' and 'appear' (or predicates such as 'be likely to' and 'be certain to'). They do not have a subject actor, and they select for an **embedded clause**, the understood subject of which surfaces as the main clause subject, e.g. 'John always seems to offend people.'

Reciprocals are **anaphoric** expressions of mutual relationship, such as 'each other' and 'one another.' See also **reflexives** and **pronouns**.

Reflexives or **reflexive pronouns** are **anaphoric** pronouns which must refer to an **antecedent noun phrase** in their local environment/domain (for example, within the same clause or sentence), e.g. 'himself' and 'herself.'

Relative clause is a **subordinate clause** which modifies a **noun phrase**. It is sometimes marked by a **relative pronoun** (e.g. 'who') or a **complementizer** (e.g. 'that').

Relative pronoun is an **anaphoric pronoun** used in **relative clauses**, e.g. 'the girl who I met yesterday.'

Restrictive relative clause specifically identifies the noun.

Resultatives are a grammatical structure which indicates that the subject has undergone some change resulting in a particular state, e.g. 'paint the wall red' and 'wipe the table clean.' See also **causatives**.

Resumptive pronouns are **pronouns** within embedded (mainly relative) clauses which refer to an **antecedent** noun phrase that appears in the main clause.

Right-dislocation is the rightward displacement of a word/phrase to a sentence-final position. It is always used to express an afterthought. See also **postposing**.

Root of an Arabic word is the set of radicals/consonants which express a particular semantic concept and form the base for further derivation of related words sharing similar concepts.

Semitic is a branch of **Afro-Asiatic languages** that originated in the Middle East.

Sentence is the largest syntactic unit, which semantically expresses a **proposition**. A sentence may consist of only one **clause**, or a number of clauses combined by **coordination** or **subordination**.

Sluicing is an **elliptical structure** which involves the use of a bare **wh-word** (i.e. **wh-sluice**).

Speech act is an utterance which is perceived as an action done by the speaker, e.g. an assertion, question, claim, suggestion, promise, oath, threat, surprise, command, request, or invitation.

Stative verbs are verbs which describe the state of being of the subject.

Stress is the perceived prominence on the syllable.

Stripping is an elliptical process in which only one element remains in the **elliptical clause** after **ellipsis**.

Subject control is a type of **control structure** in which the subject of the main clause controls/determines the subject of the **embedded clause**, e.g. 'John tried to come,' in which 'John' is the subject of 'try' and 'come.'

Subjunctive is a grammatical expression of **modality** which indicates that some **irrealis** situation is wished or imagined.

Subordination is a process of **embedding clauses** in which a clause, the subordinate, is dependent on another, namely, the main clause.

Suffix is an **affix** added to the right of a stem.

Sun letters are letters in Arabic which correspond to coronal consonants (i.e. which make use of the front part of the tongue). They license the assimilation of their preceding definite determiner. See also **moon letters.**

Superlatives are grammatical structures which express comparison of an entity to a group, i.e. express the concept of 'the most.' See also **comparatives** and **equatives**.

Suprasegmental process involves any phonological processes on the length, stress, tone, and intonation, and is usually applied to a level higher than a phoneme, e.g. syllables, words, and sentences.

Syllable is a prosodic unit in **phonology** which groups the consonants and vowels together. Syllables may have different structures (see also **syllabic structure**).

Syllabic structure is the structure of a **syllable** and is based on the number of consonants that a language allows as the **onset** and/or **coda** of the syllable.

Syntax studies the internal structure and formation of sentences, i.e. the way words and phrases combine to form a sentence.

Tags or **question tags** are short questions which follow a **declarative** or **imperative** sentence, e.g. 'Ahmad will come, won't he?' and 'Mariam must pass the examination, right?'

Tense is the linguistic expression of the time reference of a verb.

Topic is the subject of a comment clause (i.e. what the clause is 'about').

Topicalization is a grammatical structure, in which the topic of the conversation is brought to the fore, usually to a sentence-initial position.

Transitive verbs are verbs which take a **direct object**.

Triconsonantal/triliteral roots are **roots** which consist of three radicals/consonants.

Typology is the field of linguistics which deals with the classification of languages regarding their linguistic (e.g. phonological, grammatical, and morphological) properties.

Unaccusative verbs are **intransitive verbs** of which the grammatical subject is the understood object of the verb, e.g. 'The window broke' and 'The ship sank.'

Unergative verbs are **intransitive verbs** of which the grammatical subject is the initiator or doer of the event, e.g. 'Ahmad slept' and 'John danced.'

Universal quantifiers are **quantifiers** which, when applying to a noun, express that all things/people of which the proposition can be said to be true. Typical universal quantifiers include 'all' and 'every.'

Valency is the number of **arguments** determined by the **predicate**.

Verb is a grammatical category of words denoting an action, event, or state.

Verbal nouns are grammatical nouns derived from a verb (see also **nominalized verb**).

Vocative is a specific nominal form expressed as case marking and used to address directly the addressee, mainly in questions or imperative sentences.

Voice is a grammatical property of the verb which indicates how its **arguments** map onto their **grammatical functions** (such as subject and object).

Weak roots are Arabic roots which have [?], [w], or [j] as a root consonant. A weak root can be **defective** or **hollow**.

Wh-fronting is an observation in **wh-questions** in which the interrogative pronoun (**wh-word**) is at the sentence-initial position instead of its original (i.e. subject or object) position.

Wh-in-situ refers to wh-questions where the interrogative pronoun (**wh-word**) appears in the position where it is interpreted (see also **in-situ wh-questions**).

Wh-questions are information questions formed with interrogative pronouns.

Wh-sluice is the bare **wh-word** used in **sluicing**.

Wh-words are question words (see also **interrogative pronouns**) such as 'what,' 'who,' 'which,' 'where,' 'when,' 'how,' 'how many/much,' and 'why.'

Yes-no questions are questions which require an 'yes' or 'no' as an answer. See also **polar questions**.

References

Abu-Chacra, F. (2007). *Arabic: An essential grammar*. Routledge.

Al-Amadidhi, D. G. H. Y. (1985). *Lexical and sociolinguistic variation in Qatari Arabic* [Doctoral dissertation, University of Edinburgh]. Edinburgh Research Archive. https://era.ed.ac.uk/bitstream/handle/1842/6727/356390.pdf

Al Ameri, H. (2009). *A phonological description of Emirati Arabic* (Publication no. 1475967) [Master's thesis, Purdue University]. ProQuest Dissertations and Theses Global.

Al-Ani, S. H. (1970). *Arabic phonology: An acoustical and physiological investigation*. Mouton.

Al-Ani, S. H. (1978). The development and distribution of the Arabic "qaf" in Iraq. In S. Al-Ani (Ed.), *Readings in Arabic linguistics* (pp. 103–110). Indiana University Linguistics Club.

Albader, Y. B. (2016). Quadriliteral verbs in Kuwaiti Arabic. In G. Grigore & G. Bițună (Eds.), *Arabic varieties: Far and wide. Proceedings of the 11th international conference of AIDA—Bucharest, 2015* (pp. 53–64). Universităţii din Bucureşti.

Albuarabi, S. (2019). Ellipsis in Iraqi Arabic: An analysis of gapping, sluicing, and stripping. In *Purdue linguistics, literature, & second language studies conference*. Purdue University. https://docs.lib.purdue.edu/plcc/2019/papers/6/

Al-Bukhari, J. (2016). *The syntax of elliptical constructions in Jordanian Arabic* (Publication no. 10123611) [Doctoral dissertation, University of Wisconsin-Milwaukee]. ProQuest Dissertations and Theses Global.

Algryani, A. M. K. (2007). Ellipsis in Arabic fragment answers. In M. Sheehan & L. R Bailey (Eds.), *Order and structure in syntax II: Subjecthood and argument structure* (pp. 319–328). Language Science Press. http://doi.org/10.5281/zenodo.1116781

Algryani, A. M. K. (2012a). *The syntax of ellipsis in Libyan Arabic: A generative analysis of sluicing, VP ellipsis, stripping and negative contrast* (Publication no. 10049238) [Doctoral dissertation, Newcastle University]. ProQuest Dissertations and Theses Global.

Algryani, A. M. K. (2012b). Sluicing in Libyan Arabic. *Al-'Arabiyya*, *44*(4), 41–63. www.jstor.org/stable/43208723

Al Hussein, M., & Gitsaki, C. (2018). Foreign language learning policy in the United Arab Emirates: Local and global agents of change. In P. G. L. Chew, C. Chua, K. Taylor-Leech, & C. Williams (Eds.), *Un(intended) language planning in a globalising world: Multiple levels of players at work* (pp. 97–112). De Gruyter. https://doi.org/10.1515/9783110518269-006

Al Kaabi, M. (2015). *The anatomy of Arabic words: The role of the root in representations and processing* (Publication no. 3716477) [Doctoral dissertation, New York University]. ProQuest Dissertations and Theses Global.

Al Kaabi, M., & Ntelitheos, D. (2019). Rethinking templates: A syntactic analysis of verbal morphology in Emirati Arabic. *Glossa*, *4*(1), 132. https://doi.org/10.5334/gjgl.428

Al-Najjar, B. (1984). *The syntax and semantics of verbal aspect in Kuwaiti Arabic* (Publication no. 8407310) [Doctoral dissertation, University of Utah]. ProQuest Dissertations and Theses Global.

Alqassas, A. (2019). The syntax of negative coordination in Jordanian Arabic. In A. Khalfaoui & M. A. Tucker (Eds.), *Perspectives on Arabic linguistics XXX* (pp. 93–112). John Benjamins. https://doi.org/10.1075/sal.7.06alq

Alqurashi, A., & Borsley, R. D. (2012). Arabic relative clauses in HPSG. In S. Müller (Ed.), *Proceedings of the 19th international conference on head-driven phrase structure grammar* (pp. 26–44). CSLI. http://web.stanford.edu/group/cslipublications/cslipublications/HPSG/2012/alqurashi-borsley.pdf

Alshaalan, Y., & Abels, K. (2020). Resumption as a sluicing source in Saudi Arabic: Evidence from sluicing with prepositional phrases. *Glossa*, *5*(1), 8. https://doi.org/10.5334/gjgl.841

Al-Sulaiti, L. M. (1993). *Some aspects of Qatari Arabic phonology and morphology* (Publication no. U060057) [Doctoral dissertation, Lancaster University]. ProQuest Dissertations and Theses Global.

Altakhaineh, A. R. M. (2018). Identifying N+N compounding in modern standard Arabic and Jordanian Arabic. *Studia Linguistica*, *73*(1), 1–36. https://doi.org/10.1111/stul.12087

Ameka, F. (1992a). Interjections: The universal yet neglected part of speech. *Journal of Pragmatics*, *18*(2–3), 101–118. https://doi.org/10.1016/0378-2166(92)90048-G

Ameka, F. (1992b). The meaning of phatic and conative interjections. *Journal of Pragmatics*, *18*(2–3), 245–271. https://doi.org/10.1016/0378-2166(92)90054-F

Aoun, J., Benmamoun, E., & Choueiri, L. (2010). *The syntax of Arabic*. Cambridge University Press. https://doi.org/10.1017/CBO9780511691775

Aoun, J., Benmamoun, E., & Sportiche, D. (1994). Agreement, word order, and conjunction in some varieties of Arabic. *Linguistic Inquiry*, *25*(2), 195–220. www.jstor.org/stable/4178858

Aoun, J., Benmamoun, E., & Sportiche, D. (1999). Further remarks on first conjunct agreement. *Linguistic Inquiry*, *30*(4), 669–681. https://doi.org/10.1162/002438999554255

Aoun, J., & Choueiri, L. (1999). Modes of interrogation. In E. Benmamoun (Ed.), *Perspectives on Arabic Linguistics XII* (pp. 7–26). John Benjamins. https://doi.org/10.1075/cilt.190.04aou

Aoun, J., Choueiri, L., & Hornstein, N. (2001). Resumption, movement, and derivational economy. *Linguistic Inquiry*, *32*(3), 371–403. https://doi.org/10.1162/002438901750372504

Arad Greshler, T., Melnik, N., & Wintner, S. (2017). Seeking control in modern standard Arabic. *Glossa*, *2*(1), 90. https://doi.org/10.5334/gjgl.295

Atawneh, A. M. A. H. (1991). *Politeness theory and the directive speech-act in Arabic-English bilinguals: An empirical study* (Publication no. 9219306) [Doctoral dissertation, State University of New York]. ProQuest Dissertations and Theses Global.

Badawi, E. S., Carter, M., & Gully, A. (2004). *Modern written Arabic: A comprehensive grammar*. Routledge.

Bahloul, M. (1994). *The syntax and semantics of taxis, aspect and modality in standard Arabic* (Publication no. 9427887) [Doctoral dissertation, Cornell University]. ProQuest Dissertations and Theses Global.

Bahloul, M., & Harbert, W. (1993). Agreement asymmetries in Arabic. In J. Mead (Ed.), *Proceedings of the eleventh West Coast conference on formal linguistics* (pp. 15–31). CSLI.

Benmamoun, E. (1996). Negative polarity and presupposition in Moroccan Arabic. In E. Mushira (Ed.), *Perspectives on Arabic linguistics VIII* (pp. 47–66). John Benjamins. https://doi.org/10.1075/cilt.134.06ben

Benmamoun, E. (1997). Licensing of negative polarity in Moroccan Arabic. *Natural Language and Linguistic Theory*, *15*(2), 263–287. https://doi.org/10.1023/A:1005727101758

Benmamoun, E. (2000). *The feature structure of functional categories: A comparative study of Arabic dialects*. Oxford University Press.

Benmamoun, E. (2006). Licensing configurations: The puzzle of head negative polarity items. *Linguistic Inquiry*, *37*(1), 141–149. https://doi.org/10.1162/ling.2006.37.1.141

Blodgett, A., Owens, J., & Rockwood, T. (2007). An initial account of the intonation of Emirati Arabic. In J. Trouvain & W. Barry (Eds.), *Proceedings of the XVIth International Conference on Phonetic Sciences (ICPhS)* (pp. 1136–1140). Saarbrücken, Germany.

Borer, H. (2009). Afro-Asiatic, Semitic: Hebrew. In R. Lieber & P. Štekauer (Eds.), *The Oxford handbook of compounding* (pp. 386–399). Oxford University Press. https://doi.org/10.1093/oxfordhb/9780199695720.013.0027

Boyle, R. (2012). Language contact in the United Arab Emirates. *World Englishes*, *31*(3), 312–330. https://doi.org/10.1111/j.1467-971X.2012.01749.x

Brown, P., & Levinson, S. (1987). *Politeness: Some universals in language usage*. Cambridge University Press. https://doi.org/10.1017/CBO9780511813085

Brustad, K. E. (2000). *The syntax of spoken Arabic: A comparative study of Moroccan, Egyptian, Syrian and Kuwaiti dialects*. Georgetown University Press.

Bukshaisha, F. A. M. (1985). *An experimental phonetic study of some aspects of Qatari Arabic*. [Doctoral dissertation, University of Edinburgh]. Edinburgh Research Archive. https://era.ed.ac.uk/bitstream/handle/1842/26361/BukshaishaFAM_1985redux.pdf

Caubert, D. (1991). The active participle as a means to renew the aspectual system: A comparative study in several dialects of Arabic. In A. S. Kaye (Ed.), *Semitic studies: In honor of Wolf Leslau, on the occasion of his eighty-fourth birthday, November 14, 1991* (pp. 209–24). Otto Harrassowitz.

Comrie, B., Haspelmath, M., & Bickel, B. (2008). *The Leipzig glossing rules: Conventions for interlinear morpheme-by-morpheme glosses*. Department of Linguistics of the Max Planck Institute for Evolutionary Anthropology and the Department of Linguistics of the University of Leipzig. www.eva.mpg.de/lingua/pdf/Glossing-Rules.pdf

Cristofaro, S. (2003). *Subordination*. Oxford University Press. https://doi.org/10.1093/acprof:oso/9780199282005.001.0001

Davis, S. (1995). Emphasis spread in Arabic and grounded phonology. *Linguistic Inquiry*, *26*(3), 465–498. www.jstor.org/stable/4178907

Diem, W. (2014). *Negation in Arabic: A study in linguistic history*. Harrassowitz Verlag.

Eberhard, D. M., Simons, G. F., & Fennig, C. D. (Eds.). (2020). *Ethnologue: Languages of the world* (23rd ed.). SIL International. www.ethnologue.com

Eisele, J. C. (1990). Time reference, tense and formal aspect in Cairene Arabic. In M. Eid (Ed.), *Perspectives on Arabic linguistics I* (pp. 173–212). John Benjamins. https://doi.org/10.1075/cilt.63.10eis

El-Shafey, F. (1990). *Politeness strategies in spoken British English and spoken Egyptian Arabic* [Unpublished doctoral dissertation, Cairo University]. ProQuest Dissertations and Theses Global.

Farghal, M. (1995). Euphemism in Arabic: A Gricean interpretation. *Anthropological Linguistics*, *37*(3), 366–379. www.jstor.org/stable/30028417

Fassi Fehri, A. (1993). *Issues in the structure of Arabic clauses and words*. Springer. https://doi.org/10.1007/978-94-017-1986-5

Fassi Fehri, A. (2012). *Key features and parameters in Arabic grammar*. John Benjamins. https://doi.org/10.1075/la.182

Feghali, H. J. (2008). *Gulf Arabic: The dialects of Kuwait, Bahrain, Qatar, UAE and Oman: Grammar, dialogues, and lexicon*. Dunwoody Press.

Ferguson, C. A. (1959). Diglossia. *Word*, *15*(2), 325–340. https://doi.org/10.1080/00437956.1959.11659702

Gazsi, D. (2017). Language and identity among the "Arabs of the coast" in Iran and the Arab Gulf states. In S. Bettega & F. Gasparini (Eds.), *Linguistic studies in the Arabian Gulf* (pp. 105–129). Università di Torino.

Haddad, Y. A. (2012). Raising in standard Arabic: Backward, forward, and none. In R. Bassiouney & E. G. Katz (Eds.), *Arabic language and linguistics* (pp. 61–78). Georgetown University Press.

Halefom, G., Leung, T., & Ntelitheos, D. (2013). *A corpus of Emirati Arabic* (NRF grant 31H001) [technical report]. United Arab Emirates University.

Haspelmath, M. (2007). Coordination. In T. Shopen (Ed.), *Language typology and syntactic description volume II: Complex constructions* (2nd ed., pp. 1–51). Cambridge University Press. https://doi.org/10.1017/CBO9780511619434.001

Hassan, Z. M. (1981). *An experimental study of vowel duration in Iraqi spoken Arabic* [Doctoral dissertation, University of Leeds]. White Rose eTheses Online. http://etheses.whiterose.ac.uk/id/eprint/2345

Hoffiz, B. T. (1995). *Morphology of U.A.E. Arabic, Dubai dialect* (Publication no. 9534685) [Doctoral dissertation, The University of Arizona]. ProQuest Dissertations and Theses Global.

Holes, C. (1984). *Colloquial Arabic of the Gulf and Saudi Arabia*. Routledge & Kegan Paul.

Holes, C. (1989). Towards a dialect geography of Oman. *Bulletin of the School of Oriental and African Studies*, *52*, 446–462. https://doi.org/10.1017/S0041977X00034558

Holes, C. (1990). *Gulf Arabic*. Routledge. https://doi.org/10.4324/9780203218426

Holes, C. (2004a). *Modern Arabic structures, functions and varieties* (revised ed.). Georgetown University Press.

Holes, C. (2004b). Quadriliteral verbs in the Arabic dialects of eastern Arabia. In M. Haak, R. de Jong, & K. Versteegh (Eds.), *Approaches to Arabic dialects* (pp. 97–116). Brill. https://doi.org/10.1163/9789047402480_010

Holes, C. (2005). Form X of the verb in the Arabic dialects of Eastern Arabia. In G. Khan (Ed.), *Semitic studies in honour of Edward Ullendorff* (pp. 115–125). Brill. https://doi.org/10.1163/9789047415756_011

Holes, C. (2007). Gulf States. In K. Versteegh, M. Eid, A. Elgibali, M. Woidich, & A. Zaborski (Eds.), *Encyclopaedia of Arabic language and linguistics* (Arabian ed., voi. 1, pp. 608–620). Brill.

Holes, C. (2013). Word order and textual function in Gulf Arabic. In J. Owens & A. Elgibali (Eds.), *Information structure in spoken Arabic* (pp. 61–74). Routledge. https://doi.org/10.4324/9780203875834

Hopper, P. J., & Traugott, E. C. (2003). *Grammaticalization* (2nd ed.). Cambridge University Press.

Hoyt, F. M. (2010). *Negative concord in Levantine Arabic* [Doctoral dissertation, University of Texas]. University of Texas Digital

Repository. http://repositories.lib.utexas.edu/bitstream/handle/2152/ETD-UT-2010-08-1763/HOYT-DISSERTATION.pdf

Hussain, A. A. A. (1985). *An experimental investigation of some aspects of the sound system of the Gulf Arabic dialect, with special reference to duration* (Publication no. U359510) [Doctoral dissertation, University of Essex]. ProQuest Dissertations and Theses Global.

Ingham, B. (1982). *North-east Arabian dialects*. Kegan Paul International. https://ia800301.us.archive.org/20/items/rosettaproject_ars_vertxt-3/rosettaproject_ars_vertxt-3.pdf

Isleem, N., & Al Hashemi, A. (2018). *Ramsah: An introduction to learning Emirati dialect and culture*. Kuttab Publishing.

Jarad, N. I. (2015). From bodily posture to progressive aspect marker. *Lingua Posnaniensis*, *57*(1), 89–111. https://doi.org/10.1515/linpo-2015-0005

Jarad, N. I. (2017). Grammaticalization in Emirati Arabic. *Arabica*, *64*(5–6), 742–760. https://doi.org/10.1163/15700585-12341473

Johnstone, T. M. (1967). *Eastern Arabian dialect studies*. Oxford University Press.

Johnstone, T. M. (1978). The affrication of "kaf" and "qaf" in the Arabic dialects of the Arabian Peninsula. In S. H. Al-Ani (Ed.), *Readings in Arabic linguistics* (pp. 285–303). Indiana University Press.

Katamba, F. (2005). *English words* (2nd ed.). Routledge. https://doi.org/10.4324/9780203495971

Katamba, F., & Stonham, J. (2006). *Morphology* (2nd ed.). Red Globe Press.

Kiss, K. É. (Ed.). (1995). *Discourse configurational languages*. Oxford University Press.

Krifka, M. (1992). Thematic relations as links between nominal reference and temporal constitution. In I. A. Sag & A. Szabolcsi (Eds.), *Lexical matters* (pp. 29–53). CSLI.

Leung, T. (2014a). Sluicing may repair LF-constraints. In A. Beltrama, T. Chatzikonstantinou, J. L. Lee, M. Pham, & D. Rak (Eds.), *CLS 48-1: The main session: Proceedings of the forty-eighth annual conference of the Chicago linguistic society* (pp. 431–445). Chicago Linguistic Society.

Leung, T. (2014b). Preposition stranding generalization and conditions on sluicing: Evidence from Emirati Arabic. *Linguistic Inquiry*, *45*(2), 332–340. https://doi.org/10.1162/LING_a_00158

Leung, T. (2014c). Modes of interrogatives entail modes of sluicing: Evidence from Emirati Arabic. In S. Farwaneh & H. Ouali (Eds.), *Perspectives on Arabic linguistics XXIV–XXV* (pp. 207–228). John Benjamins. https://doi.org/10.1075/sal.1.13leu

Leung, T., & Al Eisaei, F. (2014). Wh-fronting and wh-cleft in Emirati Arabic. In R. Baglini, T. Grinsell, J. Keane, A. R. Singerman, & J. Thomas (Eds.), *CLS 46-1: The main session: Proceedings of the forty-sixth annual conference of the Chicago linguistic society* (pp. 221–235). Chicago Linguistic Society.

Leung, T., & Shemeili, A. (2014). Making the first step correct in syntax-evidence from Emirati Arabic sluicing. In C. Abrego-Collier, A. Kang, M. Martinovic, & C. Nguyen (Eds.), *CLS 47-1: The main session: Proceedings of the forty-seventh annual conference of the Chicago linguistic society* (pp. 167–181). Chicago Linguistic Society.

Lucas, C. B. (2009). *The development of negation in Arabic and Afro-Asiatic* (Publication no. U516160) [Doctoral dissertation, University of Cambridge]. ProQuest Dissertations and Theses Global.

Mazid, B. E. M. (2006, April). *(Translating) Emirati Arabic politeness formulas: An exploratory study and a mini-mini-dictionary* [Paper presentation]. Seventh Annual UAE University Research Conference, United Arab Emirates University.

McCarthy, J. (1979). *Formal problems in Semitic phonology and morphology* (Publication no. 0341797) [Doctoral dissertation, Massachusetts Institute of Technology]. ProQuest Dissertations and Theses Global.

McCarthy, J. (1981). A prosodic theory of nonconcatenative morphology. *Linguistic Inquiry*, *12*(3), 373–418. www.jstor.org/stable/4178229

McCarthy, J., & Prince, A. S. (1990). Foot and word in prosodic morphology: The Arabic broken plural. *Natural Language and Linguistic Theory*, *8*(2), 209–283. https://doi.org/10.1007/BF00208524

McCloskey, J. (1990). Resumptive pronouns, A'-binding, and levels of representation in Irish. In R. Hendrick (Ed.), *Syntax and semantics of the modern Celtic languages* (pp. 199–248). Academic Press.

McCloskey, J. (2017). Resumption. In M. Everaert & H. van Riemsdijk (Eds.), *The Blackwell companion to syntax* (2nd ed.). Blackwell. https://doi.org/10.1002/9781118358733.wbsyncom105

Merchant, J. (2001). *The syntax of silence: Sluicing, islands, and identity in ellipsis*. Oxford University Press.

Merchant, J., & Simpson, A. (Eds.). (2012). *Sluicing: Cross-linguistic perspectives*. Oxford University Press. https://doi.org/10.1093/acprof:oso/9780199645763.001.0001

Mohammad, M. A. (1999). *Word order, agreement and pronominalization in standard and Palestinian Arabic*. John Benjamins. https://doi.org/10.1075/cilt.181

Mughazy, M. (2005). Rethinking lexical aspect in Egyptian Arabic. In M. T. Alhawary & E. Benmamoun (Eds.), *Perspectives on Arabic linguistics XVII–XVIII* (pp. 133–172). John Benjamins. https://doi.org/10.1075/cilt.267.09mug

Mustafawi, E. M. (2006). *An optimality theoretic approach to variable consonantal alternations in Qatari Arabic* (Publication no. NR18602) [Doctoral dissertation, University of Ottawa]. ProQuest Dissertations and Theses Global.

Ntelitheos, D., & Idrissi, A. (2017). Language growth in child Emirati Arabic. In H. Ouali (Ed.), *Perspectives on Arabic linguistics XXIX* (pp. 229–248). John Benjamins. https://doi.org/10.1075/sal.5.10nte

Ouali, H. (2017). The syntax of tense in Arabic. In E. Benmamoun & R. Bassiouney (Eds.), *The Routledge handbook of Arabic linguistics* (pp. 89–103). Routledge. https://doi.org/10.4324/9781315147062

Owens, J., Dodsworth, R., & Kohn, M. (2013). Subject expression and discourse embeddedness in Emirati Arabic. *Language Variation and Change*, *25*(3), 255–285. https://doi.org/10.1017/S0954394513000173

Owens, J., Dodsworth, R., & Rockwood, T. (2009). Subject-verb order in spoken Arabic: Morpholexical and event-based factors. *Language Variation and Change*, *21*(1), 39–67. https://doi.org/10.1017/S0954394509000027

Palmer, F. R. (2001). *Mood and modality* (2nd ed.). Cambridge University Press. https://doi.org/10.1017/CBO9781139167178

Palva, H. (1991). Is there a North West Arabian dialect group? In M. Forstner (Ed.), *Festgabe für Hans-Rudolf singer* (pp. 151–166). Peter Lang.

Persson, M. (2002). *Sentential object complements in modern standard Arabic*. Almqvist & Wiksell.

Persson, M. (2006, February 18). *The use of the active participle in Gulf Arabic* [Paper presentation]. The Divisions of Culture and Heritage and of Language and Communication, United Arab Emirates University.

Persson, M. (2008a). The role of the "b"-prefix in Gulf Arabic dialects as a marker of future, intent and/or irrealis. *Journal of Arabic and Islamic Studies*, *8*, 26–52. www.lancaster.ac.uk/jais/volume/docs/vol8/v8_4_Persson_26_52.pdf

Persson, M. (2008b, August 28–31). *An interesting typological compromise: Report from a corpus based study of modal and aspectual markers in Gulf Arabic dialects* [Paper presentation]. Eighth Association Internationale de Dialectologie Arabe (AIDA 8), Essex University.

Portner, P. (2009). *Modality*. Oxford University Press.

Qafisheh, H. A. (1977). *A short reference grammar of Gulf Arabic*. University of Arizona Press.

Ross, J. R. (1969, April 18–19). Guess who? In R. I. Binnick, A. Davison, G. M. Green, & J. L. Morgan. (Eds.), *Papers from the fifth regional meeting of the Chicago linguistic society* (pp. 252–286). University of Chicago, Department of Linguistics.

Ryding, K. C. (2005). *A reference grammar of modern standard Arabic*. Cambridge University Press. https://doi.org/10.1017/CBO9780511486975

Saiegh-Haddad, E., & Henkin, R. (2014). The structure of Arabic language and orthography. In E. Saiegh-Haddad & R. M. Joshi (Eds.), *Handbook of Arabic literacy: Insights and perspectives* (pp. 3–28). Springer. https://doi.org/10.1007/978-94-017-8545-7

Sells, P. (1984). *Syntax and semantics of resumptive pronouns* (Publication no. 8500135) [Doctoral dissertation, University of Massachusetts]. ProQuest Dissertations and Theses Global.

Sharvit, Y. (1999). Resumptive pronouns in relative clauses. *Natural Language and Linguistic Theory*, *17*(3), 587–612. https://doi.org/10.1023/A:1006226031821

Shlonsky, U. (1992). Resumptive pronouns as a last resort. *Linguistic Inquiry*, *23*(3), 443–468. www.jstor.org/stable/4178780

Shlonsky, U. (2002). Constituent questions in Palestinian Arabic. In J. Ouhalla & U. Shlonsky (Eds.), *Themes in Arabic and Hebrew syntax* (pp. 137–159). Springer. https://doi.org/10.1007/978-94-010-0351-3_5

Smart, J. (1990). Pidginization in Gulf Arabic: A first report. *Anthropological Linguistics*, *32*(1–2), 83–119. https://doi.org/10.5296/ijl.v6i6.6846

Tenny, C. (1992). The aspectual interface hypothesis. In I. A. Sag & A. Szabolcsi (Eds.), *Lexical matters* (pp. 1–27). CSLI.

Thompson, S. A., Longacre, R. E., & Hwang, S. J. (2007). Adverbial clauses. In T. Shopen (Ed.), *Language typology and syntactic description, vol. II: Complex constructions* (2nd ed., pp. 237–300). Cambridge University Press. https://doi.org/10.1017/CBO9780511619434.005

van Craenenbroeck, J. (2010a). Invisible last resort: A note on clefts as the underlying source for sluicing. *Lingua*, *120*(7), 1714–1726. https://doi.org/10.1016/j.lingua.2010.01.002

van Craenenbroeck, J. (2010b). *The syntax of ellipsis: Evidence from Dutch dialects*. Oxford University Press. https://doi.org/10.1093/acprof:oso/9780195375640.001.0001

Verkuyl, H. (1993). *A theory of aspectuality: The interaction between temporal and atemporal structure*. Cambridge University Press. https://doi.org/10.1017/CBO9780511597848

Versteegh, K. (1997). *The Arabic language*. Edinburgh University Press.

Versteegh, K., Eid, M., Elgibali, A., Woidich, M., & Zaborski, A. (Eds.). (2006). *Encyclopedia of Arabic language and linguistics* (vol. 2). Brill.

Wahba, W. (1984). *Wh-constructions in Egyptian Arabic* (Publication no. 8422170) [Doctoral dissertation, University of Illinois, Urbana-Champaign]. ProQuest Dissertations and Theses Global.

Watson, J. C. E. (1999). The directionality of emphasis spread in Arabic. *Linguistic Inquiry*, *30*(2), 289–300. https://doi.org/10.1162/002438999554066

Watson, J. C. E. (2002). *The phonology and morphology of Arabic*. Oxford University Press.

Wierzbicka, A. (1992). The semantics of interjections. *Journal of Pragmatics*, *18*(2–3), 159–192. https://doi.org/10.1016/0378-2166(92)90050-L

Youssef, I. (2013). *Place assimilation in Arabic: Contrasts, features, and constraints* [Doctoral dissertation, University of Tromsø]. UiT Munin Open Research Archive. https://munin.uit.no/bitstream/handle/10037/5347/thesis.pdf

Other references written about Emirati/Gulf Arabic in Arabic:

حماد، أحمد عبدالرحمن. "الخصائص الصوتية فى لهجة الإمارات العربية: دراسة لغوية ميدانية". الاسكندرية: دار المعرفة الجامعية، ١٩٨٥

عبيد، أحمد محمد. "ظاهرة الإبدال في لهجات الإمارات العربية المتحدة". أبوظبي: هيئة أبوظبي للسياحة والثقافة، دار الكتب الوطنية، ٢٠١٣

عبيد، أحمد محمد. "لهجات الإمارات: مقدمات ودراسات". الشارقة: دائرة الثقافة والإعلام، ٢٠٠٦

المسلّم، عبدالعزيز عبدالرحمن. "اللهجة الإماراتية: مدخل عام" الشارقة: دائرة الثقافة والإعلام، ٢٠٠١

حنظل، فالح. ١٩٩٨. معجم الألفاظ العامية في دولة الإمارات العربية المتحدة. أبوظبي: وزارة الإعلام والثقافة، الإدارة الثقافية

Index

Note: Page numbers in *italic* indicate a figure and page numbers in **bold** indicate a table on the corresponding page. Page numbers followed by 'n' indicate a note.

Printed in Great Britain
by Amazon

67266449R00296